The Kastendiecks
An Immigrant
Legacy

The Kastendiecks

An Immigrant Legacy

KENNETH E. BURCHETT

Amity America, Publishers
Branson, Missouri

Library of Congress Control Number 2019912796
Burchett, Kenneth E.
The Kastendiecks: An Immigrant Legacy
xiv, 500 pages : illustrations ; 24 cm
Includes bibliographical references and index
ISBN-13: 978-1-7333006-2-9 (hardback)
1. Genealogy 2. United States 3. Family History

CS71.K19345

ISBN-13: 978-1-7333006-1-2

On the cover: *Bremerhaven* by Carl Justus Fedeler, 1848
(Bremen Fockemuseum)

For Jayme

Contents

Contents

Contents

Acknowledgements

Immigration is a topic of much interest in the making of America. Historians have tried to piece together a fair history of the impact of immigration on the formation of the United States, often with aggravation over the facts. This work will undoubtedly fall short in that respect as well. Although every effort went into rendering a true account of immigration through the lives of the Kastendieck family and an accurate description of events in Brooklyn, New York, and southwest Missouri, I take full responsibility for any errors of fact or omission.

I wish to thank the many authors both past and present whose work inspired my own. Tyler Anbinder's *City of Dreams* is a master narrative of the transforming migrations that have shaped New York. Robyn Burnett and Ken Luebbering, in *German Settlement in Missouri*, demonstrate the crucial role of German immigrants and their descendants in the settlement of Missouri. Annika Romero and Gustav Streckfuss in *A German-American Tale* give us the compelling story of a German immigrant who came to American with his two young daughters in 1834 anticipating the incredible journey of the Kastendiecks.

Acknowledgements

I greatly appreciate the encouragement and support of family and friends and the generosity of Dee Willauer and David Gay for opening their collections to me to make possible many of the illustrations in this book. With apologies to anyone who I may have missed, I wish to acknowledge the special assistance of Jim Murray, Bob Collins, Jane Cuccurullo, and Kenneth Gruschow.

Finally, thank you to the staffs of the institutions and organizations that contributed to the research: Brooklyn Public Library, Greene County Library Center, Green-Wood Cemetery, Library of Congress, Missouri State Archives, National Archives and Records Administration, NYC Municipal Archives, University of Central Arkansas, and Zion Church Archives.

Preface

The uniqueness of the characters in this book opened a window of opportunity to write a history of places that were new to me, to build a biography around a single immigrant family, and in the process widen my understanding of history.

With any writing project, there may come a few conundrums. The success of a biography rests mainly on the availability of documents and access to historical records. A study of the Kastendiecks was particularly difficult in this regard because they lived the prime years of their lives in Brooklyn, Kings County, New York. Historians of Brooklyn have complained of an uphill climb in biographical research for a long time. One frustrated writer in 1880 wrote, "Perhaps there is no county in the State, or in the United States, in a more unhappy condition owing to the absence of public records than Kings…The future historian of Brooklyn will encounter dead locks beyond which he will travel as if in a maze."

Many are the tales of carelessness and indifference in the storage of Kings County records. One county employee, for instance—taking a liking to one of the bookcases in the city hall records office—removed all the records to the floor, whereupon the janitor, thinking the papers were trash, threw them out. On another occasion, a department moved out of city hall and to expedite the move sent all the old records to the paper mill. Many official public records from 1849 to 1865 are simply nonexistent. Fortunately, the newspapers preserve much of the history of the city of Brooklyn. The one grand custodian of Brooklyn history was the press. Here we often find not only the leading events of the time but also the minor details of what it was like to live in Brooklyn in the middle of the 19th Century.[1]

Alternate spellings of the Kastendieck name add to the maze: for example, Kastendeick, Kassendeick, Kassendeik, Kastendick, Kastendieck, Keastendick, Kastenick; all further complicated by variations that commence with the letter C; e.g., Castendieck.

The four Kastendieck brothers all shared the same first name of John. The main character of the book, John Herman Kastendieck, familiarly addressed as Herman, appears in documents spelled variously as Herrman and Hermann, and appears frequently as John H. Kastendieck. This book uses the name John Herman throughout to preserve consistency in the narrative.

The book is in three parts. Part one covers the life and times of the Kastendiecks from Morsum, Germany, to Brooklyn, New York.

Part two is about the Brooklyn years.

Part three recounts events of the Kastendieck family in rural Missouri.

Part four includes chapters about some of the extraordinary accomplishments of next generations: a visionary architect, a physicist who helped to build the atomic bomb, and an educator who aided in the restoration of schools following the destruction of Japan in World War II.

1

Introduction

The Kastendieck family came from the Kingdom of Hanover, Germany. The German place names of Morsum and Bremen found in various family documents point to an origin in Lower Saxony, the Hanoverian District of northwestern Germany, touching on the North Sea.[1]

The little farming town of Morsum lies situated a half mile south of the Weser River. It sets about three and one-half miles southeast of the town of Thedinghausen, the center of the municipal district by that name in the state of Verden, which today forms a part of the geography of modern Germany.

Morsum, Germany, is a very old village mentioned in documents as early as 1486. Its location on the fertile soil of the marshlands along the Weser River made it a center of farming and livestock breeding. The town is about fifteen miles from Bremen and fifty miles inland up the Weser River from the North Sea and the port of Bremerhaven, once one of the important harbors of emigration in Europe. Emigrants went first to Bremen to book passage and then down the Weser River to board ships at Bremerhaven. From the Kastendieck home at

Morsum, it was a short boat ride down the river to ships that regularly departed from Bremerhaven for America.

The Kingdom of Hanover became a sovereign territory in 1814 with the restoration of the Hanoverian lands to George III following the era of Napoleon. The House of Hanover ruled the Kingdom in personal union with the United Kingdom of Great Britain and Ireland until 1837 when the ascendance of Queen Victoria to the British Throne broke the union because Hanover permitted only male heirs to rule the Kingdom. Hanover fell into chaos during the political changes that followed. Nevertheless, well after their homeland in Lower Saxony became a principality of Prussia, and then the German Empire, the Kastendiecks always said they came to America from the Kingdom of Hanover.

The ancestry of the Kastendieck family traces to the patriarch Johann Friedrich Wilhelm Kastendieck born in 1758. We know little about him except that he married Anna Maria Bremer on July 16, 1789, in Lunsen, a small village near Morsum in Lower Saxony. He died in the fall of 1816.[2] They had a son named Johann Dietrich Kastendieck who was born on March 28, 1792. Mention of him in family records suggests he was born also in Lower Saxony. Family tradition says that he was at one time the mayor of Morsum.[3] He married Catharina Maria Gömann about 1817.[4] Trina, as people knew her, was born on September 7, 1791, in the Hanoverian District of Lower Saxony, the daughter of Christian Gömann and Anna Dorothea (Thies) Gömann.[5] Johann Dietrich and Trina had six children: Anna Dorothea, John Friedrich Wilhelm, John Heinrich, John Herman, Mary Catharina, and John Dietrich.[6]

The elder Johann Dietrich Kastendieck died on November 29, 1842, at Morsum, leaving Trina—his wife of twenty-five years—a widow with six children in a country facing turmoil.

1. Introduction

Germany was on the brink of revolution in 1842. The oldest Kastendieck child was twenty-four, the youngest eight. With sons of military age, the widowed Trina and her six children decided to leave war-torn Germany.

Four years passed following the patriarch Johann Dietrich's death before the first of the family made the voyage to begin a new life in the United States. They immigrated to America at different times over a period of seven years. In time, all left the quiet farming community of Morsum for the bustling city of New York. John Herman came first in 1846, followed by John Friedrich and Dorothea together in 1847, John Henry came about 1850, John Dietrich in 1851, and finally mother Trina and daughter Mary. By 1855, all were located at various addresses in New York. This book describes their journeys in the order that they came, the lives they lived, and the stories preserved through three generations.

Map of Königreich Hannover (Kingdom of Hanover). This map shows Lower Saxony prior to 1837 when the House of Hanover was in personal union with the King of Great Britain and Ireland. The circle covers the general region of the Kastendieck homeland. An arrow marks the approximate location of the town of Morsum on the left bank of the Weser River in the district of Thedinghausen. Adapted from Putzger, Historischer Weltatlas, 1965.

2

John Herman and Steerage Class

The first Kastendieck to set foot on the eastern shore of America was John Herrman Kastendieck. He came in 1846, the first of his family to leave Germany among a wave of young immigrants departing the declining circumstances of Europe for a more promising if uncertain future in the United States.[1]

Many emigrant ships sailed west out of Europe in those days. Besides Germany, mass emigrations took place out of Great Britain and Ireland on a grand scale. Famine and the threat of war drove people out by the hundreds of thousands. In Germany alone, sixty-thousand Germans a year immigrated to America during the five years beginning in 1840. That number increased in 1846—the year of John Herman's emigration—to eighty thousand immigrants.[2] So many people tried to leave Europe that there were sometimes not enough ships to carry them. One historian wrote, "Because of the potato famines and other economic hardships, German immigration was so large that immigrants without tickets were warned not to come to Bremen."[3] Bremen was the popular port of debarkation.

John Herman was not yet twenty when he left Morsum.[4] He likely travelled light, taking only the amount of baggage allowed to make the trip. Passengers received detailed lists of the luggage they would need for sea travel. The shipping company furnished food, mattresses, and cooking utensils, but the company advised travelers to pack blankets and other amenities. Emigrants brought their own clothing. Women carried six shifts, two flannel petticoats, six pairs of stockings, two pairs of shoes, and two strong gowns. Organizers instructed men to have two pairs of trousers, six shirts, six pairs of stockings, two pairs of shoes, and two complete suits. Those who could afford it added extra clothing and food items to make the six-week journey tolerable. However, many poor immigrants arrived in America with nothing but a small bag, simply unable to afford more.

John Herman proceeded from his home at Morsum by cart and by foot the fifteen miles to Bremen. On the other hand, he could have walked the half mile to the Weser River and drifted by boat down the river to Bremen. At Bremen, he registered and cleared emigration authority. Certain rules governed. Bremen was the first port city to pass laws designed to improve quality of life for German emigrants. Each ship had to be sea worthy, have a minimum amount of space per passenger, and have provisions on board for ninety days at sea. Regularly inspected living spaces had to be clean. The rules required that a doctor be on board each voyage. Ship owners had to furnish a list of passengers.

After registering at Bremen, it took a day to go from Bremen to Bremerhaven. Emigrants traveled from Bremen down the Weser River by barge to Brake, Germany, from there by brig to Bremerhaven, and from Bremerhaven out onto the North Sea.

There were three classes of passengers on a typical Bremerhaven ship. Cabin passengers paid the most and enjoyed the most luggage space; intermediate class was a step down from cabin; and steerage class was the least costly and the least amenable. John Herman sailed in steerage class. Most emigrants traveled steerage, which provided very little space or privacy on board.

The high demand for travel caused ships ordinarily built for freight purposes to be refitted as passenger ships on the Bremerhaven to New York route. A "tween" deck divided ships into three layered sections that used freight space to accommodate emigrants. The bottom, or the "hold", carried provisions and baggage; the middle division was steerage; and the upper section contained the cabins and intermediate class accommodations.

Steerage consisted of partitioned cubicles that contained upper and lower berths for sleeping, usually five persons to a cubicle. Steerage passengers cooked and ate in communal fashion, sitting at long tables with benches on either side. Meals comprised salted pork and beef, peas, beans, barley, rice, potatoes, sauerkraut, and cabbage.

Shipping companies enjoyed a lucrative business in emigrant transportation. Passengers paid for travel to America; freight was then loaded for the return trip thus collecting revenue both ways and avoiding the need to load ballast on the outward voyage. Shrewd businesspeople hoped to avoid bad weather that could easily double the length of the journey.

Immigrants came to America in large numbers, mostly to escape war and famine but also to start a new life. Among them were artisans and farmers with enough funds to buy land and start businesses. Among the immigrants, also, were a few political refugees seeking to escape the turmoil in Germany that would soon become a revolution in 1848. John Herman perhaps came for many reasons. The famine was widespread and persistent, and he was of an age to serve in the military forces of the revolution.

John Herman landed in New York and opened a small grocery store in the Brooklyn community of Red Hook. Four Kastendieck siblings followed him in order of their ages beginning with the eldest, Anna Dorothea.

2. John Herman and Steerage Class

John Herman Kastendieck. The first of six members of the Kastendieck family to immigrate to America from Morsum, Germany, John Herman Kastendieck arrived in New York in 1846. This photograph dates to about 1863, a few years after he established a successful grocery business in Brooklyn, New York. Augusta Kastendieck Family Album.

Emigrants at Dinner. An 1847 wood engraving shows German steerage passengers seated at long tables eating dinner. Accommodations were similar on most immigrant ships and typical of the conditions passengers experienced on a journey to New York in the mid-19th Century. *Illustrated London News*, 13 April 1844.

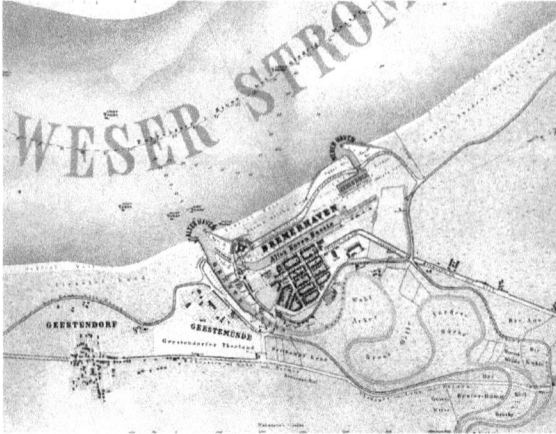

Map of Bremerhaven in 1849. Bremerhaven lies on the east side of the Weser River at the junction of the Weser and the Geest Rivers. Built on land ceded by Hanover, the Old Port (Alter Hafen) was the principal debarkation point until 1852 when the New Harbor (Neuer Hafen) opened adjacent to it. G. Hunckel, Der alter hafen in Bremerhaven.

Old Port of Bremerhaven. This scene at Bremerhaven shows ships lying at anchor awaiting passengers for the journey to America. John Herman Kastendieck would have walked this path to the port administration building at the top of the hill for final processing for the trip across the Atlantic. Lithograph *Bremerhaven* by G. Weinhold, with the depiction of the office building around 1845. Courtesy of Historical Museum Bremerhaven.

Bremerhaven. An 1848 painting depicts the busy emigrant port of Bremerhaven, Germany. The Kastendiecks left their home at Morsum, Germany, and sailed out of this port at a time when emigration out of Germany to the New World was at its peak. *Bremerhaven* by C. J. Fedeler, 1848, in the Bremen Fockemuseum.

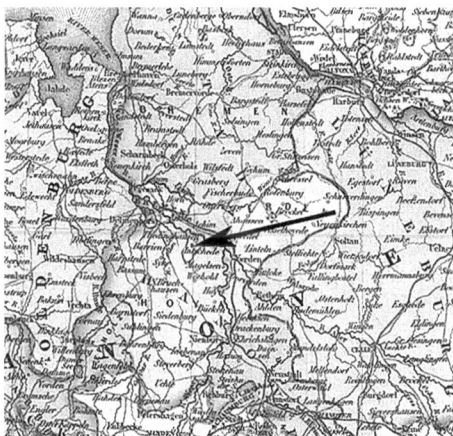

Morsum to Bremerhaven. The journey to America for the Kastendiecks began at Morsum, Hanover, Germany, (arrow) on the Weser River. They proceeded downriver a short distance to Bremen. Passage was booked at Bremen before boating down the Weser to Bremerhaven (upper left), there to board ship out onto the North Sea and across the Atlantic Ocean to New York. Adapted from J. H. Colton Map, 1855.

3

Aunt Dora

Anna Dorothea "Dorris" Kastendieck was known familiarly as Aunt Dora. Born in 1818, she grew up in Morsum, Hanover, Germany, the eldest of the Kastendieck siblings.[1] We know little of her early life, her education, or her activities in Hanover, except that the Kastendiecks of Morsum were well educated, and she appears to have been no exception.

Aunt Dora was plain; matronly some might say. Her dark hair parted in the middle and pulled back, framed features that expressed a pleasant but serious countenance. She dressed humbly in the 19th Century fashion of the German American working class.

Dora immigrated to America at the age of twenty-nine and arrived at New York in the summer of 1847 with her brother John Friedrich aboard the ship *Emma*, sailing out of Bremen, Germany.[2] By 1853, she had settled in Brooklyn, New York.

She married rather late in life to Henry Boevers, a man remembered only by the inclusion of his name on her tombstone as the husband of Anna D. Kastendieck.

The couple had two daughters, Alice and Hermina, neither of whom survived childhood. Both children died at the same time of unknown causes, buried on the same day in the Kastendieck family lot at Green-Wood Cemetery, in Brooklyn. Few details survive about the tragic loss of her children. There is no record of the birthdate of Alice. However, Hermina Boevers was born on September 25, 1853, in Brooklyn, and died on January 9, 1857, at the age of four.[3] Her tombstone survives at Green-Wood but no tombstone exists for her sister Alice. Usually, siblings buried on the same day would customarily have shared the same grave marker. The Green-Wood Cemetery Register recorded both children as buried in the Kastendieck family lot on January 11, 1857, bearing the Boevers name.[4]

The grief over the tragic death of Dora's children in the winter of 1857 added to the loss of her mother in the same year. Trina Kastendieck, matriarch of the Kastendieck family, died in the summer of 1857, in July; thus, in rapid succession interment of three members of the Kastendieck family occurred in the Kastendieck lot at Green-Wood Cemetery.[5]

Dora disappeared from the public record after 1857. Over the course of a dozen years, there was no mention of her. She surfaced again in the 1870 US Census living with John Herrman Kastendieck her recently widowed brother and his four small children, in Brooklyn.[6]

The New York Census of 1875 listed her as single and widowed, this time living with her brother John Dietrich Kastendieck and his family, in Brooklyn.[7]

We know that Aunt Dora later accompanied the Kastendieck brothers on their migration from New York to Missouri, trading the bustling cityscape of Brooklyn for the quiet solitude of rural Christian County, Missouri. She lived in Christian County the remainder of her life as a guest at different times in the homes of her brothers, mentioned, for instance, in the 1880 census at the home of her brother John Dietrich.[8]

Dora died in the winter of 1893 a few days past her 76th year. They buried her at Rose Hill Cemetery amid the farmland of the Missouri countryside, a few miles north of the town of Billings, Missouri.[9] Her plain red granite gravestone says simply, "Anna D. Kastendieck wife of Henry Boevers." The people of Billings remembered her as Anna Boevers, a widow, but to her immediate family she was simply Aunt Dora.[10]

Aunt Dora. Anna Dorothea "Dorris" Kastendieck Boevers. This studio portrait of her dates to about 1870, taken in Brooklyn when she was in her early fifties. Augusta Kastendieck Family Album, inscribed on reverse, "Aunt Dora, father's sister," David Gay Collection.

4

John Friedrich Wilhelm Kastendieck

John Friedrich Wilhelm Kastendieck bore a striking resemblance to his older sister. He was of average stature with searching dark eyes and broad lips, framed by drawn-out features accented by a high forehead. The eldest of Trina and Johann Dietrich's four sons—all with the first name of John— John Friedrich by his senior status among the four sons claimed the first name John for himself. He consigned his siblings to the use of their middle names to avoid the confusion arising from having all the boys in the family addressed as John.

John Friedrich left Morsum for America in the summer of 1847, sailing out of Bremen with his sister Dora aboard the ship *Emma*. He was twenty-six, a farmer, and one of 183 passengers who crowded on board the Bremen bark, on a June day to make the difficult and sometimes dangerous journey across the Atlantic.[1] The *Emma* was a sailing vessel about 100 feet in length. The same ship *Emma* survived a collision at sea two months earlier that sank a Dutch schooner. The *Emma* came away with her bowsprit sprung but otherwise seaworthy.[2]

The first eight years in the life of John Friedrich in America are a blank. His name surfaces in the 1855 New York Census as head of the household of the Kastendieck clan and living in Brooklyn's Eighth Ward.[3] We know only that he became a naturalized citizen of the United States sometime during those intervening years.[4] He set up a grocery store at the corner of Nineteenth Street and Third Avenue, in Brooklyn, and was a grocer off and on at that address for more than thirty-three years, taking time along the way to build a milk route.[5]

John married about 1861 at the age of forty-one, old for bachelors of his generation. His marriage to Marie Elizabeth Helmke, of Brooklyn, a tall German girl of twenty-three from Hanover, celebrated a major accomplishment for him. John was not a particularly handsome catch. Marie was, to say the least, a youthful compliment to their union. She was heartily welcomed into the Kastendieck family. She was among those celebrating the 1863 baptism of Andrew Kastendieck, nephew of John Friedrich, at the Wyckoff Street Methodist Episcopal Church, in Brooklyn.[6] The entire immigrant Kastendieck family settled in the same Brooklyn neighborhood as part of a closely-knit extended family.

By 1870, John Friedrich, Marie, (or Mary as people often called her), and their three young daughters: Margaretha, Anna, and Dora, were living in Brooklyn's Eighth Ward. Marie was a housekeeper and he a milkman, work that had netted him after a decade of marriage a modest personal estate of $600 and no recorded real estate holdings.[7] The job of a milkman was a difficult and competitive business in those days. It required long hours of driving a horse-drawn milk wagon around the city delivering milk. The *Brooklyn Daily Eagle* is replete with stories of accidents and other events attendant to the milk delivery business. Moreover, a milkman required a residence built in the city to accommodate his trade, including a barn in which to keep his horses.[8]

During the decade that followed, John Friedrich alternated his business interests between the retail grocery trade and his milk route, inserting into local business directories from time to time the occupation of grocer in place of milkman.[9] Little else changed in John's life except his family grew larger by two children, a son John born in 1872 and baby Millie who came in March of 1875. The New York census-taker appears to have been the object of a harmless prank in 1875. The census did not list daughter Anna; however, in her place and of her age was a son "Henry." There was no son in the family named Henry, although in 1879 a daughter named Henrietta came along.[10]

John and Marie eventually made their home at 653 Third Avenue, near the corner of Third Avenue and Nineteenth Street, in the Gowanus District of Red Hook, Brooklyn.[11] The couple had six children all born in Brooklyn; sadly, only three of them outlived their parents.[12] Baby Henrietta, the youngest child—affectionately called Hattie—came in the winter of 1879 and departed in the summer of 1881.[13] She would be the first of other very difficult losses the family would suffer in the coming years. Margaretha died in 1884 at the age of twenty-two on Christmas day at home, in Brooklyn. We know only that she died of natural causes.[14] She was the oldest of John and Marie's children and perhaps the dearest—ill and cared for by her parents from an early age. They buried Margaretha in the family plot at Green-Wood Cemetery beside her baby sister Henrietta buried there three years before, both at final rest a few blocks from the family home.

Three years passed after Margaretha's death almost to the day when John joined with two associates of Brooklyn to incorporate the People's Cooperative Medical Association, a company meant to furnish inexpensive medical care and relief by reputable physicians for the sick at a low charge to the people.

The *Brooklyn Eagle* reported that twelve shareholders paid $100 each to capitalize the company.[15] Whether the organization grew out of John Friedrich's personal experiences with the death of his daughter is unknown. Meanwhile, no record of the company's success exists.

It took John Friedrich more than five years to face the circumstances of his daughter's loss. He finally petitioned the surrogate court in 1890 to settle her meager estate. She never married and did not leave a will. John wrote out in a firm hand the names of her next of kin: himself her father, "her mother Maria Kastendieck and three sisters Annie Kastendieck, Dora Kastendieck and Millie Kastendieck, and one brother John D. Kastendieck."[16]

Two years later, John Friedrich's son, John D., died unexpectedly in the spring of 1892.[17] Not age twenty yet, the circumstances of his premature death are unknown. He worked as a driver, according to one account, a job that could be dangerous and even deadly.[18] Horse and wagon accidents were frequent. His gravestone marker at Green-Wood Cemetery carries his name and that of his deceased sister Margaretha both carved beneath the name of Trina Kastendieck their grandmother. The elder John Friedrich likely had the marker erected to replace the aging limestone monument that once identified Trina's gravesite and had long since become illegible.

John Friedrich lived but ten more months after losing his only son. He wrote out his will on January 6, 1893, and passed away on March 5, in Brooklyn, still working at his lifelong profession as a milkman. He was age seventy-two.[19] Kings County Surrogate's Court proved his Last Will and Testament on June 6. Marie served as executor of his small estate. Millie (Emilie) was not yet of full age, and a guardian was appointed by the court to represent her, a duty for which the guardian was paid $10. Probate law could be very strict in those days. It was required by law that all known descendants of John Friedrich be served personally with the probate summons to appear in court. Officials overlooked no legal step. Henry C. Cleveland represented the court to carry the notifications door to door. The witnesses to John Friedrich's will came into court as well. Longtime Brooklyn acquaintances Henry Nieber and John C. Kinkel showed up to swear before Surrogate George B. Abbott that they were well acquainted with John Friedrich Wilhelm Kastendieck and witnessed the signing of his will.[20] Court proceedings acknowledged that at the time of his death he held real estate property in New York worth an estimated value of $1,100; his personal property they designated simply as "nominal".[21] He died a relatively poor man and by financial comparison the least successful of the Kastendieck brothers.

Marie carried on after his death. She and her daughters occupied a residence at 282 Seventeenth Street, in Brooklyn. The Kastendieck household now comprised Marie and daughters Millie and Annie, and Annie's new husband John Leonhauser. Daughter Dora had married and moved elsewhere in the city to a place on Seventh Avenue. Dora later took over ownership of the family home on Seventeenth Street to care for her aging mother.

On July 22, 1901, the following death notice appeared on page five of the *Brooklyn Daily Eagle*. "Kastendieck—On Monday, July 22, Marie Elizabeth Kastendieck, widow of John F.W. Kastendieck, at the residence of her daughter, Mrs. C.F. Holzer, 282 Seventeenth St, Brooklyn, N.Y., in her 62nd year. Funeral will take place on Wednesday, July 24, from St. John's German Evangelical Lutheran Church, Prospect Ave., between Fifth and Sixth at 2:30 P.M."[22] St. John's Church was the all-German-speaking congregation that served as the fellowship of worship for the Kastendiecks from the date of its organization in 1866.[23] Kastendieck children grew up in German-speaking households.

There were no descendants of the Kastendieck name in the line of John Friedrich. The Kastendieck name went extinct with the death of his son. There were, however, descendants on the distaff side. The eldest of John and Marie's daughters, Dorothea—Dora to friends and family—was the first to marry of the three surviving Kastendieck daughters. She married Charles Friedrich Holzer, a New York-born butcher sales representative, in November of 1891.[24] Their daughter was Anna Henrietta Holzer who married Charles Krimmel, a printer for a box company. The Holzers and the Krimmels lived together in the same residence until Dora's death in 1934, in Orangetown, New York, a small town northwest of New York City.[25] They returned her body to Brooklyn for burial with the rest of the family in Green-Wood Cemetery.[26]

Meanwhile, Emilie—born Amelia and called "Millie" by her father—married a tailor named George Diedrich Gerken. They had four sons.[27] Emilie died tragically in the fall of 1913 at the age of thirty-eight leaving her four young boys to the care of their father. In a curious twist of fate, Emilie's widowed sister Annie Leonhauser moved into the Gerken household.[28] Annie had previously married John H. Leonhauser in January of 1893. The Leonhauser couple showed up regularly at the German Dramatic Society or other local arts events.[29] Regrettably, Leonhauser died suddenly leaving Annie a widow, too, in 1897 with their infant daughter, Margaret. When Annie's sister Emilie died, Annie and baby Margaret moved into the Gerken household.[30] Annie never remarried and raised Margaret and the Gerken boys as a single mother attached to the Gerken ménage. She died in the summer of 1929, with her remains interred at Green-Wood Cemetery alongside her early-departed husband. Emilie's burial was at Green-Wood, also, but in a different section of the cemetery next to her husband, George Gerken.

The death of Dora Kastendieck Holzer in 1934 closed out the second generation of the immigrant John Friedrich Wilhelm Kastendieck family. Dora was the last survivor of his lineage to be born of the Kastendieck name.

John Friedrich Wilhelm Kastendieck. This portrait dates to about 1870 when John Friedrich was age fifty. An inscription on the reverse, "Uncle John, father's brother," identifies him as the brother of John Dietrich and John Herman Kastendieck. Augusta Kastendieck Family Album.

Marie Elizabeth (Helmke) Kastendieck. Identified as "Aunt Mary", this portrait of the wife of John Friedrich Kastendieck was taken when she was in her early thirties. The chair and backdrop suggest that the photo was taken at the same time as the full-length companion portrait of her husband. Augusta Kastendieck Family Album.

Marie Kastendieck and Child. The child is identified as her daughter Margaretha (below) who died of natural causes at the age of twenty-two. This photograph dates to about 1870 when Marie was in her early thirties. Inscribed, "Aunt Mary [Marie], Uncle John's wife and paralyzed child." Augusta Kastendieck Family Album.

Margaretha Kastendieck. Eldest daughter of John Friedrich and Marie Kastendieck, she died December 25, 1884, in Brooklyn, New York, about the time of this photograph. Augusta Kastendieck Family Album.

5

John Henry Kastendieck

Henry Kastendieck was the fourth in line of the immigrant Kastendieck family to leave Morsum, Germany. He made the journey alone at the age of twenty-nine, and by 1852 settled into New York's Eleventh Ward.[1] Records reveal little of his early life or his decision to immigrate to America, except that like his sisters and brothers, he chose to abandon farm life in revolutionary Hanover to journey down the Weser River to Bremerhaven and out across the Atlantic to New York City.

He went into the grocery business; first in Manhattan, New York, and then in Brooklyn, opening a store in Brooklyn at 633 Court Street at the corner of Seventeenth Street.[2] His movements are difficult to trace because there were other Kastendiecks named Henry living in Brooklyn at the same time, including Rev. Henry Kastendieck, a well-known Methodist Episcopal Church minister.

Henry came into the grocery business, in part, by way of his marriage to Catharine (Benthen) Windeler, widow of the deceased Charles Windeler, a successful grocer. Four years prior to their union, an entry in the 1850 census listed Catharine and

Charles Windeler in New York's Eleventh Ward with two small children; the census listed Mr. Windeler's occupation as grocer.[3] He died in August of 1854, in Manhattan, and Henry and Catharine wed on December 31 of the same year, in Manhattan.[4] They were of the same age—Henry and Catharine—both born in 1823 and both immigrants from Hanover; she being the daughter of Ludwig Benthen, citizen of Baden; she had a brother named Henry Benthen.[5]

Henry Kastendieck did well in the grocery business by either hard work or inheritance. By 1855, the couple had established their home in Manhattan, living in a $7,000 brick residence, working the grocery trade, and taking in boarders; one of whom was Catharine's brother, Henry.[6] The youngest Windeler daughter, Margaret, died sometime prior to 1855 leaving only nine-year-old Adeline "Linna" Windeler as the lone surviving child of Catharine's previous marriage.

The Kastendiecks had three children of their own. Mary Kastendieck came along in August of 1855; joined by John Dietrich in 1859; and Henry, Jr., in 1862. The family had by now left the environs of Manhattan, resettled in Brooklyn's Twelfth Ward, on Court Street, and traded their fine brick home in New York for one of similar stature in Brooklyn.[7] Henry's stepdaughter, Linna Windeler, took the surname Kastendieck as his adopted daughter. In time, she married a French confectioner named Joseph Masson and moved away.[8]

Over the next decade, there was a downturn in the grocery business. Henry traded in his $6,000 brick residence for a frame house of less than half that value and took a job as a workhand. By the year 1875, he and Catharine were living in the house alone. Daughter Mary had wed the year before, and the boys were busy at work elsewhere in the city and boarding with a family living next door to their stepsister Linna (Windeler-

Kastendieck) Masson. The Kastendieck sons worked in the Masson and Zollinger candy shop in Brooklyn's Second Ward and at odd jobs about the city.[9]

In his early fifties, Henry took work as a laborer in New Lots, Kings County, New York.[10] New Lots was one of six towns that stood separate from Brooklyn in 1875 but later annexed to the city. Henry lived in Brooklyn and commuted to New Lots. This was a common practice of men seeking lucrative jobs outside the city limits of Brooklyn.

Henry retired in 1880, and things went downhill quickly. He and Catharine took up residence with their daughter and son-in-law, Linna and Joseph, at the Masson home in New Lots.[11] It was a brief arrangement because Linna died the next year in December of 1881, childless and a few days short of her thirty-sixth birthday—the day after her twelfth wedding anniversary. They buried her at the Lutheran All Faiths Cemetery, Middle Village, New York, and the place of interment of her biological father. Meanwhile, Joseph Masson, her widowed husband, died three years later while on a business trip to France. His interment was in France.[12]

Henry Kastendieck died in the autumn of 1885, at the age of sixty-two, in Brooklyn, with burial in the Kastendieck family plot at Green-Wood Cemetery.[13] Henry lived a life of no particular distinction, saw his businesses come and go, and departed without knowing that the Kastendieck name in his line would become extinct with the next generation. Henry's eldest son, John D., died under peculiar circumstances in the spring of 1899. John D. lived in New York and worked as a bartender, but he died at 438 Fourth Street, in Brooklyn, where his brother Henry, Jr., operated a butcher shop. John D. was thirty-eight at the time and single. His burial was in the Lutheran All Faiths Cemetery beside his adopted stepsister, Linna, and not with his father in Green-Wood.[14] No details of his death were furnished. In less than a year, his mother Catharine died. The widow of Henry Kastendieck wrote her will on April 18, 1899, coincidental with the sudden death of her son, John. She, too, died at the residence of her son Henry Kastendieck, Jr., on Fourth Street. Kings County Surrogate's Court proved her will, taking note that the value of her personal property did not exceed $1,057.[15] Meanwhile, Mary, only daughter of her and Henry Kastendieckk, Sr., followed her in death six months later.[16] Regrettably, the coincidental deaths of so many people at one time were common in turn-of-the-century New York.

The final resting places of the deceased members of the Henry Kastendieck, Sr. family were unique. Interment of Henry, Sr. was in Green-Wood Cemetery with others of the Kastendieck name. Meanwhile, his wife Catharine went to her final rest in Lutheran All Faiths Cemetery with her first husband, Mr. Windeler, and their daughter Linna. Either the family faced the dilemma of choosing to bury John D. Kastendiecck with his father in Green-Wood or with his mother at Lutheran All Faiths; his burial was at Lutheran All Faiths.[17] They buried daughter Mary, on the other hand, at Green-Wood, which adds yet another turn in the Henry Kastendieck legacy.[18]

Mary Kastendieck, oldest child and only daughter of Henry and Catharine, became the wife of Charles Gruschow, a Chicago boy originally from Hamburg, Germany. They married the year after he moved to Brooklyn on December 13, 1874. Mary was nineteen; Charles was twenty-eight. The couple had ten children; six survived to adulthood. Gruschow worked for the Armour meat company in the Chicago Stock Yards before starting his own meat supply in Brooklyn called Ships Chandler, at 50 Hicks Street, in what later was the Brooklyn Bridge area. The company supplied meat to ships near the Brooklyn Bridge.[19]

Mr. Gruschow died in the summer of 1917 in South Brooklyn. His interment was in Green-Wood Cemetery in the Gruschow plot, thus explaining why Henry Kastendieck's daughter went to rest in Green-Wood but not his sons.[20] The burial of Mary in Green-Wood was not because of her father but because of her husband.

The cemetery issue arose again when Henry Kastendieck, Jr., died in 1920.[21] He was a part-time bank guard in later years, having retired after many years of running a butcher shop on Brooklyn's Fourth Avenue. He had made some money.[22] He wrote out his will in the spring of 1919 naming as heirs his nieces and nephews of the Gruschow family. The six surviving Gruschow children were the sole descendants of the elder Henry Kastendieck, Sr., and the last to carry his legacy forward. Henry, Jr., did not marry and had no children of his own. He owned no real estate at the time of his death. However, the Surrogate's Court of Brooklyn judged the value of his personal property to be between $7,500 and $8,000 dollars. The finalized estate divided the money among the Gruschow offspring scattered across Brooklyn, with a small remembrance to the Lutheran All Faiths Cemetery, in Queens.[23] At the end of his will, he wrote out in his own hand a specific if not enigmatic, demand. "It is my wish that my Executor shall have placed in my plot in Lutheran Cemetery, Lot No 44-Map 1/B a tombstone or monument to cost from $600 to $700 with the inscription In memory of Catharine Kastendieck Born April 8th 1823 died March 28 1900—John D. Kastendieck Born Sept 20th 1859 died April 11th 1899. Henry Kastendieck Born July 21st 1862."[24] He chose burial with his mother and brother in Lutheran All Faiths and not with his father in Green-Wood. Henry Kastendieck, Sr., meanwhile, lies in an unmarked grave in the Kastendieck Green-Wood Cemetery Lot, Number 9625.

Henry Kastendieck. Family historians accept this portrait from the mid-1860s as that of the German immigrant Henry Kastendieck. The unidentified picture, taken in a studio setting identical to portraits of Kastendieck family members, was with photographs of the other Kastendieck immigrants in the Augusta Kastendieck Family Album.

Mary Kastendieck and Charles Adolph Gruschow. The oldest child of Henry and Catharine Kastendieck, Mary wed Charles Gruschow at Zion Evangelical German Lutheran Church in Brooklyn in 1874. These portraits date to about the time of their marriage. Augusta Kastendieck Family Album.

6

John Dietrich Kastendieck

The youngest child of Johann Dietrich and Trina Kastendieck's six children was Dietrich. Born in 1834, he was the fifth of the immigrant Kastendiecks to journey to America.[1] He left Morsum for the United States in 1851 to join his siblings who had made the crossing at different times over the previous five years.[2] He settled into the German community of New York where his brothers already enjoyed a good foothold in the grocery business. The 1855 New York Census found him living with his older brother John Friedrich in Brooklyn's Eighth Ward.[3]

There are many stories of Dietrich's youth in Morsum, some of which survive in the writings of his talented daughter Augusta "Gussie" Kastendieck. According to Gussie, Dietrich developed an early interest in wildlife, first hunting for pleasure in the fields and woodlands around Morsum, Hanover, and later in the parks of Brooklyn. He extended his interest in nature to the art of taxidermy to preserve the specimens taken in the hunt.[4]

He made his livelihood in the retail grocery business in the same trade as his three older brothers. At one time, they all had grocery stores in Brooklyn. There is no evidence, however, that they ever incorporated their common interest, choosing instead to maintain individual establishments in competition with each other.

One spring day in 1860, Dietrich visited John Herman Kastendieck's grocery store on Van Brunt Street, in Brooklyn, coming over from his own store on Fourteenth Street. There was a new girl in town working for his brother, a girl recently arrived from the old hometown of Morsum, Germany, and helping the Herman Kastendieck family in the role of household servant. Her name was Rebecka Röpke, a smart, petite girl of seventeen with boundless energy and a fastidious nature when it came to housekeeping.[5] They—Dietrich and Rebecka—were both born in Morsum, Hannover, and in that small-town environment knew each other growing up as children. Each immigrated to America at different times; Rebecka came later. She was the daughter of Dietrich and Katharine Magdalena "Lena" (Doppe) Röpke. Rebecka was one of a family of three sisters and a brother, three of whom also settled in Brooklyn.[6]

Dietrich visited his brother's store again, and again. It took him two years to convince Rebecka to marry him, a twenty-eight-year-old bachelor.[7] The couple married in May of 1862, beginning a journey of thirty-nine years together that would take them eventually out of Brooklyn to a place halfway across the country to the rural landscape of Billings, Missouri.[8] In the meantime, they set up housekeeping in the grocery store.[9] Taxidermy was a hobby patiently endured by Rebecka.

Business was good in Brooklyn. Soon after their marriage, Dietrich and Rebecka were able to move to a better location on Fifth Avenue where they lived and worked for nearly twenty years.

Their first child, John Dietrich, Jr., was born in Brooklyn in the summer of 1863. Helena Dorothea then came along in the late fall of 1865, but she lived for only a year. Her burial was in the usual place in the Kastendieck Lot at Green-Wood Cemetery, a few blocks from the Kastendieck home.[10]

Meanwhile, Alice was born in 1867 and Charlotte in 1870. Charlotte arrived soon after the family returned from a visit to Germany in 1869 to see Rebecka's parents at Morsum. Then unthinkable tragedy hit as it did many times in the extended Kastendieck family. Their son Herman Friederich was born in the spring of 1873 and died in the summer of that year; then Edward, born in 1875, lived but three years. In the wake of these heartbreaks, Aunt Dora, Dietrich's sister, moved into his residence on Fifth Avenue. A daughter Augusta came along in 1877 and happily survived as the fourth surviving child of Dietrich and Rebecka, allowing them a pause in the painful familiarity of the deaths of their children.

The grocery business in Brooklyn prospered for several years. Dietrich did well, resided in a $6,000 frame home at 534 Fifth Avenue, and immersed himself in taxidermy.[11] By all accounts, he became a well-respected professional taxidermist particularly among ornithology scholars. The World's Fair once exhibited his work.

A downturn in economic conditions in the late 1870s, coupled with deteriorating living conditions in Brooklyn and an unbearable string of personal bereavements, caused Dietrich's brother, John Herman, to want to leave Brooklyn. Dietrich bought out his brother through a financial arrangement that allowed John Herman to abandon the grocery business and move to Missouri. Dietrich soon made the same decision to leave Brooklyn. In 1880, he sold the businesses, gathered his family including Aunt Dora, and followed his brother to Billings, Missouri, there to live out the remainder of his life. By June of 1880, the Dietrich Kastendieck family had settled on acreage in Polk Township, Christian County, Missouri, already acclimated to Dietrich's new occupation of farmer.[12]

The move from Brooklyn to rural Missouri came with a sad irony. Dietrich left the unhealthy environment of urban Brooklyn for the restorative merits of the Christian County countryside and the promise of a better life for his family. They arrived at Billings in February of 1880, and within eight months, on September 29, 1880, his daughter Alice died. They buried her in an unfamiliar place called Rose Hill Cemetery, near Billings, Missouri, the first Kastendieck to lie at rest in Rose Hill, and not in the fabled Green-Wood Cemetery of Brooklyn.[13] Alice was thirteen years old; the fourth of Dietrich and Rebecka's seven children to die in childhood.

John Dietrich Kastendieck. This picture depicts a young Dietrich Kastendieck in his early thirties in a portrait taken about 1866 at the Sherman Photography Studio, in Brooklyn, New York. Sherman and Company at 270-272 Fulton Street, according to an 1863 advertisement in the *Brooklyn Daily Eagle*, was a leading photographer of Brooklyn. The Augusta Kastendieck Family Album.

Rebecka (Röpke) Kastendieck. She immigrated to America about 1859, married Dietrich Kastendieck in 1861, and lived in Brooklyn, New York, until the family moved to Billings, Missouri, in 1880. She gave birth to ten children. This photograph of her taken in Brooklyn dates to around the year 1866 when she was age twenty-four. The Augusta Kastendieck Family Album.

Rebecka Kastendieck and Daughter Charlotte. Taken about 1872, Charlotte was the fourth child of "Becka" and Dietrich Kastendieck. Born in Brooklyn, Charlotte grew up in rural Christian County, Missouri, near the small town of Billings. She later married and moved to St. Louis, Missouri. Augusta Kastendieck Family Album.

John Dietrich Kastendieck, Jr., was the oldest child and son of Dietrich and Rebecka Kastendieck. This photograph taken about 1866 in Brooklyn, New York, shows the common 19th Century practice of dressing young boys in dresses. Boys wore dresses until they began to wear breeches or trousers between two and eight years of age. Augusta Kastendieck Family Album.

7

Trina

The Kastendiecks came to the United States in stages over a period of years; each in turn putting down roots in New York and awaiting those left behind at the home place in Morsum. All eventually left Germany for America. Trina was the last of the family to leave Morsum. The matriarch of the family set sail out of Bremerhaven in 1852 with her daughter Mary to embark on the long journey across the Atlantic.[1]

Travel accommodations for emigrants improved at Bremerhaven after her son John Herman made the first Kastendieck voyage in 1846. A new railway from Bremen to Bremerhaven eliminated the need to crowd onto a boat for the daylong sail down the Weser River. A New Harbor went in at Bremerhaven adjacent to the Old Harbor, and a modern emigration center opened at Bremerhaven in 1850. Still, once aboard ship it took about six weeks to make the trip from Bremerhaven to New York on ships not usually designed and built for passenger travel.

There is scant evidence of Trina's presence in New York. The 1855 New York Census listed her living with her bachelor sons

John Friedrich and John Dietrich and daughter Mary, in Brooklyn's Eighth Ward.[2] The first of the many tragedies to strike the Kastendiecks happened the next year. Mary suddenly died in the winter of 1856.[3] She was next to the youngest of the Kastendieck siblings, age twenty-five and unmarried when she died. Her years in America were very brief, dating only from the time of her journey with her mother from Morsum until 1856. Her brothers purchased a burial lot in Green-Wood Cemetery, in Brooklyn, and buried her there as the first of many of the Kastendieck family who would be buried in that place.

A year later mother Trina died. Her burial was beside her daughter Mary in Green-Wood in the cemetery lot purchased by her sons.[4] Note of her passing appeared in the pages of the Green-Wood Cemetery register. "Maria Kastendieck died July 18, 1857, at the age of 65 years 10 months 9 days.[5] Interment of her remains was July 20, 1857, in Lot 9625, at Green-Wood. She was born in Germany; late residence was 19th, corner of 5th avenue, Brooklyn, New York. Cause of death was Consumption."[6] The time and memory of her in America were brief. With her death, the first generation of the immigrant Kastendiecks passed into history.

Many years went by, and the stone that marked the location of Trina's burial place gave way to the seasons. The names and dates etched into the soft limestone that once marked her grave faded away. Her son John Friedrich, upon the death of his son in 1892, erected a new stone, a gray granite marker bearing the name T.M. Kastendieck, and the names of John Friedrich's two deceased children.[7] This gray tombstone today sets nestled between markers on either side, one the original limestone of Trina and the other belonging to the later deceased wife and infant children of John Herman Kastendieck.[8] T.M. Kastendieck stood for Trina Maria Kastendieck and Trina was short for

Catharina.[9] In placing the stone at Green-Wood, her family chose to represent her as the familiar Trina by her initials and not by her full Christian name.

The Emigrants' House in Bremerhaven. Opened in the spring of 1850, the emigration house could accommodate two thousand people who were awaiting departure on overseas ships. Trina and her daughter Mary Kastendieck would have taken rooms here. Expanded rail traffic carrying emigrants directly from Bremen to Bremerhaven made the building obsolete in the latter part of the 19th Century. Lithograph by W. Casten, 1850. *Das Große Bremen-Lexikon.* Bremen: Temmen, 2003.

Three Kastendieck Gravestones. The center stone, in Section 116 Lot 9625 Green-Wood Cemetery, identifies T.M. (Catharina "Trina" Maria) Kastendieck and the deceased adult children of John Friedrich Wilhelm Kastendieck. It was erected upon the death of his son, John D. Kastendieck, in 1892. The marker on the right is for John Friedrich Wilhelm's sister-in-law, Bridget Kastendieck, and her deceased infant children. The left-hand stone is illegible but believed to be the one placed originally for Trina and daughter Mary in 1857. Photo by Bob Collins.

The Brooklyn Years

8

Brooklyn, New York

In the beginning a few Dutch settled on the marshland along the westernmost portion of Long Island, New York, to avail themselves of the excellent fishing brought on by six-foot tides that forced salt water into the streams and produced an ideal environment for oysters. One of the meandering streams they found to be especially productive was Gowanus Creek that flowed into Gowanus Bay. Soon the creek and surrounding farmland coalesced into an urban fabric of villages and towns that sprung up along the shore. Here in the mid-1650s the small town of Breuckele took shape on the East River shore of Long Island.

Two hundred years of history passed. By 1855, Brooklyn was the nation's third most populous city.[1] By mid-19th Century, the mills and landings along the creek turned into an industrial revolution that required larger navigational and docking facilities. Some local merchants advocated the dredging of Gowanus Creek into a mile and a half canal to serve as a commercial waterway. The New York State Legislature authorized the construction of the Gowanus Creek Canal in 1867 and saw the work essentially completed by 1869.

The Gowanus Canal became a hub of commercial maritime shipping. Practically overnight, the canal transformed South Brooklyn from a once rural place into a world port and industrial destination, the nation's busiest commercial canal.

Brooklyn grew exponentially. People constructed as many as five hundred buildings a year in South Brooklyn. Sewage ran downhill into Gowanus Creek. Pollution flowed into the canal unabated. The fish died off and Brooklyn a little at the same time.

John Herman Kastendieck was nineteen years old when he boarded a ship at the Old Harbor of Bremerhaven, Germany, and sailed out onto the North Sea to begin his journey to America. He landed at the Port of New York with little more than the essentials of ship travel and a desire to begin a new life. He settled eventually in the up-and-coming community of South Brooklyn, on the undeveloped tip of Long Island, on the shore of Gowanus Bay. There he established his grocery business in the 1850s, before the city's decline, and during the good times.

Sunset at Gowanus Bay in the Bay of New York. Gowanus Bay connects to Upper New York Bay bordering the neighborhood of South Brooklyn where the Kastendieck brothers kept their grocery stores. The artist Henry Gritten painted this idyllic view of Gowanus Bay c. 1851 a few blocks from John Herman Kastendieck's location. Allport Library and Museum of Fine Arts, Tasmania State Library, Austrialia.

9

Red Hook and the Atlantic Basin Riot

T he village of Red Hook grew up out of the marshes along the Atlantic seaboard and was once a separate community before annexation into the Sixth Ward of Brooklyn. Red Hook took its name from the red clay soil and the shape of the land mass that projects out into the East River. Originally named by the Dutch who settled the area as Roode Hoek, the word Hoek meant "point" or "corner" (and not the English word hook). Sometimes called Red Hook Point today, local inhabitants mistakenly added a second "point" to its original meaning.[1]

In 1841, the only business in Red Hook was a powder factory that stood at the foot of what became Wolcott Street. There was a stone house near the intersection of King and Van Brunt Streets and a few rudely constructed shanties—occupied mostly by Germans—built at the foot of Van Brunt and Wolcott Streets.[2] That was about it. Everything else was little more than a swampy meadow. People traveled there at the risk of their safety at the hands of one of the many thieves that infested the neighborhood.

In 1843, the Atlantic Dock Company laid out plans for a new dock facility, situated above Red Hook on the west shore of Brooklyn. The company engaged a number of laborers to build it at the going rate of seventy-five cents a day. The mostly Irish workers soon became dissatisfied with the rate of pay and demanded a pay increase to eighty-seven cents a day. Weary of the labor strife, the Atlantic Company sent to Germany for replacements. In this decidedly squalid and uncomplimentary setting is the earliest clue to the circumstances of the journey of John Herman Kastendieck from Morsum, Germany, to America.

In the fall of 1845, two ship cargoes of Germans arrived in Brooklyn in response to the call of the Atlantic Dock Company for laborers. They gladly availed themselves of the free Atlantic passage and wages of fifty cents per day offered to them by the Company.[3] The Irish dockworkers went on strike to demand reduced work hours and higher pay, and the Atlantic Company turned to the recently arrived German immigrants to replace about a hundred Irish laborers and break the strike. The hiring of the Germans so enraged the Irish a riot broke out. A bitter ethnic conflict erupted between the Irish and the Germans. It became necessary to call in the military to squelch the riot, eventually requiring members of the New York militia to take up a defense of the Germans and protect them in their work on the basin.

The riots broke out on the morning of April 15, 1846, when the Atlantic Dock employers attempted to replace the striking Irish workers with a contingent of German laborers. A gang of Irish immediately set upon the German party with clubs and stones and drove them off, severely injuring several in the process.[4]

All through the month of April, gangs of Irishmen lay in ambush of the Germans, many of whom lived in Manhattan, took the ferry to work, and had to pass through the Irish going to and from work. Fights broke out daily and the Germans usually got the short end of it. It was common for groups of escaping Germans to arrive at the ferry, bleeding and beaten half senseless from the blows of their attackers, their teeth knocked out and their heads and faces gashed. Rumors circulated that some died of their wounds.[5] The *Brooklyn Daily Eagle* took occasion to point out that the problem was not with the Brooklyn Irish but with the "blustering rowdies in New York" who were the guilty parties. It seems they were the ones to fan the flames of riot.

Many are the stories of the violence that accompanied the building of the Atlantic Basin Dock. One such story tells how a number of young Germans, done with their day's labor on a day in 1846, were under great distress, fearful of the Irish, and afraid for their lives in a foreign and unfamiliar place. A robust Irishman, seeing their entrapment, took pity on the tired and hungry Germans and personally guided them through the gangs of angry Irishmen to safe passage back to their homes in New York.[6] Only after the Irish went to work on another part of the project did the tensions begin to ease. In the end, both the Germans and Irish worked on the basin together. The wages settled on the laborers were eighty cents a day for those who worked on the landward side, and eighty-five cents for the dredge men, mostly Germans who actually built the basin.

While the evidence is circumstantial, John Herman arrived in New York in 1846 as a young man looking for adventure and opportunity not then available in Germany. Germany stood on the verge of revolution. He did not come in the first wave of German immigrants brought over by the Atlantic Dock

Company in 1845 but certainly could have availed himself of a later offer in time to experience the Atlantic Basin Riot. The work in Brooklyn and free passage to America paid for by a future employer had the makings of real adventure.

John Herman did not settle immediately in Red Hook and took up quarters elsewhere. Evidence suggests that he first lived either in Manhattan, somewhere in greater Brooklyn, or further north up Long Island. The Hamilton Avenue Ferry that opened for business in 1846, running regularly between Red Hook and Manhattan across the East River, connected Red Hook to greater New York. The German contingent of laborers living in Manhattan took it to work because many immigrants preferred the more amenable Manhattan to Brooklyn.

John Herman eventually did move to Red Hook, built his grocery store there, and made Brooklyn his permanent home for more than twenty years.[7] Whether he helped to build the Atlantic Basin Dock or simply opened a grocery business to take advantage of the growing demand for goods in the city we can only presume. He nevertheless experienced firsthand the opportunities and difficulties encountered in those early years of immigrant occupation of Brooklyn.

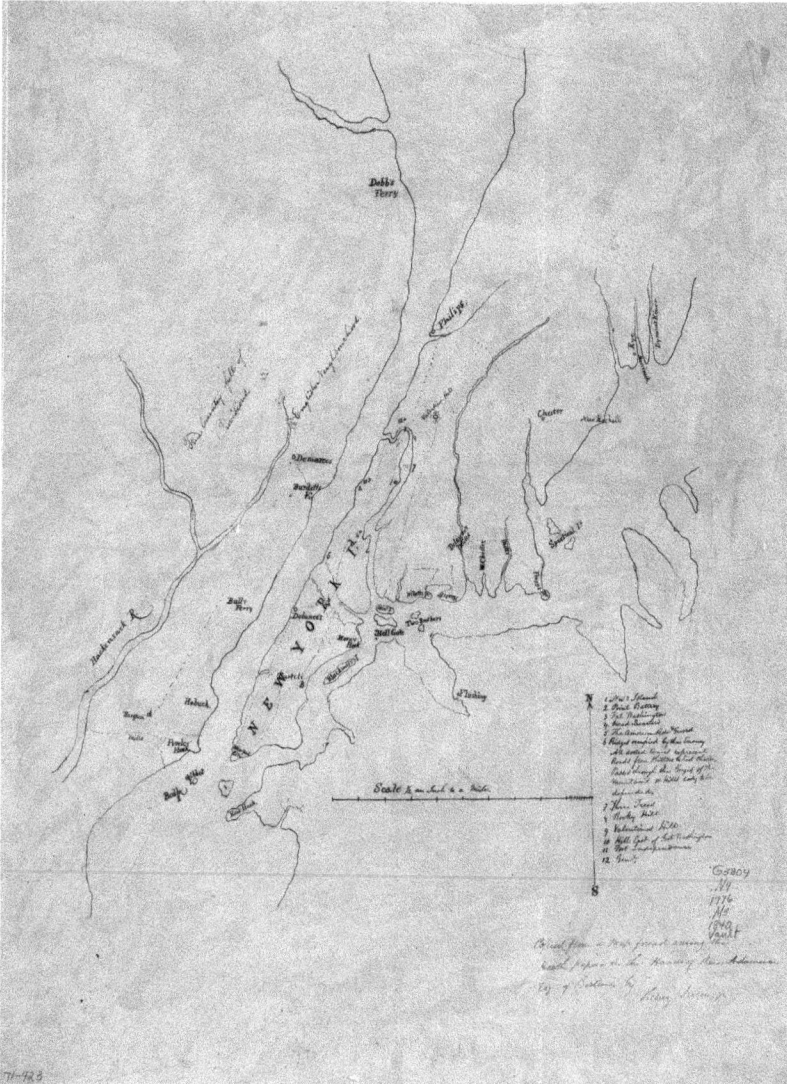

Map of New York Island and Vicinity. This early map shows Red Hook (bottom left-center) projecting out into the Upper New York Bay, set across the East River that divides Manhattan from Brooklyn. Pen and ink tracing of a map created in 1776, copied in 1840. Library of Congress.

Bird's Eye View of New York and Brooklyn. Battery Park and Governors Island are in the foreground. The East River divides busy Manhattan and the more populated region of upper Brooklyn on the right. The less-populated rural area of Red Hook is to the right and below out of view in this drawing. Lithograph by John Bachmann. New York: A. Guerber, c. 1851. Library of Congress.

Ferry House at the Foot of Hamilton Avenue, in Brooklyn. Ferry service on the Hamilton Avenue Ferry began in 1846, the year John Herman Kastendieck arrived in New York. He located his grocery store about one-half mile from the Ferry House. *Harpers Weekly*.

10

Corner of Van Brunt and Wolcott

When John Herman took up residence in Red Hook much of outlying Brooklyn was woodland with scattered patches of farmland. Developers had graded the streets of the town but there were few houses. The Atlantic Dock was new, and the Hamilton Ferry was up and running; however, South Brooklyn was a place separate from Manhattan and New York City and of a very different character.

The Atlantic Dock Company owned nearly two-thirds of the land of Red Hook. About the time that John Herman moved to Red Hook, workers were in the process of removing a large hill some forty to fifty feet in height that extended from Forth Place to Degraw Street and from Columbia Street nearly all the way to Gowanus Creek.[1] The president of the Atlantic Dock Company, seeking to make the land more profitable, undertook to move Bergen Hill. This large hill at the time constituted the only high ground in South Brooklyn. The Atlantic president contracted large numbers of new Irish immigrants literally to cut away the hill and use the dirt to fill the marshes and swamps that covered a good part of Red Hook. The Irish stayed and settled on the cleared land. Those who had the money purchased lots, while most rented paying up to $20 a lot per annum. At the same time, Red Hook divided into several smaller municipalities. Among them was Tinkerville located in the general vicinity of where John Herman eventually lived. Tinkerville comprised primarily residents of a Bohemian character. To house them initially, the Atlantic Dock Company constructed a row of shanties along the line that became Van Brunt Street where John Herman would build his grocery store. This turned out to be the first colonization of Red Hook Point, or Tinkerville, by Germans. Van Brunt Street formed the easterly boundary of the property of the Atlantic Basin, which covered about eighty acres.[2] The land lying west beyond Van Brunt was originally under water at high tide. The builders of the basin filled it in to make the lots and streets, which accounted for a sizeable portion of Brooklyn's Red Hook district.

As early as 1847, Van Brunt Street was seventy feet wide as the result of its reconstruction and a law passed by the New York State Legislature empowering city officials of Brooklyn to acquire the necessary land to widen the street and extend it northward to accommodate the docks. It was on this wide street at the corner of Van Brunt and Wolcott Streets that John Herman Kastendieck came to establish his grocery business.

We do not know how John Herman came to own his property. However, south of Hamilton Avenue, two wealthy landowners owned nearly all of what would become the Tinkerville-Red Hook section of Brooklyn. Any land not owned by the Atlantic Dock Company was in the hands of the Van Dykes and Luqueers.[3] They bought up the land early when it was a patchwork of farms cut by shoreline inlets and dotted with gristmills operated by the rise and fall of the tidewater. No deeds are extant; however, it is likely that John Herman bought property that once belonged to the Van Dykes or Luqueers on which to build his store. They sold off some of their holdings in the 1840s and 1850s and passed other parts onto their heirs in the early 1860s.

As the area of Red Hook built up, clusters of stores and businesses sprung up mostly along the waterfront and a few blocks inland. Houses went up quickly on the newly created lots practically before the earth could settle. Row houses only seventeen feet wide but three stories high rented for $250 a year, compared with the nominal price of lots on the leveled upper flats at $600 per annum.[4] Single lots usually measured twenty-five by one hundred feet. Most streets were at least twenty-four feet wide and sidewalks thirteen feet. Houses sat back from the street a comfortable distance of thirty-three feet, giving neighborhoods a spacious and well-kept appearance.

Improved ferry service from Manhattan to Brooklyn was in the works; and the first gaslights appeared in Brooklyn in the spring of 1848, the same year the newly completed Atlantic Basin officially went into operation. The early planners of South Brooklyn had a vision of a grand city.

The record is silent on how John Herman acquired his property in Brooklyn. Property records may eventually yield up an answer. Meanwhile, one of the ways that many Brooklyn citizens became landowners was through the periodic sales of real estate by the Merchants Exchange Bank headquartered on Wall Street, in New York City. The bank acquired property either through speculation or through foreclosure and periodically sold it at public auction. One such sale occurred on November 28, 1849, when the Bank auctioned property situated on the southeast corner of Van Brunt and Wolcott Streets, in South Brooklyn. The sale consisted of two small lots each twenty-five by twenty feet with a two-story brick store and dwelling on the corner measuring eighteen by twenty-five, and a two-story frame dwelling house adjoining and fronting on Van Brunt Street that measured thirteen by twenty-five in size. The properties sold together, subject to a mortgage of $1,100 for three years at 7 percent interest. Already rented, the property promised to pay a good return.[5] This was John Herman's neighborhood cornering on Van Brunt and Wolcott. This very well could have become his property. We think, however, that he settled on the west side of Van Brunt and that the tenants of these premises became his neighbors and competitors in the retail sales business. At the same time, he probably was not in a position to take on a purchase of property of this size. He was only twenty-three in 1849, in the country just three years, and not yet ready to take on the responsibility of land ownership. He nevertheless read the Merchant's Exchange advertisements in the *Brooklyn Daily Eagle* and saw Brooklyn as a place of opportunity. The Merchants Exchange also advertised in 1849 an attractive new frame store, dwelling, and lot situated on the southeast corner of Van Brunt and Dikeman Streets, down the street from where John Herman eventually bought property. Set on a lot fifty by fifty feet, the building was the same modest thirteen by twenty-three two-story affair that was a common design in mid-19th Century Brooklyn. Evidence exists that John Herman first established a store at Dikeman and Van Brunt before moving or expanding his business to Van Brunt and Wolcott.[6]

Property sold at a brisk pace in Brooklyn. Getting in on the bottom floor meant making a quick investment. Brooklyn was rapidly evolving into a city of desirable destination. A new Classical Revival style city hall building went up in 1849 at Fulton and Joralemon streets close to the Fulton Ferry and about a mile and a half from John's eventual home and store. In 1851, the *Brooklyn Daily Eagle* found it newsworthy to report that a new three-story house had gone up at the corner of Dikeman and Van Brunt, probably on the lot previously described above. "One of the handsomest frame houses to be seen anywhere," the article said, "Finished in a very tasteful and elegant fashion."[7] This is very different from the description a few years earlier that characterized the Red Hook area as a disgraceful slum filled with shanties. John Herman's future neighborhood was taking on a new look.

In May of 1851, the Merchants Exchange Bank advertised for sale an attractive offering. They listed twenty-six lots of ground in South Brooklyn, in the Sixth Ward near the Atlantic Dock and Hamilton Avenue Ferry, on the block bounded by Dikeman, Richards, Wolcott, and Van Brunt Streets—the John Herman Kastendieck neighborhood. These lots offered a good opportunity to someone like John Herman looking for an affordable way to establish a business and home in Brooklyn. The Bank would take a mortgage on part of the purchase price.[8] We cannot say that John Herman attended the noonday auction, on May 19, 1851, at the Merchants Exchange in New York City. However, it is the best circumstantial record so far that would place John at his future address in South Brooklyn as a property owner at the age of twenty-five, at the corner of Van Brunt and Wolcott Streets.

The domestic picture of Brooklyn in the 1850s was one of a bustling town replete with the dangers and petty crime of any busy city. Fires were commonplace, often from the highly combustible liquid used in many homes to light lamps. The newspapers hardly missed an edition without reporting on such an incident. A camphene lamp burst at Murray's grocery store on the corner of Dikeman and Van Brunt Streets, down the street from where John had his store, setting fire to clothing and threatening the entire house, if not the neighborhood.[9] In another incident, a thirteen-year-old servant girl died of burns suffered because of a bursting camphene lamp.[10] These lamps were especially dangerous because gas could accumulate and explode. They replaced old whale-oil lamps, which people often converted to the brighter burning camphene, and thus compounded the danger. Cheaper and slightly safer kerosene did not become readily available domestically until after the oil discoveries of 1859.

Meanwhile, across the street from the location of John's store, one John Connally broke into the home of Mr. Gilcrest at the corner of Van Brunt and Wolcott and stole a $15 coat. Police arrested and jailed him.[11] In another instance, they caught a young man who had been a bar keeper in the neighborhood and thought to be of good character, embezzling more than $600 from his employer at Dikeman and Van Brunt and stashing the gold in the chimney.[12] Both incidents occurred in John Herman's vicinity.

Criminal behavior while not rare did not rule John Herman's neighborhood. Many uplifting events made Brooklyn a desirable place to live. Police found a little girl named Jane Irving wandering the streets. Her parents had died months before and left her homeless and alone in the world. Neighbors took her in and saw her settled properly in a safe home.[13]

Such was Red Hook in South Brooklyn in the early 1850s.

The Original High and Low Grounds of Red Hook. Salt marsh and shore lines in the city of Brooklyn appear in darker gray. John Herman Kastendieck's property (arrow) stood on a site that was once marshland. The East River traces the western shoreline of Brooklyn. Excerpt from an original government survey made in 1776-77. New York Board of Health, American Photo-Lithographic Company, 1876. New York Public Library.

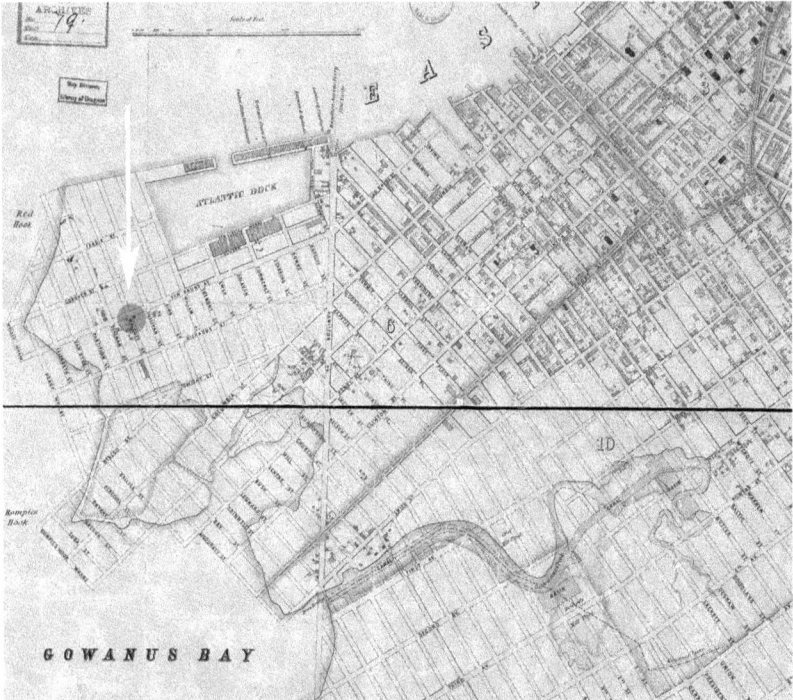

Location of John Herman's Property in Red Hook. The Red Hook area
of Brooklyn lay situated between the Atlantic Basin and Gowanus Bay.
John Herman's grocery store stood at Wolcott and Van Brunt Streets
(arrow). Modified from Matthew Dripps map published in 1850. Library
of Congress.

BROOKLYN CITY HALL.

Drawing of Brooklyn City Hall in 1850. This new Classical Revival style building in Brooklyn Heights stood about one and one-half miles northeast of where John Herman Kastendieck opened his store, in South Brooklyn. Shown are the horses and carriages typical of transportation of the day. The building still stands and is now Brooklyn Borough Hall. Lithograph by Charles Magnus, 1850, courtesy of the Brooklyn Public Library.

Camphene Lamp 1830-1860. These lamps were popular but dangerous replacements for the old whale-oil lamps that lighted early 19th Century American homes and businesses. The lamps frequently exploded causing fires, injury, and even death. The camphene fluid cost about fifty cents a gallon and burned brighter and cleaner than coal oil (the original kerosene), which was usually more expensive. Petroleum-based kerosene did not become widely available until after 1859. Courtesy of Illinois State Museum.

11

The Liquor License

The Village of Williamsburg, New York, became a city in 1851, giving Kings County two cities, Brooklyn and Williamsburg, and five towns: Bushwick, Flatbush, Flatlands, Gravesend, and New Utrecht; by now Red Hook was a ward of greater Brooklyn. Brooklyn grew rapidly. Commerce and transportation got a boost from the incorporation of the Brooklyn City Railroad in 1853. There were a good number of controversies, too, of the type that usually accompanies a politically diverse society. For instance, the editor of the *Brooklyn Daily Eagle* lost his job for supporting the sermons of Henry Ward Beecher who preached sending rifles rather than Bibles to "bleeding" Kansas. Kansas was in the initial fight to keep slavery from within its borders, a fight that ultimately led to the Civil War.

We do not know exactly when John Herman first opened the doors of his grocery store in Brooklyn, except to say that it was sometime between the time of his arrival in 1846 and 1854. His name appeared in the city directory placing him in the grocery business on Van Brunt Street. By this time, the other members of the Kastendieck family had left Morsum, Germany, and joined him in New York. His older brother John Friedrich had opened his own grocery business nearby at the corner of Nineteenth Street and Third Avenue, in South Brooklyn.[1]

One has to be careful going forward in constructing a timeline because there were many Kastendiecks in Brooklyn at the time, some of them like John Herman also in the grocery trade in Red Hook, and a few with the same or very similar names and initials. Sorting of Kastendiecks is a tricky genealogical puzzle. For example, there appeared a John H. Kassenbrock [sic] in Brooklyn in the *New York City Directory* of 1852. An entry listed him as a grocer at 85 Oliver Street and apparently living in the store at the same address, according to the directory.[2] A probable relative of his, C. Kassenbrock, also a grocer, did business at 294 Van Brunt Street less than a block from where John Herman Kastendieck kept his store. The two families had much in common and no doubt knew each other. Both Kassenbrock families eventually got out of the grocery business, selling out several years after John Herman left Brooklyn. These and others, along with the known kin of John Herman—all of his brothers sharing the same first name John— make the task of writing an acceptable history of the first Kastendiecks in America a particularly diligent one.

The earliest newspaper record of John Herman Kastendieck is of his arrest for illegally selling liquor in his grocery store. He happened to be just one of a large number of Brooklyn merchants caught in a citywide crackdown designed to rid the community of too much booze flowing illicitly from all manner of storefront establishments. On August 24, 1854, the Board of Commissioners of Excise for the Year 1854 published a resolution calling for drastic reductions in the number of merchants selling intoxicating liquors.[3] The level of such sales within the city had reached alarming proportions. Every grade of character of establishment was in the liquor sales business "from the low grogery to the gilded saloon" and included many grocery stores similar to the one John Herman owned. The Board decided to put a stop to the unlawful sale of drinks and put some teeth into the licensing requirement that sellers had heretofore largely ignored.

The Board's resolution called on the authorities of the city of Brooklyn to institute immediate proceedings against all unlicensed retail venders of liquor. Some of the more strident abolitionists blamed the situation on the Irish who they said brought with them an innate love for a drop of brew and quickly set up whisky stills in Brooklyn that led to widespread illicit distillation of spirits. In any event, the Board had the view of abolishing all illegal traffic in intoxicating drinks. All of a sudden, there was a flood of liquor license applications from establishments across the city. Every mom and pop operation all the way up to the finest saloons and entertainment houses applied for a license.

The Board of Commissioners published its liquor resolution in August of 1854. In September, John Herman Kastendieck's name appeared on a list of merchants in the Sixth Ward denied a license to sell liquor in his grocery store, at that time located at the corner of Van Brunt and Dikeman Streets. It was a long list of several hundred merchants covering all the Brooklyn wards, which reflected the concern of Brooklyn officials at the time trying to clean up the illicit sale of spirits in the city. The list ironically included a number of taverns likewise denied their liquor licenses, raising the question of what kind of tavern could not sell liquor.[4]

Apparently, the crackdown did not stop John Herman from passing a pint or two over the grocery counter because at the fall Court of Sessions of 1858, four men, including John

Castdendick [*sic*], pleaded guilty to selling liquor without a license.[5] Less than two years later, in the spring meeting of the 1860 Court of Sessions, John Kastendieck was again before the court, one of three Brooklyn proprietors this time brought before Judge Garrison and Justices Stilwell and Stryker for selling liquor without a license. It is impossible from the information to know which John Kastendieck at these various times was in trouble, because they were all named John; nevertheless, he pled guilty again and promised not to resume the business of selling liquor without a license. The judges fined him $10 with the option of spending twenty days in jail.[6]

Fudging the law on liquor sales seemed to be a quality that ran through the Kastendieck family. Years later, in 1867, the following notice appeared on the Brooklyn police blotter, "Henry Kastendack [*sic*], of Fourth Avenue, near Nineteenth Street, was yesterday arrested on a charge of violating the Excise Law in selling liquor without a license. He will be examined upon the charge next week."[7] This was John Herman's brother, Henry, who in the intervening years had gone into the grocery business at the corner of Court and Luquer Streets. It was apparently worth the risk of arrest to pass liquor over the counter with the expectation that profits would outweigh fines.

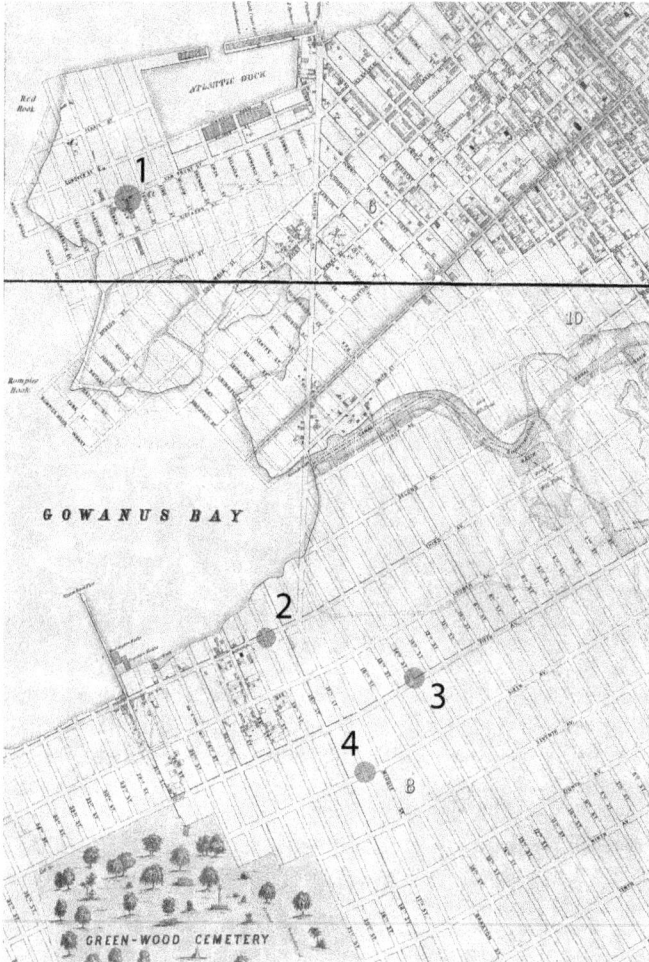

Kastendieck Grocery Stores in South Brooklyn. The four
Kastendieck brothers kept grocery stores at the same time at
four Brooklyn locations. 1. John Herman, corner of Van
Brunt and Wolcott; 2. John Friedrich Wilhelm, Nineteenth
Street and Third Avenue; 3. John Dietrich, Fourteenth Street
and Fifth Avenue; and 4. John Henry, Seventeenth Street
and Sixth Avenue. Meanwhile, many of the Kastendieck
family are buried in Green-Wood Cemetery shown at the
bottom of the map. Map modified from Matthew Dripps
map of 1850. Library of Congress.

View of Green Wood Cemetery, Brooklyn, New York. This idyllic, park-like setting a short distance from John Herman Kastendieck's residence became the final resting place of several members of the Kastendieck family, including Trina Kastendieck, the matriarch of the Kastendieck clan who died in 1857. *Lawn-Girt Hill*, engraving by R. Hinshelwood from an original work by James Smillie, 1855. *Green-Wood Illustrated.*

12

Bridget Ford of Ireland

T he Atlantic Basin Dock went into service in 1848 and soon became a prime destination for shipping. Its completion came coincidental with the famine in Ireland of 1848 and the beginning of the German Revolution of that same year. Ships carrying thousands of Irish and German immigrants crowded into the Port of New York; more and more ships docked at Red Hook. Great numbers of immigrants settled in Brooklyn, which explains, in part, how John Herman Kastendieck met Bridget Ford, of Ireland.

We know nothing of Bridget Ford's early life; she came from Ireland to America on an unknown date. Nor do we know anything of her parents and family. Conflicting information clouds the exact date of her birth. The Kastendieck Family Bible gives her birth date as September 16, 1835; her tombstone at Green-Wood Cemetery records a birth date of September 11, 1836; and, working backwards from her age at the time of her death as recorded on her death certificate, she was born December 16, 1835.[1]

Bridget was small in stature, attractive but somewhat plain, and wore her hair in the comfortable middle-parted style of the day, her dark hair combed down straight. Her dark eyes betrayed an anxious and sometimes frail look that exposed an underlying health issue that would later take her life.

She may have come from Galval, Ireland, a town unidentified today among Irish towns and villages. The name appears as Bridget's hometown on the baptismal certificate of her son Andrew.[2] One may only extrapolate from the limited information that Bridget Ford came from a very small town in Ireland. A similar supposition applies to her parents. The US Census of 1850 for New York lists the family of Jeremiah and Bridget Ford, of Ireland. They had a daughter named Mary of the same age as our Bridget in 1850. Various records refer to Bridget Ford Kastendieck also as Belinda, Melinda, and Mary, as well as Bridget. There is no proof that this is the family of Bridget Ford, and it is a leap to assume that it was. The Ford surname was very common in Ireland and New York, as was the name Bridget.

John Herman was an established grocer in Red Hook when he met Bridget Ford. These were exciting times in Brooklyn, and his business was growing with the city. In April of 1854, the New York Legislature consolidated the cities of Brooklyn and Williamsburg, setting in motion yet another phase of the city's meteoric rise to prominence and dizzying bouts of geographic reorganization.

When Brooklyn became a city in 1837—well before John Herman or Bridget arrived in the city—the founders divided it into nine wards. John Herman settled in the Sixth Ward of Brooklyn and remained there most of his life. The Sixth Ward boundary ran along Atlantic Street to Gowanus Bay, and then followed the waterlines along Gowanus Creek, New York Bay, and the East River. Records later showed John Herman in Brooklyn's Twelfth Ward. However, he never moved far from his original location. As the city rapidly grew, it added new wards and changed the geographic map much like the creation of new counties within a state that caused a family to appear to move and resettle when in fact, the geography changed and the family remained at the same location.[3] In this case, the Sixth Ward of Brooklyn split into wards Six, Ten, and Twelve. John Herman's home, originally located in the Sixth Ward, became part of the Twelfth, and he was thereafter associated with the Twelfth Ward.

About the same time John Herman Kastendieck met Bridget Ford, he became an American citizen. He was a young man of average height, of serious countenance, and with the demeanor of a respectable citizen. He combed his dark hair back to reveal a high forehead. He looked businesslike if not somewhat stern. He obtained naturalization on December 7, 1854, at City Court, Brooklyn, New York, noting for the record that he was a native of the Kingdom of Hanover.[4] Two months later on Valentine's Day, February 14, 1855, he and Bridget were married; he, the storekeeper from Hannover, Germany, a month short of his twenty-ninth birthday and she, an Irish-born girl of nineteen from Galval, Ireland. They moved into a flat in Brooklyn sharing a brick apartment building with three other couples.

If there was a celebration of their wedding, it well could have included a turn at skating on the East River, a popular pastime during the winter months in New York when the river froze to create a temporary bridge from Brooklyn to Manhattan.

In due time Herman and Bridget took up housekeeping above their grocery store on Van Brunt Street to enjoy the life that any young couple would seek, starting what they no doubt hoped to be a lifelong partnership.

Brooklyn was an exciting and interesting place in 1855 when John Herman and Bridget married. Walt Whitman published his seminal *Leaves of Grass* on July 4, 1855, out of a small print shop on Fulton Street in Brooklyn just a few blocks from where John Herman and Bridget made their home. Whitman had been Editor of the *Brooklyn Daily Eagle* back in 1846 for a couple of years before the newspaper fired him. The *Eagle*, which began publishing in 1841 and was in full swing during the time John Herman lived in Brooklyn, was the principal source of news in the United States. At one point, it was the nation's most widely read afternoon newspaper. It ran for 114 consecutive years without missing an edition. A copy cost a penny, sometimes three cents for a larger edition. As a result, *The Brooklyn Daily Eagle* provided a window into Brooklyn's past, as well as documentation of national and international events that shaped history during the Brooklyn years of the Kastendieck family. It turned out to be a mere footnote to the career of Walt Whitman.

When the winter ice thawed, the Fulton Street Ferry connected Brooklyn across the East River to New York City, bringing a daily stream of visitors and business to Brooklyn and delivering Brooklyn labor to New York City. At about the same time, the city introduced a new form of transportation in 1857. Forty-passenger rail coaches pulled by teams of horses carried people smoothly from downtown Brooklyn out to the suburbs. The innovative horse railway conveniently connected the expanding communities of Brooklyn to its commercial core and added to the budding success of grocery businesses like that of John Herman Kastendieck and the Kastendieck brothers.

By now, the entire Kastendieck family had settled in New York.[5] John Herman and Bridget lived above their store in the Twelfth Ward of Brooklyn. John Friedrich, John Dietrich, Mary, and mother Trina" shared quarters at John Friedrich's store in Ward Eight of Brooklyn. John Henry, the fourth Kastendieck brother, had his grocery business at the same time in the

Eleventh Ward of New York. The only member of the family not accounted for in the 1855 New York Census was Dora who had married and was living elsewhere.

John Herman Kastendieck. Originally from Morsum, Germany, he immigrated to the United States in 1846. This studio portrait shows him in approximately 1863 when he was about thirty-seven years old. He ran a successful grocery business in South Brooklyn. Augusta Kastendieck Family Album.

Bridget Ford. She married John Herman Kastendieck in 1855 at the age of nineteen. This studio portrait was made about 1863 when she was a wife and mother in her late twenties. Augusta Kastendieck Family Album.

Fulton Street Ferry, Brooklyn, New York. Forty-passenger horse-drawn cars carried people from the ferry by rail to outlying developing neighborhoods up to three miles from downtown Brooklyn. Only poor weather interrupted the ferry's reliability. 1857 engraving courtesy of the Brooklyn Historical Society.

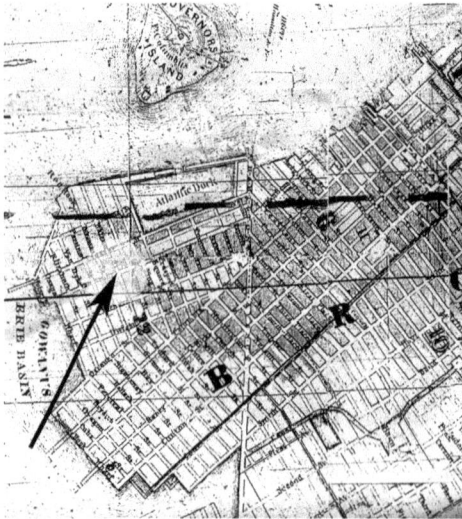

Red Hook Twelfth Ward of Brooklyn, New York. Red Hook annexed to Brooklyn in 1854. As a result, the grocery store business of John Herman Kastendieck stood at the corner of Wolcott and Van Brunt Streets (arrow) in the Twelfth Ward after the Sixth Ward divided into the Sixth, Tenth, and Twelfth Wards to organize the rapid growth of the city. Modified map excerpt from M. Dripps, New York, 1855.

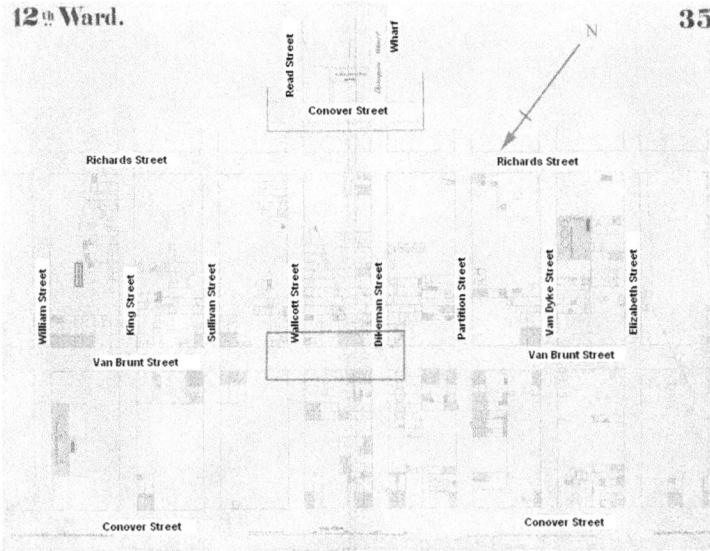

John Herman Kastendieck's Brooklyn Neighborhood in 1855. The earliest recorded address for John Herman Kastendieck was 1854 when he had a store on Van Brunt Street at the corner of Dikeman Street in Brooklyn, New York. The box shown on the map marks the approximate boundaries of his neighborhood. Modified Brooklyn Fire Insurance Map, Plate 35, New York Public Library.

New York Census. The 1855 New York Census listed Herman and Bridget Kastendieck as family 327 residing in Brooklyn's Twelfth Ward. The census was enumerated June 15, 1855, four months after Herman and Bridget's marriage in February. New York Municipal Archives.

13

Death and Life in Brooklyn

John Herman and Bridget Kastendieck had their first child—a son born on December 6, 1855—nine months and twenty-one days after their marriage.[1] They named him John Herman Kastendieck, Jr.; less than a year later, William Henry Kastendieck came along on November 27, 1857.[2]

The year 1857 was a bad time for the Kastendieck family. Dora, the sister of John Herman, lost two infant daughters both at the same time in January of 1857. The year before that, Mary, the twenty-five-year-old sister of Dora and John Herman, died. In addition, between the deaths of Dora's only children and the birth of William Henry to John Herman and Bridget, Trina Marie Kastendieck, the matriarch of the family, died in the summer of 1857. John Herman and John Friedrich pulled together enough money to purchase a lot in Green-Wood Cemetery in South Brooklyn, there to bury the four loved ones who had so quickly departed. Then, a series of new tragedies struck John Herman's household. Baby William Henry, barely a year old, died on January 8, 1858. The following November 13, 1858, Bridget gave birth to Heinrich Kastendieck. He lived only six days and died November 19, 1858.[3] The next year, baby Belinda Kastendieck came stillborn on November 25, 1859.[4]

John Herman and Bridget buried their three infants in the new family plot at Green-Wood Cemetery amid the beauty of its pastoral setting where the famous and not so famous citizens of Brooklyn shared their final rest.[5] It must have caused great anguish and sad reflection for John Herman and Bridget to see the names of so many of their deceased kin written so soon in the records of New York municipal deaths as if by a cruel turn of fate. The cause of death of the children was most likely Cholera Infantum, a particularly deadly disease in children although it struck mostly in the summer months and not in the winter when John Herman and Bridget's three children succumbed. They went on to have three more children who survived but none born in the winter months.

Life went on. In 1859, John Herman had his grocery store on Van Brunt, at the corner of Van Brunt and Dikeman. His brother John Friedrich was doing business as a grocer on Third Avenue, at the corner of Third Avenue and Nineteenth Street. No other Kastendiecks appeared in the 1859 *Brooklyn Directory*, which does not rule out by itself that the other Kastendieck brothers were not likewise engaged in their own businesses at the time.[6] There were multiple directories for New York in those days. A name might appear in one directory and not another.

Brooklyn was growing rapidly, developing a reputation as a modern city. The Brooklyn Academy of Music opened in 1859. That year saw also the introduction of the first piped water to the city, an occasion happily celebrated with fireworks at City Hall. People hoped that piped water might help stem some of the disease that sometimes swept through the city, of the kind perhaps that claimed the lives of the Kastendieck relations. Piped water also eased the difficulty of firefighting. More than one large conflagration, including the Great Fire of Brooklyn of 1848, burned out of control because of an inadequate supply of water. The closest distribution reservoir to John Herman's place was about two miles distant. Exactly when piped water reached the Kastendieck household in Red Hook is unknown. Many residents continued to rely on dug wells or the old cistern water supplies that collected rainwater in shallow, easily polluted underground storage systems. Such water supply systems could be unhealthy and often dangerous. Small children fell into cisterns sometimes narrowly escaping drowning.[7]

Down Van Brunt Street and a block over to Van Dyke, the first large-scale industrial building went up in Brooklyn in 1859 three blocks from John Herman's place. The Brooklyn Clay Retort and Fire Brick Works Storehouse (built ironically out of rock and not brick by the owner incidentally named Joseph Brick) occupied a large swath of real estate between John Herman's grocery store and the waterfront. It formed a sizable disruption of the idyllic quality that had previously favored Red Hook. Three large kiln chimneys rose through the roof of the basilica-like structure, belching coal smoke and steam, and blocking the view of the waterfront. The architecture of the building was typical of industrial structures of the mid-19th Century. The cathedral-like building, complete with clearstory windows, sat on cast iron pillars, and opened into a cavernous space filled with machinery and all the tools of manufacturing.[8] The company expanded over the years until it occupied the better part of the intersection of Van Brunt and Van Dyke Streets some distance in each direction. Still, the loss of the view notwithstanding, industry was good for the grocery business and that mattered to a young entrepreneur like John Herman trying to establish a foothold in a growing industrial climate. Red Hook and the Gowanus district would see many such structures go up in the coming decades. Some, like the Fire Brick Works Storehouse, remain today on their original sites. Others long ago disappeared to accommodate a more modern version of Brooklyn.

The 1860 US Census sealed in time a snapshot of John Herman and his Brooklyn family. For one thing, it introduced a curious twist to the identity of Bridget Kastendieck. The census showed John H. Kastendieck, age thirty-four, living in the Twelfth Ward of Brooklyn, Kings County, New York. The census confirmed his birthplace as Hanover but listed "Bellinda" not Bridget, age 25, as his wife, born in Ireland. This is of interest because her name was Bridget. The age and birthplace of Bellinda in the 1860 census was the same as that of Bridget; thus, taken with other identifying information it is clear that they were the same person. Why then was her name Bellinda in the census? The name of the couple's stillborn infant who died the previous year was Belinda. Perhaps the census entry was in the baby's honor. On the other hand, Bridget, whose middle name was Mary, may have been Belinda Bridget Mary Ford. In any event, the 1860 census showed the couple with one child, John H., age four, born in the state of New York. The census went on to record John Herman as a grocer with real estate valued at $4,000 and personal property worth $1,000, each amount representing respectable sums for an established citizen of the middle class. One of his grocery clerks, sixteen-year-old Harmon Schule, was living in the Kastendieck household; and they had a servant named Rebecka Röpke, nineteen years old, also living in the same household. Both boarders were from Hanover.[9] Rebecka turned out to be the same Rebecka Röpke, of Morsum, Germany, who later married John Dietrich Kastendieck, youngest brother of John Herman.

13. Death and Life in Brooklyn

Brooklyn was a modern city of many conveniences and entertainments, despite its often-unhealthy environment, political intrigue, and predatory business climate. Gas light came to the city in the late 1840s. Entrepreneurs had tried gas twenty years earlier, but citizens refused to sign a contract for the new-fangled lighting, and the company folded. Now, twenty years later, controversy erupted. The contentious gas industry left a sad legacy on Brooklyn. Cutthroat competition among as many as fifteen different companies—each vying to put the other out of business—made customers unsure just where their gas was coming from at any given time. Street bands seized territory and claimed customers without the customer's consent, giving rise to the term "gas-house gang" in the American lexicon. A letter to the editor of The *Brooklyn Daily Eagle* in 1861 summed up the public frustration. "We have never had anything but ill usage and miserable insult," said the writer. The public image of the Brooklyn Gas Light Company served only to fuel resentment. The company put up a new two-story office building on Court Street with brownstone façade and Tuscan style colonnade complete with high arched windows. The ostentatious, temple-like structure of new-style architecture projected itself as the hall of the nouveau rich rising up out of Brooklyn within sight of the city's own magnificent new city hall.

As the decade rolled over to the 1860s, Brooklyn enjoyed a reputation of a city of modern conveniences and good business climate. It was a city where people loved entertainment. They attended performances at the Philharmonic and programs at the Academy of Music. For those less culturally inclined, there was Coney Island and the exotic Barnum's American Museum where for 25 cents children and adults alike could experience a world of curiosities never before imagined. By 1861, residents could go by rail unimpeded via the Long Island tunnel under Atlantic Avenue to surrounding suburbs and places like Coney Island. It could be a somewhat arduous ride, especially for the daily commuter.

The inner city continued to move by horse-rail because the new steam cars were too dangerous in town. Horsecars brought passengers to the outskirts of the city where they transferred to the steam cars for the trip out to the beach resorts.[10] The rail line to Coney Island carried the dubious name of the Brooklyn Bath and Coney Island Railroad, known locally as the Dummy Road because it was so slow.[11] The Kastendieck family lived near the East River ports and likely chose a two-hour steamboat ride to Coney Island over the daylong trip by rail.

In the winter, amusement turned to ice-skating. The East River froze so hard and so thick that people used it as a bridge between Brooklyn and Manhattan. Skating was popular for both adults and children. When they were not sliding along the surface of the East River, you found them on one of the many skating ponds that dotted the city. Lessons were available at the Brooklyn Skating Hall where patrons skated to music under gas light. Another favorite pastime, winter and summer, was baseball. Teams like the Brooklyn Atlantics played the New York Mutuals before large crowds stirred up by gambling and fighting that often accompanied an otherwise enjoyable outing.

John Herman and Bridget added a second child to their family in 1861, a son named George Dietrich, born on May 18, 1861.[12] One can only imagine the fear and anticipation that must have accompanied his birth and the first years of his life. On three previous occasions, their children had died as babies. Nevertheless, George Dietrich survived to join John Herman, Jr., together the beginning of the next generation of Kastendiecks.

By 1862, John Herman, Sr., had acquired two lots and houses on Van Brunt Street between Dikeman and Wolcott. This is a matter of somewhat regrettable record because in March of 1862, his property appeared in the *Brooklyn Daily Eagle* along with several thousand other Brooklynites for delinquent taxes going back to 1860. The article served notice that property would sell for non-payment of taxes at public auction by the Collector of Taxes and Assessments of Brooklyn to any person who would take it for the lowest term of years and pay the amount of taxes owed, in John Herman's case $35.96.[13] He must have paid his taxes before the June 3 deadline because years later he was still at the Van Brunt address.

Part of the problem of delinquent taxes in Brooklyn about this time stemmed from the attempt of the New York State Legislature to consolidate the cities of Brooklyn, Williamsburg, and Bushwick into one municipal area. The collection of back taxes was a specific part of the legislation aimed at facilitating the merger, which was not popular with many Brooklyn residents. (The later merger with New York City faced similar resistance from independent-minded Brooklyn citizens.) In defense of John Herman's neglect, resistance to property taxation in Brooklyn was not unique to him. In 1894 the Litchfield heirs tried to sell a parcel of land only to discover that a debt of more than $1 million in back taxes was due dating back more than three decades to 1860.[14]

John's tax troubles probably stemmed from an assessment made against his property in 1862. Much of the neighborhood where he lived was fill dirt, dirt taken out of the original building of the Atlantic Dock. Over the succeeding years, the dirt settled, causing the city from time to time to add fill dirt to bring the lots back up to a satisfactory level. The property owners had to pay the costs. In January of 1862 city officials announced that the lots bounded by Wolcott, Richards, Dikeman and Van Brunt Streets were scheduled for fill work and owners would be added to the assessment rolls subject to payment to the Collector of Taxes and Assessments at city hall.[15] This was John Herman's neighborhood and his lots fell squarely within the area slated for assessment.

Brooklynites did not pay much attention to taxes, especially in 1862 when the nation found itself embroiled in a civil war, a war whose uncertain outcome had the potential to negate taxes and many other things.

John Herman Kastendieck, Jr., The eldest child of John Herman and Bridget Ford Kastendieck, John Herman, Jr., grew up in Brooklyn, New York, and later moved as a young man to Christian County, Missouri. He posed for this picture about 1863 at approximately age eight. Augusta Kastendieck Family Album.

George Dietrich Kastendieck. The second surviving child of John Herman and Bridget Kastendieck, he is pictured in this photograph at about age two or three. He later moved as a teenager with his father and stepmother to Missouri. Holding a ball in his left hand and steadying himself with his right, he looked unenthused at having his portrait made by the relatively new medium of photography. Augusta Kastendieck Family Album.

Fireworks at the Brooklyn City Hall. The city of Brooklyn pumped water from Long Island to reservoirs at Ridgewood and Mount Prospect for distribution to city residents. Brooklyn sumptuously celebrated the occasion with a grand fireworks display. This engraving appeared in *Harper's Weekly*, May 14, 1859. Courtesy of the Brooklyn Public Library.

Coney Island Beach Scene. People came to Coney Island for the water, sun, and cool breezes. The fashion of the 1860s called for long woolen pants and skirts with jackets, shawls, and hats despite the heat and discomfort of a summer day. Photograph taken Summer 1863. Courtesy of the Brooklyn Historical Society.

THE ORIGINAL EAST RIVER BRIDGE. CROSSING ON THE ICE IN 1852.

The Original East River Bridge. Before there was the Brooklyn Bridge across the East River, people crossed the thickly frozen stream over the ice that bridged travel from Brooklyn to Manhattan. It was a favorite venue for skating, a popular amusement in Brooklyn for children and adults. "Crossing on the Ice in 1852," *The Eagle and Brooklyn*, Vol. 1, (Winter 1852), Brooklyn Public Library.

14

The Civil War

Harriet Beecher Stowe reignited the slavery issue in 1852 with the publication of her novel, *Uncle Tom's Cabin*. This tragic subject, rendered in earnest conviction and touching detail, fueled northern sentiment against the slaveholding South. Two years later in 1854, the issue of slavery came to the forefront of political discourse when Congress passed the Kansas-Nebraska Act, replacing the Missouri Compromise that had held the nation in balance for three decades between free and slave states. The new law left it to the new states entering the Union to decide their status by a vote of the people—so called popular sovereignty.

The Kansas Territory was the first testing ground of this new law. Hostilities broke out immediately between factions trying to influence the direction of Kansas statehood as slave or free. Bloodshed followed. John Brown, an avid abolitionist and some say religious fanatic, took a small band of men from the conflict in Kansas to Harper's Ferry, Virginia, intent there on starting a slave revolt to strike at the heart of slave territory. The revolt failed, and the state of Virginia hanged Brown. Not since the Dred Scott decision in 1857 when the US Supreme Court held that slaves were property unworthy of citizenship had anything so united northerners than Brown's execution at the hands of slave owners in Virginia; they saw his execution as murder. Brown became a Christian martyr to the abolitionist movement. The South, on the other hand, saw him as a scoundrel who got what he deserved.

The chasm between North and South grew wider and the politics more polarized. The election of 1860 was the final blow to the slaveholding South when Abraham Lincoln became President. The Southern states revolted. Secession came almost immediately, and in April of 1861, Confederate forces in South Carolina fired on Fort Sumter.

The citizens of Brooklyn closely followed these events through daily dispatches of the *Brooklyn Daily Eagle*. The paper came under scrutiny by the federal government for biased reporting. Authorities forbade the *Eagle* from mailing to subscribers outside the city of Brooklyn. The government thought the paper should be more pro-Union and less balanced in its reporting of the conflict. Such highhanded tactics were unnecessary because Brooklyn was a decidedly Union city from the beginning.

There were many who championed the fight against slavery, but none perhaps more colorful or outspoken than the Rev. Henry Ward Beecher who was the younger brother of Harriet Beecher Stowe the writer of *Uncle Tom's Cabin*. From his pulpit at Plymouth Church of the Pilgrims in Brooklyn and through his editorship of the *New York Independent*, he unleashed a stream of rhetoric against the South, as powerful in its message as his sister's novel. On one occasion on February 5, 1860, speaking from the pulpit, he impersonated a slave auctioneer selling a young slave girl named Sally Maria Diggs—nicknamed Pinky—and imploring his congregation to give money to buy her freedom. His theatrical and touching performance caused the audience to toss money and jewelry into the collection plate far in excess of what was necessary to buy Pinky's freedom. The press reported it, calling attention to a particularly poignant moment when Beecher picked up a large opal ring from the collection plate and placed it on the young slave girl's finger with the words, "With this ring I do wed thee to freedom." Plymouth Church was a Calvinist Congregational church located less than two miles up Hicks Street, in Brooklyn Heights, north of John Herman's home. Although John Herman was a Methodist Episcopal and a consistent member of the Methodist Episcopal Church, he probably attended Beecher's sermons out of curiosity for the orator's spreading fame just to say he had seen and heard the great Brooklyn preacher.

The Civil War transformed Brooklyn into a critical supplier to the Union effort. At the beginning of the War, the Brooklyn waterfront was a six-mile long port that could dock more than one hundred ships. The giant warehouses of the Erie Basin and the Atlantic Docks in Red Hook, very close to John Herman's neighborhood, could store huge amounts of supplies ready for easy transfer to the war effort. The shipyards in Greenpoint along the East River about five miles northeast from where John Herman lived repaired troop ships and built battleships. Perhaps the most significant ship built there was the ironclad gunship *Monitor* built by the Continental Iron Works in 1862. History remembers the *Monitor* for its storied battle with the Southern ironclad *Merrimack*, which up to that point had jeopardized the wooden ships of the Union Navy.

The Union looked to Brooklyn and the surrounding region for men, war materiel, and money. In 1861, Brooklyn had grown to be the third largest city in America behind only New York City and Philadelphia. Although Brooklyn was a bustling industrial town, the surrounding area was largely rural farmland populated by hardworking young New Yorkers fit to take on the rigors of war. Thousands of men went to the battlefield while New York women organized to raise funds for the war effort. The 1864 Sanitary Fair, for example, raised more than $400,000 largely due to the dedicated drive of the women of Brooklyn and Long Island.[1]

There is no evidence that John Herman Kastendieck served in the Civil War, or of any other Kastendieck except an unknown Ferdinand Kastendick [sic], a private in the 193rd New York Infantry out of Albany, New York. The almost complete absence of Kastendiecks from Civil War rolls is surprising because the German immigrant population steadfastly backed the Union cause and joined the fight to put down the rebellion wherever the opportunity presented itself. In the border state of Missouri, for instance, German forces kept Missouri in the Union. It is doubly surprising not to find Kastendiecks on the rolls of the New York regiments because New York sent more Germans to the Union army than any other state. Records may surface in time to document the Kastendiecks in the Civil War. Brooklyn had strong connections to the navy and maybe that is where the Kastendieck records will be found, or in the obscure documents of minor state militia units where rolls were less apt to be kept with much accuracy. How all the Kastendieck men then living in Brooklyn escaped the war, if they did, is a mystery. There were several Kastendiecks of military age residing in the city at the time, and all of them were subject to the draft instituted in the middle and latter stages of the war. Nevertheless, not everyone fought in the war.

By August 1862, the number of volunteers coming into the Union Army had dropped off. So in March 1863, Congress passed the Conscription Act requiring all men between ages twenty and forty-five to register for the draft. John Herman was about to turn thirty-seven at the time and was within the age for draft registration required by law. However, John Herman did not always follow the law. On the other hand, he simply may have avoided selection by chance. There are at least three plausible possibilities for what happened. The Kastendiecks ignored the draft, bought an exemption, or did not qualify. There was great anger in Brooklyn and elsewhere over the conscription law, especially among the working class and poor of the city because the law allowed that if a man did not want to serve, he could pay $300 to have a substitute serve in his place. The wealthy could afford to buy their way out; the poor could not, and thus the burden of the draft fell on them. Riots over the issue broke out in July 1863 and lasted for several days. Mobs burned draft offices and directed their anger at the homes and stores belonging to anyone connected to the corrupt conscription law. Blacks became a particular target.[2] They were beaten, some lynched, and murdered. Arsonists destroyed Black homes and churches and even burned down a Black orphanage. A mob of two hundred burned two-grain elevators at the Atlantic Docks. It took the Fighting Fourteenth Regiment of Brooklyn—recently back from the Battle of Gettysburg—to put down the violence and restore order.

There were exemptions from the draft for physical and mental disability and other conditions regarding only-sons within a household, including one ridiculous provision whereby a widowed mother with two sons chose which son to exempt. There were also different classifications by age. It is possible that John Herman escaped service under one of these clauses. For instance, a man over the age of thirty-five and married—John Herman was thirty-seven and married—fell into a second class of recruits called into service after all others. Brooklyn had a draft quota of 4,000 men. If it filled its quota with men between the ages of twenty and thirty-five, and non-married men between thirty-five and forty-five, those in the second class escaped the draft. Actual selection included only about one in seven of those enrolled.[3] The remote possibility also existed that John Herman qualified for a draft exemption under one of the fifty-eight physical disabilities listed in the draft legislation, or he paid $300 to the Collector of Internal Revenue of the District and bought his exemption. After all, John Herman had a business to attend to and two small children at home, the youngest less than a year old when the war broke out. A third child came along in the middle of the war when son Andrew was born in September of 1863.[4] They baptized Andrew at the Wyckoff-Street Methodist Episcopal Church on Sunday, December 13, 1863. One of the sponsors was John Henry Kastendieck, brother of John Herman, who registered his presence at the baptism and not at war. Older brother John Friedrich Wilhelm did not attend. His wife, Marie Elizabeth, represented him as the second sponsor at Andrew's baptism.[5]

Despite the violent reaction to the draft, and the dearth of Kastendiecks who served in the war, Brooklyn fervently supported the Union cause. The city played a major part in supplying troops. The famous Fourteenth Brooklyn Regiment fought from 1861 to 1864. Personally called into service by President Lincoln, it was the only Regiment of the Civil War named after a city. The soldiers wore a distinctive red uniform during the entire war patterned after the light infantry French Chasseurs, or Hunters. Nicknamed the Red Legged Devils, they were a factor in several major battles and known by both sides for their refusal to stand down from a fight.[6]

Henry Ward Beecher. Clergyman and avid abolitionist, he preached against slavery from the pulpit of Plymouth Church in Brooklyn, a few blocks from the Kastendieck grocery store. With his sister, Harriet Beecher Stowe, author of *Uncle Tom's Cabin* published in 1852, they kindled northern sentiment against southern slavery and helped to hasten the nation toward Civil War. C.D. Fredricks and Co., c. 1860. Library of Congress.

Brooklyn Sanitary Fair. The Fair was located in the Brooklyn Academy of Music building on Montague Street near Court Street. Dances, parades, merchandise sales, auctions, and even a cattle show raised more than $400,000 to support the Civil War effort. Interior view of the Academy of Music, Lithograph by A. Brown, 1864. Library of Congress.

The Navy-Yard at Brooklyn, New York. Ships of war crowded into the harbor of the US Navy port located on the East River about two and a half miles up the river from Red Hook, in Brooklyn. At the beginning of the Civil War some 6,000 men worked at the Navy-Yard to support the Union war effort. The ship, *Monitor,* was fitted with its revolutionary iron cladding at nearby Greenpoint. By the time this picture was published these ships, shown as of June 1861, had departed for the southern coast. *Harpers Weekly,* July 20, 1861.

15

Post-War Episodes

A light of hope came into the Kastendieck family in the summer of 1866. John Herman and Bridget had their first daughter. On August 6, 1866, Bridget gave birth to Amelia Maria Dorothea Kastendieck. There were four children to raise now, John Herman, Jr., George Dietrich, Andrew, and Amelia.[1]

Amelia came into the world in the summer in a dangerous time. As Brooklyn grew so did its problems. Disease was a frequent visitor to 19th Century New York. Major outbreaks of cholera and smallpox happened on a regular basis. Almost every summer emergency actions were required in parts of Brooklyn to stem a cholera epidemic. John Herman Kastendieck and his family lived in an especially vulnerable location. The Twelfth Ward of Brooklyn was once a section of low, flat ground filled with ponds connected by a network of shallow waterways. As the Twelfth Ward of the city grew, city engineers built streets directly across these ditches without the benefit of culverts, and thus severed the natural watercourses, turning the ponds into stagnant pools. By 1866, the lack of sanitation in the city was a serious problem. The Metropolitan Board of Health took on the job of improving sewer connections, filling sunken lots, and generally cleaning up the Twelfth Ward of Brooklyn. Crews of city workers went from house to house stopping at any residence in need of cleanup. They visited John Herman's house the week of July 22, 1866, just as they did every house in the Twelfth Ward that week, except for a few situated on high ground. The cost of the mandated cleanup to residents was $10 to $20 to make their home and lot sanitary. Overflowing privies or cesspools, a dirty yard or cellar, garbage and ash boxes left unattended, all required removal and generous applications of lime to stave off disease. The cleanup suffered from the fact that there was no legal place to take the filth of Brooklyn out of the city.

Cholera also traveled by ship. The Board of Health quarantined all ships it suspected of carrying disease, much to the consternation of the ship captains because cargos were ordered dumped into the ocean when refused entry into the city. The *New York Times* reported that in the 1866 cholera outbreak, conditions neared epidemic proportions in Brooklyn. The Sanitary Superintendent wrote, "In consequence of the number of cases of cholera in the Twelfth Ward of Brooklyn and the impossibility of providing, in many instances, for their proper care at their own homes, it became necessary on Saturday last to procure at once a suitable building for use as a hospital." The vacant building known as the Columbian Bakery situated on the corner of Hamilton Avenue and Van Brunt Street became a hospital within just a few blocks of John Herman's grocery store on Van Brunt Street.[2]

The cholera outbreak of 1866 passed. There were no deaths as a result in the Kastendieck family. Baby Amelia survived, grew up, married, and raised three daughters of her own.

Things were never quite the same in Brooklyn after the Civil War. Germans celebrated the victory of the Union. The Irish were less exuberant; many of them had sided with the South. The resulting tensions recalled the old days of the building of the Atlantic Basin when riots broke out between German and Irish workers.

The Kastendieck family embodied the ethnic divide in Brooklyn, John Herman a German, Bridget of Irish extraction. There is no indication, however, that whatever hard feeling existed between the German and Irish communities that it ever infringed on the Kastendieck household. Life was difficult enough without fretting over things beyond their control.

The ethnic divide surfaced sometimes in subtle ways. One incident involving the Kastendiecks revealed something about the unscrupulous dealings of certain Brooklyn citizens. The incident does not seem to have been an isolated case. This is the story as it appeared in the *Brooklyn Daily Eagle.*

"This morning officer Geer, of Justice Cornwell's Court, arrested Joseph McCann, a resident of the Twelfth Ward and an employee of the City in the office of the Tax Collector, for forgery. When taken before Justice Cornwell for examination the following facts transpired. On the 3rd of May [1867], as alleged by Hon. James Buckley, Justice of the Second District Court, said McCann forged a process of dispossession or notice to quit certain premises, and served it upon a tenant with intention to defraud, the name of said Justice being illegally affixed thereto. The premises, three rooms on the third story of a house belonging to Mr. John H. Kastendieck, in Van Brunt, near Wolcott street, Twelfth Ward, were occupied by a Mr. Gregg, and by this forged instrument it is charged that he was made to pay the sum of $7.50, or one month's rent, which he otherwise would not have done…Justice Buckley has had many similar forgeries of his name perpetrated during the present year, and is determined to make an example of this case, which will be examined this afternoon."[3]

It is not clear what role John Herman played in the arrest of Mr. McCann or how McCann could defraud one of John Herman's tenants under his nose.

The story of the attempt to defraud one of John Herman's tenants gave additional insight into the Kastendieck property and John Herman's business practices. At least one of his houses was a three-story affair that included units renting for $7.50 a month. Since he owned multiple properties, the title of landlord adds to his occupation as grocer.

John Herman was in the right business at the right time. Brooklyn's population explosion caused a shortage of housing, especially for affordable apartments for rent to the working class. Advertisements in the *Brooklyn Daily Eagle* were a continuing testimony to the viability of the rent market. A nice three-story house rented for $300 a year, and upwards. A house of modest size in John Herman's neighborhood with water and gas might fetch as much as $400 per annum but usually less. Single rooms usually rented for about $10 a month.[4]

Meanwhile, controversy in Brooklyn found an easy beginning over just about any project. For example, Gowanus Creek divided Brooklyn in two parts. In 1867 work commenced on the long anticipated project to improve the creek by widening and deepening it into a more navigable canal and making of it something more than an inconvenient obstruction.[5] The project met immediate controversy. At one point officials disclosed that the Special Commission in charge had spent more than $70,000 to build a single bridge across the canal at Union Street.[6] Brooklyn citizens were still complaining two years after the bridge opened. The unique design of the bridge allowed for the passage of ships. People wanting to cross the bridge had to wait up to half an hour or more in the cold "for every Tom, Dick, and Harry who wants to get his boat through."[7]

John Herman was a man of modest income despite his business dealings. In 1867, the *Brooklyn Daily Eagle* ran an article listing Brooklyn residents whose incomes as returned to the Internal Revenue Service were under $1,000. Another list ran the day before showing incomes above $1,000. The modest income list showed J.H. Kastendink [*sic*] with income of $305. Allowing for $1000 exempted by law, John had an annual income in 1867 of $1,305, at least as he reported it to the IRS.[8] We know, however, that John Herman did not always pay his taxes and may have taken a similar attitude when reporting his income to the IRS.

Notwithstanding the tragedy of the Civil War for the nation and the unsettling consequences of its aftermath, Brooklyn soon regained its old dynamism. Major new projects brought new attention to the city to make it more than "the borough of homes and churches" that had identified its pre-war status. Work commenced in 1867 on the Brooklyn anchorage of what would be the Brooklyn Bridge. Even before the war ended, the newspapers and local officials lobbied to erect a bridge over the East River to connect Brooklyn and Manhattan that would become a symbol of Brooklyn pride. Well known is the history of the construction of the bridge including the death of its visionary designer who died before construction began, and the pivotal role his daughter-in-law played in seeing it to completion. Determination to build the bridge got a major boost in December of 1868 when Brooklyn's Common Council authorized a $3 million loan for its construction.

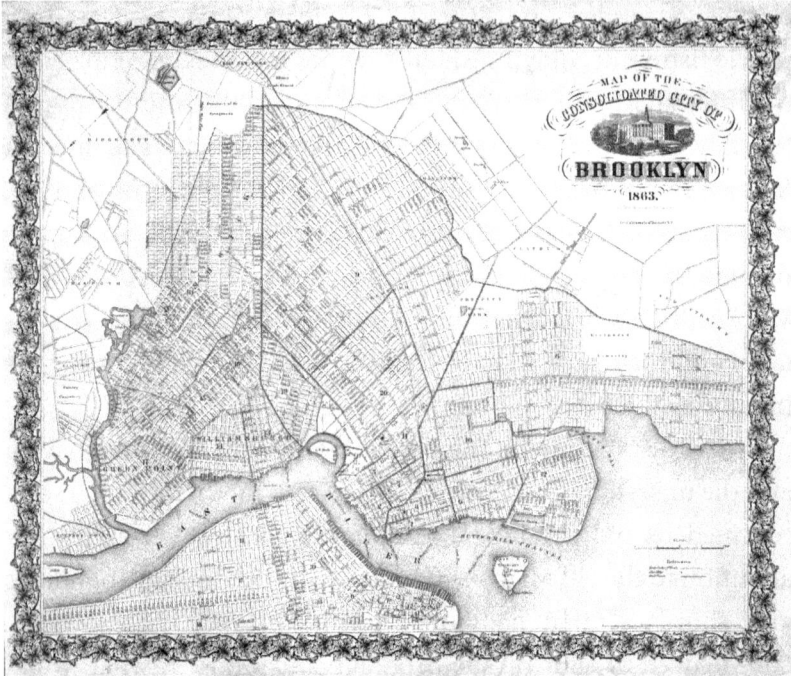

Map of the Consolidated City of Brooklyn, New York. In 1863 Brooklyn
was the third largest city in America, after New York and Philadelphia.
Maps of this period were often oriented with the East River at the bottom
and the top of the map pointing west. South Brooklyn and Red Hook
Point, where John Herman Kastendieck lived, are at the lower right just
above Governor's Island. McCloskey's Pocket Map of Brooklyn, 1863.
Brooklyn Public Library.

16

The Death of Bridget Kastendieck

In the summer of 1869, Bridget Kastendieck died. She died a terrible death from gastritis and its spasmodic complications. A general description of the disease tells a dreadful story of her last days.

Gastritis was, and still is, an inflammation of the lining of the stomach. During the 19th Century, death usually occurred from peritonitis when the stomach became perforated and its contents emptied into the abdomen. Death often came suddenly, accompanied by extreme severe pain and attended by vomiting or retching spasms.

Gastritis was a particularly painful and insidious disease that could take its deadly toll over a period of days or weeks, or after years of lingering illness and suffering. The body became exhausted and gradually wasted away until it extinguished life. In rare cases death occurred rapidly without outward signs of the disease, becoming fatal within a week's time. Usually, however, the disease was long-suffering in its sinister progress and was often mistaken for indigestion in its initial phases.

Many things could cause it. In Bridget's case, unhealthy living conditions that pervaded much of Brooklyn's south side no doubt aggravated the disease. Overeating or eating something irritating could also bring it on; or bad food that inflamed the stomach; or habitual cold and damp conditions. The deadliest cases sometimes traced to the abuse of alcohol. Other causes of a more occult nature like yellow and typhoid fever and other fevers weakened the body and made it susceptible to gastritis. Depressing mental emotions were also a large contributing cause.

We do not know the exact diagnosis of Bridget's illness. Gastritis was a common disease in 19th Century America, and yet doctors knew little about how to cure it. Medical books of the time were able to describe it but were vague on how to cure it, except by bland diet and various homeopathic remedies.[1] Bleeding stood at the head of remediate means. Leeching, cupping, and the inducement of a large blister over the affected area of the stomach were all accepted alternatives to subduing the distress of the disease. Opium was a valuable remedy, its most popular variant being Dovers Powder, a major component of which was opium. Doctors gave opium in large doses, preferably after bleeding.

The disease took a heavy toll of its victim. It began with gastric distress, nausea, and vomiting. A general lack of appetite eventually resulted in an abhorrence of food coupled with a strong desire for cool drinks, a craving not easily satisfied in South Brooklyn in August of 1869.

The prolonged suffering of Bridget, this young mother, is unimaginable. Medical descriptions of the disease in its final stages were usually hideous and very similar in every case. The patient could not eat; vomiting ensued after taking anything into the stomach. This conspired with diarrhea to cause rapid loss of weight and a weakened and emaciated condition. The skin turned yellowish brown, drawn tightly over the muscles, and produced a sallow countenance with a peculiar dark tinge. The tongue began to take on the appearance of rotting. The patient entered into a state of great depression of spirit in the last throes of the disease, dejected and morose, ill tempered and irritable. Gastritis caused a frightening aspect of countenance in its victims as prelude to death. Victims expressed great anxiety and suffering or despondency and despair. Toward the end violent vomiting and purging set in with a burning or excoriating pain in the stomach.

Bridget Kastendieck's last hours were probably like those described by Erberle in 1835, "The pain and vomiting continue with unabated violence for several days, with difficulty of respiration and hiccough, the pulse becoming smaller, more frequent, and corded, the worst consequences are to be dreaded. If, after the symptoms have continued in this progressive course of aggravation, the pain suddenly subsides, and the extremities become cold and clammy, with dimness of sight and slight delirium, a fatal termination is inevitable."[2]

Bridget's doctor was Dr. Frank Bond, a forty-one-year-old homeopathic doctor, Pennsylvania born, and a member of a large medical practice operating under the name of the Brooklyn Homeopathic Dispensary on Court Street, in Brooklyn.[3] The dispensary opened to the public in 1853 and by 1869 had taken on the scale of a small hospital, complete with city and state funding assistance. Dr. Bond became the resident physician in 1857 when the establishment moved to larger quarters at Number 83 Court Street.[4] He ran extensive advertisements in the *Brooklyn Daily Eagle.* In the years that followed, the Brooklyn Homeopathic Dispensary grew at a rate of 25 percent annually, becoming one of the largest medical practices in Brooklyn.[5]

On Monday morning of August 2, 1869, Dr. Bond made his last house call to see Bridget. The trip had taken a little longer than usual because the city was laying new Belgian Pavement along a section of Court Street.[6] A doctor's ordinary house call cost $3. All the doctors charged the same fixed price plus other professional charges. This time, however, it was just a courtesy house call; he could do nothing more for Bridget. She died the following day. It was a reflective visit. Dr. Bond's wife, Ellen, was the same age as Bridget, and they had two small children about the ages of the Kastendieck children.

We cannot say how much of Dr. Bond's treatment of Bridget included the standard practice of cupping and leaches. These cures along with bleeding were still in use as late as 1869, even on children afflicted with the disease.[7] Homeopathic medicine, however, with which Bond was associated at the Brooklyn Dispensary, generally rejected "scientific" medicine in favor of less invasive alternatives, anything from dilution of medications to applications of placebos to restore the "spiritual vital force". In its extreme form homeopathy amounted to little more than the curing effect of magic water. Dr. Bond advertised himself as a physician and surgeon; therefore, we may assume that he applied the best of both homeopathic and scientific cures and that Bridget received the best care available in 1869.

Dr. Bond listed the cause of Bridget's death as gastritis complicated by spasms.[8] She was thirty-three years, ten months, and eighteen days old when she died on August 3, 1869.[9] She was a resident of Brooklyn for thirteen years, married to John Herman Kastendieck for fourteen, and left behind four small children, three under the age of eight. A homemaker born in Ireland of long Irish descent, she died in Brooklyn at her home on the corner of Van Brunt and Wolcott Streets.

John Herman at first wanted to bury his young wife at Holy Cross Cemetery, but the next day changed his mind and announced that he would bury her at Green-Wood where their infant children lay buried.

In the week that Bridget died, there were 253 deaths in Brooklyn, seventeen of them in the Twelfth Ward where the Kastendiecks lived. Brooklyn had a population of 395,000 residents in 1869; therefore, 253 deaths was not an excessive number for the city; less than what one might expect, for example, if there were an epidemic. One hundred ninety-eight of the deaths that week were children under the age of ten. Most of the children died from Cholera Infantum, the deadly disease of children in the 19th Century that had claimed the Kastendieck infants a decade earlier.[10]

It was customary in those days in Brooklyn for the deceased to remain in the home until the funeral. An upstairs bedroom of the three-story Kastendieck home became the funeral parlor. The undertaker, William Cody—who also served as city undertaker—came over from his store on Court Street to the Kastendieck home soon after Bridget's death to prepare her for burial.[11] We do not know the exact details of Mr. Cody's work. However, looking at the description of a funeral he arranged for a Mr. Jenks at the Jenks' home on Henry Street—almost a year later to the day in August 1870—we get a general picture of Bridget's preparation in 1869.[12]

She was probably laid out in lavender with the use of sprigs of aromatic lavender along with heavily scented soap to mask the stench of decomposition long enough to have a funeral. Her death coming in the hot August summer, the corpse probably lay on a cooling board; a patented device drilled with holes and then placed above a block of ice—fancier models were concave, ice-filled boxes fitted to the torso and head. Embalming was not yet in widespread use, although it came into practice during the Civil War; and advertisements for embalming services appeared widely in the *Brooklyn Daily Eagle* as early as 1863; however, none by William Cody. Cody and his associates arranged the room for visitors who would surely come during the following days to pay their last respects to a relative and friend.

Mr. Cody came back several times over the next two days because his office was less than a mile east of where the Kastendiecks lived. About 1 o'clock Friday afternoon, he and his assistants returned for the last time on the day of the funeral to make final preparations. He had a favorite casket that he used made of rosewood. Its elegant design included silver mounting and richly patterned handles that extended out from the coffin.[13] The casket was six feet in length inside, by twenty-four inches wide, and twenty-two inches deep. At the top and bottom ran a straight strip of silver-plated relief, and at either end or side heavy substantial handles were fastened. The interior was plush satin. He sometimes draped the exterior in black velvet crepe.

Mr. Cody and his associates gently placed Bridget in her casket. They carried her for the last time downstairs, carefully easing the coffin into the coffin corner of the stairs, a niche built into most Brooklyn homes between flights of stairs for this purpose. The coffin bearers backed the casket into the corner to maneuver it around the turn of the stairs, all the while keeping it level and preserving the solemnity of the occasion. Around 2 p.m. Friday afternoon, they carried Bridget out of the house into the hot August day and placed her casket in a horse-drawn hearse parked before the Kastendieck home at 307 Van Brunt Street. Two splendid grays pulled the hearse driven by Mr. Cody himself. Carriages lined Van Brunt from the corner of Wolcott Street, waiting patiently some distance down both streets. The carriages soon fell in behind the hearse for the long and sad journey to Green-Wood Cemetery. At 2:30, the carriage carrying John Herman and the children took its place behind the hearse and led the funeral procession out of South Brooklyn.

Notice of Bridget's death ran twice in the *Brooklyn Daily Eagle*.[14] A brief announcement appeared on page three inviting relatives and friends of the family to attend her funeral in South Brooklyn. The funeral was Friday. It began at her home at the corner of Wolcott and Van Brunt Streets promptly at 2:30 on August 6. The procession proceeded up Van Brunt Street to the Hamilton Avenue intersection, made a hard right turn, and then slowly eased along Hamilton the two miles to Green-Wood Cemetery.

About midway up Hamilton, they came to the toll bridge across Gowanus Creek. The recently completed dredging of the Gowanus Canal may have caused them to detour to other crossings before reaching the cemetery. In the old days, travelers crossed the Gowanus Bridge at their own risk. On one occasion in 1848, a funeral procession to Green-Wood that included a large carriage carrying the city board of aldermen stopped while the council members got out and walked over the bridge for fear that it was not safe enough for them to cross.[15] However, that was many years before, and the new improvements across the Gowanus Canal assured safer passage than that encountered by the council members. In any event, the normal funeral route would have taken the Kastendieck procession over the Gowanus Bridge and up Hamilton Avenue until it became Third Avenue. From there they went about eight blocks to Twenty-fifth Street, and then turned left on Twenty-fifth for two blocks to the Cemetery entrance at Fifth Avenue and Twenty-fifth Street.

The procession moved into the cemetery and stopped at Section 116, Lot 9625. Here they laid Bridget to rest in the

Kastendieck family burial plot beside her three infant children who had preceded her in death a decade before.[16]

As the declining sun shone sympathetically upon the quiet beauty of Green-Wood, the mortal remains of Bridget Kastendieck went to rest in the keeping of the silent grave.

Lot Number 9625 would become the final resting place of many of the Kastendiecks of Brooklyn, once again pointing to a strong family relationship between the several families of this distinctive German name.

CERTIFICATE OF DEATH. 5816 57 73

1. Name of the Deceased, (in full,) _Bridget Kastendieck_
2. Age _33_ years, _7_ months, _18_ days. Color, _White_
3. Single (Married) Widow, or (Widower) (Cross out the words not required in this line.)
4. Occupation, _Housekeeping_
5. Birthplace, _Ireland_ (And how long in the United States, if of foreign birth.)
6. How long resident in this City, _18 years_
7. Father's Birthplace, (The State or Country.) _Ireland_
8. Mother's Birthplace, "   "   _Ireland_
9. Place of Death, No. _Van Brunt & Wolcott_ Street, _12_ Ward.
10. I Hereby Certify, That I last saw her on the _2_ day of _Aug_ 1869, that _she_ died on the _3_ day of _Aug_ 1869, and that the Cause of her Death was

[FIRST,] _Gastritis_

[SECOND, (remote or complicating,)] _Spasms_

Place of Burial, _Holy Cross_

(Date of do.) _August 6_

Time from Attack till Death.

Frank Bond M.D.,
Medical Attendant.

(Undertaker,) _Wm Cody_

(Place of Business,)   (Address,)

R. M. Whiting, Jr., Stationer and Printer, 272 Fulton St., Brooklyn.

Death Certificate of Bridget Kastendieck, 1869. The certificate lists cause of death as gastritis, a particularly insidious and painful disease. Her burial was in Green-Wood Cemetery, in Brooklyn, and not Holy Cross Cemetery as listed on the certificate. New York Municipal Archives.

DIED.

KASTENDICK—In Brooklyn, August 3d, 1869, BRIDGET, wife of John Kastendick.
  Relatives and friends of the family are most respectfully invited to attend her funeral which will take place from the cor. of Wolcott and Van Brunt st., South Brooklyn, Friday afternoon, August 6th, at 2½ o'clock.   au4 2t*

Funeral Announcement of Bridget Kastendieck. This brief newspaper announcement of the death of Bridget Kastendieck, wife of John Herman Kastendieck, appeared two times in the *Brooklyn Daily Eagle*, first on August 4, 1869, and again on August 5.

Funeral Route of Bridget Kastendieck. The Kastendieck grocery store stood at Van Brunt and Wolcott Streets on Red Hook Point, in South Brooklyn between the Atlantic and Erie basins. Hamilton Avenue, which extended out to Buttermilk Channel in the East River and connected Manhattan to Brooklyn by ferry, intersected Van Brunt Street and ran diagonally from South Brooklyn to Gowanus, connecting to Third Avenue before turning onto Twenty-fifth Street and on into Green-Wood Cemetery. Bridget Kastendieck and three of her children were buried at Green-Wood. Adapted from an 1866 engraving of A.J. Johnson's Map of Brooklyn and New York.

17

Green-Wood Cemetery

Green-Wood Cemetery was a spectacular source of pride to all New Yorkers. People spoke often of its park-like attraction. "The quick as well as the dead flocked to Green-Wood," said one observer. "On pleasant days hundreds of carriages headed for the Hills of Gowanus, took the Hamilton Avenue ferry, and then crossed Gowanus Creek over the Hamilton Avenue toll bridge. By the early 1850s, Green-Wood had become, in effect, the preeminent park for both Brooklyn and Manhattan."[1]

Green-Wood Cemetery helped to make of Brooklyn a favorite destination. Visitors from cities for miles around came to enjoy the pastoral beauty of this premier American cemetery. Horse drawn streetcars and railroads connected citizens to the many key locations in the city, and always to Green-Wood, making travel from any part of town both affordable, convenient, and pleasurable. A rail line, for example, ran from Fulton Ferry the four miles to Green-Wood. The trip cost four cents.

From the time of its founding in 1838, Green-Wood Cemetery developed an international reputation for its unsurpassed natural beauty to become the most fashionable burial place anywhere. One of the first large-scale rural graveyards, Green-Wood surpassed all other cemeteries in America for its bucolic and aquatic scenery. Crowds flocked to its grounds to enjoy family outings and carriage rides. By 1860, Green-Wood was attracting 500,000 visitors a year and rivaling places like Niagara Falls as one of the country's leading tourist attractions. Green-Wood's popularity helped to inspire the creation of public parks, including New York City's Central Park and Prospect Park, in Brooklyn.

In Green-Wood Cemetery lie the rich and famous: Louis Comfort Tiffany, Samuel F.B. Morse, Horace Greeley, Currier and Ives; and more recently Leonard Bernstein. All are buried there, the latter not far from the gravesite of Bridget Kastendieck. Buried in Green-Wood, too, are more infamous Brooklyn characters like "Boss" Tweed, and Henry Ward Beecher. Beecher went from avid abolitionist preacher to scandalous adulterer before he died.[2]

Funerals in Brooklyn were both a source of pride and complaint. We cannot describe the specific details of Bridget's funeral with certainty because we do not have a firsthand account. The procession may have stopped at one of the many churches on Hamilton Avenue for a service; however, we do not know that. Nevertheless, there is a hint at what the funeral procession might have been like in an article that appeared in the *Brooklyn Daily Eagle* in September of 1869, barely a month after Bridget's death. The article bemoans the excesses that funerals in general appear to have had. The tendency of urban funerals in the 19th Century apparently was to mount a costly display of ostentatious celebration of the deceased, "as though the only way of showing respect for the dead lay in squandering money on funeral arrangements," according to one complaint.[3]

People became afraid to bury a relative in a simple way for fear of accusal of disrespect and meanness. Those of modest means had a new fear of death, of having to provide a funeral whose cost was beyond their means. The old-fashioned coffin had become a richly adorned casket that some claimed to cost as much as a grand piano. Moreover, bystanders noticed a common disrespect from many of the funeral attendees. The first carriage or two of a funeral procession contained grieving relatives, but the larger part of the procession comprised people who stared complacently out the windows and laughed and chatted with acquaintances as if they were out for a holiday. The funeral became little more than a lavishly endowed convenience for the followers of the procession to take a pleasant carriage ride to Green-Wood Cemetery. The caring attendance of a bereaved family competed with the presence of a crowd of indifferent people.

Notwithstanding such overindulgences, which funerals may have caused, it did not detract from the singular beauty of Green-Wood Cemetery. Green-Wood was, and is, no ordinary cemetery. From the main entrance at the northwest corner of the property—where Twenty-Fifth Street turns into Fifth Avenue—a panorama of paths and lakes festoon the rolling, tree-shrouded landscape: 413 acres in 1869 when Bridget Kastendieck died, extending a mile east to west, and almost that distance north to south.

Coming up to the Fifth Avenue entrance, a seventy-five foot wide elevated grand avenue extended from Twenty-seventh Street to Thirty-fifth Street, a distance of eight blocks, lined with iron railings on either side. Coming in line with the Fifth Avenue entrance, visitors passed through the great arch three stories tall, erected there in 1851 at the exorbitant cost of $15,000.[4] More than fifteen miles of roads crisscrossed the cemetery and about an equal mileage of footpaths; so large was the whole affair that visitors became lost. The problem of disorientation became so bad that in 1871 cemetery mangers placed more than one hundred colorful cast iron arrows along the routes pointing to the entrances. The complex contained eight lakes supplied with water pumped by a steam-powered pump.

A lot at Green Wood cost $457 in 1868; several deceased persons could occupy one lot, which made it suitable for the interment of several family members. Many of the Kastendieck family occupy Lot 9625 in Section 116 of the cemetery.

A visit to Green-Wood promised a beautiful and pleasant drive although in the early days when it first opened a dangerous one. Green-Wood was the highest elevated spot in Brooklyn. One visitor described his visit in the *Brooklyn Daily Eagle* urging the uninitiated traveler to be cautious. He said, "Obtain first, old and steady horses; secondly, a good driver; and thirdly, restrict your pace to the slowest kind of trot. The road...is narrow and sinuous, sometimes curving so abruptly as to prevent you from seeing more than three or four yards of it at a time. The ground is also very hilly, and the rolling swells follow each other in quick succession. The descent to a lake, situated near the centre, is very bold, and if a vehicle were upset in making it, the party involved could scarcely escape with life."[5] Usually, however, published descriptions carried a much more complimentary tone. One visitor remembered, "With its landscaped terrain, pastoral winding paths, weeping statues, and plots enclosed by iron railings, Green-Wood was a romantic suburb for the deceased."[6]

It was a cemetery filled with monuments, tombs, and temples, of glittering marble and polished granite, highlighted by thousands of sculptures and carvings. One visiting correspondent giddy with delight at what he saw wrote, "On every hand are to be seen soft, easy slopes covered with a luxuriant growth of verdure; shady dells where the lights and shadows play incessantly and song birds warble in their wooded recesses; cool nooks where the sunlight never comes; broad hilltops catching every ray of light that reflects from the sky; placid lakes, umbrageous groves, broad, smooth drives and pleasant paths."[7]

It caused almost a state of envy for the dead buried there, and no doubt gave John Herman a bit of pride that he had buried his young wife and children in such a beautiful and famous place and that Bridget found eternal rest in the best cemetery in all of America.

Burials in the 19th Century did not always provide individual tombstones. Therein lies the story of the rediscovery of the gravestone of Bridget Kastendieck. Names were sometimes blocked on a single stone, three or more names to a stone, notably because of the expense of furnishing a separate monument for each of the deceased. This was particularly true of infants and young children. The Kastendieck family seemed always to return to these group burials, and even after the passage of many years erected new markers in remembrance of those yet long deceased.

The years covered up confusion regarding the burial of Bridget in Green-wood Cemetery. Her death certificate showed her interred in Holy Cross Cemetery, in Brooklyn. There were a number of Fords buried in Holy Cross, and Bridget's maiden name was Ford. One would expect, however, that the burial of a young mother of thirty-three would be near her deceased children, in the Kastendieck lot at Green-Wood. Yet, there was no confirmation of her burial at Green-Wood until the discovery in 2010 that someone incorrectly indexed her name in the cemetery records. Instead of Kastendieck, the recorder indexed her as "Kasbendick". After twenty years of searching, her burial had been in Green-Wood all along. The corrected record places her name on the list along with other Kastendiecks buried at Green-Wood, including her children who preceded her in death before her burial in 1869: William H., 1858; Heinrich, 1858; and Belinda, 1859. The four of them share a common gravestone lovingly engraved as the wife and children of John Herman Kastendieck.

New-York Bay, from Greenwood Cemetery.

New York Bay Seen from Green-Wood Cemetery. An 1874 engraving recorded the final resting place of Bridget Kastendieck, buried at Green-Wood in 1869. People escaped the bustling streets of Brooklyn to stroll amid the quiet solitude of the cemetery, along the paths overlooking New York Bay. *Harper's Weekly.*

Green-Wood Cemetery Brochure. This map depicted the early layout of Green-Wood Cemetery, in Brooklyn. Bridget Ford Kastendieck was buried in 1869 in the Kastendieck burial plot located in the upper left quadrant of the map (arrow). Images surround the map to record the pastoral beauty of the cemetery setting. Adapted from an engraving by W. Lawrence and J. Smillie, 1846. New York Public Library.

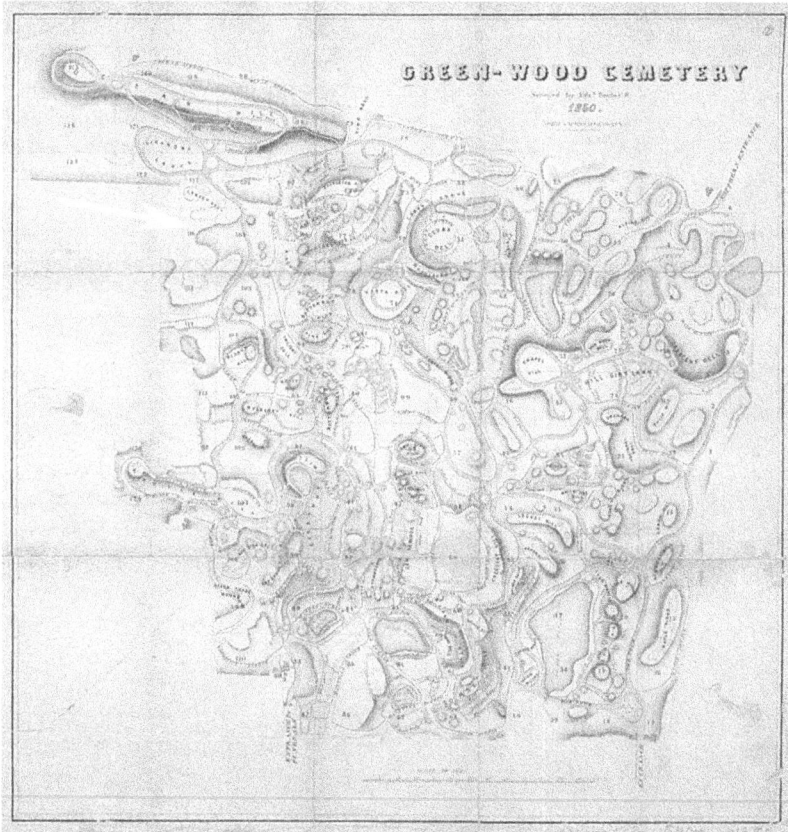

Map of Green-Wood Cemetery. An arrow identifies the approximate location of the Kastendieck Lot 9625 Section 116, in Green-wood Cemetery. John Herman and John Friedrich Kastendieck purchased the lot prior to the death of their mother, Trina Marie, in 1857. It became the final resting place of many of the Kastendieck family. The lot appeared isolated at the edge of the cemetery in this 1850 map. As the cemetery grew, streets and paths extended past the gravesite. Lithograph of Edward Boyle's 1850 Map, New York Public Library.

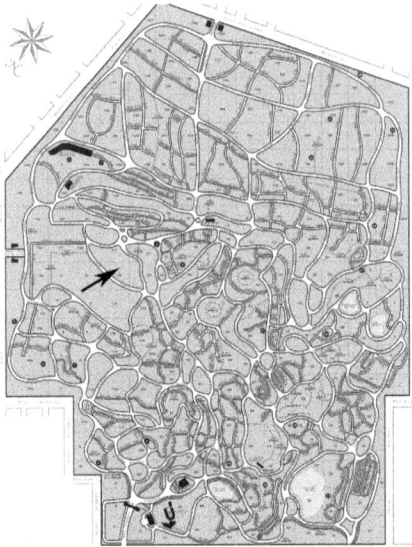

Map of Green-Wood Cemetery. The interment of Bridget Kastendieck and her children was in Lot 9625 (arrow) along with many other Kastendieck family members. Map courtesy of Green-Wood Cemetery.

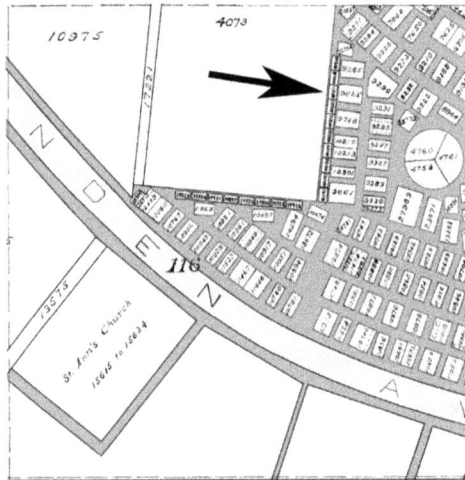

Section 116 of Green-Wood Cemetery. Bridget Kastendieck and her children were buried in Lot 9625 located in the upper right quadrant of Section 116 (arrow) not far from St. Ann's Church. The lot was accessible by the cemetery's Linden Avenue. Courtesy of Jane Cuccurullo, Green-Wood Cemetery.

18

The Seventies

A total solar eclipse occurred across the central United States on August 7, 1869. Although only a partial eclipse for persons in New York, it was nevertheless impressive to the Kastendieck family and everyone else who saw it, especially coming but four days after the death of Bridget Kastendieck and but a day after her burial. It began at a little past 5 p.m. on a Saturday afternoon, reached its maximum around 6 o'clock, and finished about 7 p.m., just as the sun was setting. The mostly cloudless sky provided a clear view of the phenomenon.

One observer described its effect as "a yellowish sickly hue which gradually and almost imperceptibly stole over the face of the city and its surroundings…It was not the natural twilight but a ghostly, indescribable half-light, which shone with a chilly subdued radiance, failing to hide even the most distant objects and at the same time making things appear void of all life and animation; like a novelist's description of the grotesque, bewitching haze that drapes the demons."[1]

A cold chill came over the land as the thermometer fell steadily. The water perhaps was the most remarkable of all in its fantastic and changing beauties. Now a sea of emerald; then a bay of crimson, crested with an occasional frothy wave; then a huge cauldron of yellow; again a sea of claret, and yet again a rolling river of somber, glittering blue and black.

Such an event did not occur again for forty years, and it left a lasting memory in the hearts and minds of the impressionable young Kastendieck children who must have wondered if the death of their mother caused such a spectacular event and what it meant. Theirs was not the only wonder. John Augustus Roebling, the engineer of the Brooklyn Bridge, died in 1869 just two weeks before Bridget died. He would not see the great bridge built, and some said the eclipse was his way of speaking from the grave.

Construction on the Brooklyn Bridge began in 1870. Originally proposed as The Great East River Suspension Bridge, or New York and Brooklyn Bridge, it created quite a stir throughout the United States. Brooklyn lay claim to it in a letter to the editor of the *Brooklyn Daily Eagle* on January 25, 1867, when a writer referred to it as the Brooklyn Bridge, and the name stuck. John Herman Kastendieck saw the first five years or so of construction of the bridge from his vantage point up the waterfront about two miles north, at his store in Red Hook. He no doubt remembered seeing its beginning with some pride in later years because upon its completion the Brooklyn Bridge was the longest suspension bridge in the world by 50 percent beyond any other such bridge; its main span bridged the East River nearly 1,600 feet. For many years, the towers were the tallest structures in the Western Hemisphere, visible for miles around as the only land passage between Manhattan and Brooklyn. The Kastendiecks left Brooklyn before the bridge's completion in 1883, but anytime talk of the world famous bridge came up, John

Herman could truthfully say he was there when they started building it.

The 1870 US Census gave an official status check of John Herman Kastendieck of Brooklyn soon after Bridget's death. In 1870, John Herman, age forty-four, was living with his children in the Twelfth Ward of Brooklyn. John, Jr., was fourteen, sons George and Andrew were ages nine and seven, respectively, and Amelia was four. John Herman's grocery business had prospered. That, and the growth of the Twelfth Ward, conspired to make him a relatively wealthy man. The 1870 Census showed him with real estate worth $30,000 and personal property of $2,000. Brooklyn in its heyday was a place where one could get rich quickly. One speculator, for instance, bought eight acres of land for $17,000 and afterwards sold it for half a million dollars.

John Herman's three sons attended school during the 1869-70 school year, and although Bridget had died the year before, the family appeared to be moving forward. Doris (Aunt Dora) Kastendieck, John Herman's fifty-four-year-old sister, was at the time living with him in 1870 as was nineteen-year-old Richard Kastendieck, probably also a relative of John Herman's. Doris was keeping house and helping with the children in the wake of Bridget's untimely death.[2]

Things were beginning to change in Brooklyn in ways John Herman found hard to accommodate. Construction of the Brooklyn Bridge was changing the entire shoreline around the old familiar Fulton Ferry; *The Brooklyn Daily Eagle* regularly protested the disposal of dead cats, dogs, horses, goats, and cows in Brooklyn waters, especially around Coney Island. Large animals shared the premises with many households. Animals stabled on vacant lots or in lean-tos attached to the houses added to the health risks. At the same time, the city was becoming too metropolitan. East New York voted by a ratio of three to one in

1872 for annexation with Brooklyn.[3] The old Brooklyn of John Herman's early days was changing into a crowded bustling metropolis.

To add to it all, John Herman had delinquent tax problems again in 1872. He had apparently not paid taxes going all the way back to 1870. By now his real estate holdings had grown to three lots and a house on Van Brunt Street, located between Dikeman and Wolcott; and a lot and house on Wolcott between Canover and Van Brunt. The tax bill was substantially more than it had been a decade earlier when he faced similar back tax problems. Taxes on the Van Brunt property added up to $314.04 while the Wolcott house and lot had an amount due of $62.03.[4] Several thousand owners of property faced an April 9 deadline to pay up or find their property on the sale block for non-payment of taxes. Once again, city assessments for the filling of low-lying lots probably contributed to John Herman's tax problems. His lots fell within the landfill project although the city assessed him for similar fill work less than a decade before.[5]

By 1872, John Herman's part of Brooklyn was not a good place to raise a family. One writer said, "Red Hook Point stands out in bold relief as being the grand central and amalgamated cesspool and sink of low life in Brooklyn."[6] Brooklyn, the writer went on, could boast of having within her boundaries localities where every crime that mind could conceive had been perpetrated. Red Hook fell prey to a denizen of river thieves who worked at night relieving schooners of whatever cargo they deemed of value usually without interference from the local constabulary. Another writer said, "There is such a state of barbarism and filth, that the entire aspect of the place is a spectacle revolting in the extreme."

John Herman may have agreed, but he stayed on, trying to make the best of his situation. *Boyd's Brooklyn Directory* of 1873 listed J.D. and J.H. Kastendieck in the grocery business, the former at 534 Fifth Avenue and John Herman at 396 Van Brunt, both addresses in Brooklyn.[7] J.D. Kastendieck was John Dietrich, youngest of the Kastendieck siblings, now in the grocery trade for himself after beginning years earlier as clerk in the store of John Friedrich Kastendieck, elder brother of the Kastendieck family. Meanwhile, John Henry Kastendieck was in business at Sixth Avenue and Seventeenth Street, thus accounting for all four of the Kastendieck brothers in the year 1873.

The Great East River Bridge to Connect the Cities of New York and Brooklyn. Currier and Ives previewed what the Brooklyn Bridge promised to look like in 1872. It was to be the longest suspension bridge by far ever constructed and the first such bridge to use steel-wire suspension. The inscription that accompanied this drawing described the planned project. "The Bridge is to cross the river by a single span of 1,600 feet, to start on the New York side from the City Hall, rising by a gradual approach of 2,381 feet in length, and on the Brooklyn side by an approach of 1,881 feet. Its elevation above the river, in the centre of the bridge will be 130 feet, its floor is to be 80 feet wide, with tracks for steam-cars, roadway for carriages, and walks for foot-passengers; it is to have an elevated promenade commanding a view of extraordinary beauty and extent; and its cost is to be about $8,000,000." Lithograph by Currier and Ives, c. 1872. Library of Congress.

Brooklyn Bridge Construction. Granite abutments pictured in a drawing from 1873 formed the foundation of the Brooklyn Bridge. Progress on the project seemed a far cry from the envisioned East River span that opened a decade later connecting Brooklyn and Manhattan. John Herman lived a short distance from the Brooklyn end of the bridge. "New York Harbor," *Harper's Weekly*, November 1873. Brooklyn Public Library.

Map of Brooklyn's Twelfth Ward. The developing neighborhood of John Herman Kastendieck's store on Van Brunt Street (circle) strategically placed him between the three docking basins that served New York Bay and most of Atlantic shipping: Atlantic Basin, Erie Basin, and Brooklyn Basin. Brooklyn grew rapidly with the completion of the Atlantic Basin to become a prime destination for commercial shipping and industry to the detriment of the neighborhood communities that once comprised the Red Hook district. Street Index of the City of Brooklyn, 1872. Brooklyn Public Library.

TWELFTH WARD

19

Out of Brooklyn

J ohn Herman Kastendieck remarried on November 27, 1870. He wed Johanna Gyridahl Hanson, a twenty-nine-year-old dressmaker and widow from Norway with three young children from her previous marriage.[1] We know little about her life except her name and her Scandinavian roots.[2] The marriage was unfortunately short-lived. Hannah Hanson died suddenly in 1872 and went to her grave in Green-Wood Cemetery. John Herman became a widower again. He added three orphaned stepchildren to raise, bringing to seven the total number of children in his family.

John Herman's life took a turn for the better on February 12, 1873, when he met and married Elida Sophia Nilson, a young Swedish girl some twenty years his junior. It was from all indications a whirlwind romance; it was her first marriage; his third. John Herman and Elida had a baby daughter, born in September 1873[3] As if their new baby was the sum of many daughters, they gave her a long name, Hermina Elida Rebecka Kastendieck; happily, they called her Minnie.[4] In due time, Elida gave birth again to two more children, this time to twins, Edward and Doris, in December 1875.[5] This brought to ten the number of children in the Kastendieck household. The oldest child, John Herman, Jr., celebrated his twentieth birthday in December 1875; George turned fourteen in May; and Andrew and Amelia were still in grammar school, as were the Hanson stepchildren. Little Minnie was three.

Then, tragedy struck the Kastendieck home yet again. Elida died on February 29, 1876, from complications of her recent childbirth. Death struck in quick succession. Baby Doris lived less than seven months until late spring of 1876. She became the fourth infant of John Herman's to die. Her death, coupled with the loss of his three wives, caused unimaginable grief. Little Doris became fatally ill and died on June 16, 1876, of Cholera Infantum, that deadly inflammatory disease feared by parents more than any other sickness peculiar to children. The insidious disease struck its victims in the summer months and was almost certain to end in death to little ones below the age of two; baby Doris was six and a half months old. It was an awful death, almost too horrible to describe. It came on suddenly as a sickness of the stomach with a fever nearing 104 degrees Fahrenheit, and then severe vomiting and diarrhea. The attack caused the stomach to fill with gas and brought on extreme thirst. Rapid emaciation followed. If a child survived for any length of time, the suffering reduced it to a veritable skeleton. At the end, the head rolled from side to side and the arms and legs flailed about. Convulsions quickly faded into a stupor or comatose state; the child gradually sunk into death.[6]

We do not know the suffering attending little Doris' condition; in the worst cases, however, children died within twenty-four hours. It is unimaginable what John Herman went through watching his motherless child suffer to the end, praying that she could somehow survive until the frost came in the fall. The Frost Cure meant simply waiting until the passing of hot weather of the summer months. The cold had an arresting effect on the disease. It was a futile wait; baby Doris died before the weather became cold enough to frost.

Cholera Infantum usually began as a case of ptomaine poisoning brought on by poor care and bad feeding. Brooklyn in the summer of 1875 was a hot, crowded city, filled with noise, foul air, and too much filth. Such conditions only helped to weaken a child's natural resistance to disease. Tobacco smoke, bad food, poor hygiene, and a myriad of other environmental factors conspired to kill the weak and unprotected.

Doris' little body put up a fight; but in such cases, it was usually a losing fight. In the worst of these cases, the child usually died under the best of care. Ironically, too much loving care could inadvertently cause the disease, too. A baby handled too much, fed too much and too often, bathed too much, not permitted to sleep enough, and so on, all could serve to weaken a small body's resistance.

On June 20, they buried her tiny body in Green-Wood Cemetery beside her mother, there amid the peaceful greenery and the sounds of nature that little Doris never grew up to know.

The loss of a child is a terrible thing. John Herman no doubt experienced the same guilt any parent would, wondering what he could have done to save his daughter.

Then it happened again. Twin baby brother Edward survived two more months and then he, too, died.

By 1875, John Herman had made up his mind to leave the squalor of Brooklyn, a place he called home for almost thirty years, a place of success and great personal sadness. On September 17, 1875, he sold his store and home on Van Brunt Street to his brother, John Dietrich. The details of the sale appeared in the *Kings County, New York, Real Estate Record and Builders' Guide*, including the sale price of $20,000.[7] The two lots in South Brooklyn comprised 6,750 square feet with 75 feet of street frontage beginning at the westerly corner of Van Brunt and Wolcott Streets and running south along Van Brunt. The lots were a generous 90 feet deep and accommodated his store and house, one lot being 50 by 90 feet and the other 25 by 90.[8]

When John Herman sold out to his younger brother John Dietrich, there was probably more to the transaction than made it into the official record. Five years earlier, the US Census showed John Herman with real estate valued at $30,000—more than a half million dollars in today's currency. Yet, he sold out for $20,000.[9]

John Herman stayed on in Brooklyn for a while after selling out; however, a string of events in 1876 convinced him for the last time to leave. Noisy steam trains were increasingly replacing the old horse drawn carts. In February 1876, things became so insufferable that citizens staged a protest against the changes and conditions coming over the city. That same month, the Brooklyn Board of Education decided not to teach German and French in any schools because, it said, "schools should not serve interests of any class of people."[10] With four school-age children still at home, such an announcement to a man of proud German heritage could not have set well. John Herman worried, too, about the general condition of the neighborhood. One never knew what to expect. Just the week before, someone had found the severed hand of a female in one of the lots on his corner at Walcott and Van Brunt. As it turned out, it was one of several body parts stored in a basement by a doctor. The doctor claimed it to be part of his medical study. The hand, he said, must have fallen out of the box when he moved his residence.[11] Because he was a doctor, the police dropped its investigation; however, John Herman had small children whose safety meant more to him than the dubious reputation of a doctor who experimented on human body parts.

Meanwhile, work began in May 1876 on the East New York end of the Brooklyn Elevated Railway promising to bring even larger streams of people of unknown character into the city.[12]

There is nothing to suggest that politics entered into John Herman's decision to leave Brooklyn although the Twelfth Ward Republican Association regularly met at Hoffman Hall, at 376 Van Brunt Street just a few buildings down the street from his house at 370 Van Brunt. They met in special session on June 20, 1876, to endorse the Republican ticket in the upcoming presidential election. The candidate for president was the popular Ohio governor, Rutherford B. Hayes. "Mr. Hayes," they said, "was a man who had not been inside the Republican Ring which had been bringing so much misfortune upon the country."[13]

In 1876, Brooklyn celebrated America's Centennial with great fanfare. Parades crisscrossed the city. Twenty thousand people gathered on July 4 at Fort Greene for a fireworks celebration a couple of miles from where John lived and well within view of his house. The celebration turned into a disaster. A large cache of pyrotechnics accidentally exploded. The fireworks caused death and destruction, followed a few months later by an even greater catastrophe.[14]

Less than two miles from John's home, the Brooklyn Theatre on Johnson Street burned on the night of December 5, 1876, killing more than three hundred people. The tragedy left a scar on the city that never healed. A kerosene lamp ignited a fire that swept up to the ceiling with astonishing rapidity and quickly turned the auditorium into an inferno. The annals of Brooklyn history had seen no other occurrence to match the panic and horror of that moment. First light the next morning revealed a pitiful sight. Layers of bodies appeared throughout the burned ruins of the theater, particularly those trapped in the upper second gallery.

City officials consigned remains to a common grave in Green-Wood Cemetery, a sad reminder of that awful event and a severe reality to an otherwise sublime setting. Nearly a year later there still was no monument to the memory of the many unidentified victims in that common grave in Green-Wood Cemetery.

In the spring of 1877, the *Brooklyn Daily Eagle* ran the headline "Twelfth Ward Troubles." The story was about politics at Hoffman Hall, but it easily could have been about John Herman Kastendieck's personal decision to leave Brooklyn. This time the Democrats—who apparently shared the hall with the Republican establishment—were in an uproar about the election of ward delegates to the General Committee. The *Brooklyn Eagle* even reported the meeting as occurring at John Herman's address, 370 Van Brunt Street, instead of 376 down the street at Hoffman Hall.[15] Meanwhile, John had $20,000 in his pocket from the sale of his real estate and business in Brooklyn, and plans for a new life away from the big city.

One can imagine that John Herman and the children made frequent visits to Bridget's grave in nearby Green-Wood Cemetery, none more poignant perhaps than the last visit before leaving Brooklyn for the last time. Green-Wood had grown to be a much larger place by the time John Herman left Brooklyn; in 1877, there were 187,000 people buried at Green-Wood. The cemetery was more beautiful than ever in those days and there was solace in leaving Bridget to rest in such an Arcadian place. When he quit Brooklyn, he left behind thirty-one years of work and memories.

John Herman left Brooklyn for good.

ATLANTIC DOCKS AND BASIN.

Atlantic Docks and Basin. John Herman Kastendieck first opened a grocery store about four blocks southwest of the Atlantic Basin around 1856. Over a period of moe than thirty years that he spent in New York, life in Brooklyn changed dramatically. By 1870 when this engraving was published, Brooklyn was no longer a rural appendage of New York City but a highly-industrialized, commercial hub. Photo from *History of the City of Brooklyn* by Henry R. Stiles, 1870. Brooklyn Historical Society.

Brooklyn Heights. When the weather was good, a stroll over to Brooklyn Heights in the north part of Brooklyn was a pleasant escape from the hubbub of South Brooklyn. This scene on the East River was about a mile and half from John Herman's store. He and Elida may have made trips here after Bridget died in 1869, remembering happier days. Elida died shortly after this engraving was made in 1874, and soon thereafter John Herman left Brooklyn for the less settled surroundings of rural Missouri. Courtesy of New York Public Library.

Clinton Street, Brooklyn, New York. Parts of the City of Brooklyn had a quiet, inviting appearance with all the amenities and idyllic character of a model 19th Century city. Clinton Street was several blocks away from the activity and noise of the waterfront. It separated Brooklyn Heights and Red Hook. Clinton Street ran roughly east and west about a mile from where John Herman Kastendieck lived. This is how the street appeared in 1874 shortly before he left Brooklyn for Missouri. Courtest of New York Public Library.

Red Hook Point, Brooklyn, New York. Red Hook evolved into a crowded, over industrialized part of Brooklyn. By 1875 when this drawing was made, it had lost much of its attraction as a place to live. John Kastendieck sold his property on Van Brunt Street and moved his family to a small farm in Christian County, Missouri. Courtesty New York Public Library.

Real Estate Sale Announcement. John Herman Kastendieck sold his property in Brooklyn to his brother John Dietrich. This announcement appeared September 17, 1875, in the *Real Estate Record and Builders' Guide of Kings County, New York*; v. 16, no. 393, p. 631.

FRANK LESLIE'S ILLUSTRATED NEWSPAPER

NEW YORK, DECEMBER 30, 1876.

THE BROOKLYN THEATRE CONFLAGRATION.

The Brooklyn Theatre Conflagration. Friends of the victims and the missing of the Great Brooklyn Fire of 1876 gathered in the room of the property clerk at the Brooklyn police headquarters to identify relics found in the ruins of the fire or on the bodies of the victims. The fire killed more than 300 people. Wood Engraving in *Frank Leslie's Illustrated Newspaper*, December 30, 1876. Library of Congress

Brooklyn Bridge under Construction. The East River Bridge rose up within sight of the demolition of buildings for the New York approach. Massive 275-foot towers loomed over New York Bay high above the East River. John Herman Kastendieck moved his family out of Brooklyn about the time this scene was captured during the bridge's construction. Wood engraving by W.P. Snyder, *Harper's Weekly*, November 1877. Library of Congress.

20

Sorting of Kastendiecks

The *1878 Brooklyn City Directory* listed John H. Kastendieck in the grocery business at 370 Van Brunt, although he had already shut his business and left the city. In the same 1878 listing was John D. Kastendieck selling groceries at 534 Fifth Avenue, and John Kastendieck selling milk from his home at 160 Nineteenth Street, in Brooklyn.[1] All appeared on the same page of the 1878 directory. These were the brothers Kastendieck: John Herman, John Dietrich, and John Friedrich.[2] The fourth brother, John Henry who had been in the grocery trade a decade earlier, had quit his business to make his livelihood as a laborer.

There were other Kastendiecks living in Brooklyn at the time and still others in New York City. Richard Kastendieck, for instance, also had a grocery store in Brooklyn at 206 Columbia, at the corner of Columbia and Sackett Streets. Likely, the same Richard Kastendieck clerked for John Herman half a dozen years earlier. He was not an offspring of any of the Kastendieck brothers, but perhaps a relative.[3]

Richard Kastendieck did not have a good reputation in Brooklyn. He apparently fatally injured an elderly customer in an argument over five cents. An old man, named Philip Collins, bought five cents worth of corn and paid the clerk with a ten-cent piece. The clerk denied this, and a quarrel broke out. Instead of trying to settle the difference, Richard took the side of his clerk, roughly threw the old man to the floor, and then ejected him from his store with such force that it broke the elderly man's leg and caused injuries that proved to be fatal. The law arrested Kastendieck on civil and criminal charges. The Collins family sued him for $5,000. We do not know the outcome of these charges; however, the court of public opinion in Brooklyn held Richard Kastendieck to be a shameless fool. One newspaper correspondent writing for the *Brooklyn Daily Eagle* wrote,

"The feelings of Mr. Richard Kastendieck, proprietor of a Columbia Street grocery store, are scarcely to be envied, if, as we are bound to suppose, he is a person of any sensibility whatever. The fact that he ejected an old and defenseless man from his store, on any provocation whatever, with such force as to fracture his thighbone and inflict fatal injuries, must cause him deep remorse."[4]

Kastendieck must have escaped a prison sentence because he appeared in the 1880 census, still in the grocery business in Brooklyn's Sixth Ward.

Richard Kastendieck was evidently a man who raised eyebrows in Brooklyn in other ways, too. The fifty-one-year-old grocer had a twenty-two year-old Swedish wife named Virginia and two small children.

By 1879, the *1879-80 Brooklyn City Directory* no longer listed John Herman Kastendieck; however, John Dietrich Kastendieck was still a grocer at his usual address, and John Friedrich Kastendieck was likewise doing business on Nineteenth Street.

In the meantime, the directory added another Kastendieck name to the list, John Herman, Jr.,

John Herman, Jr., kept his father's store open for a while at 370 Van Brunt Street but soon left to follow his family to Missouri.[5] Both John Herman, Jr., and John Dietrich Kastendieck disappeared from the Brooklyn directories after 1880 when Dietrich also moved his family and Aunt Dora to Missouri. John Friedrich, meanwhile, remained in Brooklyn and maintained his milk business until his death in 1893.[6] Henry, too, stayed in Brooklyn working as a laborer until his passing in 1885.

Henry Kastendieck was the first of the four Kastendieck brothers to pass on. Henry was something of an enigma in the Kastendieck story. He seems generally to have kept to himself. The one exception was when he attended the baptism of John Herman's son Andrew. Kinfolks represented all the Kastendieck siblings at that event except Dietrich. It may be that the interpretation of Henry as an outsider is simply a result of fewer records to identify his activities.

It does not help that there was living in Brooklyn at the same time a Rev. Henry Kastendieck. He appears to be a cousin, known by, and often associated with the Kastendieck families.[7] Highly respected in New York and New Jersey clerical circles, Rev. Henry served the German Missionary District of the New York Conference of the Methodist Evangelical Church, including Brooklyn from 1858 to 1860, and again in 1864.[8] Moreover, he was the first appointment to the new Eastern District in 1872.[9]

Photographs of Rev. Henry Kastendieck and his family, found with other photos in the Augusta Kastendieck Family Album, prompted at one time the belief that Rev. Kastendieck might have been John Henry Kastendieck the fourth

Kastendieck brother. However, they proved to be two different people.

The Kastendieck name continued to show up from time to time on the Brooklyn social register. On one such occasion in 1877, John "Kasondick" [*sic*] served as floor manager of the annual fall picnic of the Resolute Pleasure Club. Everybody agreed that the event surpassed all preceding ones. Dancing was of course the principal means of enjoyment.[10] We suspect that the John Kastendieck that helped do such a fine job of supervising the event was young John Herman Kastendieck, Jr. who had turned twenty-one in December. It was his best and last gala in the city of Brooklyn before departing to join his family in Christian County, Missouri.

21

Wives of John Herman

John Herman Kastendieck married four times; the only one of the original immigrant Kastendiecks to wed more than once. The human tragedies that visited his marital life are a sorrowful chapter in his personal story.

Over the years, the identities of his wives faded into history. The journey to rediscover them began with the notes of Hazel Kastendieck Shafer, granddaughter of John Herman. She left handwritten notes tucked inside the Kastendieck Family Bible, in which she wrote, "John Herman Kastendieck lost by death three wives, was married four times."[1] She included no names or dates, simply a recounting of a family tradition that remembered only that he married multiple times.

His first bride was Bridget Ford, a nineteen-year-old Irish immigrant. They married on Valentine's Day, 1855. John Herman was just shy of his twenty-ninth birthday. The ten years that separated their ages was common among men and women of the immigrant population. Older men, confident of a good livelihood, frequently married eligible young brides in their early childbearing years.

Bridget and John Herman were together fourteen years.[2] The accepted length of their union of fourteen years, however, portends a difficulty in deciphering the details of their marriage. Bridget's death certificate said she was thirteen years in Brooklyn at the time of her death.[3] This of course was not possible if the true length of her marriage to John Herman was fourteen years, according to the marriage date contained in the Kastendieck Family Bible. The length of time in Brooklyn recorded on her death certificate may have been an error on the part of the medical attendant who completed it. It appeared that someone first wrote ten years, and then wrote thirteen over that, suggesting they were unsure about the length of time she lived in Brooklyn. It had to be at least fourteen years to coincide with the fourteen years of Bridget and John Herman's marriage. On the other hand, they married elsewhere and later moved to Brooklyn. There is the possibility that the couple married in Manhattan or Long Island. The absence of a marriage record for them makes it impossible to verify this detail. Brooklyn did not require civil registrations of marriages until 1866; therefore, no official record of their marriage exists.[4] If a record exists, other than an entry in the Kastendieck Family Bible, it dwells in the dusty vaults of a church or other private location. There were many churches in Red Hook, Brooklyn, in those days that conformed to John Herman's religious leanings.

For example, the Pacific Street Methodist Episcopal Church stood at Clinton and Pacific Streets, where Hamilton Avenue runs diagonally across Clinton, about a half mile from where Bridget and John Herman eventually made their home on Van Brunt Street. A more likely candidate for their wedding place, however, was the First Place Methodist Episcopal on Van Brunt Street, a church that began in 1849 roughly contemporary with John Herman's arrival in America. Subsequent moves of this church to other locations took the congregation finally to a new building at First Place and Henry Streets in 1855, the year of Bridget and John Herman's marriage. This church was, incidentally, the location of one of John Herman's subsequent marriages. There is some question, however, as to whether the new First Place Church still under construction was available at the time of his wedding to Bridget in 1855.

Yet another possibility for their wedding place leads to Zion German Evangelical Lutheran Church about two miles north of their location on Van Brunt Street uptown in Brooklyn Heights close to the Fulton Ferry on the East River.[5] This all-German language church dedicated itself to speaking only the German language. In worship and church business, the congregation preserved the German heritage as Lutheran Christians. It was a favorite worship center for German immigrants.[6] It was at Zion that John Dietrich Kastendieck, the youngest Kastendieck sibling, married Rebecka Röpke in 1862.[7] Henry Kastendieck, likewise, saw his daughter Mary wed at Zion in 1874.[8]

Finally, there was the Wyckoff-Street Methodist Episcopal Church in Brooklyn where Bridget and John Herman baptized their youngest son, Andrew, in 1863, forming an obvious family connection.[9] In 1863, the Wyckoff-Street Church was one of twenty-three churches in Brooklyn. Located on Wyckoff Street near Smith Street, it added to the reputation of Brooklyn's prominence as the "city of churches."[10]

Any of these churches could have been the church home of Bridget and John Herman Kastendieck. The records may yield up a more complete and conclusive picture about their union in due time. Meanwhile, theirs may not have been a church wedding at all. A few smaller missions existed in Red Hook within close proximity of their future address on Van Brunt. None, however, has produced a record of their wedding.[11]

Long since forgotten are the circumstances of the courtship of Bridget and John Herman. Nevertheless, perhaps the birth of their first child reveals their attraction to one another. John Herman, Jr., came along nine months and twenty-two days after their marriage.[12]

Of Irish roots, Bridget wed into a German household, lived with John Herman in Red Hook, and helped him to establish his grocery business in Brooklyn. The marriage sadly came to an unfortunate end when Bridget died in the summer of 1869 at the age of thirty-three. She was the mother of four young children ranging in ages from fourteen to three—a baby daughter and three sons.

John Herman remained single in the year following Bridget's passing. His older sister Anna Dorothea, or Doris, (Aunt Dora) came to live with the family in the wake of Bridget's death. In her early fifties at the time, the past hardships of Dora's own life prepared her for the tragedy that now visited her newly widowed brother.[13] She herself had experienced the loss of two small daughters a dozen years earlier.[14] Her own painful losses would have made her particularly sensitive to the untried hardships death can bring to a family. She moved in with John Herman to help care for his four motherless children.

Johanna Gyridahl Hanson became Mrs. John Herman Kastendieck in the fall of 1870. Her rediscovery and identification as John Herman's second wife skips ahead to the 1880 US Census after he had moved his family to Billings, Missouri. The 1880 census of his household included Henry Hanson, fourteen-year-old "stepson" of John Herman. For there to be a stepson there had to be a heretofore-unidentified wife with a prior marriage to a man named Hanson. A retroactive check of the 1870 Census of Brooklyn produced the name of Hannah Hanson, a twenty-nine-year-old single dressmaker from Norway living at the time in Brooklyn's Twelfth Ward a few houses from where John Herman lived.[15] He lived at 370 Van Brunt Street, and she kept an apartment at 374 Van Brunt, two buildings up the street from the Kastendieck grocery store.[16] Johanna "Hannah" Hanson, nee Gyridahl, was the widow of Bernard Hanson who died in 1867 at the young age of thirty-five.[17] Hannah had three small children from that marriage all under the age of six: George, Cecelia, and the youngest, Henry, age four.[18] It was the second marriage for both John Herman and Hannah, or Johanna, as she wrote on their marriage certificate. Born in the coastal market town of Stavanger, Norway, Hannah was the daughter of Peter and Jorgina (Swensen) Gyridahl.[19]

After what appears to have been a relatively lengthy acquaintance and courtship, John Herman and Hannah married on Sunday, November 27, 1870, in Brooklyn. He was forty-four years old; she was age thirty. Witness to their marriage was Aunt Dora, John Herman's sister and nanny; caregiver to what now suddenly became a family grown in number from four to seven children.

John Herman apparently acceded to Hannah's wishes to be married in her church, and they were married at the Scandinavian Chapel on Pacific Street, near Flatbush Avenue. The chapel was a legation of the Methodist Episcopal Church Scandinavian Mission Society. Rev. Ola Helland solemnized the union. Rev. Helland, a Norwegian sailor, had a reputation as a mobile clergyman. When he was not preaching at the Scandinavian Chapel or one of several other missions in South Brooklyn, he was on board some ship attending to the spiritual needs of his Norwegian brethren. In his report to the church leaders in 1869, he wrote from his station at Sugar Loaf, New York, "An unusually large number of Scandinavian emigrants have come to this country this season." Rev. Helland died in

1892 counting among his lifetime of clerical service the wedding of Hannah and John Herman Kastendieck.[20]

John Herman and Hannah were together less than two years; and then, Hannah died suddenly in 1872, at home at 370 Van Brunt.[21] The details of their marriage during their brief time together and the circumstances of her premature death are scant. Her burial was in Green-Wood Cemetery in the Kastendieck family plot.[22]

In those days, the law required the US Postal Service to advertise periodically a list of letters remaining at the post office unclaimed by their addressees. The *Brooklyn Daily Eagle* ran such an official list in the spring of 1875.[23] On the women list of unclaimed mail was the name of Hannah Hanson. It is possible that this was another Hannah Hanson, but most likely, the letter went unclaimed because Hannah Hanson Kastendieck was dead for more than two years when the list appeared. What was in the letter or whether anyone ever claimed it is unknown.

John Herman was once again a widower, this time with seven small children to raise, four of his own and the three orphans left by Hannah's death.[24]

John Herman Kastendieck married a third time on February 12, 1873, in Brooklyn, to Elida Sophia Nilson, a Swedish woman nearly twenty years his junior; he was forty-six; and she was twenty-eight. It was her first marriage. A marriage certificate for this marriage found on file with the New York Municipal Archives confirms this as John Herman's third marriage. Speculation that John Herman had an unknown marriage prior to his first marriage to Bridget Ford ended with the discovery of the record of his marriage to Elida. The marriage certificate of John Herman and Elida Nilson clearly confirmed that this was his third marriage, and proved that he was indeed single during those first nine years in Brooklyn before he wed Bridget Ford.

Elida's father was John Nilson. Beyond that, we know very little about her. She came from Gutenberg, Sweden, probably newly arrived in America because in the place of residence on the marriage certificate she wrote Sweden, then scratched that out and wrote Brooklyn.[25] She may have been one of the many young women from Sweden who took jobs around Brooklyn as domestic servants. Such an occupation sheltered vulnerable immigrants until they could marry or gain experience for more substantial employment.

John Herman and Elida took their marriage vows before Rev. A.S. Hunt, Pastor of the First Place Methodist Episcopal Church, located at the corner of Summit and Henry Streets, facing First Place Street. This was most likely John Herman's church. It had its beginning back in the 1850s on Van Brunt Street where John had his store.[26] The congregation replaced that old church with an impressive new structure in the Eleventh Ward. It stood about a half mile from where John lived and was one of the more popular Methodist Episcopal Churches in Brooklyn.

John Herman and Elida did not have a church wedding per se. They took their marriage vows at the home of Rev. Hunt who lived next door to the church in the parsonage at 158 Summit Street. The day of the wedding, February 12, fell on a Wednesday. The ceremony was probably a simple, private one. The couple did not provide their own witnesses. Only one person signed the marriage certificate as a witness; that was Rev. Hunt's Aunt Jane G. Hunt.

Rev. Hunt who married John Herman and Elida was no ordinary preacher. His full name was Albert Sanford Hunt, A.S. Hunt for short. He was John Herman's age, a native New Yorker, and a descendant of a family of English Quakers.[27] Educated at the seminary, he had a degree from Wesleyan University by the time he was twenty-three. He taught at Wesleyan briefly, did some travel in Europe, and then came to Brooklyn as a member of the New York conference of the Methodist Episcopal Church about 1860.[28] A brilliant scholar and speaker, he was much in demand as a guest minister and actively promoted the growth of the Methodist Episcopal Church, chiefly by recounting its history and documenting its several congregations in New York.[29] Rev. Hunt believed in an ecumenical approach to religion, promoting the free interchange of religious thought with all denominations, ideas known from later events to correspond to John Herman's worldview pertaining to religion. Despite his personal success as a church leader, Hunt urged the church to hold to its common origin in the ordinary lives of people and not the elite.[30] He developed a national reputation within the Methodist Episcopalian faith, holding high positions within the church organization.

Rev. Hunt had a talent for art. He made one of the last drawings of Abraham Lincoln from life in 1865. It seems he was also a personal acquaintance of Ulysses S. Grant during the Civil War. He had a bent for the political; his sermon on the assassination of President Lincoln ranked among the best to come from the pulpit in the wake of that national tragedy.[31] Rev. Hunt held a number of pastorates in Brooklyn over the course of a few years, coming eventually to the First Place Methodist Episcopal Church in Brooklyn in 1872 where John Herman and Elida found him as minister when they married in the winter of 1873.

Rev. Hunt lived most of his life with his mother, never married, and amassed a sizeable fortune that he gave to charity, a large part of it to Wesleyan University to build a library. It happened, also, that at the time he married John Herman and Elida, he had a Swedish servant named Christina who was

Elida's age and doubtless one of her close friends and a connection to Rev. Hunt.[32]

John Herman and Elida had a daughter, Hermina Elida Rebecka "Minnie" Kastendieck.[33] Records are inconclusive about the date of her birth, given variously as 1872, 1873, and 1874. In due time, Elida gave birth to twins, Doris, or Dora, as she was called after her Aunt Dora, and Edward, in December 1875.

Then, Elida died on February 29, in the leap year of 1876, at the age of thirty-one from complications of childbirth.[34] Baby Doris lived but six months until late spring of 1876, and she died. Edward survived two more months and died, all three gone by August.[35] John Herman and Elida's marriage had lasted three years and seventeen days, a short burst of happiness closed out by unimaginable grief.

From the time of his marriage first to Bridget Ford in 1855 until the death of Elida in 1876—hardly a span of twenty years—John Herman saw eight members of his immediate family die; not counting his mother who had died in 1857, his sister, and numerous nieces and nephews. Of all the Kastendieck deaths recorded in Brooklyn during that period for those interred in Green-Wood Cemetery, more than half were from John Herman's household.

Burial of Elida was in Green-Wood Cemetery with her two infant children, initially in the Kastendieck plot and then for unknown reasons removed to another location in Green-Wood probably for the sheer want of space in the Kastendieck plot.[36] The new cemetery plot was also under Kastendieck ownership at the time but later transferred to a new owner. Green-Wood archivist Jane Cuccurullo described the burial arrangements this way. "The remains of Elida Sophia Kastendieck who died February 29, 1876 were interred in Lot 9625 [Kastendieck plot] on March 2, 1876.[37] On August 12, 1876, her remains were removed to Lot 21709. The remains of Doris Kastendieck who died June 19, 1876 (an infant) were first interred in Lot 9625 on June 20, 1876. On August 12, 1876, her remains were also removed to Lot 21709. The remains of Edward J. Kastendieck who died August 9, 1876 (an infant) were interred in Lot 21709 on August 12, 1876. Lot 21709 was purchased July 22, 1874 by John D. Kastendieck and Casper Ficken. John D. Kastendieck conveyed his interest to members of the Ficken family."[38]

John D. Kastendieck who sold his interest in the Green-Wood lot to Mr. Ficken was John Herman's younger brother, Dietrich. The Ficken families were longtime friends, in-laws, and business associates of the Kastendiecks in a multifaceted relationship between the two families.[39] Casper Ficken's wife Anna was the sister of Rebecka Röpke, wife of Dietrich Kastendieck. Casper's brother, Diedrich Ficken, married a third Röpke sister and lived on Third Avenue, in Brooklyn, not far from the Dietrich Kastendieck grocery store. Diedrich Ficken was also a witness to the will of Catherina Kastendieck, wife of John Henry Kastendieck, brother of Dietrich and John Herman.

It appears that when baby Edward died in August there was no room for him in the original Kastendieck lot. John Herman had evidently filled his portion of the lot. Rather than seeing his baby son separated from its mother in death, John Herman had Elida's remains along with infant Doris exhumed and reinterred at the new location. No more burials of members of John Herman's immediate family ever occurred in Green-Wood Cemetery. He left for Missouri soon after the deaths of Elida and the children.

Elida's death made of John Herman a widower for the third time, this time though for barely nine months when he married Virginia (aka Caroline Victoria) Harper Wingood on December

3, 1876.[40] He was now fifty years old; she was thirty-two. It was her second marriage. She was from the Danish West Indies, born on St. Thomas Island, the daughter of George Harper While she and John Herman had no children of their own, she helped to raise the Kastendieck children from John Herman's previous marriages. When they wed, the Kastendieck children, including the Hanson stepsiblings, ranged in ages at the time from four years to a few days short of being twenty-two years old.

Caroline's origin from Denmark's St Thomas Island contributed to the international flavor of the Kastendieck family. While she added no descendants of her own, she was a mother to all of them, children with maternal roots in Ireland, Norway, and Sweden blended with their German ancestry. Caroline accompanied John Herman to Billings, Missouri, and was his wife for more than twenty years.

First Place Methodist Episcopal Church, Brooklyn, New York. John Herman Kastendieck married Elida Nilson at the parsonage next door to this church in 1873. Dedicated in 1856, an impressive building fifty-three feet wide by seventy-five feet deep built in the Romanesque style of brick with brown stone trimmings, its spire rose from an octagon tower one hundred thirty-four feet in height. The parsonage was on the rear of the lots facing Summit Street. Photograph from Stiles, *A History of the City of Brooklyn*, 1870.

1875 New York State Census. John Herman Kastendieck's 1873 marriage to Elida Nilson enlarged the Kastendieck family to eight offspring listed here in order of their ages. Not shown is their daughter, baby Minnie Kastendieck, who was born just prior to the date of the census. The census enumerator was confused by the blended family because he mistakenly listed Andrew and Amelia Kastendieck as Hanson stepchildren on the census form. Only George, Cecelia, and Henry were the children of John Herman's second wife, Hannah Hanson. New York Municipal Archives.

KASTENDIECK—On Monday morning Dora M. J.,
daughter of J. H. and K. S. Kastendieck.
Relatives and friends of the family are respectfully invited to attend the funeral, from the residence of her parents, 370 Van Brunt st, at 2 o'clock P. M. on Tuesday.

Death Notice of Dora Kastendieck. Dora, infant daughter of John
Herman and Elida Sophia Kastendieck, died Monday morning, June 19,
1876; her funeral announcement appeared the same day; and she was
buried the next day. Her mother had died in February of 1876. Her twin
brother died a few weeks later in August. *Brooklyn Daily Eagle*, June 19,
1876, and Green-Wood Cemetery.

Marriage Certificate of Caroline
Wingood and John Herman
Kastendieck. They married in 1876
shortly before leaving Brooklyn
and moving to Missouri. Marriage
records like this were kept in New
York after 1866. New York
Municipal Archives.

Casper and Anna (Röpke) Ficken.
Elida Kastendieck and her infant
children were reinterred in the
Ficken family cemetery plot. Anna
Ficken was the sister-in-law of
Dietrich Kastendieck. When the
Kastendiecks left Brooklyn for
Missouri, the Ficken family took
over the Kastendieck share of their
common burial lot in Green-Wood
Cemetery. David Gay Collection.

22

Into Missouri

John Herman had his eye on leaving Brooklyn for some time, perhaps as long as a decade, dating back to the death of Bridget in 1869. We cannot say with certainty that her tragic demise was the reason for his disenchantment with the East Coast, but her awful death and the many other tragedies that befell his family could not have left him feeling a close attachment to the environs of Red Hook. Red Hook was in an insalubrious state, part of a steady decline in conditions generally throughout New York. One observer wrote, "New York is a study of contrasts. It has no virtue without its corresponding sin; no light without its shadow; no beauty without deformity; for it is a little world in itself."[1] What once stood as a poetic ode to America's largest city took on an ominous tone for those trapped within the sinking fortunes of the city in the decade of the seventies.

A stampede to riches followed the American Civil War, fueled by the Second Industrial Revolution and a race to rebuild the country. Corruption and unbridled speculation produced a period of rampant inflation. The era became the "Gilded Age", a time when nothing seemed worth its purported value. A government crackdown on big business stirred uncertainty in the public. The drive to root out corruption and break up monopolies caused people to lose confidence. These factors put an immense strain on the banks. In New York City, bank reserves plummeted in the fall of 1873 to one-third their normal value. Depositors panicked. The run on the banks that followed sent the New York economy into a tailspin that lasted for six years. The panic triggered a depression that spread across North America and Europe and lasted until the spring of 1879—the year after John Herman settled in Missouri.

His desire to escape the hullabaloo of New York to a place less susceptible to the financial misfortunes of the economy was a reasonable decision. He weathered the worst of it and left with the bulk of his earnings intact. Whether the Long Depression—the period from 1873 to 1879—drove him out of Brooklyn is lost to history. We know only that John Herman's brother Dietrich Kastendieck blamed the downturn in financial matters in part for his own decision to sell out his Brooklyn grocery business and follow his brother to Missouri.[2]

John Herman's choice to resettle in the Midwest begs the question why Missouri? Gleanings of anecdotal remarks preserved in family records suggest that former acquaintances from Brooklyn had moved to Missouri previously.[3] An exchange of correspondence may have extolled some of the virtues of the state, its independent nature, and rapid development, not to mention the lesser impact of the depression that gripped the rest of the world.

Missouri in 1878 was German in substantial numbers up and down the state and had been since before the Civil War. The German community wielded a robust presence especially in the city of St. Louis. At the outset of the war, the German population of St. Louis organized a formidable military response to the Confederate-leaning Missouri State Guard. Unionists credited the Germans with the muster of enough federal resistance to keep Missouri in the Union. After the war, the political and ethnic divides in St. Louis prompted many Germans, uncomfortable with lingering adversarial relationships, to abandon their businesses and move into one of the several outlying German settlements that promised conditions more agreeable in rural Missouri. Germans left St. Louis in large numbers in much the same way they abandoned their fortunes in Brooklyn and other metropolitan centers of the country.[4]

The circumstances of the German population in Missouri were of two kinds. First, they came to America in large numbers to escape the German Revolution. John Herman and the Kastendieck brothers were in this wave of immigrants, except the Kastendiecks initially chose the East Coast over the Midwest. The second circumstance owed German immigration to Missouri to Gottfried Duden, the German writer who in 1829 and for three decades thereafter drew wave after wave of German refugees to Missouri with his idyllic descriptions of a land of promise altogether as fertile and abundant as the fatherland.[5] Many who came did not find his promotion of Missouri to live up to his descriptions. They found farming too difficult and accordingly migrated to St. Louis.[6] Thus, there grew up in Missouri farming communities of Germans across the state, each anchored to an ethnic and political base in St. Louis but settled in close-knit communities that preserved their language and culture.[7] German-Americans constituted about four-fifths of the foreign population of every western city by the beginning of the Civil War.[8] After the war, the flow of Germans out of the big cities and back into the farming communities was in effect a reversal of the earlier trend toward urban settlement.

Missouri and other western states ran a steady stream of advertisements in the eastern papers seeking to recruit new settlers to grow the population and with it the young economies of the trans-Mississippi lands. Articles appeared periodically in the *Brooklyn Daily Eagle* extolling the virtues of southwest Missouri, a place of rolling prairies abundant wildlife, and clear streams. "The farmers of Southwest Missouri," said one article, "have a prodigious crop of peaches on their hands, and do not know what to do with them. No sufficient market is available."[9] Ironically, one such article appeared on the day Bridget Kastendieck died, August 3, 1869. In it, the organizers of the Missouri Colony described in detail the fertile land of southwest Missouri and the several ore mining opportunities that existed in addition to attractive farm land at a fair price, anywhere from $5 to $12 per acre, and some government land as low as $1.25 per acre. The Erie Railroad, the article said, would transport people to St. Louis at a one-third reduced price of the fare and include transport of up to three hundred pounds of baggage per person. The Missouri Colony locaters would then arrange transportation from St. Louis on to southwest Missouri.[10]

We might imagine that John Herman Kastendieck clipped out this article or one like it and kept it should the need to leave Brooklyn ever come to pass, as it finally did in 1878. If one read the Brooklyn papers closely, they also carried stories of a lawless Missouri that might give pause to anyone contemplating a move to the frontier. For example, there was the story of the judge who divorced himself from his wife in his own court, a judge acclaimed to be "at the head of the legal profession in Southwest Missouri."[11] On a more somber note was the execution of a trio of black men, captured in Brooklyn and executed for murders committed across the Midwest and South, one man for killing a farmer named Davis in Christian County, Missouri.[12] That happened in 1877, too late to serve as a warning to John Herman because he was already in the process of moving to Christian

County. Then, there was the story in the fall of 1880 about a stagecoach robbery south of Billings, in Christian County. Six well-armed masked men held up the stage that ran between Pierce City, Missouri, and Eureka Springs, Arkansas. The robbers stripped the passengers of money and valuables to the tune of about $900. A couple of passengers tossed their pocketbooks into the brush and recovered them later denying the gang another $1,500. One passenger attempted to draw a revolver and took a bullet through his coat sleeve to keep him quiet.[13] This story appeared in the *Brooklyn Daily Eagle*, but by 1880 at the time of the robbery, John Herman had left Brooklyn and likely read about it in the *Billings Times* or heard about it firsthand from a neighbor.

The Kastendiecks journeyed across country by train, but not on the Erie Railroad, as the *Brooklyn Daily Eagle* article had promised in 1869 because the Erie no longer existed in 1878 under the Erie name. Railroad conglomerates and independent railroad companies made it difficult for the traveler to know what railroad line belonged to whom. A bewildering maze of railroads emanated out of the East Coast like a spider wed spread over the northeastern states, reaching into the upper Midwest to connect with a host of independent railroads operated by a potpourri of different companies under a plethora of leasing agreements.

At the time John Herman left Brooklyn for Missouri, he most likely took the New York Central and Hudson River Railroad, which operated out of the northeastern United States headquartered in New York City. The line included extensive rail service across the states of New York, Pennsylvania, Ohio, Michigan, Indiana, and Illinois. A popular passenger line, it delivered vacationing tourists to Niagara Falls and the shores of the Great Lakes.

Just what route the Kastendiecks took is a guess. The New York Central and Hudson River Line took riders first from New York City to Buffalo, New York. There, passengers usually transferred to the Michigan Southern Railroad that took them around Lake Erie and on to Chicago. From there, the Chicago and Alton Railroad or the Illinois Central took travelers south on into St. Louis.

On the other hand, the Kastendiecks could have taken a more direct rail route once out of New York on less travelled lines out of Cleveland, cutting across Ohio to Cincinnati, and from there on into St. Louis via the Ohio-Mississippi Railroad. Either way, the thousand-mile trip from New York took them through at least four states passing through the changing vista of the American landscape. From St. Louis, it was another two hundred miles by rail connection with the Frisco Line on to southwest Missouri, overall about a four to five day trip from New York.

Rail travel into the Ozarks was a relatively new experience. For a long time, there was no railroad to that part of Missouri at all. By 1860, construction efforts to build one had advanced as far as Rolla, Missouri, before the Civil War stopped it. Section men dropped their shovels and picked up muskets to join either North or South in the war. Plans to link St. Louis to southwest Missouri by rail went on hold. After the war, a series of bankruptcies and receiverships held off progress on the extension of the rails until 1870. That year, crews laid track from Rolla to Springfield, Missouri, and then on down to the railway town of Plymouth Junction, Missouri, or Gonten (present day Monett), before continuing in 1871 on across southwest Missouri to the Missouri-Oklahoma state line.[14] The dream of the St. Louis and San Francisco Company to reach San Francisco, California, to connect the East and West Coasts of the nation, never happened. The Frisco fell short by a thousand miles, but other companies in due course made it a reality.

The unbridled race to reach the Pacific by rail caused numerous big investment fiascos that contributed to the Panic of 1873 and the Long Depression.

When John Herman and his family transferred to the Frisco Line at St. Louis in 1878, the trains to the Ozarks carried a steady stream of newcomers eager to begin a new life far removed from the one they left behind. The train that brought John Herman to Missouri dropped him into a new world, one vastly different from the hurried streets of Brooklyn, out of the routine of city life, and into the pleasures and hardships of rural living. He rekindled ties to nature he had not known in its fullness since leaving Morsum, Germany, more than three decades before.

No one remembers exactly why he decided to shut his grocery business in Brooklyn in 1878 and move his family to the frontier of the country. Perhaps it was for health reasons or maybe the downturn in Brooklyn's economy. New York was still struggling in 1878 to recover from the collapse of the banks in 1873. Maybe he came to Missouri purely for personal reasons, to give his children the same joys of rural upbringing that he had once experienced in his own youth. His kids were in their formative years: George turned seventeen in May. Andrew and Amelia were teenagers, too, and Minnie was just starting grade school. The Hanson stepchildren were all in their teens. Only John Kastendieck, Jr., had reached adulthood, approaching the age that John Herman was when he first struck out across the Atlantic on his adventure to America. Missouri would be a different story than Red Hook and Brooklyn.

The Panic of 1873. The Run on the Fourth National Bank, New York City. The financial crisis of 1873 caused the Long Depression, a crisis felt worldwide. It remains the longest running price and economic recession in history. Its six-year duration caused many businesses to fail and forced their owners to close and relocate. Wood engraving illustration in *Frank Leslie's Illustrated Newspaper,* October 4, 1873, p. 67. Library of Congress.

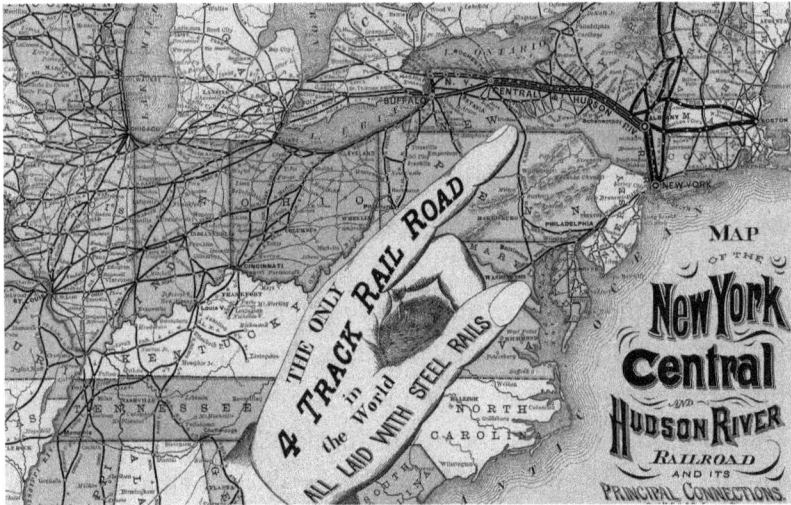

New York Central and Hudson River Railroad and Its Principal Connections. By 1876, railroads linked major cities on the East Coast to the main population centers of the Midwest. This map of the eastern half of the United States shows the railroad network. Main lines are indicated in heavy black. No railroad connections appear in the south where the hand indicator is located. The more heavily travelled routes linked the northern tier of tracks from New York to Chicago. Excerpt from Rand McNally, 1876. Library of Congress.

The Railroad Scene. Well-dressed passengers wait as the Illinois Central Railroad train pulls into the station. The Illinois Central was one of several railroads John Herman Kastendieck could take on his journey from New York to Missouri. A large globe displays the United States and the extent of the I.C.R.R. lines. Swain and Lewis lithography, c. 1882. Library of Congress.

Frisco Steam Locomotive. The Kastendieck family arrived in Billings aboard a passenger train pulled by a steam locomotive similar to this Manchester engine built in 1880. Passenger service into southwest Missouri was relatively new when the Kastendiecks came to Christian County in 1878. Frisco Archives, Springfield-Greene County Library.

23

Christian County

At the tip of the panhandle of Christian County, Missouri, lies one of southwest Missouri's most fertile regions.

Spread along the highlands of the Ozarks Plateau, the area went largely undiscovered by white settlement until well after Missouri statehood in 1820. It was at one time Indian land. The first inhabitants wrote their presence in the flint arrowheads and fragments of broken pottery strewn over the fields that the Indians once called home.

It was not until 1835 that the government surveyed the public lands of Missouri. In 1837 Samuel Garoutte, a man of New Jersey roots, located his home four miles north of the future town of Billings. George M. Laney, among others, came the same year, and from 1845 until 1860, the community rapidly grew.[1]

Christian County did not exist formally until shortly before the Civil War when the Missouri legislature created it in 1859, some thirty years after statehood. They carved the county out of the existing counties of Taney, Lawrence, and Greene Counties. Stone County refused to give land; hence, the Christian County

Panhandle that extends along the original boundary of Stone County.[2]

The name Christian County came from Christian County, Kentucky; named, according to tradition, at the request of a local resident who wished to see the county named for her home state that supposedly first adopted the name from a Revolutionary War veteran named William Christian. In the spring of 1860, the government established a post office at Elba, future site of the town of Billings.[3]

Christian County was strongly pro-Union during the Civil War. Political views aligned with the names of the county townships. Names like Polk, Porter, and Benton represented Union men. The township of Breckenridge, named originally for a southern politician, changed at the outset of the war to Galloway Township in honor of a local Union soldier killed at the beginning of the war. Meanwhile, Lincoln Township honored the President.[4] If county officials had known that Jefferson Davis, President of the Confederate States, was a native son of the county's namesake in Christian County, Kentucky, Christian County, Missouri, today might have a different name.[5]

Like many Missouri counties, Christian County residents suffered greatly from the Civil War in a state torn by sectional division that often surfaced in acts of hostility and unlawfulness against innocent people.

Following the war, the panhandle of Christian County entered a period of quick recovery; the business life of the community began to take shape. The first store went up in 1865 in the Plymouth community, named for a land development adjacent to the Elba Post Office. Soon there was a produce market, drug store, hardware store, wagon shop, a lumberyard, and brick yard to supply materials for the burgeoning residential and commercial structures going up in the community. By 1871, the St. Louis and San Francisco Railway Company, the Frisco, reached into Christian County, swept past Elba, and on to the Oklahoma border and beyond.

One of the Frisco officials was Frederick H. Billings. The community wanted a church. As more people settled, the attendant need for a school and especially a church became a priority. Mr. Billings, being a civic-minded representative of the railroad, contributed the land and $1,000 to the building of a union church. With slight prompting from the donor, the community responded by renaming the Elba community Billings—and Billings it has been since 1872. Such quid pro quos were common. Down the track from Billings is Pierce City, Missouri, a town also named for another railroad official.

Billings was a wayside destination, one of the stops of the Frisco train on its southwesterly route out of St. Louis that amounted to little more than a wide place in the road where the train paused to take on water and check equipment for the ride on down the line. Nevertheless, with the arrival of the railroad came Billings' first hotel. Two more hotels added in relatively quick succession made Billings a trendy destination. In 1875, John A. Owen moved his mill to Billings from Illinois.[6]

A wave of German speaking immigrants flowed into southwest Missouri from all parts of the country and from their homelands, places like Germany, Austria, and Switzerland.[7] The railroad offered land for sale along its corridor and ran advertisements in eastern newspapers promising free rail passage to anyone willing to partake of the comparably inexpensive land. At the same time, homestead acreage was available to anyone able to pay the modest cost and improve the land for a stipulated period. Moreover, a newcomer could always purchase land at the going market price wherever he wanted and do whatever he pleased with it.

John Herman Kastendieck came to Missouri in the fall of 1878, bought a parcel of ground southwest of Billings, built a house, and settled into his new life. He apparently never entertained the idea of restarting a grocery business in Billings. He left that all behind in Brooklyn and at the age of fifty-two took up farming.

A contemporary description of his new rural surroundings is in a letter written by a neighbor in July of 1880. Nikolaus Rauch, writing to his family back in Germany, wrote,

"We have the impression that the neat little village [Billings] where we bought our land is going to grow. There are many Germans there, all of whom have settled during the past five years. There are only about two hundred inhabitants, but there are two churches and schools, a doctor and pharmacy. Lumberyards; everything one would need. The land we bought is right on the city limits of the town…the land cost $11 an acre. All the brothers will be able to find land close to ours and they will buy as soon as possible…There is native corn as well as good wheat, grapes and other fruit, including peaches. There is also flat higher ground and a healthy climate. Game is available including large and small deer and numerous rabbits. Wild grapes and wild plum are also plentiful. The humming bird is the smallest bird in the world and there are many to be found in this area."[8]

By 1880, the Kastendiecks accounted for a sizable presence in the Billings community. John Herman's family of ten included his stepchildren and son John Herman, Jr., who had closed out the last of the grocery business in Brooklyn and rejoined the Billings clan. John Herman, Jr., George, Andrew, and stepson Henry Hanson made out as farmhands; Amelia and Minnie went to school. Stepson George Hanson, recently married to

Sarah Keithley in Christian County, took up farming, and occupied a farm in Polk Township close to the Kastendiecks. Cecelia Hanson, meanwhile, worked as a live-in cook for a family in nearby Marionville, Missouri.

The youngest immigrant Kastendieck brother, Dietrich Kastendieck, followed John Herman's lead, sold out his Brooklyn business in 1879, and journeyed by train with his family and Aunt Dora to Christian County. He purchased farmland and went into farming not far from John Herman's place. Dietrich's household brought to fourteen the number of Kastendiecks of that name who formed the ancestral base of the southwest Missouri Kastendiecks.[9] John Friedrich Kastendieck and Henry Kastendieck remained in Brooklyn, splitting up the immigrant Kastendieck family for the first time. All would remain in their chosen locations. Eventually, time forgot the familial connections between the Billings and Brooklyn lines that once shared the same beginnings in the ancient farming community of Morsum, Germany.

The Southwestern Missourian began publication in Billings in 1879, changed its name to *The News-Record*, and sold in 1881 to W.W. Kinloch. Kinloch renamed it *The Billings Times* and for more than seventy years, it brought the news to southwest Missouri.[10] It kept local citizens in touch with national and world events. Back in Brooklyn, for instance, the East River Brooklyn Bridge was nearing completion, and electric light appeared for the first time in Brooklyn in Loeser's store on Fulton Street. On the social calendar, the Society of Old Brooklynites organized in the spring of 1880, a probable nostalgic bit of news to John Herman who likely would have been included in its membership had he remained in Brooklyn. When John Herman left Brooklyn, he left for good. His old address at 370 Van Brunt Street became the address of Lawrence Fogarty's Store.[11]

Population alone told the story of John Herman's decision to relocate from New York to Missouri. The number of people living in Brooklyn in 1880 approached 600,000; the nearest large city in southwest Missouri, meanwhile, was Springfield with a population of 6,500, or about 1 percent of the Brooklyn number; Billings, meanwhile, counted 129 souls.[12] The sparse density of the farming community of Polk Township, in Christian County, spread out around Billings and beyond and added to the census count of the Billings community but nothing approaching the size of Springfield, and far below the scope of imagination when measured against Brooklyn.

John Herman Kastendieck spent half of his life in Brooklyn blended into the work and culture of metropolitan New York, watched it change, and took notice of the great bridge rising over the East River. Billings, Missouri, was a lot like going home to Morsum, Germany.

Map of Christian County, Missouri. John Herman Kastendieck and the Kastendieck family settled in Polk Township at the extreme western end of the panhandle of Christian County. This 1874 map was drawn a decade and a half after the county's organization in 1859. The town of Billings is shown at the upper left of the map situated on the Frisco Railroad. *Campbell's New Atlas of Missouri,* 1874. Springfield-Greene County Library.

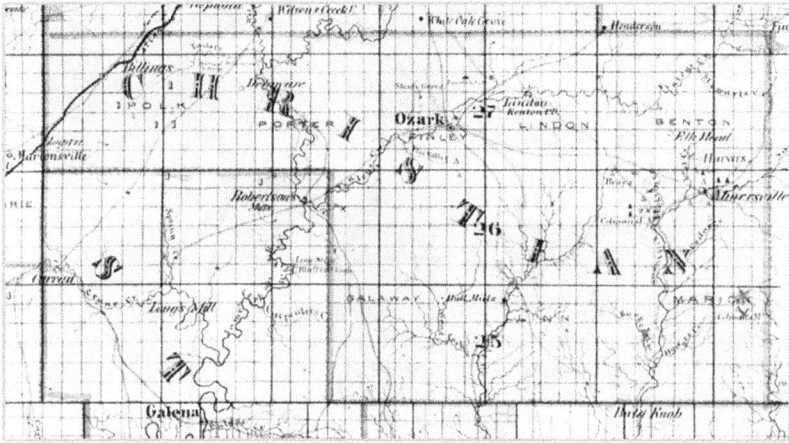

Farm Scene near Morsum, Germany. The quiet rural landscape of Morsum has changed little since the Kastendieck family left it to start a new life in America in the mid-1800s. The land around Morsum is fertile farmland similar to the countryside where the family ultimately settled in America, in the panhandle of Christian County, Missouri. Photo courtesy Yousef79.

Harvest Time. Shocks of grain cut and tied by the horse-drawn binder machine shown in the background sit stacked to dry awaiting thrashing. Harvest time meant long days in the field. This undated photograph is believed to be a picture of unidentified members of the Kastendieck family. David Gay Collection.

Brooklyn Bridge. The East River waterfront at the Fulton Ferry in Brooklyn was a familiar sight to John Herman Kastendieck before he moved to Missouri. He saw the start of construction of the Brooklyn Bridge in 1870 and watched the activity of workers some two miles northeast of where he kept his grocery store on Van Brunt Street. Photomechanical collotype print c. 1889. Library of Congress.

24

Taxes, Churches, and Bald Knobbers

The move of the Kastendiecks from Brooklyn, New York, to Billings, Missouri, caused a necessary shift in their accustomed urban lifestyle, although probably not as dramatic as Dietrich Kastendieck liked to portray it to his friends back in Brooklyn. His daughter remembered him telling how he lived in a floorless one-room log cabin on his Christian County homestead, kept a cow, a few chickens, some pigs, and a yoke of oxen.[1]

John Herman Kastendieck dutifully paid his taxes in Christian County, something he had not always done in Brooklyn. Taxes in Christian County were substantially lower than in Kings County, New York. In 1879, the Christian County Assessor listed John Herman with modest personal property holdings valued at $92 and taxes of $1.12.[2] The reported size of his estate showed a startling reduction from a decade before when he had estimated his Brooklyn personal estate to be $2,000; and just five years ago, he was living in a $12,000 brick home on Van Brunt Street, part of real estate holdings valued overall at about $40,000 in 1880 currency.[3] Time has covered up the full range of his financial affairs. We do not know exactly how much money he arrived in Missouri with after the sale of his Brooklyn business and property, or if by some pecuniary misstep, he lost most of his wealth. The law required taxpayers to report all property to the Christian County Assessor, including the amount of cash and its equivalent, along with numbers and values of horses, mules, cattle, hogs, sheep, and the value of household items.

A general disdain for taxes caused many a creative individual to find ways to shelter wealth from the assessor. We know only that John Herman had a nest egg sufficient to retire to the country and take up farming in Christian County, Missouri; and he did not report it all to the tax assessor.

Billings, Missouri, became an incorporated village in 1884 on the land originally laid out by the railroad company. The town added a jewelry store, drug store, hardware and dry goods stores, all destined to be prominent companies for many years, run by descendants with names like Watkinson, Andrews, and Neyer. The year 1884 was also the year that J.W. Sanders opened the Sanders Mercantile Company (later the Berghaus Mercantile), a well-stocked store known throughout the region as a leading commercial establishment.

Billings boasted all manner of products and services meant to meet the needs of local residents. Anything not available in Billings could usually be found in Springfield a few miles up the road, or ordered delivered by train to the buyer's doorstep. A group of local citizens pooled $10,500 in capital and chartered the first bank in Billings. It opened for business in part of the Sanders Mercantile.

Discontent hardly existed in Billings. One observer commented, "This whole community being of a peaceful character is manifested by the fact that Billings, Mo., has only two lawyers."[4]

Goodwill fraternal organizations sprung up. Generations of Kastendiecks joined the Billings Lodge Number 379 of Ancient Free and Accepted Masons almost from the date of its founding in 1879. There were also the Independent Order of Odd Fellows, Daughters of Rebeckah, Modern Woodmen, and Royal Neighbors to name a few that flourished, their good deeds in the community often going unheralded and known only to the members.[5]

A plethora of churches sprung up. The Kastendiecks were of the Methodist Episcopal faith shading to the evangelical side, as were most if not all of the large German community that populated the town of Billings and the farms that dotted the countryside around the town. The farms formed the backbone of the Billings neighborhood.

Church life was an integral part of community life from the beginning. There were five congregations in Billings as early as 1871 but no church building until Mr. Billings, the railroad official donated the money to build a union church and a community building. The five congregations came together as trustees, plus "one for the world," to manage the building until they moved out into buildings of their own.[6]

The first all-German services were in a local mill in 1878. The desire for German-speaking churches soon led to the organization of an Evangelical Congregation in 1879—the year John Herman arrived in Billings. The following summer the congregation erected St. Peter's Evangelical Church of Billings on June 20, 1880. Two other churches also served the German Evangelical parishioners. There was a German Lutheran Church and a German Methodist Episcopal Church; both churches counted German settlers among their charter members.

John Herman and the Kastendieck family faithfully attended the Methodist Episcopal Church for many years following its construction in May of 1882.[7] The church originally stood on a triangle of land near Hamilton and Oak Streets across from today's United Methodist Church. It served the community into the 20th Century when the congregation divided. Many of its members gravitated to St. Peter's Church. Meanwhile, no records remain of the history of the Billings German Lutheran Church that once stood in the three hundred block of South Pine Street.[8]

Schools, too, were a big part of the fabric of the Billings community. Education was always of primary interest to the Kastendieck family, an interest they brought with them from Morsum, Germany, to New York to Missouri, and one that already existed in Billings.

The first school in Billings opened in 1859 in a local blacksmith shop. The German population was so heavy that an all-German school was established. A public school district organized in 1877 to build the first school building in the community. Shortly after the Kastendiecks settled into the community, the first brick schoolhouse went up in Billings in 1884 to house a grade school, which was the highest level of education for Billings' youth until 1912 when teaching high school began.[9]

Not all was always peace and quiet in Christian County all the time. While the serenity of Polk Township in the panhandle of the county was relatively immune from crime, tranquility was no guarantee, especially in the southern part of the county.

During the Civil War, Christian and surrounding counties divided in political sentiment. Men went away to fight for their respective sides. In their absence, lawless men called bushwhackers terrorized citizens left unprotected. Neighbor robbed neighbor; stealing, burning, and sometimes killing defenseless people. Lawlessness ruled and crime often went unpunished in many communities.

Frustrated one time when a court tried and released a murderer without punishment, several citizens of Taney County—the county abutting Christian County on the south— organized under the name "League of Law and Order." Their purpose was to assist in the enforcement of the law. The organization soon gained the name Bald Knobbers after the isolated, elevated locale it chose for its meetings.

The Bald Knobbers gained members rapidly and soon spread to Christian County where about 500 members, good citizens with laudable purposes, joined the Christian County bands.

Instead of calling law authorities, the Bald Knobbers summarily proceeded to mete out whatever punishment they thought a transgression merited. Any type of perceived bad behavior in the community met with corrective actions by a visit from a delegation of masked representatives or a bundle of hickory switches left on the offender's doorstep as a warning to change his behavior.[10]

Under pressure from state officials, the Taney County Bald Knobbers disbanded in 1886 but not so, in Christian County; they became a magnet for rash and irresponsible individuals seeking to satisfy some personal vengeance. Unjust actions happened in the name of the Bald Knobbers. Consequently, the Bald Knobber numbers dwindled until only a small group of reckless wrongdoers remained to roam the countryside burning and destroying property.

The Bald Knobber Chief was a man named Dave Walker. Walker saw the ongoing impropriety of the organization and moved to end it. However, his own son, a sixteen-year-old hothead, refused to disband and instead pledged to right a situation in the county that he regarded as a personal insult to him and his family. Someone had made disparaging comments about the Bald Knobbers, saying they were no better than sheep-killing dogs. The last project of the Christian County Bald Knobbers was to be a visit to the offending party.

On the night of March 11, 1887, Walker's small band rode to the man's home where he and his family were sleeping. In the melee that followed, the man's home was broken into and shots fired. When the fighting was over, two men lay dead, and another seriously injured. One of the Bald Knobbers was unmasked in the struggle and identified. Arrested and under threat of a mob lynching, he confessed and named the twenty-five other men involved, including Dave Walker, the leader who wanted to end the organization, but looked on helplessly during the deadly raid.

Authorities rounded up the Bald Knobbers and charged them with multiple offenses, including murder. The *Osage City Free Press* reported, "At the term of the Christian County, Missouri, Circuit Court, which is now in session at Ozark, Missouri [seat of Christian County], sixteen Bald Knobbers are to be tried. There are 242 cases pending against these men. Twenty eight are for murder, ninety five are for whippings administered to citizens, eighty-seven for unlawful assemblies, four for perjury, and four for disturbing the peace."

People came by the hundreds and camped out for more than a week to see the trials. A jury found Walker and his young son with two others guilty of murder and sentenced them to hang. A witness to the hanging remembered, "Every road into Ozark was clogged with continuous traffic of horses, wagons, buggies, and people on foot. As the morning advanced, the prisoners could see through the open but barred windows of the jail the sunlight of a cloudless day playing on the maples of the Highlandville Hill to the South."[11] At 9:30 on the morning of May 10, 1889, the three men mounted the scaffold. (One of the four condemned prisoners escaped from jail and evaded recapture). David Walker climbed the scaffold first, followed by his son, each stepping firmly. The third man followed, unsteadily. Executioners fitted nooses around each man's neck. Precisely at 9:55 a.m., the trap door sprung and the men fell. "A cry of horror went up from the few spectators in the enclosure," said a witness. "The new ropes stretched and Dave Walker's feet touched the ground. The noose about William's [Walker] neck had come off and he lay on the ground, unconscious." The elder Walker ceased to struggle. They hoisted his son, regaining consciousness, back on to the platform. When he saw that they intended to hang him again, he lamented, "For God's sake, hurry".

The saga of the Bald Knobbers dissolved into folklore, their well-meaning objectives kept alive by their descendants and their atrocities remembered by the children of the victims of their deeds.[12]

The eventful period of the 1880s ended, and the calendar rolled over to the final decade of the 19th Century. Billings had more than tripled in size in the ten years since John Herman Kastendieck's arrival, but still a relatively small town with a population of 464 in 1890. The life-blood of the community was in the many prosperous farms that ringed the town and sustained its commerce. Owners wrestled these farms from an overgrowth of oak and hickory saplings, thick underbrush, and knobby timber that once punctuated the landscape.[13] The rock fencerows and rock piles strewn around the cleared fields attested to the hard labor of claiming the land.[14] The industriousness of the Kastendiecks and their German-speaking neighbors brought an old-world language and deeply rooted culture to southwest Missouri.

J.W. Sanders Mercantile Building on Elm Street, in Billings. From a small beginning the Sanders Mercantile Company grew to be one of the flourishing enterprises in southwest Missouri. It later became the J.B. Berghaus Mercantile. The Bank of Billings first opened for business in part of this building on May 14, 1889. Collection of the Bank of Billings.

Busy Day in Billings. Billings, Missouri, was a flourishing town when John Herman Kastendieck moved his family there from Brooklyn, New York, in 1878. Market days and fair events drew large crowds from the farms that made up the larger community of Billings. Undated photo, Author's Collection.

Kastendieck Farm near Billings, Missouri. Farmhands identified only as Kastendiecks, plow the land that first prompted the Kastendiecks to leave Brooklyn, New York, for the fertile ground and promise of Christian County, Missouri. Based on the estimated ages of the individuals in the photograph and the bearded older figure, they may be Dietrich Kastendieck and his son John Dietrich, Jr., Undated photograph, David Gay Collection.

25

Caroline's Court Case

Caroline Kastendieck, wife of John Herman, opened a
millinery shop in Billings. She was a dressmaker. Her
store stocked a number of women items from hats to
notions, enough merchandise of different choices to cause one
visitor to characterize her place as a country store. It is unclear
exactly when she opened her shop but probably sometime in the
mid-to-late 1880s, a while after the Kastendieck family arrived
in Billings. Hermina the youngest Kastendieck finished grade
school in 1886 easing some of the demands of parenting.
Meanwhile, John Herman's property taxes doubled in 1889
indicating a sizeable investment like an inventory for a millinery
shop might incur.

Hardly had Caroline's business commenced when someone
sued her. The lawsuit, though not historically significant, was a
window into the state of the courts of the late 19th Century, and
into how the judicial system worked at the local level—or in
Caroline's case, how it did not work.

On January 17, 1891, Keet and Rountree Mercantile and
Company, a wholesale business in Springfield, Missouri,
presented a bill in Christian County Circuit Court for Mrs. C.

Kastendieck ongoing from September 1890 to January 1891 that showed an outstanding balance of $270.44. The company alleged that the unpaid debt represented purchases of goods from Keet and Rountree.[1] The company's petition to the court read, "defendant is justly indebted to plaintiff in sum of two hundred seventy dollars and forty four cents...for goods wares and merchandise sold and delivered [to the] defendant."

Had the petition stopped there, the case might have been a simple matter of debt collection. But the petition went on to accuse Caroline of fraud, arguing in the affidavit that the account was past due and the plaintiff had "good reason to believe that the defendant fraudulently conveyed or assigned her property or effects so as to hinder or delay her creditors." The plaintiff further alleged that the "debt sued for was fraudulently contracted" and concealed, removed, or disposed to hinder her creditors; essentially saying that Caroline never intended to pay for the property in the first place, and to avoid confiscation of her property assigned it to a third party so that technically she did not own the property anymore.[2] The plaintiff asked for a writ of attachment to collect the debt. A writ of attachment in a civil action meant a court could confiscate property owned by the defendant to satisfy the alleged debt.

Circuit Clerk M.V. Gideon wrote out an attachment order, which the clerk could legally do without oversight pending approval by the circuit judge. The writ of attachment instructed Christian County Sheriff C.P. Gibson to seize all of Caroline's property to the extent needed to cover her debt and court costs. The summons ordered Caroline to appear in court at Ozark before Judge W.D. Hubbard, Judge of the 21st Judicial Circuit of Missouri, to answer the complaint at the February Term of Court.[3]

Events moved quickly. The sheriff served the writ of attachment on the same day Keet and Rountree filed its complaint. The clerk recorded the complaint in Ozark at noon on Saturday, January 17, wrote the attachment order immediately, and had it served on Caroline in Billings by 1:30 p.m. that afternoon. It is a bit of a mystery how the filed complaint, writ of attachment, and service of summons could occur all on the same day in a matter of less than an hour and a half. The courthouse at Ozark was close to twenty-three miles from Billings. A good horse and rider could cover that distance by horseback but at a speed that would have added a measure of unnecessary urgency to the complaint. The attachment order may have gone by telegram or been called ahead by telephone. Such a means, however, meant the confiscation of Caroline's property took place without a signed document in hand.

Nevertheless, Sheriff Gibson took into his possession dry goods, groceries, notions, and "such articles as are usually kept in a country store…all the goods and stock of millinery and dry goods general[ly] kept in a millinery store…bonnets, hats, ribbons, lace, linings, braids, and notions," sufficient in amount, he estimated, to satisfy the plaintiff's demand.[4]

On January 21, 1891, Keet and Rountree filed a petition with Judge Hubbard to sell Caroline's personal property then in the possession of the sheriff. Judge Hubbard ordered Sheriff Gibson to sell everything at auction to the highest bidder.[5]

Caroline Kastendieck was no shrinking violet. She put up a fight. A smart person, she proved to be a step ahead of Keet and Rountree at every stage of the proceedings. She had at her back her husband John Herman and the Kastendieck family, all seasoned in business dealings in the rough and tumble environs of Brooklyn, New York.

Caroline faced off against the law firm of Wolf and Tipton, high-powered Springfield attorneys for Keet and Rountree Mercantile, a company with a reputation for suing its customers.[6] Josiah T. Keet was a longtime businessperson with offices on the Springfield Public Square.[7] The partnership of Keet and Rountree Mercantile had recently ended its retail business to be exclusively a wholesale company, the only wholesale dry goods, and boot and shoe house in the city of Springfield. Their market reached out 150 miles in all directions south of Springfield.[8]

Caroline hired an attorney; a Virginia-born, Tennessee-reared lawyer named George Julius Bradfield, son of George Washington Bradfield, a country lawyer who had risen to the position of Probate Judge of the Fourteenth Missouri Circuit in Lebanon, Laclede County, Missouri. Young Bradfield had recently opened a law office in Billings, in 1888.[9] A relative newcomer to the community, he was thirty-seven years old and in the prime of his law practice when he took Caroline's case.

On February 25, 1891, the third day of the February Term, the Circuit Court convened in Ozark, Judge W.D. Hubbard presiding. Bradfield was ready. He immediately filed for an abatement to the Keet and Rountree attachment demanding that the court lift the seizure of Caroline's property. The plaintiff's attorneys soon discovered they had a worthy opponent in G.J. Bradfield. Using the familiar legalese of the defense, Bradfield began his petition, "Now comes the defendant... [She] denies each and every allegation by plaintiffs." Bradfield asked the court for abatement of the attachment, that the court release Caroline's property, and that the plaintiff pay all costs.[10]

The remarkable quality of attorney Bradfield's argument was that he denied the charges of Keet and Rountree in the exact same words the plaintiff used to make them. The plaintiff was put on the defensive with the task of having to prove every allegation made in their complaint, including the charges of fraud; or abandon the suit and return Caroline's property with costs. Keet and Rountree chose to go to trial. Their attorneys retired to their offices in Springfield to prepare for court.

Bradfield waited until the twelfth day of the court term, and then filed a motion on March 7, 1891, to dismiss Caroline's case for want of prosecution. "Because," he said, "plaintiffs failed to prosecute this action without delay"—as they stated they would in their initial petition.[11] Bradfield's move forced the plaintiff's attorney to file an application for continuance of the case until the August term. The Court sustained the motion and ordered the case continued at cost to the plaintiff Keet and Rountree until next court term.[12] Bradfield had thus bought valuable time to construct a defense.

Meantime, the court released Caroline's property to her, but that proved to be short lived. Keet and Rountree filed another attachment order at the end of March asking the court to secure the goods again and order Caroline to appear in court at the August term.[13]

On April 1, 1891, Sheriff Gibson read the new court summons to Caroline, seized her property again, and placed the attached goods in the hands of S.N. Lafollette, Constable of Polk Township in Christian County. The inventoried goods comprised, in part, calico, gingham, cashmere, percale, and other goods generally found in a millinery shop—including a particularly large stash of calico and gingham. The goods were altogether valued at $72.43, less than a third of the $270.44 allegedly owed to Keet and Rountree. Where was the rest of it? What had transpired between the first attachment and this one? The court would want to know.[14]

August 1891 rolled around and the August Term of the Circuit Court lay just ahead. On August 14, Sheriff Gibson began delivering subpoenas in preparation for trial set to begin August 26, at the courthouse in Ozark. Among the first subpoenas to go out were to George Hanson, Hanson's wife, and several of the Knightley family, all called on behalf of the plaintiff, and not Caroline although Hanson was Caroline's adopted stepson who married a Knightley. The case began to look as if it could harbor ulterior motives. A few days later, subpoenas went to Dietrich Kastendieck, Andrew Kastendieck, and banker Andrew J. Howard, all called as witnesses on behalf of Caroline.

Meanwhile, Keet and Rountree had a new attorney. G.M. Sebree who made his presence known by filing an affidavit with the court restating the original complaint and noting that Caroline's account was "now past due."[15] He added that she was about to sell or dispose of her property fraudulently. Caroline's attorney Bradfield responded in a point-by-point retort denying each charge, including the one alleging fraudulent disposal of property. The plaintiff's attorney now had to produce evidence that proved intent to defraud, a high bar in a civil suit.[16]

More subpoenas went out; several to witnesses for the plaintiff, including former attorney T.M. Wolf and Constable Lafollette; about an equal number went out for Caroline, including stepson John Herman Kastendieck, Jr.,

A twelve-person jury convened. Dr. Fred Brown of Billings sent over a few medical requests asking to excuse some people from jury duty because they were unable to travel from Billings all the way to Ozark.[17]

Court set to begin.

On August 29, 1891, the attorneys appeared before Judge Hubbard and pronounced themselves ready for trial by jury—

before twelve men. To the astonishment of all, Judge Hubbard declared there was insufficient time to hear the case that day. The jury was "respited" until 9:00 a.m., Monday morning, August 31. Any witnesses who had traveled any distance to Ozark were obligated to retrace their steps or stay over in Ozark until Monday.[18]

Monday came and court got underway again.

No transcript of the testimony of the day survives, except that attorney Bradfield pointedly denied each allegation, baiting the attorney for the plaintiff to produce evidence proving every charge. Altogether eight witnesses testified for Keet and Rountree, and nine witnesses for Caroline. The Jury after hearing all the evidence, arguments of counsel, and instructions of the court retired to consider their verdict.[19]

Judge Hubbard kept sending in handwritten notes of instruction for the jury to consider. Meant to be points of law, the notes decidedly slanted in favor of Caroline. The judge pointed out, for example, that with regard to the fraudulent concealment to avoid her creditors, the evidence should show if the removal of the goods occurred before or after January 17. That was the date of the attachment, and should show if removal to her home of goods was simply to make more room in her shop without any attempt to defraud creditors. The jury should also take into consideration, he advised, Caroline's previous record of paying her debts. (The jury rejected this instruction as irrelevant). The judge further opined that if Caroline wanted to convey her property to others to satisfy bona fide debts, such was not fraudulent. She had a right to do it. (The jury rejected this as well.) The judge pointed out that there was no evidence to prove that Caroline fraudulently contracted the debt as the plaintiff claimed; meaning Caroline did not buy the goods with the intent of defrauding anyone. Furthermore, he said, never presume fraud. Under the law, the plaintiff must show evidence. If there is no evidence of fraud, then presumably she acted honestly.

By this time, Judge Hubbard had laid out a convincing rebuttal of the plaintiff's charges. He went on. With regard to concealment to hinder her creditors, Judge Hubbard wrote, the jury should take into consideration the time and manner in which she removed her goods.

As the day wore on, Judge Hubbard apparently took note of his seeming bias and added the instruction, "On the other hand, if the evidence showed intent to defraud the jury should so find."

He instructed the jury, "If they [the jury] believe from the evidence that a short time before the bringing of this suit the defendant was engaged in business in the town of Billings, Mo., running a millinery store and was indebted to this plaintiff and others and that she had removed a part of the goods from said store and had the same concealed with intent to either hinder or delay her creditors in the collection of their debts, then you will return a verdict for the plaintiff."

Meanwhile, the plaintiff discovered during testimony that Caroline had executed a deed of trust on her store of goods to secure a note of two hundred dollars to the Bank of Billings. Judge Hubbard pointed out, "If the bank did not have such a note at the time the case was filed [on January 17, 1891], it should be considered fraudulent. The details of this mortgage were never revealed, nor was it settled as to whether this was a loan meant to pay Caroline's debt to Keet and Rountree or if she intended to transfer ownership of the mortgaged goods to the bank and, therefore, out of reach of Keet and Rountree.[20]

It turned out to be a hung jury. Twelve men could not agree. Judge Hubbard ruled that the "jury disagrees and are dismissed." He declared, they heard all the evidence, went into deliberations, and "report that they are unable to agree on a verdict herein and they are by the Court ordered discharged." Court adjourned until the November Term for retrial of the case.[21]

The saga of Caroline's court case was not quite over. On November 10, 1891, court opened a day late because of the absence of Judge Hubbard detained elsewhere. Out of the gate, the attorney for Keet and Rountree filed a petition for a change of venue. "The defendant has an undue influence over the inhabitants of Christian County," the petition said, "and the same state of facts exists in Taney County." They had become aware of this, they said, after the mistrial. Judge Hubbard agreed and awarded a change of venue to Greene County. He ordered Christian County Circuit Clerk Gideon to make a transcript of court proceedings in Christian County Court and forward it to Greene County, which he did.[22]

By the middle of December, court fees were adding up. The sheriff got at least one dollar for every subpoena delivered, and he charged a dollar a night for sleeping in Caroline's store for nine nights to guard seized property. Moreover, according to the policy of the day, court costs paid witnesses to testify. George Hanson and his wife were witnesses against Caroline for two days, racking up forty-six miles of travel costs. Andrew Kastendieck testified for five days, as did John Dietrich. John Herman, Jr., testified for one day. Ironically, John Herman, Sr., did not testify on his wife's behalf. Nevertheless, one senses from the proceedings of the court that he never remained far removed from what was going on. After all the charges were added up, it cost $148.10 in fees to try the case in Christian County, more than half the amount of the alleged debt Keet and Rountree sought to recover.[23] Without a jury verdict in its favor, the plaintiff was by law, according to their attachment bond, responsible for all costs.

The day after Christmas, 1891, the county clerk filed the Christian County transcript at the Greene County Courthouse in anticipation of a new trial next year.

On January 11, 1892, the second Monday of January and first judicial day of the January Term of Greene County Circuit Court, Caroline's attorney George Julius Bradfield shocked the court by petitioning for a change of venue. He used the same kind of tactic he had used previously in refuting the charges of Keet and Rountree; that is, he mimicked the language their attorney had used to secure a change of venue from Christian to Green County. He wrote, "Plaintiff has an undue influence over the inhabitants of the said Greene County."[24] The tactic worked again. The judge heard and sustained Bradfield's petition for a change of venue and awarded the venue to Webster County in the Fourteenth Judicial Circuit. He ordered the Greene County Circuit Clerk to prepare a transcript of proceedings for Webster County.[25]

Attorney Bradfield had now managed to stall proceedings against Caroline for a year. He had lined up witnesses and convinced a jury of her innocence to the point that it ended up a hung jury. He had by his latest move, convinced the judge to move the case to Webster County, next door to Laclede County in the same Fourteenth Missouri Circuit Court in which his father was a judge.[26] Judge Bradfield was a circuit court probate judge and unlikely to be scheduled to hear the case. Nevertheless, the judicial fraternity was small, and the success of his son in Caroline's case resonated with a father's pride.

On February 6, 1892, Greene County Circuit Clerk W.W. Donham completed a transcript of the case proceedings up to that date. Then, it disappeared. A month later, on March 21, 1892, the attorney for Keet and Rountree wrote a two-page affidavit to the Webster County Court complaining that as of

January 11, 1892, the case was pending in the Circuit Court of Greene County. Greene County had had some sixty days between the removal order and the first day of the Wester County Court term. Greene County had "neglected or refused" to transmit a copy of the transcript, they said. The plaintiff's petition asked the Webster County Court to make an order for Greene County to show legal cause why it had not complied with the proper process of the court in not transmitting the transcript.[27]

The record of Caroline's court case ends with the Webster County petition. We do not know whether Greene County ever delivered a transcript to Webster County. The Greene County Clerk made the transcript in February 1892 but oddly, did not file it until 1893 under the 1893 Green County Term of Court although all the records in the file dated to 1891 and 1892.[28] What happened after the Webster County petition on March 21, 1892, is likewise unknown. A judge possibly dismissed the case, or there may have been an out-of-court settlement.

George Julius Bradfield left his practice in Billings in 1893, shortly after the conclusion of Caroline's case. He moved to San Antonio, Texas.[29] He died there the following year at the age of forty-two.[30] Caroline apparently closed her millinery shop. John Herman's property taxes dropped substantially in 1891 as if his taxable assets had greatly diminished.

George Julius Bradfield. Attorney Bradfield, of Billings, Missouri, defended Caroline Kastendieck in her lawsuit with Keet and Rountree Mercantile Company of Springfield. His legal tactics spread the case across three counties in two different judicial circuits over a period of two years until the suit against her ended. Courtesy of Kay Herndon-Foglesong, Find A Grave.

Christian County Courthouse. Caroline Kastendieck's court case took place in this building. The courtroom was on the second floor. The building originally stood at the center of the Ozark, Missouri, Square and was built at a cost of $7,775. It continued in use until 1914 when it was torn down. Photo from the *Ozarks Mountaineer*, July 1958.

26

Rose Hill

News came from Brooklyn from time to time. Family members there kept in touch with their Billings kin, sending John Herman articles now and again from the *Brooklyn Daily Eagle* and writing about the day-to-day lives of those back in Brooklyn. The Brooklyn Bridge had opened and experienced its first bridge tragedy. An 1883 Memorial Day crowd panicked out of fear that the bridge was about to collapse. The stampede, which took place hardly a week after the bridge opened, left twelve dead and many more injured. The city hastened to open a trolley car service across the bridge.[1] At the same time, not satisfied with going over the East River, the New York Legislature introduced a bill for a tunnel connecting Brooklyn to New York under the river, an idea surely bordering on fantasy to the citizens of Billings.[2]

In other news, Henry Ward Beecher the great abolitionist died and the *Brooklyn Daily Eagle* issued a six-part memorial of his colorful and controversial life.[3] On the lighter side, Coney Island introduced the hot dog. Electric rail cars began running to the popular recreation spot, replacing the sluggish old steam trains that had once been part of the Kastendieck experience.[4]

Over the next few years, more somber news came as the immigrant siblings died one by one. Henry Kastendieck passed in October of 1885; John Friedrich Kastendieck, the elder brother, died in March of 1893, each interred in the Kastendieck lot at Green-Wood Cemetery. The year that followed saw the death of Aunt Dora in February of the winter of 1894, not in Brooklyn but in a place far from there in the little town of Billings, Missouri. They buried her not in Green-Wood in the picturesque, parklike setting surrounded by statuary, fountains, and the graves of the famous but amid the plain tombstones of her Christian County neighbors with only the bare trees of the winter season standing sentry over her grave in a small, rural resting place called Rose Hill. Aunt Dora's grave stone was inscribed simply, "Anna D. Kastendieck wife of Henry Boevers," recalling a happier time a quarter of a century ago in Brooklyn when she was married with two small children before the cruelty of life took it all away.

Like many old cemeteries, Rose Hill Cemetery began as a family graveyard when John Leonard buried his Irish-born wife there in 1876. Little more than a tree-covered hill sloping off to a small stream at its base, it was here also that Diedrich Kastendieck chose the pleasant setting for the burial of his young daughter, Alice, in the autumn of 1880 when she died suddenly shortly after the family arrived in Christian County. In the year 1882, William and Sarah Conrad, who had interred family members there since 1877, gave the land thereafter designated as Rose Hill Cemetery.[5]

Rose Hill became the chosen cemetery of the Methodist Episcopal branch of the Kastendieck family whose remains occupy Lot 36, Block 2 of the cemetery.[6] Twenty-six of the nearly 1,300 graves at Rose Hill bear the Kastendieck name or names of their descendants, some returned from distant places, their remains brought back to Christian County to honor a last request for burial in Rose Hill.[7]

There were, of course, stories imbedded in the folklore of Rose Hill that told of its haunted past when the deceased—so the tales go—arose from the grave to chill the spine of more than one cemetery visitor. One time a couple came from out-of-state to visit the grave of a lost relative recently rediscovered at Rose Hill. When they arrived at the cemetery, they found the gate locked and were unable to gain entry. It was about noonday so they decided to spread a blanket on the ground beneath a shade tree outside the fence to enjoy a picnic lunch. When they finished and prepared to leave, they froze. The locked gate now stood wide open as if to invite them into the cemetery.

The ritual from life to death in the Kastendieck family routinely required the services of the family physician, Dr. Eli Bedford Brown. Dr. Brown visited John Herman Kastendieck several times in the winter of 1896. The accumulation of the seasons had taken their toll on John Herman, now in the twilight years of his life. His frailty began to give way to a particularly bitter winter. Everyone hoped that Dr. Brown could pull him through to the warmer days of spring. Billings depended a lot on Dr. Brown.

Dr. Eli Brown was a pioneering physician of Christian County. He opened his practice first at Ozark, Missouri, in 1867, and then moved to Billings in 1888. Dr. Brown was a Confederate Army veteran and a staunch Democrat, a man who in the early years of his practice rode on horseback to the homes of his patients. He married Sarah Ann Clapp in the spring of 1871 and had nine children all educated in the Billings School, six going on to graduate from institutions of higher learning, three of the six to become doctors.

Exactly how many Kastendiecks came under Dr. Eli's care over the years is untold. Those generations of Kastendiecks that he did not see, he passed on to his son, Dr. Fred Brown. Many a death certificate in Christian County bears the name of a Dr. Brown, the final record of a Kastendieck on the way to Rose Hill Cemetery. Dr. Eli Brown continued his practice in Billings until his death in 1926, after which Dr. Fred Brown prolonged the Brown medical tradition into the 1940s.[8]

The Christian County Tax Assessor filled out John Herman's tax bill in 1897, adding a new extra charge to pay for upkeep of the road that ran past his farm. Beginning in 1897, county Special Road District assessments amounted to an added tax of $2.50 for people living in surrounding areas outside the town of Billings. John Herman had moved into Billings in his waning years but still owned property southwest of town. Some individuals paid the added tax, but many did not. John Herman did not. He died on January 16, 1897.[9] The assessor made a note in his records, "lives in Billings, dead before assessment."[10] John Herman thwarted the reality made famous in the often-repeated quotation of Benjamin Franklin who declared that death and taxes were the only true certainty of life. John Herman accepted the one but avoided the other. He likely would not have paid the extra road tax anyway because the $2.50 charges were only for men ages twenty-one to sixty. John Herman died at the age of seventy years, ten months and two days.

His brief obituary mentioned his life in Brooklyn and subsequent move to Billings, the reserved lifestyle that he lived, and the esteem with which the Billings community held him. It did not mention his survivors by name, content instead with the notice that he left behind a "companion, children, relatives, and friends." His burial was in Rose Hill beside a small sapling. It grew to be a large tree; its roots pressed hard against John

Herman's grave, dislodged the stone, and toppled it to the ground. The tree grew, never cut, and allowed to stand as a symbol of the perseverance of nature and life over death. The mended marker will set up right again, kept as a monument to an American original, a reminder of a life that ended far from where it began; from the lowlands of Morsum, Germany, to Billings, Missouri, the place that John Herman Kastendieck chose to call home.

The borough of Brooklyn, New York, became the fourth largest city in the United States the year John Herman died. The city merged into Greater New York City in December 1897. Brooklynites called the merger the "great mistake."[11] The *Brooklyn Daily Eagle* opposed consolidation to the end. For several days the *Eagle* ran a leader on its editorial page calling Brooklyn "a city of homes and churches" and New York "a city of Tammany Hall and crime government."[12] The self-governing borough of Brooklyn and the life of John Herman Kastendieck, the city's independent-minded former citizen, poignantly ended in the same year.

Caroline Kastendieck was fifty-two years old when her husband died in 1897. She had the promise of active years ahead of her. The last of the Kastendieck children were out of the house and on their own. She had her millinery skills and dressmaking trade to fall back on, not to mention a part of John Herman's estate promised by law to the widows of deceased spouses. Whether personal animosities arose in the course of events that surrounded John Herman's death no one knows. Probate records do not appear to preserve a record of his estate. Absent any personal recollections of the matter, Caroline's improbable estrangement from the Kastendieck family is not part of the record of the final years of her life. In one of the regrettable chapters of Kastendieck history, and for reasons left untold, none of the children she helped to raise stepped forward to help her in her final years, more than a dozen years of which she spent alone in a home for the aged. Caroline had no children or family of her own. She spent twenty years of her life in the role of stepmother, surrogate aunt, and caregiver to the Kastendieck and Hanson children but forgotten by them in the end.

Caroline stayed in Billings but a short time after John Herman's death. She left Christian County in the summer of 1898 and moved north to the small town of Washington, Missouri, in Franklin County, situated on the south bank of the Missouri River about fifty-five miles west of St. Louis. How she came to be there is speculation. She took a job as cook at the McLain Memorial Old Folks Home. Sometime later, she entered the Bethesda Home for Old People in St. Louis. Why she chose to leave Billings so soon for a seemingly unfamiliar place is not clear.

Caroline, however, did know someone in Franklin County. Her step-niece Charlotte Kastendieck Froeschle lived in Franklin County. Charlotte's minister husband had a family connection that may have opened the door to the retirement community network in the St. Louis area. The Froeschles like the Kastendiecks were Methodist Episcopal adherents, and the St. Louis Alliance of the German Methodist Episcopal ministry included generous support and management of several orphan's and old people's homes in and around St. Louis. Charlotte's husband served as one-time trustee and president for one such home. He had an older brother also connected to the Alliance. The Froeschles kept an active presence in church affairs dating to 1885, sufficient to credibly to recommend Caroline's entry into one of the ministry's retirement establishments.[13]

Caroline took up new quarters at the McLain Memorial Home for Old People on Stafford Street, in Washington.[14] She identified herself as a dressmaker familiarly known among home residents as Vicky, short for Caroline Victoria. She was both resident and a cook for some twenty residents of the Old Folks Home, which was one of several businesses in Washington, otherwise a farming community of about 3,000 people. Businesses included flourmills, a cob pipe factory, and a zither factory, all situated convenient to the town brewery. Caroline was not totally isolated in Franklin County because the Missouri Pacific Railroad passed through Washington and connected to Billings, St. Louis, and places elsewhere, but there is no indication that she ever returned to Billings.[15]

In early December of 1900, the Bethesda Home for Old People opened in St. Louis, and Caroline moved from Washington, Missouri, to St. Louis. Established in 1889 as the Biblically inspired "house of mercy", Bethesda encompassed several missions in a spreading complex of charitable centers.[16] Caroline's new home was The Home for Incurables, the last of the structures added to the Bethesda complex by way of a large gift from wealthy St. Louis executive and philanthropist, Richard M. Scruggs.[17] The St. Louis press applauded his generosity as an exception to the general disregard of charity by the St. Louis rich when compared with the civic pride of cities along the Atlantic seaboard.[18] Admirers singled Scruggs out for praise notwithstanding that authorities once arrested him for smuggling jewelry into the county.[19]

Caroline's stay at the Home for Incurables was brief. Her failing health soon took her to the Bethesda Hospital as an inmate, the name given at the time to residents and patients. By the spring of 1910, her health had deteriorated to a point that at age sixty-four she was one of about fifty patients in the acute care hospital wing of Bethesda.[20]

Caroline died in the winter of 1912 after a long battle with liver cancer. She was sixty-seven years old. Bethesda attendants knew little about her. They filled in her name on her death certificate as "Virginia [*sic*] Caroline", marked her parents as unknown on the form, and even indicated that she was married, which she had not been since John Herman's death fifteen years before. Whoever completed the form did not remember, either, that she was born in the West Indies. Originally, she came from the Danish West Indies, immigrated to the United States at a young age, and was for thirty years a resident of Missouri— sixteen years at Billings and the last thirteen years and six months in the lonely setting of a St. Louis healthcare facility.

Caroline wished to come home to Billings when she died, and so caretakers entered her wishes in the final record. The Meek-Dickman Mortuary in St. Louis charged with the responsibility to return her remains to Billings for burial at Rose Hill, for reasons undisclosed, did not follow her wishes, and buried her in St. Louis.[21]

A Good Citizen Gone.

John Herrman Kastendieck, Sr., was born in the Province of Hanover, Germany, in 1826; died, near Billings, Christian county, Mo., January 16, 1897.

He emigrated to New York in 1846 and was for 31 years a resident of Brooklyn. He then moved to Christian county, Mo., where he resided until his death. He leaves behind a companion, children, relatives and friends to mourn the loss of a loving husband and father and a true friend. He was a consistent member of the M. E. Church, always in attendance at church services when possible, always striving to lead an exemplary christian life, rather reserved in his profession but true to the principles which he believed to be right. He had lived to a good old age. God had spared him to live out his allotted time. The body has gone back to the dust and the spirit to God who gave it.

His funeral sermon was preached in the M. E. church Monday, January 18, at 1:30 p. m., attended by a large company of weeping relatives and friends. His remains were interred in Rose Hill cemetery, there to await the general resurrection. His death was triumphant, his hope reached into the realm of better life.

> When the spark of life is waning.
>   Weep not for me;
> When the feeble pulse is ceasing.
> Start not at its swift decreasing,
> Tis the fettered soul's releasing
>   Weep not for me.
>
> Christ is mine—He cannot fail me!
>   Weep not for me!
> Yes, though sin and doubt endeavor
> From His love my soul to sever,
> Jesus is my strength forever!
>   Weep not for me.
>   C. BAKER.

FUNERAL NOTICE.

The Funeral Services of

JOHN HERRMAN KASTENDIECK,

born March 14th, 1826, died January 16th, 1897, aged 70 years, 10 months and 2 days, will be conducted at

The M. E. Church,

At 1 O'clock p. m.,

Monday, January 18, 1897.

Interment in Rose Hill Cemetery.

Friends of the family are cordially invited to attend.

Good Citizen Gone. John Herman Kastendieck Funeral Announcement and Obituary. These newspaper clippings of unknown sources were found pressed between the pages of the John Herman and Bridget Kastendieck Family Bible. The funeral service took place at the Methodist Episcopal Church, in Billings, with burial at Rose Hill Cemetery. The hymn at the end of the obituary is from a poem by Rev. Thomas Dale, a Cambridge University student, written in 1819. Jayme Schaumann Burchett Collection.

Rose Hill Cemetery. John Herman Kastendieck and members of the Kastendieck family are buried in this small, secluded cemetery in Christian County, Missouri, near the town of Billings. Burials in Rose Hill numbered fewer than 1,300 souls when it closed, a number in stark contrast to the almost 400,000 graves of Green-Wood Cemetery, in Brooklyn, New York, where John Herman buried many of his Kastendieck kin before moving to Missouri. Photo by Mark and Kay, Find A Grave.

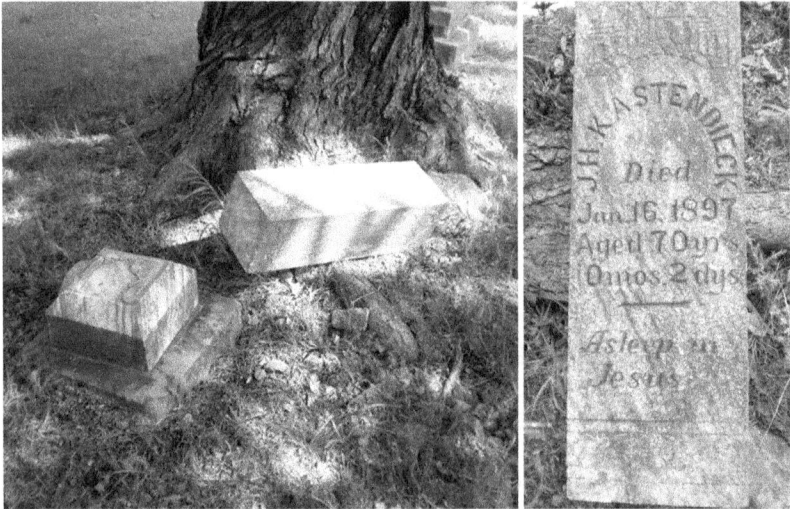

Tombstone of John Herman Kastendieck. The plain gravestone that once marked his grave awaits repair in Rose Hill Cemetery, pushed aside by the tree that for more than one hundred years stood sentry over his final resting place. Photo by Mark and Kay, Find A Grave.

27

The Last Immigrant

The brothers—John Herman and John Dietrich Kastendieck—were close as family. Beginning in Morsum, Germany; sharing the adventure to America; the years together in Brooklyn; and then Missouri, John Herman and Dietrich stayed close in place and time for sixty years. They had much in common, but much, too, that made them different as brothers. They were alike in matters of business; and both shared a deep love of family and a quiet inner strength that carried them through many unspeakable personal tragedies. Dietrich, the kid brother of John Herman by eight years, grew up with a love of nature that sustained a lifelong interest in birds. He pursued the cultivation of knowledge about birds through the art of taxidermy. John Herman had no such avocation. John Herman was quiet in demeanor, reserved in public, and handsome in his younger years.

Dietrich—known to business associates as John D. and to family and friends as Dick—tended to be more outgoing, especially when it came to sharing knowledge about his bird collection. Five feet nine inches in height, of medium build, light-brown hair, and hazel eyes, his angular features set him apart in appearance from the other Kastendieck brothers. A pale complexion acquired during the indoor Brooklyn years stood in distinct contrast to his sharp nose and rangy facial structure born of Germanic ancestry on a farm in Morsum.[1] No less striking in looks than his other brothers—John Friedrich Wilhelm, John Herman, and John Henry—Dietrich could have been anyone else's brother if judged by looks. Yet, his steady gaze and self-assured presence left little doubt about his character; that he, too, was a Kastendieck who could be trusted.

Friends and neighbors called him Uncle Dick, but few in Billings outside his extended family knew much about his beginnings in the Kingdom of Hannover, about his youth in Morsum, growing up on the Weser River, or about his journey to America and his Brooklyn past. He was born in 1834 on the family farm, in Morsum, the youngest brother of two girls and four boys in a household of four sons who all shared the same first name, John. He loved the out-of-doors, fished in the summer, and skated in the winter. He was a child of nature in some ways, free to roam the countryside, enjoyed the many fruit trees of pear and cherry that surrounded the Kastendieck home, and delighted in the birds that made their nests in the apple trees.

He had an interest in bird life from an early time.[2] A person who knew him in those days told of the plight of one nest of feathered fledglings after the birds' parents died. "Dick adopted the orphaned youngsters and fed them. They thrived under his care and came at his call even after they were grown. When cherries were ripe they would perch close to him as he picked the cherries, and wait for him to feed them some of the luscious fruit."[3]

His father died when he was eight years old, opening a void in his life that never filled. His formal education was in Morsum, enlarged by the natural surroundings along the Weser River, and under the watchful tutoring of his mother and older siblings. He dreamed of becoming a sea faring man situated, as he was, on the Weser a few miles upstream from the port of Bremerhaven and the open sea. A sea captain uncle offered to take him with him to sea.[4] He would have been a natural fit if stories about his sea journeys were true. Those who knew him said he never got seasick. On one occasion, so the tale goes, during a severe storm, he, the captain, and one other passenger out of two hundred or more cabin passengers were the only ones to appear in the dining hall to partake of the steward's excellent dinner prepared for that day.[5]

Dietrich immigrated to America in 1851, traveling alone at the age of sixteen, sailing out of Bremerhaven destined for New York to join his siblings who had previously made the trip and settled in Brooklyn. He went to work as a clerk in his brother's grocery store making $2.50 a month and board. In due time, he opened his own grocery store in Brooklyn and spent the next twenty years as a successful businessperson.

The American Civil War began in April of 1861. In June, Dietrich went to the Court of Brooklyn and officially became a citizen of the United States. Whether the two events—citizenship and the war—were connected is unknown. He was always immensely proud of his citizenship, but he did not serve in the Civil War. Whether by choice or chance, the war passed him by.

In the meantime, he met and married Rebecka Röpke, a seventeen–year-old German girl from Morsum eight years his junior who worked as a domestic in the household of his brother John Herman. They married in 1862 and began housekeeping in the rooms above Dietrich's grocery store. As business prospered, they soon were able to purchase property in Brooklyn at the corner of Fifth Avenue and Fourteenth Street. They had seven children; three died in infancy, buried in the Kastendieck lot at Green-Wood Cemetery, in Brooklyn.[6]

In the summer of 1869, Dietrich, Rebecka, and their two children, John, Jr., and Alice ages six and ten months respectively, returned to Germany to visit the old Kastendieck homestead at Morsum.[7] Not much is remembered of the details of the trip because that was also the year that Bridget Kastendieck, John Herman's wife, died in Brooklyn. Her death began a lengthy series of family tragedies and misfortunes that eventually caused John Herman and Dietrich to abandon Brooklyn for the unknown fortunes of southwest Missouri. Financial reversal brought on by the banking crisis and ill health aggravated by the deteriorating conditions in Brooklyn prompted Dietrich to move his family to Missouri, following John Herman who had made the move a couple of years before.

Dietrich arrived at the Frisco depot in Billings, Missouri, in February of 1880. He inquired of an old Brooklyn friend who met him, "Where is Billings?" To which the friend replied, "It is still invisible."[8] Dietrich bought a small farm near Billings, a parcel of land with a brook flowing through it, and settled into a new occupation in life as a farmer. Hardly had the family arrived when tragedy struck. Alice, a little past her thirteenth year, took ill with diphtheria in September of 1880 and died. They laid her to rest in a little brush-grown cemetery near Billings later called Rose Hill.[9]

After a decade of farming in Missouri, the opportunity came to take up a new business interest in Billings, something Dietrich had steered clear of up until the year 1891. He had money to invest from the sale of his grocery company in Brooklyn and invested it in milling, an up-and-coming trade in southwest Missouri. The grinding of grain into household staples, along with the production of animal feed was a lucrative business that furnished the fuel for the livelihood of many a farmer in southwest Missouri.

Several gristmills sprang up in and around Billings in the decades after the Kastendiecks arrived. In partnership with others, Dietrich took over the operation of the Billings Flour and Feed Mill that operated under the firm name of Wolf-Blades Milling Company, a sprawling complex of buildings located on a large millpond east of Billings. The name of the Wolf-Blades mill changed in 1892, reincorporated as the Kastendieck-Blades Milling Company of Billings.[10] The partners of Blades, Kintzel, and Kastendieck invested capital stock of $15,000.[11] The company did well for many years and was a widely respected milling operation throughout the country.[12] It advertised itself as a manufacturer of all grades of flour marketed under fanciful brand names like Whiterose, Harvest Queen, and Baker's Extra, each brand available in carload lots.[13]

Business in Billings like anywhere else had its adverse times. In 1894, Dietrich and associates found it necessary to sue Marion Stone for not paying his milling bill. Delinquent debt lawsuits were common occurrences in Christian County. Dietrich was already a witness in the case of his sister-in-law Caroline Kastendieck in a similar court petition against her that was winding its way through the court system in 1894.

The suit against Marion Stone had another twist. The wife of Dietrich's nephew was a Stone. Nevertheless, a petition filed in the Christian County Circuit Court ordered Marion Stone to appear at the February Term of Court. The court issued an order of attachment to secure Stone's property in an amount equal to the alleged debt of $347.02. The sheriff dutifully took into custody Stone's lots in Billings and a sizeable undivided piece of real estate in Polk Township. The court received lengthy lists of unpaid purchases by Stone as proof of Stone's debt to Kastendieck-Blades. The attachment had the desired effect. Stone came into court complaining that he knew nothing of the attachment, confessed that he owed the debt to Kastendieck-Blades as they claimed, and planned to pay it all along. Whether Stone lost his property, we cannot say. The clerk filed the case away in circuit court and history forgot it.[14] Such was the normal course of events in 19th Century Christian County.

From an early age dating to his youth in Morsum, Dietrich held an interest in birds. One of his pastimes after coming to New York was to pursue recreational hunting in the extensive parks around Brooklyn and in lengthy walks over Long Island. He developed a habit of taking the game from these excursions to a taxidermist as trophies to be mounted. Before long, he took up the hobby himself, a hobby he practiced for many years, eventually to wide acclaim; first for the East Collection in Brooklyn, and then for the Missouri Collection in Billings. He spent fifty years working on his bird collection beginning in 1860 in New York and continuing in Billings until his death.

The Kastendieck bird collection became like a museum. People came from everywhere to see it. A new building went up at the Kastendieck farm, adding special rooms to accommodate the growing number of species. The greater part of the East Collection was disposed of when Dietrich moved to Christian County, but he steadily replenished it with specimens native to the Ozarks. For instance, the millpond overflowed in 1895, and Dietrich did not miss the opportunity to collect a number of shore birds that came into the area. Over time, the Kastendieck collection gained critical acclaim, catching the attention of noted taxidermists and ornithologists.[15] His artistic skill in mounting birds caused experts and casual observers alike to remark, "They are not dead."[16]

Wherever there was an opportunity to add a species of a bird not in his collection, he found a way to include it. He brought back a number of European birds taken during his trip to Germany in 1869. When he moved to Billings, passenger pigeons were still plentiful. He took two in the fall of 1880 with the intent to add them to his collection. However, that was the year that Alice died suddenly in the same month. The now extinct pigeons were never mounted but remained in the collection as reminders of that awful month when Alice died.[17]

Time passed. Both Dietrich and Rebecka suffered for many years from attacks of acute ague. Rebecka, Dietrich's wife of thirty-nine years, died in the early summer of 1901. A tidy housekeeper by her nature, she had long patiently endured having kitchen and living room turned into the taxidermist's workshop. Her death was a great loss as the calendar rolled over to the 20th century. More sadness came when their daughter Charlotte died in 1905.[18]

The Bank of Billings moved into its new quarters in 1908 signaling a new milestone in the developing prosperity of Christian County. Nevertheless, by 1914, the downturn of economic conditions brought on by large corporations that squeezed out the small manufacturers and hastened, in part, by the outset of World War I, led to financial misfortune. The flourmill passed into a state of litigation. Farmlands and savings all but disappeared in the court settlements that followed.[19]

Never afraid of adversity, Dietrich Kastendieck lived to a ripe old age. In time, the brook that once flowed through his land lay lifeless and dry reduced to a wet weather stream. Frail and emaciated, sick with the infirmities of old age rapidly multiplying but undaunted in spirit, Dietrich passed away on the night of December 5, 1923.[20] He became ill in early November. Dr. Brown came out from Billings to attend to him, but it was clear that the infirmities of old age had taken a toll. Dr. Brown came for the last time on November 11 hoping no doubt that recovery might still be possible but knowing the meager chances. The diagnosis was Lobar Pneumonia usually fatal among the aged. Dietrich held on for a few weeks and then passed away quietly ten months shy of his ninetieth birthday, laid to rest at Rose Hill on December 8.[21]

Dietrich outlived his siblings by several years. He was the last of the original immigrant Kastendieck family to pass. Overcoming declining health after many years in an unnatural urban setting, the open countryside of rural southwest Missouri restored him to the good old age of eighty-nine. Like John Herman, he, too, left a legacy of beliefs and a concept of honest living that generations of Kastendiecks followed. Together, the two brothers—John Herman and Dietrich—proved able stewards of the Kastendieck name and the pride of Missouri descendants who carried on the Kastendieck ways.

Rebecka (Röpke) and Dietrich Kastendieck. The younger brother of John Herman Kastendieck, Dietrich (aka Dick) married Rebecka in 1862 and later moved his family from New York in 1880 to follow John Herman to the Midwest. He sold a successful grocery business in Brooklyn and took up farming near his brother in rural southwest Missouri. Augusta Kastendieck Family Album.

Citizenship Diploma of Dietrich Kastendieck. The Kastendiecks were German, attended German language churches, and made German the first language of their day-to-day lives. They valued their German heritage. Nevertheless, they took pride, too, in their status as citizens of the United States. Each of the immigrant brothers became citizens of the US, and the family mentioned the accomplishment at every opportunity. City Court of Brooklyn, New York. David Gay Collection.

Billings Frisco Depot. Dietrich Kastendieck arrived in Billings in 1880. He stepped from the train onto a new frontier in southwest Missouri. He brought with him his wife Rebecka and their four children from the bustling surroundings of Brooklyn,

New York, to the quiet landscape of a small farm near the country town of Billings. This picture of the depot dates to 1910. Rodger McKinney Collection.

The Bank of Billings. Pictured during the 1910 Billings Street Fair, the new Bank of Billings opened in 1908. A two-story Greek-revival structure, it was built of Carthage stone and brick. The traffic light above the intersection of Washington Avenue and Elm Street was a signal of the recent arrival of automobiles in Billings, Missouri. Collection of the Author.

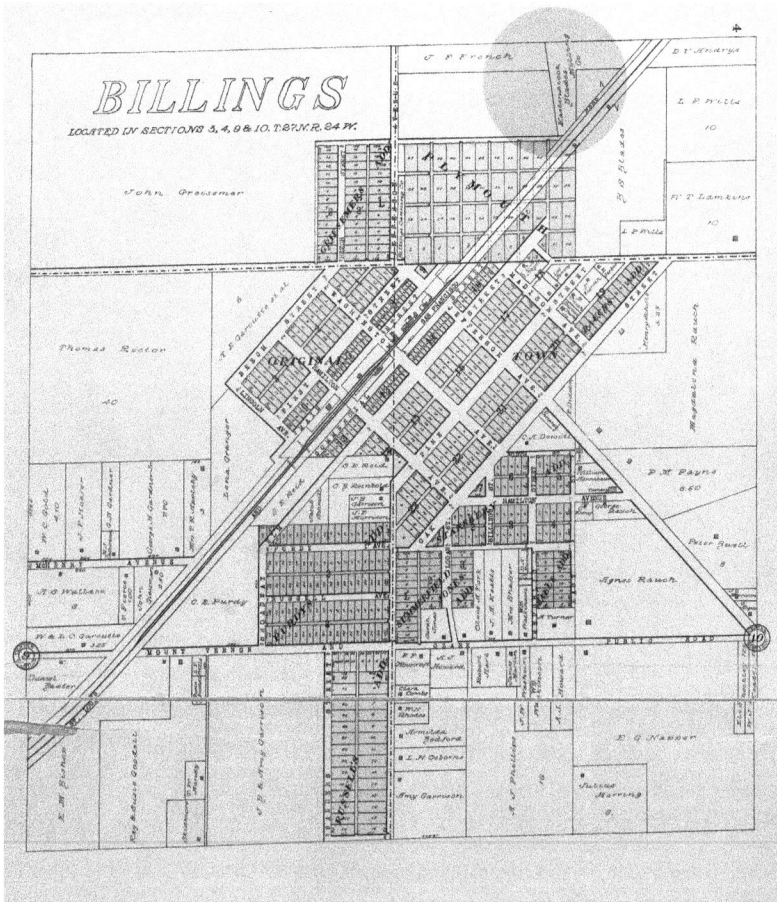

Map of Billings, Missouri, Showing the Kastendieck-Blades Milling Company. The mill stood at the northeast edge of Billings (upper right) next to the Frisco Railroad tracks on the west side of the tracks about where Mill Street turned into Zell Road. Remains of the old millpond still exist. Christian County Plat Book, 1912. Springfield-Green County Library Center.

Memorial Card of Rebecka (Röpke) Kastendieck. The card's all-German text reaffirmed the Kastendieck family's ongoing practice and dedication to the German language and the ways of the Old Country. The inscription beneath her portrait reads "Gone but not forgotten." The touching poem that followed was probably written by her daughter, the writer Augusta Kastendieck. David Gay Collection.

John Dietrich Kastendieck the Taxidermist. The stuffed owl specimen held by an aging John Dietrich is thought to be the Great Horned Owl named Blinky, his prized pet and feathered companion in life for eighteen years on the Kastendieck homestead near Billings. Dietrich enjoyed a national reputation as an expert taxidermist. David Gay Collection.

28

Children of Dietrich and Rebecka

Dietrich and Rebecka (Röpke) Kastendieck reared four children, three of them to adulthood. The devastating loss of Alice who died at the age of thirteen shortly after coming to Missouri never left Dietrich's mind. The expressed anguish he felt at her loss must have outwardly veiled a feeling of guilt for bringing her to an unknown place that she never lived to see in all its opportunity. Her burial in Rose Hill Cemetery made her the first of the Missouri Kastendiecks interred there. Many of her relatives would follow her in the passing years to a final resting place on the gentle slope of Rose Hill.

The oldest surviving daughter of Dietrich and Rebecka Kastendieck was Charlotte Anna Mavis Kastendieck—known at different times in her life as Anna and Charlotte. Born in New York, she grew up on the family farm in Christian County. When in her early twenties, she met David Froeschle, a young preacher in his first preaching assignment at the German Methodist Episcopal Church at Billings.[1] An Ohio boy of German descent, Rev. Froeschle had just begun his ministerial career when the two met. They married in the fall of 1892. Their son, Clarence Walter Froeschle, was born to them in the late summer of 1893, in Billings.[2]

It often happened in those days that ministers moved from church to church, sometimes in quick succession. David's job took him next to Owensville, Missouri, in Gasconade County. Two more children, Edgar Dietrich and Ethyl Rebecca, each with middle names from their Kastendieck grandparents, were born to the couple—Edgar in Owensville, Missouri, in 1897, and Ethyl in Franklin County, in 1900. Each birth marked along the way a new stop in their father's mobility as an Alliance preacher.[3]

The family settled for a brief time in Berger, Missouri, in Franklin County, a small town set on the floodplain south of the Missouri River about seventy miles west of St. Louis. Here tragedy struck. Charlotte became ill. After a struggle to regain her health, she died in 1905 in a St. Louis hospital. She was thirty-four years old and the mother of three young children, ranging in ages from twelve to five. Her family returned her remains to Billings for burial in Rose Hill Cemetery.[4]

Rev. Froeschle moved the family to Jamestown, Missouri, where he married again in 1906 to Minnie Schumacher, a music teacher from Illinois and like him a graduate of Central Wesleyan College, in Warrenton, Missouri.[5] They had two children of their own. His church work in the St. Louis German Conference afterwards took him and his family to more places in multiple states. In 1930 he retired, first to Illinois and then eventually to Orange County, California, where both he and Minnie died and were buried at Santa Ana, California.[6]

Charlotte's children generally followed their father's movements. Clarence came of age during World War I and served for the duration of the war, a difficult time for soldiers of German descent like him. For reasons of his own, he returned to his mother's Kastendieck roots in Missouri and married a local girl named Elizabeth Peiter; he took up farming in Stone County.[7] He located south of Billings near Marionville not far from his grandfather's old place across the county line in Christian County. Meanwhile, Edgar and Ethyl had long careers as teachers: Edgar first in Vinita, Oklahoma, where he met his future wife, Ruby Young. He and Ethyl later taught school for many years in Santa Ana, California.[8] Ethyl Froeschle never married, but Edgar and Clarence raised families that continued the Kastendieck line. Not of the Kastendieck name, they were nonetheless descendants of Dietrich Kastendieck through his daughter Charlotte.

The eldest of Dietrich's children was John Dietrich Jr. who came to Missouri from New York with his sisters and parents at the age of sixteen, the same age as his father when his father immigrated to America, coming from the rural German community of Morsum to the bustling city life of Brooklyn. John Dietrich, Jr., in a reversal of settings came out of the crowded wards of Brooklyn into the open rural farming community of Christian County. With an eighth-grade Brooklyn education and his father's love of nature, he settled comfortably into making friends in Billings and the work of helping to build a new place in time. He married Louisa Franck, an Ohio-born girl of German parents who came to Christian County by way of Cincinnati.[9] The Kastendiecks—John Dietrich Jr., and Louisa— had four children: Clarice M. (known as Clara), Karl Dietrich, John Paul (aka Paul J.), and Willie Andrew. Willie died in infancy in 1904 three days past his first birthday.[10]

John Dietrich Jr., was a dairy farmer and sometime merchant who built a respectable farming operation southwest of Billings.[11] Starting on rented property, he eventually bought his own place in the south part of Polk Township.[12] By 1908, his farm was one of the good producing spreads that furnished milk to the Billings Creamery.[13]

He built a modest house for his family (valued in 1940 at about $1,500, one-fourth of the value of the home he grew up in in Brooklyn in 1875) and dedicated his whole life to the hard work of farming, cows fed and milked daily, sometimes twice a day. There were crops to attend to, hay to put up, and the regular chores of repairs and maintenance of machinery to keep everything in good order. Even with the help of his sons and occasional hired hands, it was arduous work. At the age of seventy-five, he was still putting in sixty-hour workweeks.[14]

The sad end of John Dietrich, Jr's., household came in an unusual way. He, Louisa, and Clara all died in the same year within a few months of each other. Infirmities of old age and the irreversible consequences of illness took their toll. There were no odd circumstances, except for the comparatively young age of Clara at the time of her death. Clara died in the spring of 1943 at the age of forty-seven and was the first of the three to pass. She never married and lived at home as homemaker and caregiver to her aging parents. It was an accepted tradition among some families that the youngest daughter remained single to care for the old folks. This tradition seemed to appeal especially to the German community of Billings where several examples inside and outside the Kastendieck circle existed. However, Clara's cause of death revealed multiple health problems that likely impaired her day-to-day life, contributed to her regrettable appearance, and ultimately caused her death. According to Dr. R.W. Marshall who last attended her, she died of acute nephritis (kidney failure) brought on by a long battle with thyroid disorder that caused a condition called Leontiasis Ossea, or Lion Face Syndrome, a rare medical condition characterized by an overgrowth and disfigurement of the face.

In her case, it also evidenced itself in a large goiter and bulging eyes. It was a hideous disease for someone who in her youth was an attractive young woman. Life ultimately became too much to bear, and she passed on the evening of April 24, 1943, and was buried the following Monday at Rose Hill.[15] John Dietrich, Jr., passed two months later a month short of his eightieth birthday of terminal pneumonia, at Billings, on June 30, 1943. He succumbed after a lingering illness from a protracted heart condition.[16] Louisa, meanwhile, held on a few more months before passing in the early morning hours of October 30, 1943. She died of a stroke due to pneumonia following months of being under a doctor's care for the inevitable illnesses of old age. She was seventy-six years old, fifty years a companion, mother, homemaker, and beloved citizen of Billings.[17] Clara, Louisa, and John Dietrich, Jr., went to final rest side by side at Rose Hill Cemetery beneath a common gray granite gravestone plainly marked with their names and life dates showing that each died in the year 1943.

John Dietrich, Jr's., surviving sons carried on the Kastendieck name and the family trade of dairy farming. Karl Dietrich the eldest son married Minnie Peiter, sister of Elizabeth and wife of Clarence Froeschle, Karl's cousin.[18] Karl and Minnie had a large family. He followed the occupation of his father as farmer and dairyman on his Billings farm in Polk Township.[19] He died at Baptist Hospital in Springfield, Missouri, in 1953 at the age of fifty-six; Minnie passed in 1988, after living thirty-five of her ninety-one years as a widow. The Billings community remembered both Karl and Minnie for their devotion to church and family, each one buried in Saint Peters Evangelical Cemetery.[20]

Paul J. Kastendieck, meanwhile, married Maud Wolf.[21] They raised a son and a daughter. Both Paul and Maud lived to a good old age. Their burial was at the Marionville Independent Order of Odd Fellows Cemetery, in Lawrence County, a short distance down the road from where they were born at Billings.

Therefore, it was that the Kastendieck name on Dietrich's side of the family continued through the two sons of John Dietrich, Jr., whose descendants in turn proudly counted themselves among southwest Missouri's best dairy farmers.[22]

John Dietrich, Sr., and Rebecka's youngest daughter—the last of the Missouri Kastendiecks to be born in New York—was Augusta. She was five when the family moved to Missouri, a spritely little miss who embodied her father's creative muse and mother's passion for learning and all things worth pursuing. All who knew her knew her affectionately as Gussie. She grew up to be an artist, writer, and devoted raconteur of Kastendieck history. She never married, apparently content to devote her considerable talents to promoting her father's interest in ornithology while chronicling his accomplishments and collecting memorabilia of the Kastendieck name. Many of the family photographs in this book are from the Augusta Kastendieck Family Album, a collection of pictures and memories of Kastendiecks and friends representing the first Kastendieck generation going forward. The album was a remnant of her work rediscovered in an attic in 2010. Among her writings was a touching memorial of the life of her father.

Gussie wrote her undated four-page memoir of Dietrich Kastendieck about 1933 based on the recollections of her childhood and stories told to her by her father.[23] There were things that she did not say about him perhaps out of the desire to skip the details and simply paint a brief and poignant portrait of his life. On the other hand, perhaps it was because the difficulties he faced in later life were too difficult to recount, some of which she may not have known. We know of the great anguish he suffered upon the death of Alice shortly after he moved his family from Brooklyn to Christian County, Missouri. Alice was not the first of Dietrich and Rebecka's children to die but surely was the most painful. He and Rebecka had lost three children in Brooklyn. Helena, Herman, and Edward all died in infancy, their remains placed in the Kastendieck lot at Green-Wood Cemetery, in Brooklyn.

When her mother died in 1901, Gussie became helpmate to her father, taking care of the household, looking after his bird collection, and collaborating with him on the addition of specimens up until his death in 1923.[24] In the intervening years, she cultivated her talent in writing, music, and art, studying in New York, Chicago, and St. Louis. Critics singled out her painting for special mention in the 1909 National Academy of Design exhibition, in New York.[25]

In the modern vernacular, Gussie was an activist. As early as 1920, she was an editorial contributor to the American Civil Liberties Union.[26]

In 1927, she loaned the Kastendieck Bird Collection to the newly founded Ozark Wesleyan College at Carthage, Missouri. Springfield newspapers heralded the opening of a new museum at the college that would feature the collection. "It includes specimens of virtually every variety of bird and animal native to this region as well as specimens of wildlife from many parts of the world," the article said. The hyperbole of the reporter who wrote the article was wedged into a lead story that announced the opening basketball game of the season between Wesleyan and Draughon's Business College of Springfield set to follow the opening of the museum bird collection.[27]

Ozark Wesleyan College opened in 1925 as a merger of three Methodist Colleges, including the one at Marionville, Missouri, near Billings that had been Gussie's school in the early days.

Ozark Wesleyan was a small liberal arts college with a campus built in the middle of Carthage. It enrolled about 180 students. Gussie moved from Chicago to Carthage to be near the Kastendieck collection, and in 1929 joined the faculty at Ozark Wesleyan following three years of work at Chicago. She took charge of art classes at Wesleyan, the first time the college offered art classes.[28] She spent the next several years as an artist-teacher, working at the college, watching over the bird collection, and living alone.[29]

The great stock market crash came in 1929, and the wealth of a burgeoning Carthage declined with it. Reduced to ruin during the Civil War, Carthage had rebuilt itself in succeeding years of recovery to a point at one time when it boasted the most millionaires per capita than any other city in the United States. The market crash and Great Depression that followed led to hard times in Carthage. The financial promise of Wesleyan College never materialized, and in 1932, the Methodist Conference closed Ozark Wesleyan and moved its records to Central Wesleyan College in Warrenton, Missouri. Gussie stayed in Carthage. She set up her own art and taxidermy business in her home at 311 East Thirteenth Street, and at the age of sixty-two followed in the footsteps of her father.[30]

Gussie wrote proudly of Dietrich's stuffed bird collection. She was the artist behind the dioramas that formed the backgrounds for many of his most prized specimens. She organized an exhibition of his best specimens for the Golden Gate Exposition of San Francisco in 1939. She followed that the next year with a catalog and exhibition at the Missouri Building of the New York World's Fair of 1940 when she returned to her birthplace in New York to celebrate, as it were, the rare bird collection taken from her new home in Missouri. She eloquently expressed in a brochure that accompanied the exhibit the pride that Dietrich took in his taxidermy work and gave personal glimpses of how he came to be a taxidermist. Nevertheless, she only briefly alluded to the considerable reputation the Kastendieck Bird Collection enjoyed in the circles of professional ornithology. Scholars cited the collection, for instance, for its excellence in the *Transactions of the Academy of Saint Louis* and referenced it in the *National Historical Magazine.* The collection accounted for about one-third of the species examples included in *The Wilson Bulletin,* an important publication of Missouri birds.[31]

A full account of the life of Gussie Kastendieck would not be complete without mention of her little-known work as a missionary among the Jewish people of Chicago. Hardly any evidence remains of her work or its nature. Nevertheless, she wrote a number of pamphlets and articles, made speeches, and distributed literature in Chicago and elsewhere. Gussie was a deeply religious person, although perhaps not in the modern sense. One might say she was a Christian in the Orthodox sense. She adopted a peculiar theology in which she saw Judaism as the ancient basis of Christianity and the fortuitous choice of the Hebrews as the chosen ones. The fulfillment of Biblical prophesies, she felt, depended on converting Jews to Christians. She was deeply critical of modern religion and railed against all contemporary versions of it without favor to any of them. She wrote a number of religious political tracts expounding her ideas. In her book, *The Jew: The Hub of the Nations,* which she based on her interpretation of biblical prophecy, she delivered a resounding recounting of the scriptures prophesizing the Promise Land. She once wrote, "The nation that possesses Palestine is destined to rule the world; it will be the axis of power [because of its strategic location]."[32] Very little of this material appears to have survived. Her poems and general writings make no mention of this chapter in her life in the late 1940s.[33]

Over the next decade, she outgrew her modest home on East Thirteenth Street, in Carthage. By 1947, she had relocated to a place on South Main Street.[34] She left Carthage around 1953 and moved to Springfield, Missouri, where she spent the last twenty years of her long and eventful life.[35]

The Kastendieck Bird Collection found a new home at the Museum of the Ozarks (later the R.M. Good Museum and then Ralph Foster Museum) at Point Lookout, Missouri, on the campus of the School of the Ozarks. She first loaned the collection to the museum and then gave it as a gift to the school. The remnants of the Kastendieck collection remain a main feature of the Ralph Foster Museum on the campus of what is today the College of the Ozarks. After one hundred fifty years, some of the mounts show their age. The museum discarded the original wood and glass cases in the 1970s, but the Kastendieck Bird Collection remains where Gussie placed it as a gift to the school many years ago.[36]

Gussie lived on to a venerable old age. She had no children, instead was matron to the extended families of all the Missouri Kastendiecks. Known in later life by family and friends alike as Great Aunt Gussie, she painted, wrote poetry and books, and savored her collection of family history, long and full of memories. She lived until 1974 when she at last took her place in Rose Hill Cemetery, the last of the children of the immigrant Kastendiecks.[37] With her death, the history of the Kastendieck legacy passed to the next generation.

The Kastendieck line carried on into the third generation and beyond. With each passing generation, cousins, aunts, and uncles went their separate ways, each building on the proud heritage of the immigrant generation in their own time and way. The natural consequences of distance and time dispersed the family to many parts of the country but always with its nuclear center at Billings, Missouri. The occasional family reunion and the mail kept them in touch for a while but in time, those faded, also. When Great Aunt Gussie died in 1974, the last bond that held the family together was gone. The record of her efforts, however, remains. It is from her that we know about the life and times of her father and of many of the descendants of her immigrant Uncle John Herman Kastendieck.

Charlotte Kastendieck. She lived in many different places in Missouri and elsewhere before her premature death in 1905. This photograph of her dates to 1893, picturing her the year after she married Rev. David Froeschle. Augusta Kastendieck Family Album, David Gay Collection.

Augusta Kastendieck. Augusta "Gussie" Kastendieck had the distinction of being the last of the Missouri Kastendiecks to be born in Brooklyn, New York. She was a writer, poet, artist, and traveler who took great pleasure in her work and in the community of Billings. Many of the illustrations in this book came from her photo collection, the Augusta Kastendieck Family Album.

John Dietriach, Jr., and Louisa (Franck) Kastendieck. The second generation son of the immigrant Dietrich Kastendieck, John, Jr., moved with his family from Brooklyn, New York, to Christian County, Missouri, in 1880 when he was sixteen years old. This picture is thought to be their wedding portrait of 1893. Augusta Kastendieck Family Album.

Four Generations. The immigrant John Dietrich Kastendieck, Sr., posed with his son John Dietrich, Jr., grandson Karl Dietrich, and great granddaughter Josephine Elizabeth. This photo was taken at the family farm near Billings in the year Dietrich, Sr., died, in June of 1923. He was in his eighty-ninth year. David Gay Collection.

Progeny

29

Kastendieck Family Bible

The John Herman and Bridget Kastendieck Family Bible is a large book measuring twelve by sixteen-and-a-half by five inches in size (pages measure eleven by sixteen inches). It is brown in color with a leather embossed cover and gold filigree border and inscription. Illustrated with steel engravings from paintings by "the most eminent artists," the Bible contains 1,030 pages including the Old and New Testaments and the Apocryphal Books. No publication date is given. However, the Johnson and Fry edition, of which this is a copy, published in New York in 1875.[1]

Compiled originally by the Scottish minister and author, Rev. John Brown, the work first appeared as *Brown's Self-Interpreting Bible* in 1778. The Kastendieck copy is a more recent English edition of Brown's work by Rev. Henry Cooke, the Irish Presbyterian leader who published an expanded version in 1855. The Kastendieck Johnson and Fry edition first appeared in 1875. Brown's Bible remained a popular reference for more than a hundred years. It stayed in print in various forms well into the 20th Century.

An embossed cover inscription on the Kastendieck Bible reads, "Holy Bible, John H. & B. Kastendieck." The family register contains birth and death dates for John and Bridget Kastendieck and their children, plus the marriage date of John Herman and Bridget. We do not know when the family purchased the Bible, who made the entries, or when. Most of the early entries appear to be in the same handwriting. At least some dates appear entered post hoc after John Herman died in 1897. The last date in the family register is 1931. The death dates of children who died after the final birth entry of daughter Hermina in 1873 are in a different hand and ink color. Someone later added the name of Hermina to the list of children of John Herman and Bridget although she was a half-sister and not Bridget's daughter. The entry of Bridget's name and none of John Herman's other wives suggests the register was started contemporaneously while he was still in New York but after the Bible's publication date of 1875, and about the time the Kastendieck family moved to Missouri. The coincidence that the authors of the Bible were of Scotch and Irish descent like Bridget may or may not have influenced the selection of this particular edition of the Bible.

According to family tradition, the Bible passed to John Herman's eldest son, John Herman Kastendieck, Jr., in 1897. When he died in 1935, his heirs sold his home along with his possessions, including the Kastendieck Bible. Apparently, no member of the Kastendieck family stepped forward to claim it, and the Bible passed out of the Kastendieck family. After several years of living in the home, the buyers sold the house and its contents, including the Bible. Frank A. Kastendieck, grandson of John Herman, Sr., purchased the Bible; thus, it returned to the Kastendieck lineage.

The Bible may have gone from Frank Kastendieck upon his death to his sister Hazel Kastendieck Shafer about 1969. Her folded notes were in its pages. From Hazel's estate in 1981, the

Bible came to her niece, the great granddaughter of John Herman, Sr., Valentine Kastendieck Schaumann. It passed on to her daughter, Jayme Schaumann Burchett in 2002.[2]

Aside from the relatively brief time after the death of John Herman, Jr., when the Bible was in other hands, it has been in the Kastendieck family through five generations, a living testimony to the past.

Indelibly written in the pages of the Family Bible were the names of the children of John Herman Kastendieck. Not written there were the memories forever etched in the formative years of their young lives. Life studied through the eyes of a child is telling. Amelia Kastendieck turned three on the day of her mother's funeral. A three-year-old cannot know much about death and birthdays, but the loss of a mother to a small child has no equal in human sorrow. Amelia's brother John Herman, Jr., was fourteen when Bridget died and the only Kastendieck child old enough to remember her completely, except perhaps for George Dietrich who had turned eight in May of 1869; Andrew was not yet six when she died.

Without a mother, survival of small children could be difficult in 19th Century urban America. Infant mortality was very high. Aunt Dora Kastendieck came to live with the family in Brooklyn for a while after Bridget's death to help take care of the Kastendieck children, especially little Amelia. Dora stayed long enough to help them through the most difficult time, and then she left.

When Amelia was about five and the other Kastendieck children likewise older, John Herman, Sr., married the widow Johanna Hanson. Johanna's sudden death just a year later again left Amelia and her siblings without a mother. Because of Johanna's sad and unexpected departure, the Kastendieck family lost a wife and stepmother but gained two more brothers and a sister. Johanna's previous marriage to Bernard Hanson had produced George, Cecelia, and Henry Hanson, the youngest about Amelia's age. The Hanson children were without a father and now with no mother either. John Herman raised them as his stepchildren, orphans of his late wife, and brothers and sister of the Kastendieck children.

John Herman soon married a third time, this time to Elida Nilson. The Kastendieck and Hanson children welcomed yet another mother into their lives. Amelia was now six going on seven. John Herman, Jr., was nearly eighteen, clerking in the Kastendieck grocery store, in Brooklyn, and working odd jobs around Red Hook in South Brooklyn. The other Kastendieck children, and now the Hanson stepchildren, busied themselves with school and tried to assume a normal life of kids growing up in a big city.

A new addition to the family came along in 1873 with the birth of Hermina Elida Kastendieck, born a month after Amelia's seventh birthday. A baby sister—albeit half-sister—meant Amelia was no longer the youngest in the family.

A lot had happened in four years' time; a little happiness was a welcome change. However, life in the Kastendieck household did not stay happy for very long. Death again visited them when Elida died, on Leap Year's day, February 29, 1876. A day that occurs but once every four years, it marked the death of still another Kastendieck wife and mother, as if it were an omen. John Herman Kastendieck turned age fifty in March of 1876, a widower once again. Another crushing blow followed when the two infant children of John Herman and Elida died suddenly within a year of each other.

His family was a family knit of many ethnic threads. Four children from his marriage to Bridget Ford were German-Irish: John Herman, Jr., was twenty-one; George Dietrich, fifteen; and

Andrew, thirteen. Amelia was approaching her tenth birthday in 1876. The stepchildren, the Hanson siblings, were Danish and Norwegian: George, age fifteen; Cecelia, twelve; and Henry now ten. Then, there was little Hermina—they called her Minnie—of German and Norwegian blood who was not yet three in 1876. Amelia knew the heartbreak that her little stepsister felt when Elida died; both Kastendieck girls lost their mothers when they were barely three.

In the cold ground of Green-Wood Cemetery lay the rest of John Herman's family of three wives and four infant children. It is almost unimaginable that a man could endure that much loss in a lifetime. From his marriage to Bridget Ford in 1855, but twenty years had passed.

John married a fourth time exactly nine months and four days after the death of Elida. He married Caroline Wingood, December 3, 1876, adding yet another exotic touch to the ethnic fabric of his family. She was English by way of the West Indies. As if not to tempt fate, John and Caroline did not have children. She became the mother of the Kastendieck children and stepchildren who until then had not known much degree of permanency. John and Caroline were together for twenty-one years, longer than his three other tragic marriages combined.

The Kastendieck family left Brooklyn in 1877, for the rural countryside of southwest Missouri. John, Caroline, and the kids—all eight of them—came to Billings, a thriving young town springing up in the panhandle of Christian County, Missouri. Here the children took up new lives far from the crowded streets of Brooklyn.

Out of the five immigrant Kastendieck siblings who first came to Brooklyn, Aunt Dora's line went extinct first. She never remarried after the death of her infant children.

John Friedrich Wilhelm Kastendieck, of Brooklyn, left no surviving son to preserve the Kastendieck name. Three daughters extended his descendants under the names Leonhauser, Holzer, and Gerken.

Meanwhile, the only son of John Henry Kastendieck, also of Brooklyn, died childless, and the Kastendieck name likewise became extinct in Henry's line. His daughter continued his descendants under the name Gruschow.

Of all the Brooklyn Kastendieck siblings, besides John Herman, Dietrich Kastendieck produced the lone male heir in the person of his son John Dietrich, Jr., His daughter Charlotte added descendants to his line in the name of Froeschle.

John Herman Kastendieck knew many heartaches and unbearable losses in his lifetime, as did the entire immigrant Kastendieck siblings. And yet, after all the seemingly unending tragedies, John Herman and his surviving children did the most in terms of numbers for the next generation to carry on the Kastendieck name and populate the Kastendieck legacy. Three sons and two daughters, each of whom contributed to the third generation of the Kastendieck heritage and beyond, survived him.

When John Herman died in 1897, he left eleven grandchildren. Five more grandchildren were born after his death upping the total to sixteen descendants in the third generation, more than all the rest of his four Kastendieck siblings combined. He had nine granddaughters and seven grandsons. Of the seven grandsons, four carried the surname Kastendieck to sustain the Kastendieck line.[3] In due time, marriages on the distaff side produced new names, some lines became extinct, and others existed in names besides Kastendieck. Nevertheless, John Herman's heritage lived on in the lives of his five children and their descendants duly recorded in the Kastendieck Family Bible.

Family Page from the John Herman and Bridget Kastendieck Bible. Entries date to a period sometime after the publication of the Bible in 1875, and at various other times up until the last entry in 1931. Collection of Jayme Schaumann Burchett.

Facsimiles of Bible pages follow.

PARENTS.

BIRTHS.

John Herman Kastendieck   the 14. day of March 1826
Bridget Ford   the 16 day of Septr 1835

CHILDREN.

John Herman Kastendieck   the 6 day of December 1855
William Henry Kastendieck   the 27 day of November 1857
Heinrich Kastendieck   the 13th day of November 1858
Belinda Kastendieck   the 25th day of November 1859
Georg Dieterich Kastendieck   the 18th day of May 1861
Andrew Kastendieck   the 18th day of September 1863
Amelja Maria Dorothea Kastendieck   the 6 day of August 1866
Hermina Elida Rebecka   16 " September 1873

MARRIAGES   DEATHS

the 14th day of Feb 1855   the 16th day of Jan, 1897
the 14 day of Feb 1855   the 3th day of August 1869

                                  the 8th of Januar 1858
                                  the 19th day of Novemb 1858
                                  the 25th day of Novemb 1859
                                  The 24 day of October 1927
                                  The 1st day of May 1912
                                  "   die by July 1918
                                  "   2d day of August 1931

30

Andrew

We begin the second generation of the Kastendiecks with the youngest son, Andrew Kastendieck, because Andrew was the first of John Herman Kastendieck's children to pass.

Andrew Kastendieck was born in Brooklyn, New York, the youngest son of John Herman and Bridget (Ford) Kastendieck.[1] They dutifully recorded his birth in the Kastendieck Family Bible: "Andrew Kastendieck the 18th day of Septemb [sic] 1863."

Civil War raged across the country when Andrew was born. He was born on the same day confederate troops began the Battle of Chickamauga, determined to push Union forces out of Tennessee. The war never reached Brooklyn to the extent that it did elsewhere. People went about their day-to-day lives without much interruption.

Four months after Andrew's birth, the Kastendieck family gathered for his baptism on a Sunday, December 13, at the Wyckoff-Street Methodist Episcopal Church, an all-German language church of Brooklyn that embodied the religious and cultural traditions of the Old Country. The minister completed Andrew's baptismal certificate in German and noted, "empfing und den Namen: Andreas." The baptism of Andrew was a family affair. Uncle John Henry Kastendieck, brother of John Herman, and Aunt Marie Elizabeth Kastendieck, wife of Uncle John F.W. Kastendieck, another brother, appeared as the sponsors. Afterwards, the elaborate baptismal certificate that recorded the event became a family artifact, put away, and kept for future generations as a remembrance of that special day in 1863. The old Wyckoff-Street church where the ceremony took place once stood near Hoyt and Smith Streets, in Brooklyn. Gone now, it was still standing as late as 1897.[2]

Andrew's early schooling was in Brooklyn. He came to Missouri as a boy of thirteen when the Kastendiecks left New York and moved west. There was no high school at that time at his new location in Billings, Missouri. He spent his teenage years on the Kastendieck farm in Polk Township learning to farm. The move away from city life, and his job as a sometimes grocery clerk in Brooklyn, thrust him abruptly into the rural agricultural prospects of Christian County.

Family life was busy. The Kastendieck clan was a relatively large family by Billings' standards. Besides his father John Herman and stepmother Caroline, there were brothers John Herman, Jr., and George; sisters Amelia and Minnie; stepbrothers George and Henry Hanson; and stepsister Cecelia Hanson. It was a crucible of the modern family long before its time. Andrew and stepbrother Henry Hanson were about the same age. Half-sister Minnie was the baby in the family.[3]

By the time Andrew reached his early twenties he had acquired enough personal property to pay taxes, which he did beginning in 1890; he continued to pay in varying amounts every year thereafter for the remainder of his life. Andrew paid his taxes regularly and unlike his father was never delinquent. He was not a wealthy person; his tax receipts suggest that he was a person of modest means. The highest personal property tax he paid up to the turn of the century was $3.23 in 1897;[4] other years' taxes ran anywhere from 60 cents up to $1.89. Personal property taxes varied widely from year to year in Christian County. Andrew's assessments ranged from values of about $80 in 1890 and 1898, to around $210, still a figure that did not represent much personal wealth. His higher tax bill in 1897 most likely included property acquired from his father's estate because that was the year John Herman died.

For a long time, Andrew remained one of Christian County's most eligible bachelors, a strapping lad of German and Irish heritage who cut a wide swath in social circles of the mostly German community of Billings. Tall, lean in physique, his engaging eyes set beneath heavy eyebrows, and blessed with unusually large hands, he commanded an authoritative appearance. Like many of his friends, he sported a full mustache that made him look older than his years.

In some ways, Andrew followed the example of his father in marriage. John Herman had waited until he was in his thirties to marry Bridget Ford, and only then after he had acquired enough resources to support a family. Andrew's single status ended at age thirty-one when he met and married Mary Ann Dewey, a young woman ten years his junior born June 4, 1873. Her name was Mary Ann, but everyone called her Mollie. Missouri-born from Greene County, her family came originally from Wisconsin. Orphaned at age four, Mollie grew up as the adopted daughter of Ranson D. and Gillie S. Blades.

She lived in southwest Greene County just over the Greene County line, bordering Christian County. Taking into account Andrew's location south of Billings, courting amounted to a distance of about five miles. Still, on a regular basis, it took romantic determination to travel by horseback or on foot.

Mollie and Andrew married November 28, 1894, before Magistrate A.M. Hall, in Christian County.[5] They settled on a small farm in the south part of Polk Township in the panhandle of Christian County.[6] Their surrounding neighbors represented the solid German farming community that established Billings as one of the top agricultural centers in Missouri. Nearby neighbors with names like Zoller, Schaefer, Hutter, Oetker, Utke, Ebert, Herring, and Wiles, to name a few, were the industrious beginnings whose descendants long thereafter occupied the same rich farmland of their ancestors.

Andrew owned forty acres at the intersection of present Highway 413 and County Road 13-B, about two miles southwest of Billings, and approximately a mile from the Lawrence County line.[7] He was not the only Kastendieck in his immediate vicinity who had property in that area. The Kastendiecks altogether owned 280 acres in this same general location, most of it in the hands of Uncle Dietrich and Dietrich's son John Dietrich, Jr., who together owned one hundred sixty acres near to or adjoining Andrew's property on the west. Uncle Dietrich Kastendieck, Sr., occupied eighty acres just north of Andrew's forty; while John D., Jr., farmed another eighty to the east of him; and Andrew's brother George lived on a forty bordering him on the east. Dietrich, Sr., had another forty acres directly across the road to the north—overall a relatively compact family settlement.

Andrew's house stood about two hundred yards off the road. A mile and a half east of him was several large farms: William Tipper's Brightside Stock Farm, C.L. Gardner's Park Lake Stock Farm, and Walnut Row Farm owned by J.F. Ward, to name some.

We cannot say for sure what network of roads connected these different places because what was once the Old Marionville

Road changed after 1912. Many of the old connecting roads realigned to the new traffic patterns. Some of the roads disappeared in time leaving only a trace of their previous roadbeds. One feature remained constant, however. The familiar sound of the Frisco train regularly passing a half mile to the north gave a reassuring rhythm to the daily routine of farm life around Billings.

Andrew and Mollie had two daughters. Verda the eldest came along in September of 1895, almost nine months to the day after their marriage; and Pauline arrived March 7, 1898. These were eventful years. In between the births of the girls, the immigrant patriarch John Herman Kastendieck died, in January of 1897, severing the anchor that had long held the Kastendieck family together through many personal tragedies. Andrew's daughters never knew the elder John Herman. The memories of Verda and Pauline of their grandfather could only be those related to them second hand.

Education was an essential quality of all the Kastendieck family. Andrew and Mollie were both literate at a time when that was not always the case among early Christian County residents. They saw to it that their daughters studied. There were two elementary schools in the neighborhood, one about three-quarters of a mile east of the Kastendieck home; the other a mile and a quarter northwest as the crow flies; a couple of miles up the road was the Billings school.

The national goal expected children in the United States to attend school until the age of sixteen; in practice, most kids never finished the eighth grade. They went to work on farms, in factories, and in some places coalmines to add to family incomes. Some kids went to high school and a few went to college, but in those days hardly any women went to college—Verda and Pauline did. They grew up attending school regularly and got the best education available in rural southwest Missouri, stepping from grammar school, to the new Billings High School, and then to college.

Farm life seemed to agree with the family as the girls grew up in the countryside of Christian County. Andrew and Mollie had a mortgage on their farm and house where they lived but they made payments regularly. Andrew had a streak of obstinate independence. He took pride in the ownership of his own farm, which he worked on his own account. He kept a few head of livestock, raised crops, and milked a small herd of dairy cows that produced enough milk to sell the excess to the Billings Creamery for a few extra dollars. Andrew's annual milk check totaled about $50.

A good dairy cow could produce enough milk to justify a good-sized herd. Tom Garoutte's farm, for example, produced enough milk to account for a herd of some sixty cows. The milk production on the farms of the Kastendieck clan, on the other hand, came from smaller herds anywhere from one or two animals up to about a dozen.

Mollie did the housework, helped with chores, and gathered the eggs that added to the family income. Eggs from her prized flock were in demand. A neighbor wrote, "Mollie, Will you please save all the eggs you get the rest of this week and bring them in for this Sunday morning. We want to set the incubator—we have about 100 already engaged. I wish you could get as many as that if possible. Do you think you could get any from Elmer?"[8] Farm families incubated their own chicks to produce not only future additions to a flock but also to stock a valued source of food. Mollie had her own incubator that she put into service whenever the need arose.

Reading was a favorite pastime in the Kastendieck household usually in the evenings by the light of a coal oil lamp after chores.

Andrew loved to read and often read aloud to Mollie and the girls. A highlight of the week was delivery to the mailbox on Thursday of the latest copy of the *Billings Times* newspaper.[9]

Andrew had a talent for music, too, and knew many songs. He never had a lesson but could play drums. He always had some rib bones trying to shake along with his singing. On a winter evening, he would come in out of the cold, put his feet on the oven door, sing, and clatter his bones.[10] Anyone who knew him liked him. He was a friend to everybody. Witty and upbeat, he liked a good practical joke, which seemed at first out of character with his serious German heritage until he made the point that he was as much Irish as he was German.

The Kastendiecks took time to socialize. Sundays usually found them at Sunday school and church dressed in the fashion of the day. There were the occasional pie suppers and community events to attend, not the least of which was the annual Billings Fair when people for miles around converged on Billings in the fall to sample the best produce, home brew, and confectionary concoctions the year had to offer.

Andrew was a dedicated fraternal man, too, basking in the social status that a club brought and engaging in the opportunities membership afforded to serve the community. He was a member of the order of Select Knights of America, a quasi-masonic order that originated as part of the Ancient Order of United Workmen, the first of many post-Civil War fraternal benefit societies to offer life insurance. The organization took care of widows and children when the head of the house died unexpectedly.[11] Andrew's reason for being a Select Knight was practical a well as social.[12]

Andrew and Mollie's fifteenth wedding anniversary rolled around in 1910. They had two teenage girls in school, and farming provided the needed livelihood. There was still a mortgage on the farm, but that was common because in 1910 mortgages existed on most of the farms in Polk Township.

The extended Kastendieck family circle grew ever wider with the births of nieces and nephews. John Herman, Jr., built a house next door to Andrew in a growing Kastendieck neighborhood. The census taker visited Andrew and John Herman, Jr., consecutively in 1910, going first to the home of John Herman, Jr., at dwelling 107 and then to Andrew's at 108.[13] Otherwise, the neighborhood stayed essentially the same, as it had been a decade earlier with other relatives making up the Kastendieck community of Polk Township.

The spring season was at its peak, flowers were in full bloom, and the trees awakened all green with life from their winter's rest. Then, Andrew Kastendieck died on May Day, 1912. He was forty-eight years old. He became ill on April 23 with what progressed to Lobar Pneumonia; he never recovered.[14]

Lobar Pneumonia was a bacterial infection rarely seen today because of modern treatments; however, in Andrew's day it was common, especially for some reason in men of his age, and often fatal if a doctor did not diagnose it early and aggressively treat it. We do not know what caused the apparent sudden attack; several things could have contributed to his illness. It often came on after a bout of influenza or some other previous condition that weakened the lungs and made an individual more susceptible. We do not know Andrew's personal habits; however, smoking could have been a contributing factor, and too much alcohol tended to weaken the immune system as well. There is no indication, however, that either played a role in Andrew's death.

He got progressively sicker as the week of April 23 wore on. It had come on suddenly with chills and fever, the usual indicators of the flu. It had been a colder than usual spring, and it was flu season. When he did not get better in the first few days, he rode into Billings to see Doc Shafer—Dr. W.W. Shafer. Whether Dr. Shafer misdiagnosed the problem or the disease had advanced too far to stop, Andrew's condition rapidly deteriorated. Dr. Shafer visited him at his home on May Day, the last time that he saw him alive. Andrew died that evening. His family was there; Mollie and the girls and friends and neighbors had come and gone during the day. His brother informed authorities of Andrew's death and took control of arrangements for the funeral. When John Herman, Jr., filled out the death certificate, he inadvertently made an entry that has long confused genealogists. He wrote the maiden name of their mother as "Bilinda Ford" in handwriting that looked like "Bilinda Pond". Transcribers of the death certificate naturally interpreted the entry as Bilinda Pond, very different from Bridget Ford, the actual name of their mother. The mistake recalled an earlier record in 1866 when Amelia Kastendieck's birth certificate in Brooklyn named Melinda Ford as her mother. Other documents showed Bridget's name as Bridget M., also at different times as Belinda, Bridget, Melinda, and Mary. John Herman, Jr., did not exactly remember his mother's name more than forty-two years after her death. However, he did remember that she was born in Ireland.

R.E. Thunney, the undertaker, came out from Republic to prepare Andrew's body for burial. Notification of his death went out. The beautiful design of the funeral announcement gave exactly the right touch of dignity to the occasion. Laid out in Roman serif type centered on an eight by five inch card and surrounded by a black border of mourning, it said simply, "Died at his home near Billings, Wednesday, May 1st, 1912. Andrew Kastendieck, aged 48 years, 7 months and 13 days. Funeral services at the M.E. Church, Saturday, May 4th. At 10 o'clock a.m. Interment Rose Hill Cemetery."[15] The first of the second-generation Missouri Kastendieck siblings to die went quietly to rest beside his father in Rose Hill.

Andrew Kastendieck Family. Looking the part of the well-dressed Billings family that they were, the Kastendiecks sat for this portrait about 1903. Identified clockwise, Mollie, Pauline, Andrew, and Verda seated in front. Dee Willauer Collection.

Thrashing Season. Machinery and thrashing crews were a regular sight around harvest time in the farming community of Billings. The thrasher and steam engine stayed in use well into the 20th Century. Neyer Hardware did a booming business for many years. This undated postcard was addressed to Mrs. Andrew Kastendieck, Billings, Mo. R.F.D. No. 1, Dee Willauer Collection.

Billings Fair. Pictured in 1910, the Eighth Annual Street Fair, Agricultural Exhibits, and Trades Carnival was a time for local citizens to parade their livestock and exhibit gardening and homemaking skills. Held each September, in Billings, the festivities included competitive shows in such categories as horses, mules and jacks, cattle, swine and sheep, poultry, agriculture, and textiles, and household goods. Photo Courtesy of Gorath, The State Historical Society of Missouri.

Andrew Kastendieck Script. This autograph card written in 1888 in the hand of Andrew Kastendieck—when he was about age twenty-four—was added to the autograph collection of his cousin, Gussie Kastendieck, when she was ten. The popular schoolbook jingle, a mainstay of autograph books, is from the lyrics of an old folk song by an anonymous writer. August Kastendieck Family Album.

Sunday School Class. In this photograph taken about 1908, Pauline Kastendieck stands at the far left of the photograph in the white dress and dark stockings. Her sister Verda (in glasses) is in the middle row in the jumper dress in front of their father Andrew who stands framed in the window. Mollie is on the right with the high collar. The elderly bearded gentleman (back left) is thought to be Dietrich Kastendieck, the lone surviving immigrant Kastendieck brother. Dee Willauer Collection.

31

Three Women

The Kastendieck family gathered at the bedside of Andrew Kastendieck in his last days, but his disease took him in a matter of a week. On the evening of May 1, 1912, at 8:50 p.m., he passed away—about the time he would ordinarily be reading or singing and clattering accompaniment on his bones.[1] The house went deathly silent, never again to revive the gaiety it had once known.

Andrew Kastendieck died at the age of forty-eight, much too young everyone said. There was a nice funeral at the Methodist Episcopal Church where he had happily lent his voice in song, where he and Mollie had diligently raised their daughters to value the teachings of Christianity.

They buried him in Rose Hill Cemetery in the Kastendieck plot next to his father. Upon his grave they placed a small gray tombstone of granite plainly inscribed, "In Loving Memory—Andrew Kastendieck, 1863-1912, Father."[2]

Verda and Pauline Kastendieck were in their teens when Andrew died; Verda was sixteen, Pauline fourteen, both old enough to understand fully their loss and to miss their father very much.

There were only three in the family now—Mollie, Verda, and Pauline—left to survive on forty acres of poor land in a place that challenged the best of men, let alone a widow in her thirties and two teenage daughters. It is fearful to think what might have happened to Mollie and her girls had it not been for the extended Kastendieck clan, Mollie's adopted family, and the help of her orphaned brothers, brothers who came together to help her despite having grown up apart orphaned in time and distance. Mollie and her brothers lost both of their parents as small children.

Memories were insufficient to fill the great depth of loss that Mollie, Verda, and Pauline felt. Daunting was the prospect of facing the future without the steady guidance of Andrew. They did not retreat into the past, however, but inwardly dedicated themselves to rise above the provincial life of Polk Township, to go steadily forward, and to steer a new course into the 20th Century.

When Andrew Kastendieck died in 1912, Billings was on the verge of becoming a boomtown, more than a convenient stop on the Frisco railroad. It had a population of 860 and all the services of a modern town. The new Billings Bank stood at the corner of Elm and Washington Streets; businesses ranged up and down Elm Street, from Sanders Mercantile, Neyer Hardware, and grocery and dry goods stores, to a drug store and Watkinson Jewelry, plus various other sundry and convenience shops. Local residents liked to brag about the peaceful nature of Billings by pointing out that in the whole town there were still only two lawyers.[3]

Good jobs were plentiful in Billings at either the Canning Factory or a host of other manufacturing concerns around town. The Billings Creamery cooperative was in full swing, and local farmers marketed their products through the Creamery Station.[4]

Local agents represented several insurance establishments, including the large Farmers' Mutual Fire Insurance Company that covered four counties. The Kastendieck-Blades Mill was a going business on the northeast corner of Billings, near the railroad tracks. The mill was a partnership between Dietrich Kastendieck and the Blades family, part of the same Blades family who had raised Mollie when her parents died.

Billings boasted something for everyone. Built next to the railroad tracks it rapidly became a shipping hub, which greatly benefited the outlying farming communities. It was common to read in the newspaper, for instance, "Hodges shipped two cars of hogs from here last week; Mr. John Stine shipped out a carload of tomatoes Saturday."[5]

The Indian trails and dirt roads of the early days changed to gravel-paved thoroughfares, greatly increasing the value of both city and farm property. Meanwhile, the city had a good start on sewer and water works. A telephone system connected the town with rural districts, as well as Springfield, St. Louis, and all neighboring towns. Almost within a decade, Billings grew from a brush-covered wayside to a full-fledged town.

The new Billings high school went up in 1912. "This is a large, modern structure well lighted, ventilated, and steam heated," the local press reported, "supplied with the best apparatus, and located on high and beautiful ground in the south part of the city." The reporter also took the opportunity to say, "The school board of Billings has always done all in its power to employ the best teachers and principals available and bring educational work to its present standard."[6]

The new high school was a substantial improvement over the first Billings school started back in 1859 in Dayman's blacksmith shop (where the Canning Factory later stood). Steady improvement in the schools over a half century of time stood as proof of the community's dedicated interest in education.

The Kastendieck sisters—Andrew and Mollie's girls as folks around Billings affectionately knew them—were sisters in every way except looks. To see them together, one would not suspect they were siblings unless they knew before.[7] Exactly one year and six months separated them in age and a noticeable difference in their height confounded the situation; Pauline stood a good two inches taller than her older sister did.

The petite Verda was for sure one of the prettiest girls in the county. Her wire-rimmed glasses, which she wore from an early age, did not disguise her attractive features. The spectacles, however, and a slight squint did punctuate a scholarly appearance that caused one to think Verda was a teacher long before she entered that honorable field. Pauline later wore eyeglasses, too; however, in the Billings years, glasses helped set the sisters apart as two individuals with very distinct looks and personalities.

The Kastendieck girls—Verda and Pauline—went on to graduate from Billings High School, Verda first and then Pauline. Verda finished high school, went to college, and became a teacher.

Pauline was one of twelve students in her 1914 high school class comprised of three boys and nine girls. The class picture showed all twelve graduates with Principal Phillips seated front and center.[8] Looking at the graduation picture, one could easily mistake it for a funeral instead of graduation day. No one smiled. Smiling in front of a photographer was apparently a talent that few in Billings possessed. Pauline looked intently into the camera with that same arresting gaze she had showed the Sunday school photographer a few years before. The three young men in the picture wore the obligatory suits and ties, looking like fashion models but fooling no one. The young women, each in a long white graduation dress, made new for the occasion, plainly overshadowed their male counterparts in the photograph.

Two of the twelve graduates were Pauline's cousins making the class 25 percent Kastendieck. In addition to Pauline there was Katherine, Uncle George Kastendieck's daughter; and Mildred, daughter of Uncle John Herman, Jr.,

Members of Pauline's graduating class went their separate ways after graduation. Mildred Kastendieck married and went to St. Louis. Classmate Edgar Turner went into the Army and served as a sergeant in World War I, until his discharge in 1918. Helen Watkinson went to Kansas City with Elizabeth Griesemer and both became bookkeepers there. Helen later returned to southwest Missouri and died in Aurora, Missouri, at age ninety-seven.

About half the class became teachers, yet another nod to the high value put on education by the Billings community.[9] Laura Conrad taught at a Springfield business college. Katherine Kastendieck taught in the public schools. She later married a veterinarian and moved to Iowa. Ruth Ely likewise became a public school teacher, and so did Celestine Leitensdorfer who was the youngest daughter of Dr. J.N. Leitensdorfer, the town physician. Dr. Leitensdorfer died in 1908, giving Celestine and the Kastendieck girls the unfortunate common circumstance of graduating from high school without their fathers.

Miss Celestine never married and spent her entire life teaching in the Billings community.[10] A common practice in those days expected the youngest daughter in a family to remain single in order to care for an elderly parent. This tradition produced many an unmarried woman. Traditional families also expected their daughters to marry in order of age. Woe was it to a younger daughter who married before her older sister.

Following her graduation from Billings High School, Pauline entered Springfield Normal School, in Springfield, Missouri. She attended summer sessions for teacher training with the intent of following her older sister Verda into teaching. The primary purpose of Springfield Normal at the time was the preparation of teachers for the public school system.[11] Pauline got a job in Springfield and tried her wings at teaching for a very brief time but quickly gave it up because she did not think she liked it.[12]

Mollie worked to keep the family together. For a long time— ever since Andrew died—Austin and Willard Dewey, Mollie's brothers, tried to get her to move to Wisconsin. The brothers had left Missouri to resettle in Wisconsin more than twenty years before. The Dewey family was originally from Wisconsin. Their parents married there and three of their six children were born in Wisconsin before they moved to Missouri in 1870. Wisconsin was home. Austin and Willard returned to the old homestead in Grant County, Wisconsin, as soon as they were old enough to leave their adopted families in Missouri to resettle in the Dewey homeland.

Despite the fruitful promise of southwest Missouri, Wisconsin was the new land of opportunity at the beginning of the 20th Century. Grant County, Wisconsin, and Iowa County next to it grew rapidly around the turn of the century because of the rich lead and zinc deposits in that region of the country. Opportunities were abundant. Lancaster, the county seat of Grant County, grew to be an important hub of mining activity. Towns like Fennimore offered opportunities for merchants and farmers to provide the necessary goods and services that mining required.

Prospects of a new beginning for the Kastendieck women in Wisconsin were increasingly attractive. Austin finally convinced Mollie that a future in Fennimore, Wisconsin, for a widow and two young daughters looked brighter than life on a broken forty-acre farm in southwest Missouri. The family began to think about leaving Billings.

The exodus of the Andrew Kastendieck family from Billings did not occur all at once. Austin had tried to get Mollie to join him in Wisconsin starting soon after Andrew's death. However, Pauline was still in high school, and Mollie did not want to leave until Pauline graduated. Therefore, Mollie moved the family and their household goods into a house in Billings at Hamilton and Oak Streets, nearer to the high school, and two blocks northwest of the Methodist Episcopal Church where Andrew used to take the family on Sunday. The house stood a few houses southwest of where Andrew's brother George kept his carpenter shop on Pine Street.

Mollie did not try to keep the farm going. She sold it, paid off the mortgage, and by October of 1917 had left Billings for good.[13] Three years after Andrew's death, she returned to the Dewey family seat at Fennimore, Wisconsin.

Mollie moved to Wisconsin by herself, leaving Verda and Pauline behind in Billings.[14] Verda remained in Billings for the time being and continued her teaching job. Pauline graduated from high school in 1914, qualified herself to teach in Springfield briefly, quit teaching, and then joined her mother in Wisconsin in 1917.[15] Verda sold the family goods at auction in 1918. "Having decided to change our location," Verda wrote on the public bill of sale, "I will sell at our home in the town of Billings, corner of Pine Street and Hamilton Avenue Saturday April 20, 1918, our household belongings."[16] Shortly thereafter, Verda joined Mollie and Pauline at Fennimore.

Mollie opened a millinery shop in her new home in the Second Ward of Fennimore, Wisconsin, using the proceeds from Andrew's life insurance policy and the sale of the Billings property. She knew the millenary trade from her stepmother, Caroline Kastendieck, who for some years ran a dress shop in Billings. Together with Pauline, Mollie made and sold hats for a living. The Kastendieck Millinery advertised an exclusive general assortment of hats with all the latest ideas in materials in all the accepted colors. The shop also carried many distinctive novelties in flowers.

Verda, meanwhile, became a schoolteacher in the public schools of Grant County, Wisconsin. The 1920 census found both girls living at home with Mollie, now in their twenties and still single.

Mollie did not remarry. She lived and worked in Fennimore at her hat shop until sometime after 1924 when she moved west of Fennimore to live with her then married daughter Verda and son-in-law Oscar Brandemuehl.

Mollie delighted in nature, studied it, and kept busy working among her flowerbeds. Many were the times when someone sick or shut-in in the community received a bouquet to cheer their day. She had a special interest in young people and did much to improve educational opportunities for children in the Fennimore community. Having joined the Methodist Church at an early age, she also devoted as much of her life to her church as her strength and health permitted.

She had a presence in the community. Her family and many intimate friends and relatives affectionately called her "Aunt Mollie." Little did anyone know that she was also an active member of the Women's Christian Temperance Union, a national movement organized in 1873 by women to fight the destructive power of alcohol and the problems it caused families and society.

As time went by Mollie's health began to fail despite the loving attention of Verda and Oscar in whose home she received every kindly care and consideration. She had her final illness on Sunday, April 19, 1942, when she suffered a stroke. She was never able to leave her home afterwards and steadily grew weaker until the end came on a Wednesday, May 13, 1942. She died at home with Verda and Oscar where she had lived for the past eighteen years. Rev. G.A. Bird of Mt. Hope preached the funeral service along with Rev. Lockhart at the Fennimore Methodist Church on Saturday at 10:30 in the morning. They laid her to rest that afternoon in Prairie Cemetery.[17]

Mary Ann (Dewey) Kastendieck—Mollie—died just short of her sixty-ninth birthday. She made the most of a difficult life. Orphaned at age four and widowed before she was thirty-nine, she raised two daughters as a single mother and never wavered from her insistence that they get the best possible education; she saw to it that they received college educations. Although burdened in her last years by poor health, she always found the strength to help others and to give of her talents and time to her church and community whenever she was able. At the end of her life, her epitaph said simply, "It can truthfully be said of Mollie Kastendieck, she hath done what she could."[18]

By the time Mollie Kastendieck died, the passing of the old generation had made way for a new one blessed with new offspring. Nevertheless, in 1942 the living descendants of Mollie and Andrew Kastendieck numbered but four: their daughter Verda Kastendieck Brandemuehl and grandchildren Ruth and David Brandemuehl; and daughter Pauline Kastendieck Jeidy, then living at Oroville, California.

The Kastendiecks of Christian County eventually lost touch with Andrew's family in Wisconsin. Hazel Kastendieck Shafer, later writing down her recollections of her Wisconsin cousins knew only that "Andrew Kastendieck married Molly." She did not remember Mollie's last name. "They had two daughters, Verda and Pauline," Hazel wrote. "Verda married Oscar Brandenmuhl [sic]; they had one son and a daughter, David and Ruth. Verda is deceased (lived and died in Wisconsin). Pauline married Melvin Jeidy who is deceased, she now lives in Ventura, California; had no children."[19] It is a scant biography but probably not intended to be more. What it misses and what Hazel could not have known at the time was the degree of success that Andrew's children and his descendants would accomplish in life.

Andrew and Mollie instilled a love of learning in their two daughters. Verda went on to continue the legacy of teaching with the dedication instilled in her by her parents. Her son became a widely respected lawmaker in the Wisconsin Legislature. Pauline rose to new heights in her life to infuse the art of teaching with the aim and purpose of humanity that she first knew back on her father's farm in rural Christian County. She became an education leader in California, selected at the close of World War II to help oversee the rebuilding of the elementary schools of Japan.[20]

Billings High School Graduation Class of 1914. This photograph caught a moment in time when no one in the class smiled, including the teacher. Front Row Seated (left to right) Mildred Kastendieck, Helen Watkinson, Principal Phillips, Ruth Ely, Callie Frank; Back Row Standing (left to right) Edgar Turner, Lucille Andre, Luia Conrad, Herbert Berger, Katherine Kastendieck wearing a pendant, Pauline Kastendieck in white hair band, Harold Turner, and Celestine Leitensdorfer. Collection of Dee Willauer.

Verda and Pauline Kastendieck. This studio portrait of the daughters of Andrew and Mollie Kastendieck, Verda (left) and Pauline (right), dates to about 1915. The photographer was Robert E. Hinchey who kept a photography studio in Aurora, Missouri. In the 1920s, the city of Aurora made him the town's official photographer. He traveled around southwest Missouri doing portrait work. One of his most famous photos was a 1926 picture of Uncle Ike and Son made famous by Harold Bell Wright's novel, *Shepherd of the Hills*. Collection of Dee Willauer.

Portrait of Molly Dewey-Blades Kastendieck. Orphaned as a small child and widowed at the age of thirty-eight, the wife of Andrew Kastendieck left Billings, Missouri, and moved with her two daughters to Fennimore, Wisconsin. She did not remarry. Collection of Dee Willauer.

PUBLIC SALE

Having decided to change our location I will sell at our home in the town of Billings, corner of Pine Street and Hamilton Avenue

Saturday April 20, 1918

our household belongings consisting of:

1 Bedroom Suite of Three Pieces,	*1 Good Incubator*
1 Wooden Bed,	*1 Clothes Wringer*
1 Feather Bed	*1 Boiler and Wash Board*
3 Rocking Chairs,	*Dishes, Irons, Churn, Oil Stove,*
1 Heavy Stand Table	*Oven, Flour Bin, Lamp,*
1 Spool Table,	*Flower Pots, Dishpan,*
8 Chairs,	*2 Teakettles, and other cooking*
1 Safe	*Utensils*

A 50 Gallon Steel Coal Oil Barrel, Hoe, Rake Crowbar and Post Hammer and numerous other small articles

Sale Starts 2:00 O'clock in Afternoon

Verda Kastendieck

OWNER.

John W. Washam,   -   -   Auctioneer

Public Sale Bill. Verda Kastendieck was the oldest daughter of Andrew Kastendieck and the last of his family to leave Billings, Missouri. She managed the sale of the family's household goods in 1918 before joining her mother and sister in Wisconsin. Dee Willauer Collection.

Verda, Mollie, and Pauline Kastendieck. Andrew Kastendieck died in 1912 leaving a wife and two daughters on the family farm near Billings, Missouri. Using money from a life insurance policy, they first moved from the farm into Billings and later sold the farm to move to Fennimore, Wisconsin. Both Verda and Pauline became teachers. Mollie lived with Verda until her death in 1942. Dee Willauer Collection.

32

Amelia

Amelia Kastendieck knew unimaginable tragedy as a child. Three days before her third birthday, her mother died in the summer of 1869. When she was six years old, her stepmother died; and before she turned ten her second stepmother died. Altogether, she lost three mothers—and two infant siblings—all gone before a child's eyes.

Her full name was Amelia Maria Dorothea Kastendieck—her middle name Maria was after her Grandmother Kastendieck and Dorothea for her Aunt Dora. By right of inheritance of the Kastendieck name, she was the youngest child and only daughter of John Herman and Bridget Kastendieck. She was born on August 6, 1866, in Brooklyn.[1] She started school in Kings County, New York, in Brooklyn's Twelfth Ward.[2] At age eleven, the Kastendieck family left Brooklyn and moved to Christian County, Missouri. She finished her schooling in Polk Township, trading the friendships of a set of urbane classmates for a group of a distinctly more pastoral character. She answered to the nicknames "Melia" or "Emilie", the latter iteration a name she later discarded and never used again.[3]

Her new home in Billings was not like Brooklyn by any means, but it was German, which added a degree of comfort to an otherwise ambivalent culture shock. Her half-sister Minnie, a few grades behind her, made school for the Kastendiecks in Polk Township an all-girl's affair. Her older brothers had passed their school age years in Brooklyn and therefore never experienced the gift of a country education.

The record is silent on the life of Amelia for seven years in Billings, until romance entered at the age of twenty in the person of Thomas Sherman Kinlock, an Illinois-born lad a couple of years her senior. The Kinlock family came from Canada, that part of the country at the southern tip of the province of Ontario, nestled between Lake Huron and Lake Erie where Ontario touches Michigan, not far from the city of Detroit. The Kinlocks were farmers in the township of Buddulph, a rich agricultural region west of the city of London, Ontario.[4] The patriarch, George James Kinlock, emigrated from Scotland; his wife Elizabeth was of Nova Scotia birth.

The Kinlocks left Ontario for the United States around 1863—at the height of the American Civil War—and settled in Fayette County, Illinois. Sherman Kinlock was born in Illinois in September of 1864, the ninth child of eleven kids and the first of the Kinlock clan to be born in the United States.

In the summer of 1870, the family moved further south to Phelps County, Missouri.[5] George James Kinlock supported his family as a laborer working at jobs around Rolla. Shortly thereafter, the Kinlocks left for Christian County where they took up farming in Polk Township and became part of the Billings community.[6]

Christian County proved to be a good fit for the Kinlock family. Although they were of Scotch and English descent, not German, they were Wesley Methodists the same as the

Kastendiecks.[7] Church in those days was a dependable setting for an eligible young person looking to strike up an acquaintance.

The Kinlock family brought a variety of talents to Billings: everything from carpenter, newspaperman, and telegraph operator, to stage driver and railroad worker.[8] Perhaps the most colorful of the Kinlock offspring and the oldest of the eleven Kinlock children was Wallace W. Kinloch who kept the old Scottish spelling of the Kinlock name that he preferred. Wallace was publisher and editor of the *Ozark Christian County Republican*. He bought *The Billings Times* newspaper and printing plant, and published it concurrently with the Ozark newspaper. His colleagues described Wallace as an "affable and business-like gentleman." Nevertheless, he was an opinionated fellow when it came to politics and used his positon as newspaper editor to promote his Republican Party views. He later bought the *Versailles Morgan County Democrat* newspaper and promptly changed the masthead to the *Morgan County Republican* in the interest he said, "of the editor and the Republican Party," a point of view that he likewise brought to *The Billings Times* and to his Kinlock siblings.[9] It was an easy sell because almost everyone living in the panhandle of Christian County was a Republican.

Sherman Kinlock, the Illinois cum Missouri farm boy of Scotch ancestry, probably met Amelia Kastendieck at church or in school, having in common their relatively recent arrivals in Christian County; they were the new kids both arriving at Billings at about the same time. Their relationship grew steady and Amelia and Sherman exchanged vows on July 21, 1887, before Justice of the Peace John Welker.[10] Amelia was two weeks shy of her twenty-first birthday.

Their first child was born in February 1888, exactly nine months after their marriage. They named her Lela Pearl. The new family lived for a brief time at home in Missouri before moving on to Texas. In Texas, two more daughters were born: Nellie V. in June of 1891 and Florence M. who came along in September of 1893.

We do not know much about the couple in the early years of their marriage except that Sherman abandoned farm life for a job with the railroad. In this, he followed the example of his brothers, one brother a brakeman and the other a telegraph operator. Sherman became a locomotive engineer, a career that shaped his life's work and by association that of Amelia. We know the adult life of Amelia primarily through the accomplishments of her husband.

Sherman became a locomotive engineer at a time when steam engines still pulled trains. By 1900 he and Amelia had followed the railroad business first to Texas and then to the Choctaw Nation, in Indian Territory. They rented a house on Tyler Avenue, in South McAlester, Oklahoma.[11] Here they raised their three daughters, Sherman working fulltime for the railroad, the girls going to school in McAlester, and Amelia keeping house although she never seems to have consented to allow record keepers to identify her as a homemaker. That line on the census form always remained blank.

Amelia and Sherman were among the early pioneer families of Oklahoma. They were residents of Indian Territory well before Oklahoma became the forty-sixth state of the Union in 1907.

Most people know about the early history of Indian Territory, how the US Government forced the Five Civilized Tribes to abandon their land in the American South for reservations on the western frontier. The inhumanity of the Trail of Tears ranks second only to the terrible scourge of slavery that stained the checkered history of the United States. No matter how far west the Native population relocated, white settlers followed, finding ways to break treaties and usurp Indian land. The United States Government was ever complicit in the takeover. In 1887—the year Amelia and Sherman married—Congress passed a law that divided the lands of the individual tribes into parcels of land for individual Indian families, ostensibly to encourage private land ownership among Native Americans. In the process, the Government confiscated almost half of Indian reservation land, making the land available to outside white settlers and to the railroad companies. Major land runs followed, the most memorable coming in 1889 when settlers lined up at the border of Indian Territory to race to claim unassigned land on a first come first served basis. Some jumped the gun and slipped across the line sooner than intended, and Oklahoma thereafter forever carried the brand of those zealous white settlers who created the Sooner state.

There is no evidence that Amelia and Sherman personally participated in the land grabbing fever that swept the nation in the late 19th Century. They lived instead in Texas when those events occurred. However, the Kinlocks did benefit from the rapid expansion of the railroads into Indian Territory. Sherman and Amelia left Texas and moved to McAlester, Oklahoma.

McAlester, Oklahoma, traced its earliest beginning to 1838—long before the land runs—to the crossing of the east-west California Road with the north-south Texas Road in what was once Tobucksy County of the Choctaw Indian Nation. During the Civil War, Union forces burned the original town of Perryville that first occupied the crossroads, and it never again reached its prewar status. When the Missouri-Kansas-Texas Railroad, the "Katy", came to the region in 1872, businesses began shifting toward the railroad trading post at nearby Bucklucksy. Railroad officials renamed the place McAlester after the trading post owner, and that was the end of Perryville.

Amelia and Sherman lived in South McAlester, which had its own independent history. Interest picked up in 1885 to build an east-west rail line to connect with the north-south Katy-Texas line. Financers established the Choctaw Coal and Railway in 1888 but were unable to secure right of way through McAlester. Therefore, the organizers and investors bought land south of McAlester's Depot and named it South McAlester. Where the two railroads crossed in South McAlester became a bustling boomtown. South McAlester and North McAlester, or North Town, operated as separate communities until 1907. By that time, Sherman Kinlock was well into his career as a railroad man stationed at South McAlester. (The two McAlester communities joined under one municipal government about the time Oklahoma gained statehood.)

In time, the Kinlocks left McAlester, Oklahoma, sometime before 1909 and moved seventy-five miles west to Shawnee, Oklahoma, in Pottawatomie County, where they lived in Shawnee's Second Ward.[12] They rented a house on North Kickapoo Street. Sherman's job with the railroad brought them to Shawnee. Several rail lines converged at Shawnee. By now, he was one of the railroad's experienced locomotive engineers.

Shawnee was still a relatively new community when the Kinlocks arrived. Established in 1895, it was a boomtown by 1903. Land was available for purchase for $5 an acre. Shawnee quickly went from Indian Town to thriving trading center. The first train of the Choctaw, Oklahoma, and Gulf railway (The Rock Island Line) pulled into Shawnee on July 4, 1895; the Santa Fe Railroad came to Shawnee in 1904; and the Texas and Oklahoma Line soon followed. Freight receipts in Shawnee doubled that of any other city in Oklahoma. Both the Santa Fe and Rock Island rail companies employed several hundred men.

Despite its commercial success, Shawnee had all the characteristics of a frontier town. Amelia and Sherman Kinlock and their three daughters arrived to a scene of unpaved roads hub-deep to the wagons when it rained and so dusty in dry weather, it was impossible to see across the street. Wooden sidewalks lined either side of the busier thoroughfares. It was an experience very different from the comfort of Brooklyn that Amelia had once known and decidedly more hectic than the settled pace of Billings life. Streetcars afforded a small bit of comfort when the cars came to town in 1903; that is, when they were able to run. One line ran along part of Kickapoo Street where the Kinlocks lived. It could take you all the way to Baptist University on Georgia Street.

Shawnee sat on a rise of ground immediately north of the North Canadian River and took its name from the Indian tribe that first made their home there. Most of the streets carried the names of early settlers, or their wives. The city had no central square, just Main Street fronted by every imaginable type of store and business connecting to the outskirts of a town girded on three sides by railroad tracks.

All the railroad companies had stations; each one vying to best the other in an architecture contest that most agreed the Santa Fe won easily. Shawnee's growth was the result of the railroad industry. By 1907, an average of forty-two passenger trains and sixty-five freight trains arrived each day!

It could be a rough town. When the Choctaw, Oklahoma, and Gulf passenger trains rolled into town, the conductor could be heard announcing, "Shawnee—twenty minutes for lunch and to see a man killed."[13]

The thriving business climate meant that almost any kind of store one could imagine set up shop in Shawnee, including a generous number of saloons. The proprietors of the saloons were considerate enough to arrange themselves along one side of the street to allow the people to walk on the other side. Blacksmiths, mule barns, and wagon yards kept busy; a good Studebaker wagon cost $125. A good wage in town was about $3.50 a day.

Shawnee was the shipping hub of the region. On some days, cotton bales lined Main Street for more than five blocks, so close you could jump from one pile to the other without ever touching the ground. Boxcars of livestock and farm produce went out daily by the carload. South of the railroad tracks, out Kickapoo Street where Amelia and Sherman lived, some three thousand longhorn steers grazed on the lush pastureland. Steak was 10 cents a pound. From the time of the land run into Pottawatomi County in 1891 to a dozen years later in 1903, Shawnee grew to be a population of more than 12,000 citizens, close to the same size as Oklahoma City.

To temper the brawl that goes into the formation of a new town, Shawnee was also a church town, mostly Baptist. Two colleges went up in the city at about the same time. Oklahoma Baptist University started in 1910 and Catholic University of Oklahoma began construction in Shawnee that same year. Catholic University did not open its doors until 1915. The name of the school changed to St. Gregory's College in 1922. We cannot say that any of the Kinlock girls attended any of these colleges. By that time, Lela and Nellie had married. Many residents for years saw the schools as consolation prizes when Oklahoma City outpolled Shawnee to become the state capital; Shawnee also lost out in its bid for the headquarters of the Frisco Railroad.

There was plenty to do in Shawnee. A shopping trip to the Monmouth mercantile took one to arguably the best department store in all of Oklahoma and a landmark of the high level of retail activity along Main Street that also had numerous soda fountains for social gatherings to occupy the teenage Kinlock sisters. Residents took to evenings of entertainment, especially on Saturday nights when patent medicine shows flourished on the street corners. The Becker Theater brought in big-name actors. The actor Sarah Bernhardt once played there; everything from vaudeville to opera gave the town an edge of culture. The great actors, Dorothy and Lillian Gish, grew up near the tracks of the Santa Fe, in Shawnee. St. Gregory's College art collection offered residents another dimension of culture available at the time in few other frontier towns. Then there was Woodland Park a couple of blocks north of Main Street. Carnegie Library later located in the park surrounded by fountains and formal gardens. It welcomed such luminaries as William Jennings Bryan. On a lighter note, one might see Tom Wright taking his daily walk up the middle of Main Street, followed by his pet goose. Pleasure seekers bound for a picnic at Benson Park lined the road to Tecumseh, Oklahoma, on Sundays. The park, complete with a rollercoaster and a giant swimming pool, was one of the things that the rival towns—Tecumseh and McAlester—shared. The two towns had an ongoing and sometimes bitter competition over rail lines. Which town should be the county seat of Pottawatomi County? Shawnee won. Adventurous lass of the town, Annette Kellerman, once caused a local scandal at the park when she wore a sleeveless and legless bathing suit for a dip in the pool.

Amanda and Sherman lived out the remainder of their lives at Shawnee. Two of their daughters married in Pottawatomie County. Lela Pearl married a Shawnee bank cashier, an Irishman named Francis J. Fleming in 1909.[14] They later moved to Okmulgee, Oklahoma. They lived comfortably in Okmulgee, helped out by their Black maidservant, Bessie. Mr. Fleming became an insurance sales representative and later district manager at Oklahoma City.[15] Meanwhile, Nellie Kinlock married Norborne L. Williams in 1911. He was also in the insurance business, in Oklahoma City.[16] They moved back to the old home grounds near McAlester, in Pittsburgh County, Oklahoma, and went into farming.[17] Sherman and Amelia's third daughter, Florence, appears not to have married. She graduated from Shawnee High School in 1913, became a schoolteacher, and lived with her parents in Shawnee.[18] It was still sometimes the custom in the early 20th century for the youngest daughter to eschew marriage for the duty of caring for aging parents.

Amelia Kastendieck Kinlock regrettably did not live to old age. She died on July 19, 1918, a few days before her fifty-second birthday. Her interment was in Fairview Cemetery, in Shawnee.[19] Within a couple of generations, Kastendieck descendants all but forgot her as often happens when families move apart. Hazel Kastendieck Shafer, Amelia's niece, only remembered in 1931 "Amelia was married to a man by the name of Kinloch [sic]; she had three daughters, Lelia [sic], Nell, and Florence."[20]

In Fairview Cemetery, a small gray-pink stone marks Amelia's grave bearing the simple inscription "Amelia M.", no last name, and the dates "Aug 6 1867–Jul 19 1918".[21] Someone did not remember that her birth date was not 1867 but 1866. A larger family tombstone stands next to her marker. Inscribed across the top of the face of the stone is the name "Kinloch" instead of Kinlock. The spelling was a memorial to the Scotch origin of the name, put there by Sherman Kinlock in anticipation of his own death.

It is a curious note that sometime around the time of Amelia's death; Sherman started to identify himself not as Sherman but as Thomas. His full name was Thomas Sherman Kinlock, which he wrote in the early records as Sherman T. or T. S. Kinlock; by 1920, however, it appears as Thomas S. Kinlock, and then Kinloch.[22]

After Amelia's death, Shawnee had another growth spurt in the early 1920s with the beginning of the Oklahoma oil boom. By this time, however, Amelia had died, and there is no reason to believe that any of the Kinlocks left their railroad jobs to dabble in black gold. It must have been tempting, nevertheless, because Pottawatomie County oil wells produced enough oil for Shawnee to promote itself as the Hub of the World's Largest Oil Fields. Oil brought a new wave of home construction to Shawnee, but by now agricultural production declined and much of the commercial activity that once fueled Shawnee's growth shifted to Oklahoma City. The Kinlock daughters were out on their own, Sherman Kinlock was in his late fifties, and the Dust Bowl years of the Great Depression were looming just over the horizon.

Sherman continued to live in Shawnee and work as an engineer after Amelia's death. When he was just short of his fifty-ninth birthday, he married the widow Minnie Wilkinson, a woman thirteen years his junior. The two had known each other for years when they were neighbors in Shawnee's Second Ward but had lost touch.[23] Minnie's husband, Edward Wilkinson, died in the spring of 1911, and Minnie moved to Oklahoma City.[24] Thomas (aka Sherman) and Minnie married October 1, 1923, in Oklahoma City. It was a whirlwind wedding. They picked up their marriage license at the courthouse on Monday morning.

They then proceeded immediately to the First Presbyterian Church, and married at the church all on the same day.[25] Minnie moved back to Shawnee with Sherman where she lived as Mrs. Kinlock for nine years until her death in 1932.[26] Her burial was in Fairview Cemetery beside her first husband.[27] Sherman lived on for another dozen years. He died the day after Christmas, 1944, laid to rest beside Amelia in Fairview Cemetery, having outlived her by twenty-six years. [28] His grave is unmarked. If there was once a stone, it has disappeared. Only the large stone marked simply "Kinloch" stands beside Amelia's small marker. Amelia and Sherman were not famous; few who rest in Fairview Cemetery were, with one notable exception. In the burial plot due west across the road from their graves is the grave of Dr. Brewster M. Higley who wrote the lyrics to the epic song, *Home on the Range.*[29] He lived in Kansas at the time, wrote the words to the song in 1872, and got fiddler Dan Kelly to put the poem to music. Dr. Higley later moved to Shawnee, Oklahoma, where he died in 1911.

Many of the original Kinlock family lie at Rose Hill Cemetery, in Christian County, Missouri, but Amelia and Sherman did not return to the old home grounds except for the occasional visit. Shawnee, Oklahoma, became their home and there they remained.

Amelia (Kastendieck) and Thomas Sherman Kinlock. This rare photograph of Amelia Kastendieck shows her as a young woman in her late twenties around 1894, a few years after she married Sherman Kinlock, in Billings. The couple moved to Oklahoma when it was still Indian Territory and lived there until her death in 1918. Augusta Kastendieck Family Album.

McAlester, Oklahoma. This view up Choctaw Street from Union Station in 1907 shows the trolley system that connected North McAlester to South McAlester where Amelia and Sherman Kinlock lived. Collection of the Author.

South McAlester Indian Territory Oklahoma Railroad Depot. The McAlester Station of the MK&T (Missouri-Kansas-Texas) Railroad, familiarly known as the "Katy", marked the relocation of the town at the McAlester junction. Unidentified patrons flank a steam locomotive of the type Sherman Kinlock operated as an engineer. Public Domain Postcard.

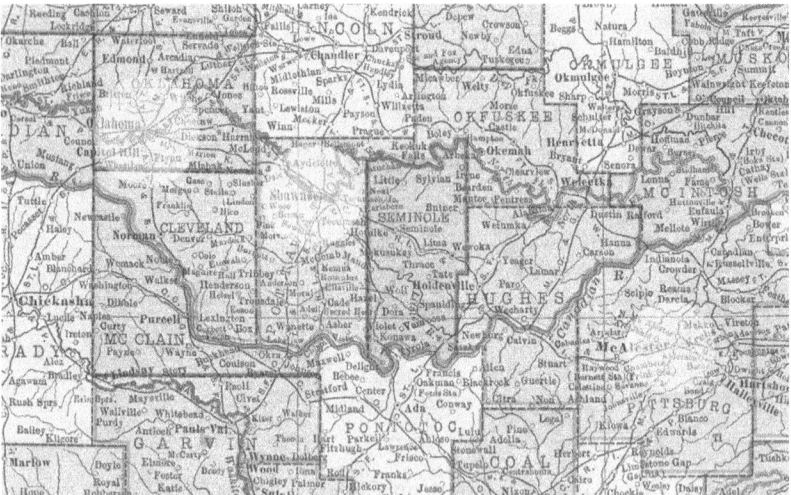

Map of Oklahoma Railroads. Highlights show main rail centers at McAlester, Shawnee, and Oklahoma City. The Kinlocks followed the railroad business from McAlester to Shawnee. Oklahoma City was a short train ride to the west. Modified excerpt from C.S. Hammond's *Handy Atlas of the World*, 1910.

Shawnee Oklahoma Main Street. Amelia and Sherman Kinlock moved to Shawnee in the early 20th Century around the time this photograph was taken in 1910. The light above the intersection identifies electrical power in the city. The rail tracks served an electric street car. This scene at Union and Main Streets took place a few blocks from where the Kinlocks lived on Kickapoo Street. Oklahoma Historical Society.

Santa Fe Passenger Station, Shawnee, Oklahoma. This photograph was taken in 1906 three years after the station was built in 1903. The Kinlocks moved from McAlester, Oklahoma, to Shawnee about 1910. Today the station is home to the Santa Fe Depot Museum. Oklahoma Department of Libraries, Oklahoma City.

33

George Dietrich

George Dietrich Kastendieck was the second child of the second Kastendieck generation, born as the second surviving son of the immigrant John Herman Kastendieck in Brooklyn, New York, on May 18, 1861.

He was born at a sad time in the nation's history.[1] A wartime baby, the Civil War began barely a month before his birth, a birth that came not just with anxiety toward the war but with understandable anxiety, too, in the personal lives of the Kastendieck family. Three other Kastendieck children had already died in infancy in the years leading up to George's birth. Baby William had lived less than three months; Heinrich, born the following November, died within days; and little Belinda who came the following November was stillborn. Each had been born in November at the outset of winter. Hope in the Kastendieck home rested precariously now on the spring birth of this new baby; perhaps a new season would change a string of devastating tragedies, and it did. George's birth in 1861 was the first of three successful pregnancies for Bridget after a gap of some five-and-a-half years since the birth of her firstborn John Herman, Jr., in 1855. After George, Bridget gave birth to

Andrew in 1863—another Civil War baby—and Amelia in 1866. Suddenly at the age of thirty-three Bridget died. George celebrated his eighth birthday in May 1869, and his mother died that August.

The next few years went by quickly for George, but sadly. There were the vicissitudes of happiness, disappointment, and new tragedies in the Kastendieck household. His father remained single for a while following Bridget's death, trying on his own to run his grocery business and be a single parent to his four young children. Aunt Dora and a cousin Richard Kastendieck came to live with John Herman as his housekeeper and store clerk; and then, they left. Dora took up residence with another Kastendieck brother, and Richard opened his own grocery business.

It happened in those days that children sometimes lost one or both of their parents. Kids grew up in households where surrogates stepped in to replace the untimely loss of a mother or father. Such situations occurred an inordinate number of times in the Kastendieck families, especially in the sad events that befell John Herman, in which some of his children knew four different mothers.

During the next seven years, John Herman married three times; happily, at first but twice with heartrending consequences that added more trauma to the lives of George and his siblings. After Bridget died in 1869, John Herman married Johanna Hanson, widow of Bernard Hanson. She died and left orphaned her three children: Henry, George, and Cecelia Hanson. John Herman raised them as his stepchildren. John Herman married a third time to Elida Nilson. They had one child, Hermina. Then more tragedy came. Elida died in 1875; and then, two of their infant children died.

Young George made many trips to Brooklyn's Green-Wood Cemetery. His was a childhood punctuated by death and funerals. They were sad years, almost unimaginable. He witnessed the burial of his mother, two infant siblings, and two stepmothers, all within a period of six years.

By 1876, as the country celebrated its centennial, Brooklyn, New York, had changed. The city's rapid growth, overlaid with too many sad memories, began to weigh on John Herman Kastendieck. He sold his grocery business, gathered his family, and left the congested wards of Brooklyn for a new life in the countryside of southwest Missouri.

When Elida died, John married a fourth time to Caroline Wingood who was West Indies-born and nearly twenty years his junior. She was young, energetic, and ready to be the mother that the Kastendieck children needed at the time. Caroline came to Missouri with John Herman, there to help raise the Kastendieck and Hanson children in a place far removed from Brooklyn in both geography and society.

George Kastendieck turned seventeen the year the Kastendieck family came to Christian County, Missouri.[2] He quickly threw off his past work experiences in the Kastendieck grocery store to take up the new chores of farm life.

The family joined the congregation of the Wesley Methodist Episcopal Church in Billings, known locally as the Home-Like Church, with a reputation for friendship that it tried truly to exemplify.[3] For the first time in a long time, everything appeared stable. The family was together, including stepbrother Henry Hanson. (The older Hanson siblings were out of the house but not far removed from the location of the Kastendieck family). Uncle Dietrich Kastendieck and his family had followed from Brooklyn and likewise settled into farming nearby in Polk Township.

The Billings community was an easy fit for the Kastendiecks. The largely German settlement readily welcomed these New York additions. The Kastendieck children were the latest of about fifty New York-born souls in Christian County in 1880; forty of them were in Polk Township. Altogether about a hundred German-born citizens anchored this mostly farming community around Billings, Missouri. The Kastendieck family had the distinction of being of both kinds—of German descent and from New York—and in John Herman's case the only family with as much multicultural and ethnic diversity that included under one roof German, Irish, Norwegian, Danish, West Indies, and New York roots.

By the year 1880, George was single at the age of nineteen and living with the Kastendieck family on a farm in Polk Township.[4] The next eleven years of George's life from 1880 to 1891 is mostly a blank, except that we know he became a member of the Masonic Lodge in Billings.[5] He may have attended college but if and where are uncertain. He remained a bachelor through this period up until May 13, 1891, when five days short of his thirtieth birthday he married an attractive twenty-three-year-old farm girl named Elizabeth Ann Keast. His union to Elizabeth introduced into the Kastendieck ethic mix a solid strain of English blood.[6]

Elizabeth Keast was the only surviving daughter and eldest child of George Lord Keast and Catherine Herring, both of established British heritages.[7] A daughter Selena and son William both died in infancy; son George Horace was three years behind his older sister Elizabeth.

George Lord Keast was originally from Tintagel, Cornwall, on the Atlantic coast of England, born there April 19, 1839.[8] Cornwall forms the tip of the southwestern peninsula of Great

Britain, bordered on the south by the English Channel and on the west by the Atlantic Ocean.

George Lord and Catherine were married in Cornwall on March 30, 1866. The newlywed Keast couple made their home at Camelford, Cornwall, about five miles inland from Tintagel, south of the Bristol Channel.

Elizabeth Ann Keast was born at Camelford on September 17, 1867. Her baby brother George came along January 19, 1870. When Elizabeth was about age five and George was barely age two, George Lord and Catherine brought their family to the United States, traveling across the Atlantic Ocean from Cornwall with their two small children.[9] John Francis Keast was a Christmas Day addition to the family in December 1877.

The Keasts immigrated to America in 1872, settled first in Pennsylvania, and then moved on to Missouri in the early part of 1880.[10] George Lord Keast took up farming in Polk Township, Christian County, Missouri, along with his brother John Harper Keast who came to Billings about the same time. George Lord, his wife Catherine—everyone called her Kitty—and their daughter Elizabeth and sons George and John Francis lived five farms over from Uncle John Harper and his family.

In the fall of 1880 another addition to George Lord's family came along, this time a daughter named Asenath Selena, a pretty name if a bit eclectic. The year 1880 was also the year that little John Francis died at the age of two, barely a month after the birth of his sister Asenath.[11]

The Keasts like the Kastendiecks were Methodists. George Lord was one of seven dedicated charter members who came together in May of 1882 to establish the Billings Methodist Episcopal Church. Uncle Keast, as everyone called him at the time, laid the foundation for the church made out of natural stone quarried locally and sand from the roadside. Completed in November of 1882, George Lord served as Sunday-School Superintendent at the church for many years thereafter.[12]

Elizabeth Ann Keast was a thirteen-year-old teenager who answered to the nickname Lizzy when she arrived at Billings.[13] George Kastendieck as a more mature sixteen-year-old could not have helped but notice the perky girl from England when their paths crossed on visits into Billings. Nevertheless, nothing approaching a serious romance developed for several years. A decade passed, Elizabeth grew up, a relationship developed, and the couple married in 1891 in the church that her father helped to build.

George Kastendieck and Elizabeth Ann Keast shared a common history of family loss. When placed together it is a history of uncommon bereavement. George lost five brothers and sisters and his mother, not to mention two stepmothers. Elizabeth's life was less traumatic but equally tragic. She lost four brothers and sisters who all died young and never reached adulthood, including little John Francis Keast who died within a few months of the family's arrival at Billings. He was the first of the Keast family buried in Rose Hill Cemetery.[14] Two of Elizabeth's infant siblings died before leaving England, buried in Cornwall; Asenath Selena died in Billings in 1887 at the age of six.[15] Only Elizabeth and her brother George of the Keast siblings survived to adulthood.

They made a good-looking couple—Elizabeth Ann Keast and George Kastendieck. She looked younger than her twenty-four years, and he hid his elder status behind a full bushy, dark mustache, heavy eyebrows, and a healthy head of dark hair to match. He was short of stature and so was she; petite would be a way to describe her. She liked to wear her auburn hair short in the style of the times with a cluster of curls gathered in front. It was a perfect look to set off her attractive features, bright dark eyes, well-formed nose, and full lips. Although a farm girl by birth, she was every bit a modern woman of her day. George was a handsome man, despite his masquerade of manly hair fixtures. He carried an air of loneliness about him. A friendly person and ever willing to donate his time and expertise to the Billings community, he nevertheless seemed not to fully escape the tragic Brooklyn years, experiencing periods of reflection that often dented the façade of his confidence.

George and Elizabeth's first child came along on April 1, 1892, with the birth of Frank Andrew Kastendieck. George Herman came along on August 17, 1894, then Katherine Viola on November 16, 1896, and finally Hazel Mary born on May 30, 1900; Hazel became the first Missouri Kastendieck to be born in the 20th Century. Happily, none of the infant mortality so prevalent in the Kastendieck and Keast families visited George and Elizabeth. All four children were healthy and grew up to lead interesting and productive lives. There is a portrait of Elizabeth Ann taken during her childbearing years. She is dressed in a full length 19th Century dress with high-buttoned collar and a generous trim of lace running full length down its front. Her usual tight hairstyle and curled bangs frame a face that is a model of self-assurance and dignity. It is a stunning photograph of an ordinary person of extraordinary beauty. There is a striking resemblance to her children as if the English bloodline prevailed over the more eclectic German Irish line.

George paid personal property taxes beginning in 1896 and each year thereafter. The taxes never amounted to much in any given year, an indication usually that he was not a rich person but a working class citizen of adequate but modest means. The most he paid in the first five years was $1.37, and that came in 1898 as the result of some added property from his father's estate; John Herman Kastendieck died in the winter of 1897.[16]

George and Elizabeth owned acreage outside Billings but made their home in town. As the 19th Century rolled over to the 20th Century, Billings, Missouri, was an up and coming community of 702 souls. Served by the Frisco rail line and a network of solid rock roads that were once Indian trails and dirt paths, Billings had grown from a brush-covered plot of land to a good business town. The old businesses were prospering and new ones came at a rapid pace. A canning factory went up in 1891 "equipped with the best labor saving machinery." Processing of large quantities of tomatoes every season added to farm income and jobs. Meanwhile, a cooperative creamery organized in 1899 likewise supplemented overall farm revenue in the community to the tune of around $5,000 a year, a number that increased six-fold over the next decade.[17] New businesses and well-built houses appeared on a regular basis; Billings had a reputation as a place of opportunity.

George held a variety of jobs. He tried farming although on a relatively small scale; he worked for a while as the secretary of the Kastendieck and Blades Milling Company, at Billings, no doubt courtesy of his Uncle John Dietrich who was part owner of the mill.[18] These jobs notwithstanding, married life required a more promising career than gentleman farmer and sometimes secretary. He became a stationary engineer for the local power company, a job that inferred a host of different talents. Sometimes called operating engineer or power engineer, a stationary engineer was a tradesman who operated heavy machinery and equipment usually to provide some kind of mechanical or electrical power to residential and commercial buildings. The work usually entailed steam-generated power to provide electricity to a community. Being a stationary engineer placed one in good company; automaker Henry Ford began his working life as a stationary engineer. However, the field was starting to lose some of its high promise for George . He was out of work for three months in 1900.[19] Maybe it was time to change to a new occupation. He was about to turn forty; he owned his house free of mortgage; and his family was complete, spread out in ages at manageable intervals. His oldest son Frank was in grammar school; Hazel was a newborn in May of 1900. (A month later, they were still contemplating what to name her.) Elizabeth was more than capable of looking after the household as she and George started their tenth year of marriage. It seemed a perfect time to start a new career. George had some savings, a little extra money from his father's estate, and enough financial backing to build a carpentry shop in Billings. His older brother John Herman, Jr., was a building contractor, and it looked like a better life than a lifetime of being a stationary engineer. Besides, his stepbrothers worked in the building trade as plasterers and his brother-in-law was in the retail lumber business over in Marionville.[20] Billings was booming and the need for houses and carpentry work had never been greater.

George located his carpentry shop on the north side of Pine Street in Billings about four blocks from the railroad depot.[21] His shop was a mostly wood frame building with a brick partition. A black pot-bellied coal stove was the heating plant. A long workbench ran down the center of the shop. It had a series of jigs fastened to one side for cabinetry work. When that part was not in use, the entire side of the bench dropped down on hinges to make more room to move about the shop. The usual woodworking hand tools attested to a well-furnished workspace. Hammers, handsaws, planes, and a good selection of wood finishing products made it a modern early 20th Century wood shop.[22] He had an electric saw and one of the new electric planers that so concerned the Sanborn Insurance Company that they included the locations of these tools on one of their fire hazard maps.[23]

For the next twenty years, George was a carpenter. He took great delight in informing whoever asked that he was self-employed, owned his own business, and worked on his own account.[24] He was a skilled house builder and cabinetmaker reputed from time to time to be a tad zealous at his trade. There is a family tradition that he built a house at the future site of Clever, Missouri, the other Christian County panhandle town later situated near the crossroads of the Springfield Road and Old Wire Road. The tale tells how for unspecified reasons, he moved the new house to Billings.[25] A capstan apparatus, so the story goes, winched the house across the fields. It is a farfetched tale—one that strains the imagination—but certainly the kind of adventure that George would have undertaken.

He and Elizabeth continued to live on Pine Street, the kids went to school in Billings, Elizabeth dutifully signed their grade cards as Lizzy, and there was never a better neighbor than the Kastendieck family. His reputation as a community leader extended beyond Christian County to Lawrence County where he reached out to his Masonic brethren to join the Marionville Chapter of the Masonic Lodge. At the same time, his unbroken relationship with the Wesley Methodist Episcopal Church in Billings added to the fond memories of the Kastendieck family. He quietly but surely often spoke of his devotion to the church. He frequently volunteered his talents as a carpenter in the service of the church.[26] His work was as much a passion for helping people as it was an occupation. George built houses in and around Billings, including his own neatly crafted two-story home on Pine Street complete with finely planed, solid black walnut trim.

His neighbors on Pine Street made up a good cross section of Billings citizens. Peter Laney lived a couple of houses down from George and kept a blacksmith shop. The wheelwright Louis Herring lived on one side of George; next-door on the other side were the family of Dr. Eli B. Brown and his large brood of nine children including Eli's son Dr. Frederick H. Brown, already himself a physician at the early age of twenty-three. The Browns had a corner on medical practice in Billings. In addition to having two doctors living under the same roof, another son, John B. Brown, who was a druggist, lived there, too.

In the house down one building from the Browns lived nurse America Wisham and her son Charley. Charley worked as a stationary engineer the same as George had once done. Then came the Landon Garrison family; Landon was a saloonkeeper, and after him Caleb Bales, editor of the local newspaper.[27] Overall, the Kastendiecks lived in an interesting neighborhood comprised of interesting people from different if not class-bound lifestyles. Only in Billings perhaps could you find a blacksmith and a wheelwright, not to mention a stationary engineer and a saloonkeeper, living in perfect harmony on the same street with a house full of doctors and a newspaper editor.

George Dietrich Kastendieck and Elizabeth Ann Keast Kastendieck. This undated photograph is believed to be the couple's wedding portrait taken in 1891. The photographer was Simon H. Wickiser who had a photography studio on Benton Avenue, in North Springfield, Missouri. Jayme Burchett Collection.

Three Generations. George Lord Keast is seen seated on the left; reading clockwise is his daughter Elizabeth Ann Kastendieck, wife Catherine "Kitty" Keast, and baby Frank Andrew Kastendieck. Both girls and boys wore dresses until a certain age. Elizabeth's eyes look distorted in this picture because they were magnified for the camera by the lenses of her eyeglasses. The undated photo was taken about 1893. Jayme Burchett Collection.

Elizabeth Ann (Keast) Kastendieck. A native of Cornwall, England, she was the wife of George Kastendieck, mother of Frank Andrew, George Herman, Katherine Viola, and Hazel Kastendieck. Photocopy of an original photograph; undated but believed to date to around 1900. Collection of the Author.

34

Good Times and Bad Times

L ife in the early part of the 20th Century in Billings was much the same as it was in many other parts of the country. The Kastendieck kids when not in school worked on the farm and at odd jobs around town. There was plenty of local entertainment, and if not in Billings, Springfield was a stone's throw up the road, or Marionville and Aurora were easy visits just across the Christian County line. Something was always going on.

Take for example the southwest Missouri girls' basketball championship of 1915. Hazel, the youngest of the George Kastendieck household, loved sports. Her best sport was basketball, and Billing's High had a girls' team. The annual championship came down to a final game between Billings and the 1914 champs Marionville, on Marionville's home court, with the home team the decided favorite to take the honors.

In a surprise upset, though, Billings won by a score of seventeen to sixteen. The *Springfield Republican* newspaper reported, "The game was fast and hard fought, and not until the final whistle blew was the result of the game certain. Kastendieck, Billings' diminutive forward, was the star of the game, making every point that the winners got."[1] The article did not give Hazel's first name, but her age made her the only Kastendieck it could have been.

The Billings girls' team became legendary in high school sports. On their way to the championship, they beat the Marionville College six by a score of twenty-nine to nine, and chalked up three wins in a single week to become the undisputed victors of 1915. As if not to overlook the boys' basketball team, the *Springfield Republican* noted that the Billings boys' second team fell to the Marionville High boys in the preliminary game in a rough outing that saw forty fouls called in the course of the game.

Frank Andrew Kastendieck, the eldest son of George Dietrich, married Lucy Ann Keatts in 1913—the first of the second-generation Kastendieck offspring to tie the knot—and took a job with one of the regional electric companies.[2] A serious electrical accident ended his career as an electrical engineer and nearly killed him. For the rest of his life he wore the scars of the burns on his left leg and across his right shoulder.[3]

Frank Andrew registered for the World War I draft on June 5, 1917. He and his brother George Herman went together on the same day to register. Frank had turned twenty-five and George was twenty-two. Frank escaped induction and did not serve in the war.[4] By 1917, he was a farmer with a wife and child solely dependent on him. His family status and the residual effects of his accident, including his poor eyesight, qualified him for a deferment. Following the war, the 1920 census found him, Lucy, and their two children, Richard and Valentine, living in a rented place next door to his grandfather George Lord Keast.[5]

Meanwhile, George Herman Kastendieck, the second son of George Dietrich, was at the time of the war still single, living in an apartment at 589 East Elm Street near the Frisco rail yard in

Springfield. He went into the Army on April 26, 1918, giving up a good civil engineer job with the Frisco in the office of Ozark Division Superintendent, J.G. Taylor. On June 4, 1818, George departed for duty overseas.

George Herman Kastendieck served two years as a private in World War I, including a year in overseas assignments with the 89th Division, first with Company C of the 356th Infantry, and then with Company B of the 314th Engineers.[6] He wrote home regularly from the war front describing army life, telling one time how his unit occupied a captured German dugout fitted with all the comforts of home for German officers.[7]

The war ended and George sailed for home out of Brest, France, on May 16, 1919, aboard the USS Montana arriving at Boston ten days later.[8] Three months later, he married Irene Hayes, an up and coming twenty-two year-old professional, courthouse stenographer, and secretary of the local civil service board.[9] The couple lived for a short while with Irene's parents at 974 North Jefferson Street until George could reestablish his civil engineering career.[10]

In 1920, life in Billings was good with the George Dietrich Kastendieck family. The war was over. Sons Frank and George completed college, married, and went out on their own. Katherine finished her degree, too, and was teaching in the public schools while still single and living at home with her parents.[11] Hazel was nineteen, single, and still in school, and living at home, too, but not for long. She married in 1922 in a quiet ceremony at home in Billings. She married an accountant in the oil industry by the name of Walter Shafer, a World War I veteran.[12] Family tradition said she stole him from Katherine. Hazel and Walter settled in Tulsa, Oklahoma, where Walter worked.

Katherine later wed in 1924. She married William Andrews, a veterinarian, and the two moved to Milton, Iowa. Hazel and Katherine left Billings for other more adventurous parts of the country. The Kastendieck boys, on the other hand, stayed closer to home.[13]

The nest was empty. As the years went by, George Dietrich began to show the wear of the passing of time. He retired from the carpentry trade but still spent days in his woodshop mostly to putter around or do some special project for a friend or neighbor. Clutter overran the shop, and it fell into disarray. Nevertheless, one might see George there on any given day in high-bibbed overalls, still sporting that full moustache now white with age, and usually wearing a stylish black fedora hat covering a noticeably thinner head of hair than in the olden days. Behind his wire-rimmed spectacles, however, was the same warm-spirited George Kastendieck who had endured so much sadness in youth but gratefully tempered by the happiness that he and Elizabeth had known up to this point in their marriage.

Nothing lasts forever. The 1920s brought a return of personal grief to the Kastendieck family. Amid the happiness of grandchildren and home life, death came unexpectedly as it often does. It began in 1921 when Elizabeth's mother, Catherine—affectionately called Kitty—died suddenly on May 26, 1921, from a stroke. Then in September, Elizabeth's twelve-year-old nephew died of diphtheria. It seemed that no sooner had the funerals closed than on February 17, 1926, Elizabeth's younger brother George contracted typhoid fever and died at his home in Lawrence County at the age of fifty-six. The next year, George Dietrich Kastendieck died.

For some time, George had been in failing health. He grew tired easily, had trouble catching his breath, and fought off recurring bouts of dizziness and nausea. He chalked it up to the aging process and went about his regular routine. Life was good in Billings and he had helped to make it that way. In Billings, Missouri, in 1927, you could have a new Dodge 4-door sedan for $875 or a new Pontiac for $745. A good used cream separator went for $45, an essential item if you owned dairy cattle as most farmers around Billings did. A year's subscription to *McCall's Magazine* and *The Billings Times* cost $1.75; Gary Cooper in *Arizona Bound* was playing at the Pavilion Theater in Billings while the actor Art Acord in *Hard Fists* was at the Princess Theatre in Aurora.

George cared little about such entertainments and in the final days grew uncharacteristically quiet and reflective, as people had seen him do so long ago when thoughts of his mother Bridget and lost siblings clouded his otherwise sunny outlook.

However, he did not lose his usual positive demeanor. Even as the end drew near, he eagerly sought out Pastor Leland H. Koewing, Minister of the Wesley Methodist Episcopal Church. The two of them heartily discussed plans for the church's future; George wanted to make sure that the church benefitted from his life-long commitment to it.[14]

Neighbors along Pine Street paid short visits to George's home from time to time. Most knew that he was in poor health. Their neighborhood had not changed much in twenty years. Louis Herring still operated his wagon-making shop next door. The Brown medical family lived on the other side. A few new houses sprung up along the north side of Pine and the town was growing, but the neighborhood was much the same as it was a decade ago.[15]

By September of 1927, George's health kept him mostly confined to his home. It was not a gentle disease; few are. Sudden agonizing attacks of cardiac asthma came on, causing him to gasp for breath for long periods at a time. Startling visible

327

pulsations of the arteries were so strong they caused his head to shake involuntarily. He grew pale, his cheeks sunken. His moist eyes widely dilated gave the appearance of staring at nothing in particular. The discomfort was so great that he slept sitting upright. His old friend and neighbor Dr. Fred Brown visited him on October 1. Congestion was setting in, and George's heart was failing rapidly. The aortic valve of his heart was allowing blood to flow in the opposite direction. There was little that doctors could do. Today, modern treatment would call for surgical replacement of the valve, a procedure that greatly reduces the mortality rate. It was 1927, however; the condition was usually fatal, and surgery sometimes hastened the outcome.[16]

George Dietrich had the best medical care available in southwest Missouri for a man in his condition at the time. Fred Brown (who had lost his own father in the past year) was at the peak of his medical career, still keeping a general practice in Billings while serving at the same time on the medical staff of Springfield Hospital.[17] Neither he nor any other doctor, however, had the means to keep George Dietrich alive.

The end came October 24, 1927, at 3:00 o'clock in the afternoon at home in the presence of his family. He was sixty-six years five months and six days old.[18] The official cause of death was "Aortic Insufficiency"; his heart simply gave out. Frank, George's eldest son, officially informed county officials of his death and provided the necessary information that summed up his life on a single page of his death certificate. Dr. Brown did not attempt a lengthy explanation of the cause of death; he made a brief entry and signed it.

A.S. Wallace of Billings had charge of the funeral. They buried George Dietrich in Rose Hill Cemetery near the grave of his brother Andrew and father John Herman, beneath a maple tree, its flaming autumn color radiating like a beacon across the

Christian County countryside. Many were left to mourn his passing, none more so than his family. His older brother John Herman Kastendieck, Jr., survived him, as did half-sister Minnie Kastendieck Riggins living at the time in Talihina, Oklahoma. The rest of the family of the Brooklyn-years family was gone: Amelia, Andrew, all except for a stepbrother Henry Hanson who still lived in nearby Greene County. George Dietrich left five grandchildren and a host of other relatives and friends to mourn his loss.

His obituary appeared in the *Billings Times* November 10. Penned by a dear family member, two lines especially summed up how he would have wanted to be remembered, "Memory of him will be vivid for years to come, and though absent, yet will he be present in the lives of his dear loved ones. May the ties of love, fraternity, and friendship bind our hearts to the cherished hope of meeting him on the glory shore."[19] George Dietrich Kastendieck was a good man. He lived an honest and exemplary life, cut too short by the medical circumstances of his time.

The weather was changing again. Winter would soon blanket the gentle hills with frost and more. A freeze Sunday morning marked the end of the growing season for the year in the Ozarks region. The mercury dropped to 27 degrees by nightfall and a stealthy black frost killed and blackened vegetation without the appearance of the familiar heavy white frost. It would be a lonely winter for the Kastendieck family.

A few days after the funeral, on November 3—Thursday after the black frost on Sunday—George Lord Keast took his daughter Elizabeth—now the widow Elizabeth (Keast) Kastendieck—along with Elizabeth's daughter Katherine (Kastendieck) Andrews and her husband Doc William Andrews—in town from Iowa for the funeral—to visit family and friends in Aurora, Missouri.[20] After a painful loss of a family member, it is better to adopt the philosophy that life goes on than to hide away in secluded mourning. The patriarch George Lord understood that because no one in the family had known more sorrow over the past few years. His wife Kitty had died six years earlier; his grandson died; and only last year he buried his only living son George; and now his son-in-law George Dietrich.

Each tomorrow became another day for Elizabeth and then slipped quietly into the past. The kids stayed with her for a while after the funeral to keep her company; however, they had their own lives to live. Hazel went back to Tulsa and Katherine returned to Milton, Iowa. Frank and George lived closer and looked in on her occasionally to see that she had what she needed. Life went on. The familiarity of a daily routine tempered her grief.

She and George Dietrich were in their thirty-sixth year of marriage when he died and had always kept faithful to the "Home-Like" Methodist Episcopal Church. Elizabeth had joined at an early age and now found extra solace in its activities. Thanksgiving came and then Christmas; the girls came back from Tulsa and Iowa. It was good to have the family together, but George's chair was empty and with it, the holidays seemed vacant, too.

Elizabeth lived alone in the house that George Dietrich built on Pine Street. The months marked bittersweet memories. Her late brother's birthday on January 19; her parent's anniversary on March 31; George Dietrich's birthday on May 18, a day they always found time to celebrate; her mother's birthday on September 17, so close to her own on September 1; and the anniversary of George Dietrich's death in October. Barely had the cycle of memories passed once when they began again.

Then, her father died. George Lord Keast died March 25, 1929, two weeks short of his ninetieth birthday. He came down with a bad case of the flu, and within a week, he died. Elizabeth buried him at Rose Hill and thus inscribed more dates on her circle of memories.

Elizabeth lived another ten years after the death of George Dietrich, surviving the era of the Great Depression and its hardships, keeping her family close, helping out with church activities as she could, and watching her seven grandchildren grow up. At different times in 1938, she noticed a lump in her breast that seemed to get larger as the year went on. Around Christmastime, she promised to go to the doctor after the first of the year. The New Year's activities behind her, she saw Dr. Fred Brown on January 6, 1939. He diagnosed her with cancer. He performed a biopsy that confirmed his diagnosis. Elizabeth was seventy-one; the treatments for cancer in patients of advanced age were few. She underwent x-ray treatment. As was usually the case, x-rays did not arrest the cancer; the treatment contributed to her death.

Dr. Brown last saw her on March 19. In the intervening eleven days, we do not know the intensity of her suffering. We assume that Fred Brown did not leave her to suffer alone but prescribed something to ease the pain and perhaps assigned a nurse to look in on her.

The winter season rolled over. Maybe the spring equinox would bring a miracle of healing as it did the promise of new life. It did not happen. Even the birds of spring were hushed on that quiet Thursday morning, on March 30, 1939. Almost to the day a decade after her father died, Elizabeth Keast Kastendieck died at 5:25 a.m.[21] Frank Kastendieck carried the news of his mother's death to county officials just as he had done for his father before; and Fred Brown signed the death certificate as he had likewise done before, too. A.S. Wallace the undertaker came once again to the Kastendieck home on Pine Street.

Funeral services were at the Methodist Church on Friday at 2:30 p.m.[22] Rev. D.S. Frazier spoke before a congregation of Elizabeth Kastendieck's family, neighbors, and friends, many of whom knew and loved her for almost sixty years from the time they first saw her in Christian County as a young English girl from Tintagel Parish. She was the last of her English family. Her parents and five siblings had gone before her. Her English legacy ran strong in her offspring, however.

None who knew her ever forgot Lizzy (Keast) Kastendieck.[23] She grew up in the countryside of Christian County, and then lived forty-eight years in the town of Billings in the house her husband built. They placed her body in Rose Hill Cemetery, there amid the budding trees and spring flowers. Two new dates entered the cycle of memories: September 17 when she was born and March 30 when she died at the age of seventy-one years six months and thirteen days.

Billings returned to business as usual in April. A year's subscription to the *Billings Times* was $1.00; a pound of marshmallows was 14 cents; a head of lettuce was a nickel; a woman's print dress went for 59 cents. A pound of coffee cost 20 cents, and a five-pound bag of sugar was 23 cents. Corn Flakes sold two packages for 15 cents. A radio could cost from $10 to $25. Playing at the Princess Theater in Aurora was Gary Cooper and Merle Oberon in *The Cowboy and the Lady*.[24]

The Kastendiecks had an estate sale in May. It was the fairest way if not the best way to divide Elizabeth's belongings among the family and to dispose of the items she had kept of George Dietrich's. Her daughter-in-law, Lucy Kastendieck—Frank's wife—bought several items: a steel bed and slats for 50 cents; wash stand for a dollar; table and rocking chair for 60 cents and 50 cents respectively; and a couple of dressers, one for $3 and the other for $5. Lucy's son-in-law, Arthur Schaumann, purchased

120 feet of heavy manila rope paying $4.10 for it and added as a keepsake a sickle and pinchers for 50 cents. One hundred five items sold at the sale, altogether amounting to $113.01. Lucy and Arthur bought some of the most expensive items. The highest priced item to sell, however, was George's coal stove that kept his shop warm for many winters. Mrs. Ralston bought it for $7.00.[25]

The Kastendieck children went their separate ways again, back to their homes but never far removed from each other as a family. Hazel and Walter Shafer bought a home at 811 South Jamestown, in Tulsa. Walter's job in the oil industry was more than enough to support their modest lifestyle in the Tulsa community. The couple did not have children. Walter became a distinguished figure in the Boy Scouts of America helping to guide many young people through the twists and turns of growing up.[26]

Katherine continued to live in Van Buren County, Iowa, a helpmate to Doc Andrews in his veterinary practice at Milton.[27] They adopted a baby boy and named him William Frank, the pride and joy of their lives. One summer day in July 1944, Billie, as everyone knew him, rode his bike into the path of a truck and died instantly. He would have been a junior in Milton High in the fall. Workers had cut down a large tree that blocked part of the view of the street. Billy did not see the truck that hit him until it was too late. Members of the community crowded into the Milton Methodist Church banked full with beautiful flowers, a tribute of the community to the popular young man who met a tragic and unexpected death.[28]

George Herman Kastendieck opened an engineering office in the McDaniel Building on the Springfield Pubic Square and established his engineering credentials early on as secretary of the Missouri chapter of the American Association of

Engineers.[29] He worked for a time for the state as Resident Engineer Inspector for the Missouri Public Works Administration, a job that frequently took him to Jefferson City, Missouri.[30] On one occasion in the spring of 1930, the census taker counted him as a Jefferson City resident before crossing out his name and writing that his enumeration belonged with his wife in Springfield, where they lived.[31]

George entered politics and won election as County Surveyor for Greene County, a post he held for many years until his retirement. George and Irene had two sons and two daughters, in order of their ages: Robert (Bob), Florence Lee, Dorothy Ruth, and Joseph (Joe). Bob and Joe, along with Frank's son, Richard Kastendieck, out of all the descendants of John Herman the immigrant were the lone progenitors of the Kastendieck name past the third generation. Sadly, George Herman's wife Irene died in 1944. He married Florence Remington in 1948.

Meanwhile, Frank Andrew Kastendieck, Lucy, and their two children settled into farm life in Greene County. Frank and Lucy built a house just over the Christian-Greene county line in Pond Creek Township on land that was a wedding present from Lucy's father.[32] They moved their small cabin that once stood in Christian County to the new location and in successive years replaced it with a modern rock structure complete with a slate roof, a basement, and an upstairs; a home having all the conveniences of early 20th Century living.

They build a large barn equipped with the latest electric powered milking machine to support a modest milk production business.[33] A machine shed, chicken house for egg production and Lucy's peacocks, and grain bins rounded out the Kastendieck quarters.

On any given day one might see Frank going about the chores and work of farming wearing his distinctive pith helmet. The pith helmet or sun helmet, also known in European circles as the safari helmet, was a cloth-covered, brimmed hat made of lightweight pressed fiber material routinely worn by the military in hot climates. It was popular with civilian travelers in the mid-19th to the mid-20th Century. Frank wore one as a farmer for the obvious reason to shade him from the hot summer sun. Nevertheless, the common association of the pith helmet with a military purpose gave him a unique identity.

Frank was a small man in physical stature—barely five feet seven inches tall and one hundred sixty-five pounds, but a giant in the Billings community.[34] He lived a mostly quiet life, his fifty-year association with the Masonic Lodge United No. 5 of Springfield being one of his most valued connections. In rural Green County in a place he built with his own hands, Frank spent his life farming. He died of a heart attack in the early evening of March 11, 1969, at home in his living room where his grandson found him slumped over sitting in his favorite easy chair.

Frank Kastendieck died a month short of his seventy-seventh birthday. His funeral was in the usual place at the Methodist Church in Billings, Rev. Roy Wilson officiating. There was a full Masonic service conducted at Rose Hill.[35] Ironically, the year before his death, Frank joined with his siblings and the children of his deceased Uncle Andrew Kastendieck to contribute $100 to the Rose Hill Cemetery Association Trust Fund for perpetual maintenance of the Kastendieck burial lot.[36]

The Carpenter. George Dietrich Kastendieck posed for this photograph in his woodshop on Pine Street, in Billings. He was a lifelong carpenter who built many of the houses in and around Billings. This picture of a cluttered workspace was taken in the early 1920s after his retirement. Jayme Burchett Collection.

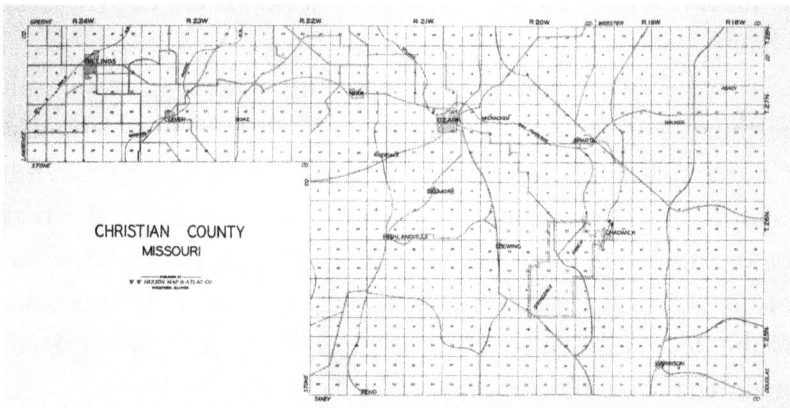

1930 Plat Map of Christian County. The town of Billings was established in Polk Township in the extreme west end of the panhandle of Christian County. The Missouri Kastendiecks first settled there in 1877. By the year 1930, none of the family of John Herman the immigrant remained in Christian County. However, his grandson, Frank, lived on the county line in Greene County on a farm north of Billings. University of Missouri-Columbia, Ellis Library Special Collections, Missouri Secretary of State.

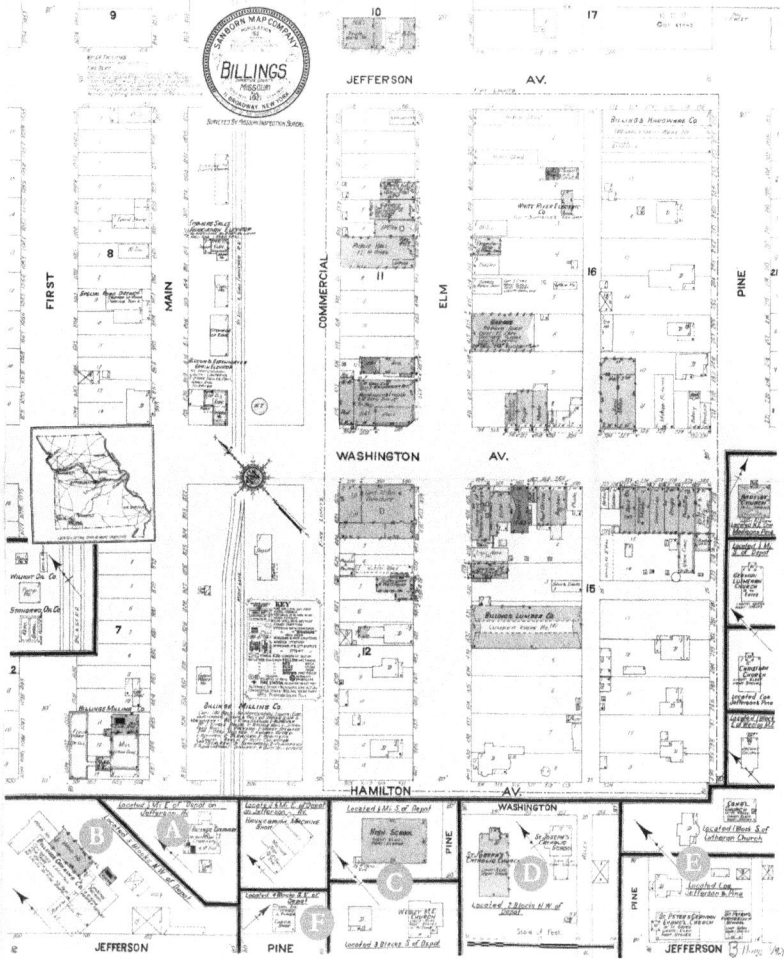

Sanborn Map of Billings. Several addresses important in the life of George Dietrich Kastendieck are shown as insets on this 1921 fire insurance map. The addresses are shown as insets on the map because they were located outside the limits of the main downtown Billings area of the map. Among them are the Cannery and Billings Creamery on Jefferson Street (Insets A and B); the high school and Wesley M.E. Church (Inset C); St. Joseph's Catholic Church and school (Inset D); St. Peter's German Evangelical Church and school and the old Congregational Church (Inset E). George Dietrich's woodshop was located on Pine Street four blocks southeast of the depot (Inset F). Ellis Library Special Collections, University of Missouri-Columbia.

Frank and Lucy (Keatts) Kastendieck. A Christmas photo taken about 1954 pictures the couple in the living room of the house that Frank built. They married in 1913 and were together for more than fifty-five years until Frank's death in 1969. Jayme Burchett Collection.

35

Hermina Elida

Out of all of the immigrant John Herman Kastendieck's children, the least is known of his youngest. Her full name was Hermina Elida Rebecka Kastendieck, known to family and friends as Minnie, or Minna.[1] She was born in Brooklyn, the only surviving child of John Herman's third wife, Elida. There are unresolved contradictions regarding her birthdate. According to the inscription on her gravestone, she was born September 24, 1872; the Kastendieck Family Bible says September 16, 1873, and the 1900 US Census recorded a date of September 1874.[2] She was not on the 1875 New York Census and the 1880 US Census listed her as age six as of June 1880. No birth certificate for her has been located. The 1872 tombstone date is unlikely because it predates the date of John Herman and Elida's marriage in 1873.[3] The date of 1873 is more plausible although it, too, means she came along seven months after the marriage; that leaves September 1874, the date recorded in the 1900 census. These dates are of interest because they reveal not only the pitfalls of family history but also perhaps something about the circumstances of John Herman and Elida Kastendieck's marriage.

Before Hermina was age two, her mother died in the winter of 1876 after giving birth to twins. The twins lived but a few months after Elida Kastendieck died, leaving Hermina as the lone half-sister of her four older Kastendieck siblings.[4]

The only mother Hermina ever knew was Caroline Kastendieck, fourth wife of John Herman, who raised her to adulthood. Hermina left Brooklyn at the age of three and came with the Kastendieck family to Christian County, Missouri. She entered school at the age of six and spent the next dozen years growing up in the community of Billings. Of German Swedish extraction, she was one generation removed from immigration and living under the watchful eye of her extended Kastendieck family in a German-speaking household.[5]

Toward the end her teenage years, she met Andrew Jackson Riggins—known as Andy or A.J., a southern-bred man ten years older than her and lately of Talihina, Oklahoma. Mr. Riggins appeared in Billings seemingly unexpectedly because there was no one of the Riggins name living anywhere near Christian County at the time.

We know little about Riggins' early life, except that he came from Cherokee County, Georgia, born in Canton, on December 5, 1863, of native Georgian parents.[6] As a youth, he came to Arkansas and was educated in the schools of Plainview, Arkansas. When Hermina met him, he was in his mid-twenties, active, and ready to end his bachelor standing.

One suspects that the liaison between Hermina and A.J. had something to do with the railroad. Andrew Riggins was a railroad man. He worked for the Frisco, and the Frisco came through Billings on a regular basis. He began his service with Frisco Lines as a supply man in the summer of 1887, at Talihina, Oklahoma. He served as hostler and fire stoker, and at the time he met Hermina, he stood on the threshold of promotion to engineer.[7] As a hostler, his work confined him to one place, moving trains around the rail yard, but as stoker of the firebox, he kept the steam engine stoked and went wherever it went, including Billings.

The St. Louis-San Francisco Railway, the Frisco, was one of two railroads approved by the government to lay tracks across Indian Territory. (The other was the Missouri-Kansas-Texas, the "Katy"). After a series of bankruptcies, the Frisco emerged to become the principal rail line serving the Midwest. The company's plan to extend tracks all the way to San Francisco fell short by a thousand miles, and the line never went west of Texas. The Frisco operated out of its main rail yard and headquarters at Springfield, Missouri. One of its main lines ran from Springfield, past Billings, to Monett, Missouri, through Hugo, Oklahoma, and on down to Paris, Texas.

Hermina and Andrew wed on a Sunday, November 26, 1893, at the Billings Wesley Methodist Church, Rev. A.M. Hall officiating. Rev. Hall was new and freshly appointed by the St. Louis Methodist Conference as minister of the gospel for Billings.[8] He was a circuit rider for the Springfield District that included Billings and a number of other churches in southwest Missouri.[9]

Almost a year to the day after their marriage, Andrew Riggins got his promotion to locomotive engineer for the Frisco in November of 1894. The job took the couple to Lamar County, Texas, south of the Red River, and to the city of Paris, Texas. Paris was the largest town Hermina or Andrew had ever experienced. The city boasted a population nearing 10,000 residents in 1900. Situated amid gently rolling terrain, Paris was a center for trade and farming that built its economy as a major cotton exchange served by the railroads. The city had a checkered past. Just a few years before in 1893, the town had lynched a black teenager for the alleged murder of a young white girl. Thousands watched him be "tortured and burned to death on a scaffold."[10] Three years later, a fire swept through Paris as if by reprisal burning several blocks of the city. On the plus side of the town's history, on the other hand, Paris was the home of pioneer cattleman John Chisum, of Chisum Trail fame, and one of the town's earliest residents buried there.

The Riggins newlyweds rented a house on the northwest outskirts of Paris west of the Frisco rail yard, in a part of town that escaped the 1896 fire. The engineer job kept Andrew employed year round. Hermina—Minnie to friends and family—dived into the duties of homemaking. The couple eventually had enough money to start a family. Omer Edwin Riggins came along in the fall of 1898, a welcome addition to Andrew and Hermina after six years of childless marriage.[11] Two more sons followed: Harry Baldwin Riggins in September 1900 and Paul Andrew in December 1902.[12]

In due time, railroad work took Andrew and his family to Talihina, Oklahoma—back to the town where his railroad career began. The frontier town of Talihina dated to 1887 when the Frisco built a line through the Choctaw Nation in Indian Territory for the purpose of shipping cattle, timber, and cotton to markets in the East. The name Talihina came from the Choctaw language meaning, "iron road". By 1905, Talihina had a population of 400 souls; Oklahoma statehood came along in 1907; and the population of Talihina edged up to 491 by the time the Riggins arrived. That was about the same size as Hermina's hometown of Billings.

Situated between the Kiamichi and Winding Stair Mountains in Le Flore County, amid an Arcadia-like setting, about half way down the state on the Arkansas-Oklahoma border, Talihina was the kind of small town Andrew and Hermina knew well. Forests of dazzling fall foliage, abundant wildlife, and rivers and streams that meandered through the valley made Talihina an enviable place to live. By 1910, residents enjoyed telephone and electric service and by 1918 a number of churches, stores and two sawmills served the local economy. The beauty of the surrounding landscape and the agreeable healthy climate caused it oddly to become the location of two tuberculosis sanatoriums between 1915 and 1921.[13]

These were the fruitful years of the Riggins family. Andrew and Hermina bought a house on Dallas Street on Talihina's west side and paid for it with cash.[14] They enjoyed all the amenities of home life. The city built concrete sidewalks along Dallas Street in front of their house, and Talihina moved closer to full civilized status.[15] The Riggins sons were out of the nest and winding their way through high school. Omer and Harry remained in Paris, Texas, to finish school while their parents moved to Talihina. Relief swept the Riggins household when they learned that the two escaped injury in a devastating fire in 1916, another conflagration like the 1896 fire that destroyed a major part of Paris where Omer and Harry later lived. Omer finished high school at Paris in 1916 and Harry soon followed.[16]

The two boys—Omer and Harry—were independent at an early age. The Talihina newspaper enviously noted, "Omer and Harry Riggins came up from Paris and visited over Sunday with their parents and their new Ford."[17] Omer set up his own restaurant and grocery store in Talihina. He took out an advertisement on page four of the *Talihina Tribune* that read, "The Frisco Restaurant and Grocery, Omer Riggins, Prop[rietor]." The ad boasted, "Night and Day Prompt Service. Fresh Bread, Pies, and Cakes Baked Daily! Full Line of Groceries and Lunch Hoods, Best the Market Supplies! All Kinds of Cold Drinks! Near Frisco Depot."[18] Overall, an ambitious enterprise for a youngster of nineteen, which one suspects included his parents Andrew and Hermina somewhere in the background.

Moreover, Omer went out of his way to be part of the community. He helped to organize a ball team for Talihina, an arduous task because the town had no ballpark. Nevertheless, Omer took on the job of soliciting uniforms.[19]

The entrepreneurial itch satisfied, by the time they were in their early twenties, Omer and Harry were living at home and working at steady jobs as telegraph operators for the Frisco.[20] For whatever reason, son Paul was living elsewhere and enrolled in school at the age of nineteen at Talihina, according to the US Census.[21]

Meanwhile, Andrew Riggins contented himself with his subscription to the *Talihina Tribune* and Hermina took time to tune up her social connections.[22] She had been married for twenty-five years dutifully following her husband's Frisco assignments. Nevertheless, she had her own personal interests. Hermina was a member of the Order of the Eastern Star, the women's female companion organization to Freemasonry. How she gained entry into the Eastern Star is speculative. A woman received an invitation to join the organization if she had a qualifying relationship to a man who was an affiliated Master Mason. She could not join on her own merit. The relationship rule included literally any kind of even the most distant kin. Family bonds could be by blood or marriage, in which case she may have doubly qualified. Two of her brothers and at least one nephew were associated with Freemason organizations, and it is possible that her husband was as well, although the symbol carved on his tombstone was for the Shriners and not the Masons, which by itself did not qualify Hermina for the Eastern Star. It appears that the Masons came from the Kastendieck side. Hermina's nephew, Frank Kastendieck, was a longtime member of the Masons, and her brother Andrew had membership in the Select Knights of America organization, a quasi-masonic order. It is possible, too, but unproven that Freemasonry in the Kastendieck family extended to the immigrant generation of her father John Herman.

The Order of the Eastern Star was a secret organization. It had as its motto the acronym F.A.T.A.L., which ostensibly stood for "Fairest Among Ten-thousand, Altogether Lovely." It made an appropriate memoir to the deceased on grave markers without betraying the Freemasonry secrets that many think it actually represented. The acronym F.A.T.A.L. had a potentially more sinister ceremonial meaning. According to the Eastern Star Ritual, when a woman initiated into the Order, she confessed it would be fatal to the character of any woman of truth to disclose the masonic secrets. Its cabalistic origins came from the Biblical Song of Solomon, masked by words that contain in part some of the language but not the entire motto.

The three Riggins sons went their separate ways but never ranged far from home. Omer moved to Tuskahoma, Oklahoma, and married a local girl named Nora Haynes.[23] Tuskahoma was a small town in Pushmataha County located on the Frisco tracks a short distance up from Hugo, Oklahoma.

Meanwhile, Paul married a Talihina, Oklahoma, girl of Swedish descent named Nell Bringelson.[24]

Harry married Effie "Dude" McGee, an attractive girl of Choctaw Indian Nation ancestry.[25]

In 1927 Talihina, where Andrew and Hermina continued to live, was still a relatively isolated place, located as it was at the base of the Kiamichi Mountains on the western edge of Le Flore County and north of prairie country. Black bears, coyotes, and other wildlife frequently came down from the foothills and crossed over to one of the many rivers and streams that flowed through the valley. At the same time, beyond the outskirts of the town, Indian residents living in the out-country were a reminder that this was still, in the minds of many, Choctaw Nation.[26]

There were anecdotal stories from time to time that revealed the day-to-day life of a railroad man like Andrew Riggins. For example, one fall day in 1926, he was on the hill engine (an engine that added push power to the main engine) and noticed something that looked like a small trunk in the grass alongside the track.[27] When he went back the next day to retrieve it, the box contained films labeled "Overland Limited". The Overland Limited was a posh passenger train that served points west all the way to the West Coast. Andrew turned the box over to his supervisor who sent it on to its intended address. No one ever revealed what the films were or where they went.[28] On another occasion, the Frisco singled Riggins out for meritorious service for enabling trains at the Talihina rail yard. It seems that Frisco properties at that point ran out of water. Andrew and a couple of his co-workers got the city fire hose, connected it to the city water main, and took care of the problem.[29]

The calendar rolled over to the year 1930. Andrew and Hermina owned a $4,000 home in Talihina, a comparatively nice house for the times; they had a radio set, telephone service, and electricity; and there were grandchildren to occupy them. Son Harry and his wife Effie were renting a house next door. Harry had a good job with the Frisco as a telegraph operator; Effie taught school in the public schools.[30]

Meanwhile, Omer—Hermina and Andrew's oldest child— his wife Nora, and their young brood followed Omer's job as a Frisco agent to Bokchito, Oklahoma, in Bryan County. (Omer had since gone out of the restaurant business.) At Bokchito, the couple owned a modest home and enjoyed many of the amenities that had existed in Talihina, including a prized radio set. The town of Bokchito was a little farther away than Hermina and Andrew would have liked, a few miles east of Durant, Oklahoma, and a good three hours from Talihina. Still, the telephone kept them in touch and able to keep up with the activities of Omer's three little ones: Virginia not yet a year old, Edwin the three-year-old, and most of all grandma's namesake Hermina the second grader.[31]

The third and youngest of the Riggins family, Paul, and his wife Nell lived in Durant, Oklahoma, a short drive from Bokchito along recently designated US Highway 70. They rented a place there while Paul worked as an electrician for the Oklahoma Pipeline Company.[32]

Life was good for Andrew and Hermina Riggins. Andrew was about to retire with a railroad pension, the children were comfortably settled into their lives, and all were well respected in their circle of Oklahoma friends. Then, Hermina died. She was by best accounts a couple of months short of her fifty-seventh birthday when she passed away on August 2, 1931, although her true age has never been resolved. They buried her in the Old Talihina Cemetery on a hillside west of town, over toward Rock Creek, and not far from where she had lived most of her life on Dallas Street. Her remains were not returned to her hometown in Billings; she was one of only two of the original New York-Missouri Kastendiecks not to be buried in Rose Hill Cemetery, the only other being her half-sister Amelia.

The decade of the 1930s that followed Hermina's death was inexplicable in many ways, a decade far removed from anything that had come before. The stock market crashed in 1929, bringing on the worst depression in the nation's history. Moreover, a period of severe drought and dust storms across the Great Plains devastated large regions of Oklahoma. Although the Riggins were never farmers in Oklahoma, the two catastrophes—the Great Depression and the Dust Bowl—proved emblematic of the fortunes of the Riggins family.

Shifting job assignments at the Frisco contributed to a sense of instability. For instance, in a period of three months in 1933, Omer had three assignments as agent: at Springdale, Arkansas in March, then to Moyers, Oklahoma for a week in April, and then to Arkinda, Arkansas, before coming back to Springdale the next year.[33] At the same time, Harry moved to Dunbar, Oklahoma, as agent in April 1933. He made weekend trips back and forth from Dunbar to Talihina to visit his father and friends, traveling with Effie and their new baby daughter, Lillie Jeanne—the granddaughter Hermina never knew. Harry eventually returned on permanent assignment to Talihina as Frisco agent in August 1933.[34]

Andrew Jefferson Riggins retired as engineer in the Central division of the Frisco on December 5, 1933. He retired coincidental with his seventieth birthday, having reached the mandatory age limit for retirement. He worked for the Frisco forty-six years and six months, service that entitled him to a pension of $89.65 a month.[35] He died at Sebastian, Arkansas, on October 20, 1939. The family returned his remains to Talihina for burial beside Hermina in Old Talihina Cemetery.[36]

The personal hardships of the decade of the 1930s were unfortunately not over with the deaths of Hermina and Andrew. Omer was now at Hugo, Oklahoma, stable in his Frisco job as telegrapher. His now grownup daughter Hermina had married a California boy named Paul Echols, and Omer's son Edwin had also married. Both couples moved in with Omer and Nora; none was working in 1940, and all living in Omer's small $1,500 house on his annual salary of $2,300.[37]

Harry Riggins, meanwhile, followed the Frisco and moved to Kosoma, Oklahoma, in Pushmataha County, moving there from

Antlers, Oklahoma. His job as a depot agent for the Frisco was not at the same pay grade as his brother's as a telegrapher (Harry made $1,440 a year in 1940), but he made enough to rent a nice place on Miller Moyers Road at $15 a month, the work was steady, and little Lillie Jeanne was doing well in school.[38]

The saddest story of the Riggins family was with Paul, the youngest son of Andrew and Hermina.[39] He married young to Nell Bringelson. The couple had no children, and after a series of personal tragedies in her Bringelson family, Nell had a nervous breakdown.[40] She entered the Oklahoma State Hospital at Norman, Oklahoma, when she was thirty-five years old. It was 1939. Mental health care was inadequate and so was the facility. The hospital grew out of the 1915 part of the legislative "Lunacy Bill" that created several state asylums. Intended as a treatment center at Norman, people continued to refer to the facility pejoratively as the Central State Hospital for the insane. We do not know the exact nature of Nell's illness. However, it effectively ended her sixteen-year marriage to Paul. He moved to Wewoka, Oklahoma, in Seminole County and took a room on South Hitchita Street. He took odd jobs as an electrician that brought in about $700 a year.[41] He went to Denver, Colorado, and then back to Arkansas where in 1941 he married the much younger Cora Bell Freeman of Heavener, Arkansas, and left Nell behind.[42] Paul died in 1970 at Heavener, Oklahoma, buried there at Memorial Park Cemetery.[43] Nell, meanwhile, lived to a good age. She died at Yukon, Oklahoma, outside Oklahoma City, in 1980 at the age of seventy-six.[44] She never remarried and retained her married name as Nell Riggins.[45] When she died, relatives returned her remains to Talihina for interment at Old Talihina Cemetery with other members of the Bringelson family.

With the passing of Paul, the Riggins brothers were no more. Omer had died suddenly of a heart attack at Wister, Oklahoma, many years before, in 1951, buried at Heavener, Oklahoma, where he spent the last years of his life.[46] Harry died in 1968, buried at Mount Olivet Cemetery in Hugo, Oklahoma, a unique site for a final resting place.[47] Mount Olivet Cemetery had a section called Showmen's Rest filled with animal-themed pedestals and gravesites. The town of Hugo was once famous as Circus City USA and consequently became the final resting place for many circus performers.

The legacy of Hermina Elida Kastendieck continued through her grandchildren, especially her granddaughter, family historian Lillie Jeanne Riggins-Doyle, only child of Harry and Effie Riggins. With Lillie, too, went the heritage of the immigrant John Herman Kastendieck of Billings, Missouri, her great grandfather. Lillie carried the Kastendieck legacy well into the 20th Century. She died in 2008.[48]

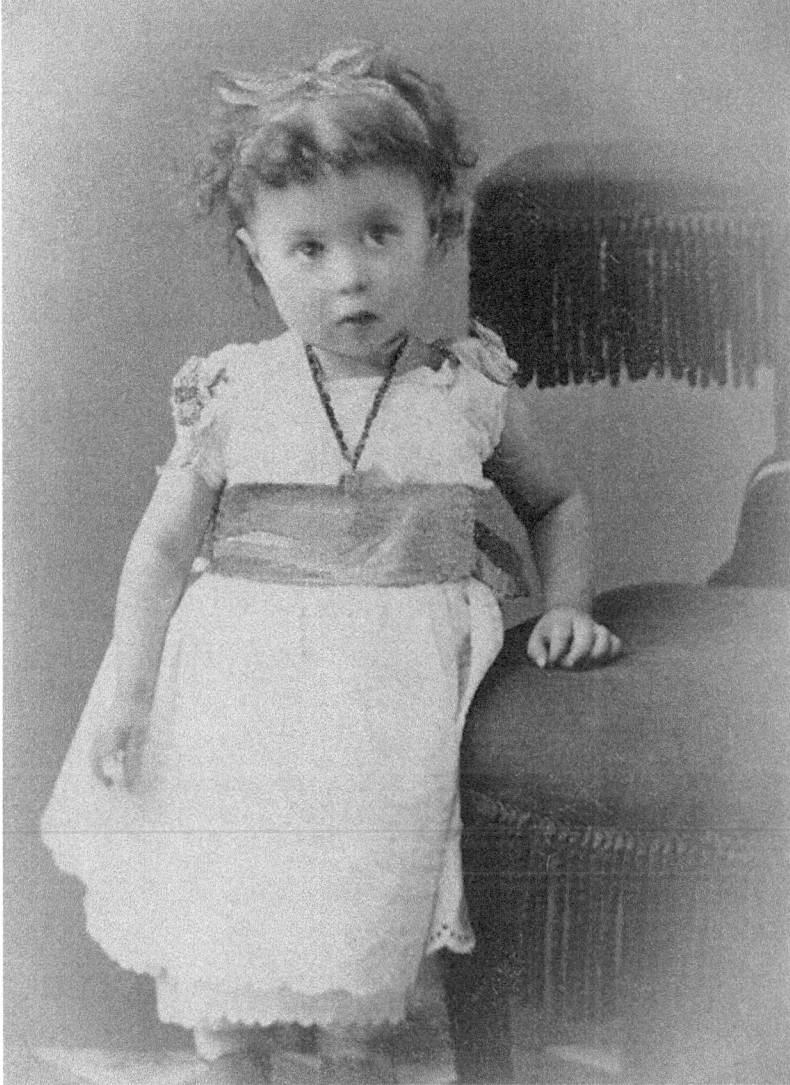

Hermina Elida Kastendieck. This picture of Hermina as a little girl was taken soon after her mother died in 1876 and about the time the Kastendieck family moved to Billings, Missouri. Augusta Kastendieck Family Album.

Old Talihina Depot. Long abandoned, the Talihina passenger and freight depot was in service in 1924. It stood near the terminus of Dallas Street, the street on which Andrew and Hermina Riggins lived at the time. Photograph taken in the 1950s. Frisco Archives.

Texas-Oklahoma Map. Circles mark the locations of Hermina and Andrew Riggins at the Frisco stations of Paris, Texas, and Talihina, Oklahoma (Talihina was not recorded by name on this 1911 map). Towns where the Riggins sons worked for the Frisco included Durant and Hugo. Hermina's sister, Amelia Kinlock and her husband, lived at the Frisco rail center at McAlester, Oklahoma. Modified excerpt from Clason's Map of Texas, Baylor University.

Andrew Jackson Riggins. Mr. Riggins worked for forty-six years for the Frisco Railroad as a locomotive engineer. He and Hermina (Kastendieck) Riggins lived and raised their family at Paris, Texas, and Talihina, Oklahoma. This portrait appeared in the *Frisco Employees' Magazine* upon on his retirement in 1933.

1909 Frisco Locomotive. The man with his foot on a block is William Thompson Fuller, locomotive engineer and probable co-worker of Andrew Jackson Riggins. Engine number 1259 was built by Baldwin Locomotive Works in 1909 and made the run from Paris, Texas, to Monett, Missouri, through Billings. The other members of the crew are unidentified. The photo dates to about 1915. Baldwin Locomotive Works Archives.

Parade around the Public Square of Paris, Texas. Citizens gathered in a scene of downtown Paris, Texas, on the day the town lynched an accused murderer. This picture taken in 1893 shows the architecture of the city shortly before Andy and Hermina Riggins moved there. Library of Congress.

Effie McGee. A Native American descendant, Effie McGee was a tribal member of the Choctaw Nation. This portrait dates to 1922, four years prior to her marriage to Harry Riggins, grandson of the immigrant John Herman Kastendieck. Effie claimed the distinction in the McGee family of coming into the world as the only baby delivered by her father. Photograph, Collection of the Author.

36

John Herman, Jr.

It looked for the longest time like John Herman, Jr., would be the only child to be born of John Herman and Bridget Kastendieck. After his birth on December 6, 1855, five-and-a-half years went by.[1] Three times Bridget became pregnant, and three times the babies did not survive. Then came a succession of brothers and sisters that filled the Kastendieck household: George Diedrich, Andrew, Amelia, and Hermina.

John Herman, Jr., was always the big brother in the fittest sense of sibling relationships. He began school in Brooklyn well ahead of his siblings and finished before his youngest sister was old enough to begin. He was thirteen when his mother died, a teenager old enough to feel the full impact of her loss. He was the big brother thereafter to whom the younger Kastendieck children always looked for support and guidance.

Many years have passed since those formative beginnings in Brooklyn, New York. Memories of the childhood of John Herman, Jr., were lost in the dust of time. We can only imagine that aside from the pain of death that too often visited the Kastendieck household, growing up in Brooklyn was like that of any other young man coming of age. He went to school, made friends, helped out in his father's grocery store, and knew the routine of living amid the sprawl of a large metropolitan place like New York, situated as it were on the adventurous waters of the Atlantic Ocean.[2] There is no reason to think he was enamored with fishing and boating, but he surely made such activities part of his youth. It is easy to imagine, too, that he accompanied his Uncle Dietrich Kastendieck on frequent trips to Prospect Park a few blocks from his home on Van Brunt Street, in Brooklyn, to hunt wildlife and add to Dietrich's growing taxidermy collection.[3] Prospect Park was then a sprawling expanse of several hundred acres of lakes and forest on its way to becoming a protected natural habitat along with Central Park in Manhattan.

John Herman, Jr., was popular if a story that appeared in the *Brooklyn Eagle* is any indication. It seems he ran the 1877 Resolute Pleasure Club fall picnic. He organized it to the grand pleasure of all who attended, complete with dancing and all the accoutrements of a good picnic. The *Eagle* said, "Everybody agreed that the event surpassed all preceding ones.[4]

By this time John Herman, Jr., had reached his twenty-first birthday and entered the world of "coming of age" as it legally applied in those days.[5] His father had moved the Kastendieck family to Missouri, to a farm in Christian County, and left John, Jr., behind in Brooklyn to tend the grocery store on Van Brunt Street.[6] His Uncle Dietrich had arranged with John Herman, Sr., to take over the Brooklyn grocery enterprise. Two years later, John Dietrich sold out and followed his brother to Missouri. John Herman, Jr., followed suit and left Brooklyn to rejoin the Kastendieck family in Christian County, Missouri. He was near the same age as his father when John Herman, Sr., had years before left the rural comfort of the old Kastendieck home in Morsum, Hanover, Germany, for the adventure of the New

World and a life in the city. John Herman, Jr., reversed the adventure, leaving the big city for the unknown prospects of frontier life in the small town of Billings.

Down the road, a short distance from the Kastendieck farm in Polk Township was Thomas Stone's place. Mr. Stone was a millwright by trade—a machinist who kept the equipment running—who had moved his family from Carbondale, Illinois, to Billings to follow the milling business.[7] Another miller, John Owen, had already moved his mill to Billings in 1875.[8] Milling became a quick success in Christian County with several mills spread across the county, a ready livelihood for a man of Thomas Stone's skills.[9]

Mr. Stone, a Kentuckian by birth, and his Tennessee-bred wife, Esther May had a large family, parceled out by gender four to three in favor of daughters including twins. The youngest daughter was Mary, born on January 14, 1859, in Illinois, next to last in the age hierarchy of her siblings.[10] The Stones arrived in Billings sometime after 1881. It did not take long for Mary to catch the attention of John Herman Jr., an up and coming young man with adult responsibilities. He paid his personal property taxes in October of 1884, a modest 91 cents on a comparatively small property estate of $75 but large enough to qualify him as an eligible bachelor with an attractive upside.[11]

A romance blossomed, and the couple married June 17, 1885, at the Billings Christian Church—the avowed faith of the Stone family but not necessarily the Kastendiecks.[12] Nevertheless, it was a Wednesday, weekday wedding, holding to the Kastendieck tradition of having very few Sabbath day weddings. John Herman, Jr., was age thirty when he married; Mary was twenty-six, not yet an unmarried woman by definition but a bit past the usual age for marrying as it was in the 19th Century.[13]

The newlywed couple bought forty acres of land in Polk Township doubtless with the intent to pursue a livelihood in farming like Uncles Dietrich and Andrew Kastendieck and like most young men of John Herman's age in Christian County.

The forty acres he bought lay in Township 27, Range 24—specifically the southwest quarter of the southwest quarter of Section 16 located toward Marionville at the extreme west end of the panhandle of Christian County, and a stone's throw from the Frisco tracks.[14] The property was about two miles southwest of Billings. The certificate of sale designated the land as "Township School Land," making of it a good investment both in property and in the establishment of schools.

Beginning with the admission of Missouri to the Union in 1820, the federal government gave this type of land to the state of Missouri to benefit public education in the various counties. Township School Land was available for purchase in Missouri until 1900. The law allowed the sale of land from each Section 16 in every township in the state with profits going to build schools or pay teachers. John Herman paid $170 for his forty acres. At $4.25 per acre, that was the going price for land around Billings in 1885.

There is no indication that John Herman, Jr., ever seriously engaged in the work of farming, or that he ever intended to. His name never appeared on the rolls of farmers of the Billings Creamery like that of his Uncle Diedrich or his brothers did, the latter being at least token farmers if not totally committed to agriculture. The land that John Herman purchased was the kind of hardscrabble acreage that entertained the scrub oak and flint rock of parts of Polk Township that quickly took the romance out of agriculture.[15] He quit farming, bought a house on the north side of Oak Street in Billings, paid his property taxes, and moved to town; noticing at the time that the assessed value of his personal property had gone up a few dollars but his taxes had gone down a dime to 82 cents.[16] All heads of household plus those people within a household who had their own separate livestock, money, or household items paid taxes in Christian County. Taxes went up and down depending on property owned in any given year.

Mary and John Herman, Jr., began what would soon become difficult times in starting a family. They wed in June of 1885, bought the Township School Land in August of that year, and by 1886 had lost their first child. The maturity of their years helped to sustain them in the first trying years of their marriage. The curse of infant mortality reared its head again.[17] It was particularly rampant in Billings. In one church alone—St. Peter's Church—in a period of twenty years from 1880 until 1900, church records recorded one hundred deaths, of which seventy-five were infants and children.[18]

John Herman, Jr., and Mary went on to have six children; only four survived infancy. Ralph died in the summer of 1886 barely a year after their marriage.[19] Ceceil came along in 1887, lived but a short time, and died in 1889.[20] By now, Mary had turned thirty, still in her childbearing years but childless. The next years proved to be fulfilling. Son John Leroy "Roy" Kastendieck was born in the spring of 1890, followed at two-year intervals by Minnie in 1892, Raymond in 1894, and Mildred in August of 1896. All lived to adulthood.

Billings was bustling. People streamed into town in large numbers; in wagons, on foot, and by train. John Herman, Jr., saw a growing need for new housing. He cast off the mantle of farmer and became a carpenter, a builder of houses. No one remembers exactly how he acquired the trade of house builder or who taught him how to be a carpenter. He invested in the tools of the trade, built a wood shop, and went into business. His business was not limited exclusively to homes; if there was a need for carpentry work, he was available. People knew him as the contractor for the new St. Peter's Church.

The founding of the Billings St. Peter's congregation dated to 1879, about the time the Kastendiecks first arrived in Billings. The Germans were predominately of the Evangelical faith, but there was no Evangelical Church in Billings. Up until then, itinerant evangelical pastors met their spiritual needs, holding services in homes. The Home Mission of the German Evangelical Church of North America, an outgrowth of the German Evangelical Church of the Union in Germany—a combination of the Lutheran and Reformed churches of Germany—encouraged the organization of a German church in Billings. A year later in the summer of 1880 the first building went up at Jefferson and Pine Streets dedicated on June 20, 1880, on land provided by the Frisco Railroad for the generous fee of one dollar.[21] The building served the congregation as a house of worship for more than a dozen years when church leaders decided that the church needed a larger and more sumptuous sanctuary. They moved the old building to the back of the lot to make way for the new structure. (The old St. Peter's served for many years as the church's Sunday school and fellowship hall before being torn down in 1967.)[22] In the summer of 1892, the church awarded the contract to construct the new church to John Herman, Jr., and on October 30, 1892, they laid the cornerstone.[23] The entire town celebrated. An article appeared in the local newspaper that summed it up.[24] "Never in the history of our little city [Billings] has any event, political, social or religious ever created so great and undivided enthusiasm, as did the laying of the cornerstone of the new German Evangelical church on Sunday last. On Saturday evening people from the country began pouring in from every direction by wagon loads and took up quarters with their German friends for a night's rest."

The article continued, "The morning trains from east and west brought additional visitors. As the morning hours wore along, the sun began to thrust its friendly rays through the foggy crust of the autumnal sky, seemingly anxious to add its charm to the solemnity of the occasion…and by nine o'clock, the hour appointed, fully 400 people covered the church lot."[25]

The crowd moved over to the nearby Christian Church building for a service. The St. Peter's congregation continued to worship at the Christian Church courtesy of the hospitality of the Christian elders during construction of the new St. Peter's. Moreover, the Christian Church and not the German St. Peter's Church was where one might most often find John Herman, Jr., because it was the site of worship of the Stone family and John Herman's wife Mary Stone, although he was by longstanding tradition of the Kastendieck family a Methodist Episcopalian.

It took John Herman, Jr., about a year to build St. Peter's at a final cost to the congregation of $2,351.[26] Eighty-two church families donated some $2,000 toward the overall construction budget, including John Herman's contract. Nine years later, the congregation retired a debt of about $800. Part of that was the cost of the church bells, cast by a St. Louis company and delivered by the Frisco at a total cost of $292.30, more than 10 percent of the cost of the building. Workers installed the bells, tuned to D and F sharp, in the tower of the new sanctuary for $3.50.

St. Peter's Church remains a time-honored tribute to the carpentry skills of John Herman, Jr., and a living example of his attention to detail. The elegant high arched ceiling, Germanic interior and Gothic pointed windows reveal the best of artistry in the finely dressed woodwork. Behind the slightly elevated pulpit, high on the end wall in large German script from the Gospel of St. Luke is the proclamation imperfectly translated, "Ehre sei Gott in der Höhe Friede auf Erden, und den Menschen ein Wohlgefallen" ["Glory to God in the highest, and on earth peace and goodwill to all people"]. It stands as an enduring testimony to the all-German language congregation that once called St. Peter's home. Dedication of the church was on September 24, 1893.[27]

Having a construction business in Billings could have its downside. Such a case involved John Herman, Jr., one time when he took on too much debt and ended up in court. Shortly before he contracted to build St. Peter's Church, he co-signed a promissory note along with his brothers-in-law, William M. Stone and Henry H. Stone, for $345.01, on August 1, 1891, payable in one year at 8 percent interest to Gustave E. Eis. The transaction took place at the Old National Bank of Centralia, Illinois, under the scrutiny of Eis' attorney W.T. Lamkin. Mr. Eis was a well-to-do manufacturer and jobber of cigars and tobacco—among his many other business interests—who lived in Centralia, Illinois. His Big Injun cigar factory was one of the most successful such enterprises in the United States.[28] How and for what reason the Billings trio sought him out for a loan is unknown. Eis was reputed to invest in entrepreneurial ventures like, for example, a construction company, or anywhere such a loan might foreshadow success and add to his considerable wealth. The loan deal may also have been a matter of old acquaintances. The Stone family came from the same part of Illinois as Mr. Eis; the Stones were originally from Jackson County and Eis lived in nearby Marion County, Illinois. In any event, John Herman, Jr., and the Stone brothers defaulted on their loan, and Eis filed a lawsuit in Christian County Circuit Court seeking a judgment against the borrowers. The Court issued a summons on February 3, 1894, for the defendants to appear at the courthouse in Ozark, Missouri, and answer Mr. Eis' petition. Sheriff D.F. Thompson delivered the writ of summons to Henry Stone but was unable to serve William Stone or John Herman, Jr., because, he said, they were "not found in my said county". The sheriff added $2.40 in fees for his trouble in trying to locate them.[29] In the end, nothing came of the matter. The plaintiff filed no further action with the court, indicating that the debt was paid and the complaint settled out of court.

John Herman, Jr., never defaulted on another loan, at least not one that required court action. However, a few years later in 1915 circumstances reversed when John Herman filed suit in circuit court against Herschel Garoutte for the collection of an alleged balance of $1,195 on a building contract. That suit, too, settled out of court and nothing more came of it.[30]

John Herman Kastendieck, Jr., The oldest son of John Herman and Bridget Kastendieck grew up and was educated in Brooklyn, New York, before moving to Christian County, Missouri. This portrait dates to about the time he left Brooklyn around 1878 when he was in his early twenties. From Augusta Kastendieck Family Album.

St. Peter's Church. John Herman Kastendieck, Jr. built this church in 1892-1893. Workers moved the old St. Peter's church, visible in the rear and later torn down in 1967, to make way for building of the new structure. He originally designed and constructed the elaborate steeple shown here. However, storm damage caused its replacement by a plain enclosure of a lower profile. Known as St. Peter's Evangelical for many years, the church today is St. Peter's United Church of Christ. Photo courtesy of David Gay.

37

Life on Oak Street

John Herman, Jr., was a responsible member of the Billings community who met his financial obligations. He dutifully paid his taxes each year with receipts recorded in the county records under a bewildering array of ways to misspell Kastendieck.[1] From records, it is hard to sort out the tax receipts between John Herman, Sr., and John Herman, Jr. The Christian County records did not always distinguish between the two, except that John, Jr., usually, though not always, paid his taxes at the first of the year. John Herman, Sr., on the other hand, always waited until the last minute to pay up, harkening back to a time in Brooklyn when paying taxes was not one of his more responsible characteristics.

One would not want to accuse John Herman, Sr., of trying to dodge the assessor. He had money from the sale of his grocery business in Brooklyn but never reinvested it to any extent in personal property. Compared with his brother Dietrich's investment in the Kastendieck-Blades Milling Company, for instance, on any given year John Herman's property value averaged anywhere from $50 to $200 while Dietrich 's personal property sometimes exceeded $4,000!

The taxes of John Herman, Jr., increased noticeably in 1897 and 1898, most likely because of county administration, inventory, and reassessment of property upon the death of his father in 1897.[2]

House building provided a good living to John Herman and his family. (Following his father's death, he dropped the sobriquet, Jr.) There was usually work year round, except in some years when a hard winter shut down construction for a couple of months.[3]

Carpentry occupied others of the Kastendieck family and their associates. George Dietrich, John Herman's brother, opened a shop on Pine Street and built houses but specialized in cabinetry and trim work. John Herman and George Dietrich's adopted brothers, George and Henry Hanson, were both in the plastering trade; and both George Dietrich and John Herman each had a brother-in-law in the lumber business. This conglomerate of trades all related to house construction but never became a formal entity. Each operated independently and remained self-employed in much the same way that the immigrant Kastendieck brothers had run their grocery businesses in Brooklyn. Each had a grocery store but no business partnership ever formed.

The twentieth century brought new challenges and opportunities. The average worker in the United States made $12.98 a week for fifty-nine hours of work. The automobile made its entrance but not for a while in Billings. The industrial age was in full swing. Mass production meant lower prices that ushered in the decade of materialism and consumerism. People read the catalogs of Sears Roebuck and Montgomery Ward more than any book except the Bible. The catalogs were a fixture in most rural outhouses. The *Billings Times* followed the great events that swept the nation—good and bad. The assassination of President McKinley was in 1901; the first flight of the Wright Brothers at Kitty Hawk occurred in 1903; and the devastating San Francisco earthquake killed more than 700 people in 1906.

On the political side, the United States Supreme Court ruled in 1904 that African Americans had no right to vote, accenting some of the worst of the Jim Crow years. The number of blacks lynched across the country rose to 115 during the decade, including several in the Ozarks.[4]

On the lighter side, people purchased sheet music to the most popular songs at the dime store, especially *Sweet Adeline*, the most popular song of the decade. The hand-cranked Victrola went on the market in 1903. Moreover, of course, the era of silent films did not bypass Billings, Missouri.

John Herman turned fifty-four in 1910, still living on Oak Street, in Billings. The kids were all teenagers at various stages of their educations and intent on completing high school and beyond at a time in America when only one-third of children enrolled in elementary school and less than 10 percent graduated from high school. Education was always a point of pride for the Kastendieck family going back at least to the years in Brooklyn. John Herman took out a mortgage on his home, in part to fund college.[5] Then World War II came. John Herman watched a nephew and both of his sons go to war, the first Kastendiecks to fight in an American war.

The war ended and all the Kastendieck boys came home.

In time, the Kastendieck children moved away from Billings and went their separate ways. By 1930, there were only three families of the Kastendieck name still residing in Polk Township: John Dietrich, Jr., his son Karl, and John Herman, Jr.[6]

John Herman and Mary lived out their lives in Billings, never wanting for much, and satisfied with the joys of raising a family and the meager entertainments available to them. They were irregular but good churchgoers and supportive of the Billings community. They bought themselves a radio set, one of the guilty indulgences of their old age.[7]

John Herman Kastendieck, lifelong builder and contractor, died at home with his family at his side on August 2, 1935, at the age of seventy-nine. Dr. Fred Brown came by the house to see him for the last time in the afternoon but nothing more could be done to reverse the chronic heart disease (Myocarditis and Arteriosclerosis) that had afflicted him for the past several years; he died quietly late on the evening of August 2, of old age.[8]

The funeral occurred as John Herman would have prescribed it. Rev. Arthur Gray came to the Kastendieck house and led a simple service in the place that John Herman had called home for most of his adult life. Never a stickler for religious preferences, the undertaker noted in his report simply that John Herman was protestant. His sons paid for his burial at Rose Hill.[9] He was the firstborn of the immigrants John Herman, Sr., and Bridget Kastendieck and the last of the Kastendieck siblings to pass away.

Mary Stone Kastendieck lived on for another eleven years and nine months. The end for Mary came on May 26, 1947. She died of a heart attack—in medical terms, embolism of the left femoral artery. She went to Springfield Baptist Hospital where she hung on for four days. The auricular fibrillation caused by the attack proved to be too much and she succumbed on the afternoon of the twenty-sixth, a Monday.[10] The front page of the *Christian County Republican* sadly announced her passing. She did not die at home in Billings, as she would have wanted. Nevertheless, the funeral service took place at home on a Wednesday afternoon in the same house on Oak Street where she and John Herman had lived together for fifty years, her last years alone on a small income from unspecified sources.[11]

Her children came home from all parts: Roy from Bristow, Oklahoma; Ray from Gary, Indiana; Minnie from Joplin, Missouri; and Mildred from Clayton, Missouri. The congregation of the Billings Christian Church where she had married and been a lifelong member gathered to pay respect to the venerable citizen from Illinois who for sixty of her eighty-nine years was a resident of Billings, Missouri. She went to rest beside John Herman, Jr., in Rose Hill Cemetery.[12]

Hazel Kastendieck Shafer, reflecting from memory on her Kastendieck genealogy, wrote in her notes, "John Herman Kastendieck—married to Mary Stone—they had six children; two died in infancy or childhood—four lived: Roy, Minnie, Ray, and Mildred. Ray lives in [the] Terra Haute, Indiana, area and is an architect. Roy and Minnie are deceased. We think Mildred is still living somewhere in Florida."[13]

Roy Kastendieck—christened John Leroy Kastendieck—followed his father's example as a building contractor.[14] Born in 1890, he claimed the distinction of being the first surviving grandchild of the immigrant John Herman, Sr., firstborn of the third generation of Missouri Kastendiecks.[15]

He finished college—the first Missouri Kastendieck to do so—and took a job with the Empire District Electric Company as Building Superintendent, in Riverton, Kansas, but soon left that for a teaching job in Collinsville, Oklahoma.[16]

Then World War I came in July 1914. For a brief time it looked as if President Woodrow Wilson would keep the United States neutral in the conflict, but in April 1917 the country entered the War. The next month, Roy registered for the draft on May 29, 1917, the first Kastendieck to offer himself in an American War. He registered in Cherokee County, Kansas, where he worked but gave Billings as his home of residence on the draft form.[17] A year later, almost to the day, his registration number came up and on May 28, 1918, he traveled to Ozark, Missouri, and joined the Army. He served overseas from August 16, 1918 to February 12, 1919, with Company E of the 313th Engineers until honorably discharged in July of 1919 at the rank of corporal.[18] He came home to Billings and moved back in with his parents on Oak Street, picked up the carpentry trade of his father, and prepared for whatever came next. He was age twenty-seven and single.[19]

Not an imposing figure but of average height and medium build, Roy Kasetndieck stood about five feet nine inches tall; nevertheless, his dark brown eyes, black hair, and light complexion gave him a distinctive appearance. [20] He was working contentedly in Billings in January 1920; by April 21, 1920, he was married and back in Oklahoma. How and when he met Virgie Irene Anderson is unknown. He had taught in the Collinsville, Oklahoma, schools before the War. She was an Oklahoma girl, eighteen years old at the time, and eleven years Roy's junior. He took her out of high school, married her in Bristow, Oklahoma, and became an Oklahoman ever after.[21]

Roy and Virgie started their family in Bristow where two daughters were born. They left Oklahoma for La Feria, Texas, where another daughter was born in 1926.[22] Roy gave his occupation then as farmer on his daughter's birth certificate, no doubt in part because he now owned the Christian County forty acres deeded to him as the oldest son by his father.[23] However, Roy more often worked as a contractor, following jobs wherever the work took him. He next settled in Harlingen, Cameron County, Texas, rented an apartment at 1126 East Fillmore, in Harlingen, and took a carpentry job at the local cement plant.[24]

Roy and Virgie came back to Missouri for a short time in 1931 but did not remain long and returned to Bristow, Oklahoma, sometime before 1934 when the last of their four daughters was born.[25] Their four children were Mildred D., Rhea Luella, Virginia Ruth, and Mary Ann. Roy rented a place for $20 a month at 230 East Eighth Street, in Bristow, and settled into his acquired trade as a building contractor.[26] Here, in Bristow, the couple lived out the remainder of their lives.

Roy registered for the World War II Draft in 1942, as all men under the age of sixty-five were required to do, but never served in that war. He was age fifty-one when the war broke out, overweight for his height, with an ominous knot on his temple, and in a class of draft registrants born before 1897 unlikely wanted by the draft.[27] He listed himself as a building contractor on his registration card.[28]

Roy Kastendieck died on February 4, 1954, at a hospital in Muskogee, Oklahoma, buried with military honors at Bristow. Virgie requested a plain granite marker for his grave but the Army installed one in bronze, a tribute to his World War I service inscribed "Oklahoma Cpl Co E 313 Engineers World War I." Remembered on the plaque as an Oklahoman from his adoptive state, he was actually at the time of the war, a Missourian.[29] Back in his home town of Billings, a brief announcement of his death appeared in the *Billings Times*.[30]

His death preceded Virgie's by more than thirty-seven years. She never remarried and died in 1991.[31] Interment of both Roy and Virgie was in Oak Lawn Cemetery, in Bristow, Creek County, Oklahoma.[32]

Hermina M. Kastendieck was second in line after Roy of the children of John Herman, Jr., and Mary Stone Kastendieck. She took the name of her Aunt Hermina. Affectionately called Minnie, her life was less adventurous than that of her siblings but nevertheless fulfilling and relatively prosperous. She grew up in Billings, graduated from Billings High, and took a job in the Billings Bank as a bookkeeper. The War came on and for a while, the nation's attention remained fully riveted on its outcome. On June 3, 1918, Minnie turned twenty-seven. The end of the war was not yet in sight. She still lived unmarried at home with her parents.

The war interrupted many a romance in those days. A young man went off to fight in a distant land leaving a sweetheart behind to await anxiously his return. We cannot say that the war was the cause of Minnie's hesitancy to wed. Marriage turns on the right person at the right time. When it came to marriage, cautious hesitation ran in the Kastendieck family. Minnie's mother, for instance, did not tie the knot until she was past her twenty-sixth birthday.

All of that changed for Minnie in 1920, about the time of the enumeration of the 1920 census. No official document has been uncovered of her marriage, but the census preserved a record of its circumstances. She met William Weaver Davis, a bachelor closing in on his fortieth year and ten years Minnie's senior. William was in the lumber business. Kansas-born out of Elk City, Kansas, he lived in Webb City, Missouri, and served as general manager for the Webb City lumberyard and other yards in his geographic area.

The details of the courtship of Minnie and William have passed from memory, but one imagines that their paths may have first crossed in Billings. Minnie's father was a building contractor with an obvious demand for lumber. It is doubtful that Billings came under the management oversight of William Davis; nevertheless, one can see how two people living apart but with much in common could bump into each other.

Events progressed. Minnie quit her bookkeeping job in Billings and moved to Webb City to take a similar job as a bank stenographer. Perhaps a career move serendipitously took Minnie to William's hometown. Perhaps she met William for the first time in January of 1920, the month her name appeared in the census. She and William lived near each other in Webb City. She rented a house on Third Street, and he lived in a rented cottage nearby. At this point, the census weaves a tangled web. The census takers counted Minnie in Webb City on January 2, working at the bank, and single.[33] On January 7, they counted her again in Billings living with her parents on Oak Street.[34] Meanwhile, the same 1920 census caught William on January 13 in Webb City living as a lodger just off Liberty Street—married to Minnie![35]

Census taking was not a high art form in the early 20th Century. As mysterious as events seemed, there was no doubt a simple explanation. The result was that the couple married about 1920 and perhaps then told Minnie's parents about it later. In any event, Minnie settled into housekeeping in Webb City.

Despite their relatively late marriage, it was the first marriage for both of them. Their first child, a daughter Helen Frances, came along in 1923, followed by William, Jr., in 1924. They soon moved to nearby Joplin, Missouri, bought a nice house in the two-hundred block of North Joplin Street, and Minnie took up homemaking. William did well in the lumber business, progressing from manager to owner of multiple lumberyards.[36] Minnie kept house and looked after the kids. A radio was their common source of enjoyment.[37] They lived in the same house on Joplin Street for many years, moving later to a place on North Sergeant Avenue, in Joplin. Time went by without much interruption in the normal course of events. A surprise came along in 1932 in the person of son Richard Davis.

Minnie stayed in touch with kinfolk in Billings, exchanged visits, and shared good and bad times. Her father, John Herman, died in 1935; his funeral was in the home that Minnie had shared for the first twenty-seven years of her life. Another war came and went.

Minnie's mother, Mary Kastendieck, came to see her for the final time in 1946 upon the marriage of Mary's grandson William Davis, Jr., a celebratory event that took up a large section of the society news of the *Joplin Globe*.[38] Mildred, Minnie's sister, accompanied their mother on the trip from Billings to Joplin. Mary, frail, ill, and approaching her ninetieth year saw her grandson marry well, to a popular college-educated girl with high professional promise. It was a fitting capstone to Mary and John Herman Kastendieck's dedication to the education of their own children. Mary died within a few months of her visit to Joplin, and everyone again convened in Billings at the house on Oak Street.[39] In 1954, Minnie lost her brother Roy in Oklahoma. The announcement of his death remembered her as part of his surviving family.[40]

Cancer claimed the lives of both Minnie and William Davis. William died in the early morning hours of November 22, 1961, at St. John's Hospital, in Joplin, of lung cancer.[41] A year after William's death, Minnie was diagnosed with breast cancer. She fought it for eighteen months and died mid-morning of March 25, 1964, at home on Sergeant Avenue at the age of seventy-two, forty-seven of her years as a resident of Joplin.[42] Both William and Minnie's burial was in Ozark Memorial Park Cemetery in Joplin, a place of beauty but far away from the pastoral surroundings of Rose Hill Cemetery at Billings where Minnie's parents and many of the Kastendieck family lay at rest.[43] None of the remains of the children of John Herman, Jr., and Mary came back to Rose Hill. Each child left Billings to seek opportunities that a small town could not afford. As the years went by, a new community somewhere else became their address, but none ever forgot that their roots remained in a little town in Christian County, Missouri, that was home.

Minnie Kastendieck. Miss Mary Lunda Brown posed with her
kindergarten class at Billings in 1897. Minnie is standing in the second
row, third from the left. Missouri State Historical Society.

Forty-Acre Farm. John Herman, Jr., and Mary Kastendieck owned forty
acres in Section 16 of Polk Township at the far western end of the
Christian County panhandle (arrow). Shown in this 1912 plat map is the
original footprint of the town of Billings, Missouri. State Historical
Society of Missouri.

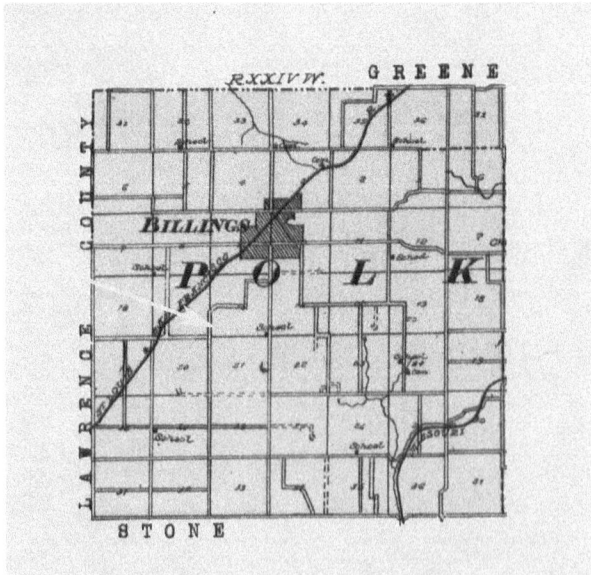

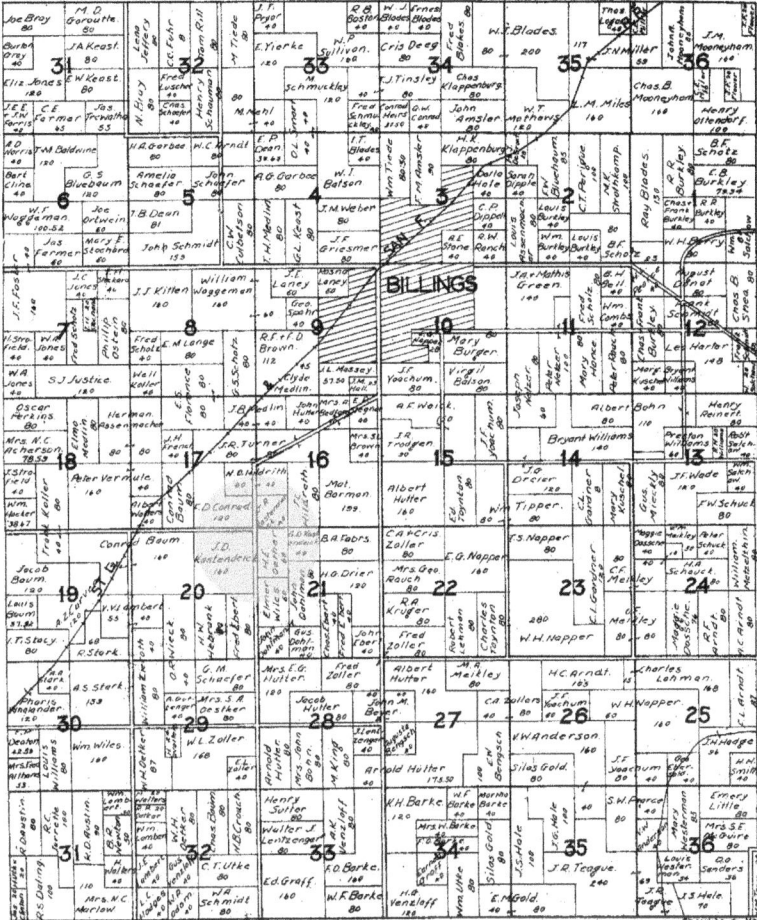

1930 Plat Map, Polk Township, Christian County, Missouri. Kastendiecks owned acreage in sections 16, 20, and 21. J.R. (John Leroy) Kastendieck owned the original John Herman forty in Section 16. J.D. Kastendieck's one-hundred-sixty acres belonged to John Dietrich, Jr., George Kastendieck died in 1927 but his forty in Section 21 remained listed in his name. Andrew Kastendieck who once owned forty acres in this vicinity died in 1912. His forty was sold by his widow. University of Missouri-Columbia, Ellis Library Special Collections.

38

The Architect

Raymond Stone Kastendieck became an architect. It was a natural career choice for the son of a builder who grew up on a steady diet of construction work.

Becoming an architect did not come easily nor quickly for Raymond. Born on the last day of August 1894, the youngest son of John Herman, Jr., and Mary Stone Kastendieck, he grew up in the family household on Oak Street, went to school in Billings, Missouri, and graduated with a diploma from Billings High School.[1] He skipped college and headed west to Oklahoma where he had family connections.[2] His Aunt Amelia and Aunt Hermina lived in Oklahoma; and his brother Roy taught school in the Collinsville city schools.[3] The elevation of Oklahoma Territory to newly conferred statehood meant opportunities for a young man like Raymond.

He taught school at Collinsville, Oklahoma, for a while until World War I broke out. It looked as if his life might change forever as did the lives of many young men who went away to fight in a distant land in the conflict euphemistically called the "war to end all wars."[4]

Raymond registered for the draft at Billings; and then waited for a call to duty.[5] The call came in June 1917, which sent him to boot camp in Arkansas.[6] He was there until August 8, 1917, when officially inducted into the Army two weeks short of his twenty-third birthday. He did not go overseas immediately. The government sent him to students' training camp to become an officer. He spent the better part of a year with the Sixth Company Twelfth Regiment Citizens Training Camp at Fort Logan H. Roots, Arkansas, where he trained with Battery B of the Field Artillery.[7]

Fort Roots was the camp of the 87th Division located a short distance upriver from Little Rock, Arkansas. It began as a training camp for men drafted from surrounding states but soon became too small to accommodate the 87th Division. Enlisted men moved down to nearby Camp Pike in North Little Rock, Arkansas, leaving Fort Roots as a training camp for officers.

Raymond trained here in idyllic surroundings. The parade ground featured a breathtaking view of the Arkansas River.[8] He came out of camp a newly commissioned first lieutenant assigned to Battery B of the 335th Field Artillery and second in command of the battery.

On August 31, 1918—Raymond's twenty-fourth birthday—the men of the 335th Artillery boarded His Majesty's Transport the HMT *Lancashire* in New York Harbor and sailed for Europe with the 87th Division. Four officers shipped out with Battery B: a Massachusetts boy, one from Mississippi, another out of New York, and Raymond who did not list a street address. Everyone in Billings would know where he lived. In case of emergency authorities should contact J.H. Kastendieck, his father.[9]

They went ashore in France on September 1, 1918, as part of the 87th Division. Upon arrival in France, surprisingly, the division drew assignment to the Service of Supply section ordered stationed at Pons (Charente-Inférieure), a commune of about 4,000 residents. The division was broken into units and placed in various support roles. It was here, near Pons, France, that Raymond served out his time during World War I with Battery B backing up the front lines.[10] None of the units of the 87th Division was in combat, including Raymond's 335th Field Artillery. The 87th provided support for men in the forward trenches.

The War ended. Raymond sailed for home, leaving out of Pauillac, France, on February 22, 1919, aboard the *Martha Washington*, originally an ocean liner pressed into service as a transport ship. The 87th Division returned to the United States to Fort Dix, New Jersey, and deactivated there in February 1919.[11] Raymond received an honorable discharge on March 8, 1919, and headed for home, having spent eighteen months in uniform, six months of that in theater, minus a few days of sea travel.[12]

Raymond came home safe—one of the lucky ones. Of the more than 4.5 million Americans who served in World War I, 53,500 perished in combat; another 63,000 died of illnesses and disease. Two hundred four thousand came home wounded and needing help. The government had not been ready for war, and it was even less prepared for peace. More than 40 percent of the nation's gross national product had gone toward the war; the government had little to spend on programs for veterans. By 1919, four million Americans were out of work. Veterans had to fend for themselves.

Raymond went to college. There was no government program to pay for college, but by the fall of 1919, he had enrolled in the architecture program at Washington University.[13] He graduated in 1923 with a degree in architectural engineering.[14] Upon graduation, he landed a job with the prominent St. Louis architectural firm of William B. Ittner, a nationally known architect of schools celebrated for the change of the architectural style of old prison-like school buildings into schools that featured inviting exteriors, natural light, and classrooms tailored to specific subjects.[15]

Ittner assigned Raymond to help design a school at Sedalia, Missouri—the now famous Smith-Cotton High School.[16] He moved to Sedalia in 1924 and spent the better part of a year working on the project. There he met Lillian Pruess. A natural attraction blossomed between them. Both born and raised in small Missouri towns; Raymond of Billings, the war veteran and budding architect, tall, slender, brown hair and eyes; and Lillie from Holden, Missouri; a 1923 graduate of Central Missouri Teachers' College, Warrensburg; a high school teacher set to occupy the new Smith-Cotton School; and a gifted and attractive musician, among her many accomplishments.[17] The couple wed privately before relatives and friends on Independence Day, July 4, 1925, at the home of Lillie's parents in Holden, Missouri, where she had grown up on the family farm and gone to school. She was the daughter of Elizabeth and Augustis Pruess, a German-speaking immigrant from Poland.[18]

Lillie gave up her teaching job, and the bridal couple left Sedalia for Raymond's next architecture assignment in Wilkes-Barre, Pennsylvania.[19] By the year 1926, they had left Wilkes-Barre and settled in Gary, Indiana, where Raymond represented his employer—William Ittner Architects—as resident engineer for the construction of several school buildings in the now famous Wirt school system.[20] The Wirt system advocated among other things innovative scheduling in the use of school facilities that involved auditorium teaching and other activities to stimulate student learning and to maximize spaces that otherwise often went underutilized.

The 1930 census taker found Raymond and Lillie living at 489 Grant Street, renting a place at $53 a month, and enjoying their new life in Gary, Indiana. Moreover, the census taker found something else, too. The census showed that Raymond had a brother named James Kastendieck, reputed to be a clothing sales representative in Gary; except Raymond had no brother by that name. Despite the otherwise accurate description of the census data as to a possible family relationship, a James Kastendieck of that age and description is unaccountable anywhere in the Kastendieck genealogy. Either the census taker made a mistake, fell victim to a practical joke, or there was a mysterious brother named James Kastendieck heretofore unknown.[21]

Lillie died suddenly. Despite its first rate facilities at the time, Mercy Hospital in Gary failed to successfully complete a surgery procedure that ended Lillie's life.[22] She died on the morning of September 9, 1931, in Gary where she worked as a substitute teacher and kept up an active community schedule. Well-liked in social circles, she was part of the sisterhood of the Philanthropic Educational Organization (PEO), and a member of the fraternal Order of the Eastern Star, accomplishments all gone at the age of thirty-two. Raymond and Lillie's family took her home to Johnson County, Missouri, for funeral services at Holden, and buried her in Sunset Hill Cemetery at Warrensburg.[23]

In 1933, Raymond ended his affiliation with Ittner of St. Louis to begin his own architectural engineering firm in Gary, Indiana. He opened offices at 673 Broadway and hung out his shingle, R.S. Kastendieck and Associates, a company that would become one of the leading architectural firms of its time.[24]

Raymond remained a bachelor for ten years after Lillie's death. In the summer of 1941, he married Marion Williams, a teacher in the Gary schools who specialized in the Auditorium part of the Wirt system, the nationally known method of instruction started in Gary.[25] Born in 1903, Marion was from Illinois, the daughter of Mary and Charles Williams, a Bushnell, Illinois, attorney.[26] She was an educator to the core from an early age. A product of far flung geography, she attended Ward-Belmont School for Girls in Nashville, Tennessee; went to Tallahassee State College in Tallahassee, Florida; and graduated with a major in linguistics from Northwestern University in Evanston, Illinois. She was a fifteen-year veteran of the Gary schools and head of the Auditorium Department at Horace-Mann High School when she met and married Raymond.[27]

Far way in another part of the world the volatile cauldron of World War II boiled over. In December 1941, Japanese warplanes attacked Pearl Harbor. Raymond again registered for the draft in April 1942. Still trim at age forty-seven: six feet, one hundred seventy-five pounds, dark hair and eyes, ruddy complexion.[28] Raymond's category of the draft was called the "Old Man's Draft" because it registered men who were forty-five to sixty-four years old at the time. Raymond stayed stateside in World War II serving as an intelligence officer for northwestern Indiana, a quasi-counter-intelligence job to ostensibly guard against the infiltration of spies into the United States.[29]

The war ended, and Raymond turned his full attention to his architecture business and the networking tasks that went with it. In 1951, he campaigned for and won election as District Governor of Rotary International, the first time in a decade that northern Indiana had brought home the honor.[30] The office carried with it opportunities to travel throughout the United States and Europe representing Rotary.[31] His travels took him and Marion to Great Britain in 1953, flying Trans World Airlines out of New York to London aboard a Lockheed L-749 Constellation.[32] The four-engine plane was the first to fly regularly across the Atlantic Ocean non-stop. Although TWA had acquired jet planes as early as 1950, they had not yet replaced the prop models on most flights.

Raymond's social status took another upturn in 1957 when he became Potentate of Orak Shriners International, placing him among the elite of the Shriners organization. His reputation as an architect grew likewise. In 1960, he won the contract for what would be his signature architectural accomplishment.

It began in 1953 when the Indiana General Assembly voted to construct a new state office building. The assembly appropriated a sum of $30 million to bring some twenty-two separate state government agencies spread across Indianapolis under one roof. The structure that Raymond designed in collaboration with a Chicago architectural firm not only met the Assembly's desire to house all agencies of government, it added a distinctive accent to the Indianapolis skyline. Built of steel and concrete in a Modernist style, it rose more than two hundred feet above street level. The design featured more than two thousand windows in keeping with Raymond's interest in bringing natural lighting into the workspace. A 900-seat cafeteria and large outdoor plaza highlighted the modern design. Underground tunnels connected the State House, State Library, and nearby parking facilities. Patrons moved from place to place without the need to brace for cold Indiana winters. Its 970,000 square feet of space contained the world's largest air condition units with advanced technology that controlled both cold and heat depending on the seasons.[33]

Dedication of the Indiana State Office Building was in December 1960 when it opened for use widely acclaimed. However, by the mid-1960s, few in his immediate family still lived to share the pleasures of Raymond's success. Lillie had been dead for more than thirty years; Raymond's father died in

Billings in 1935, followed by his mother in 1947; his brother Paul passed in 1954; and Minnie died in the spring of 1964. Only he and his sister Mildred remained of the house of John Herman Kastendieck, Jr.,

Raymond retired from architecture, stayed active in community affairs, and lived comfortably at his home on Glen Park Avenue, in Gary, Indiana.[34] He gathered his papers and gave the files to Indiana University.[35] He lived to a good old age and died on April 21, 1983.

Unlike the old days at Billings, Missouri, in the past, the family plot at Rose Hill Cemetery did not claim the remains of Raymond Kastendieck, nor did Indiana; a place he called home for most of his adult life. Instead, Marion buried him in Illinois in Bushnell Cemetery in McDonough County, Illinois. Illinois was the home of the Williams family and the original address of Raymond's wife, Marion Williams. Raymond was buried at Bushnell where Marion would join him in due time. A simple, well-proportioned, red granite monument marked his grave.[36]

Raymond left a legacy in line with the Kastendieck tradition of a good man of good deeds. More than two-thirds of his lengthy obituary was devoted to his professional and community involvement. It listed Rotary District Governor, President of the Northwest Indiana Symphony, Fellow of the American Institute of Architects—AIA national director and Treasurer, President of the Indiana Society of Architects, honored National Boy Scout leader, YMCA board member, member of the American Legion, and Shriner Potentate, to name a few of his many accomplishments.[37] Among his several architectural contributions, he seems to have prized most his designs for schools, of which there were many starting with Smith-Cotton High School in Sedalia, Missouri. Many other times he donated his architectural talents to create Boy Scout and YMCA facilities.[38]

Raymond never exploited his fame nor held himself above his Kastendieck roots. Though separated geographically, his Kastendieck relatives knew of his endeavors and found pride in knowing that he was one of them. Cousin Pauline Kastendieck Jeidy—writing to a relative about two of her young Kastendieck kin studying architecture at the University of Texas—wrote, "The Texas boys say Ray is very well known. They read about him in books and hear him mentioned in lectures."[39] Perhaps the only regret about Raymond Kastendieck was that he died childless. His obituary mentioned survival by nieces and nephews but none were of the Kastendieck name. With Raymond's passing, the Kastendieck name expired in the line of John Herman Kastendieck, Jr.,

Marion Williams Kastendieck lived to be ninety-eight years old, forty-one of her ninety-eight years as the wife of Raymond Kastendieck. After Raymond's death, she left Gary, Indiana, to return to her home state of Illinois and entered a retirement home in Macomb, Illinois.[40] She died there at Wesley Village on November 4, 2001, with burial in the family plot at Bushnell Cemetery in McDonough County, Illinois, beside Raymond.[41]

Raymond Stone Kastendieck. Shown at the height of his success as an architect and community leader, he was in his early sixties when this photograph honored his selection as Potentate of Orak Shriners International Temple. It was during this time that he collaborated in the design, and oversaw the construction, of the Indiana State Office Building. Official Portrait, Orak Shrine Center, Michigan City, Indiana, 1957.

Smith-Cotton High School, Sedalia, Missouri. Dedicated May 14, 1925, Smith-Cotton was Raymond Kastendieck's earliest architecture project. The design featured an expansive façade of windows, with natural light filling classrooms uniquely planned around specific subjects. It was in Sedalia while working on this project that Raymond met Lillian Pruess his future wife. Smith-Cotton postcard, private collection.

Indiana State Office Building, Indianapolis. Raymond Kastendieck's premier architectural accomplishment, the building houses the state offices of practically all state government agencies. At the time it was constructed in 1960, it was the largest state office building in the nation. Extensive renovation was undertaken in 1993, which among other repairs replaced the aging limestone skin shown in this 1964 view. Postcard, private collection.

39

Mildred and Harry

Mildred was a willful girl; creative, intelligent, attractive, a lover of nature, and an adventurous soul. Some said too adventurous.

She entered the world in November 1896, the youngest of John Herman, Jr., and Mary's four surviving children. She grew up in the family home on Oak Street, the daughter of a building contractor, went to school in Billings, Missouri, and graduated from Billings High School in 1914 in a class of twelve students, looking more mature and experienced at age seventeen than most of her classmates.[1]

The world changed in 1914. World War I began; Mildred started to college to become a teacher; and she became engaged to be married.[2] A smart, nice-looking girl from a good family could choose as she pleased from the eligible young men of Billings, in as much as marrying stock existed in the panhandle of Christian County. Instead, she ventured into the environs of Marionville, down the road a ways from Billings, and over the county line in Lawrence County. She caught the eye of Harry Wilks Fulbright, a blond-headed, blue-eyed, muscular boy three years older than she was. How they met, no one remembers.

Billings and Marionville lay about seven miles apart, a twenty-minute ride on the Frisco. The two schools regularly competed in sports and other activities.

Harry Fulbright, like Mildred, was the youngest of four siblings and the only son of a moderately well to do, cantankerous, and demanding farmer who styled himself as a general farmer when not hawking his specialty as a fruit grower.[3] William Neely Fulbright alone should have been a warning to Mildred, but she apparently missed the clues.

Harry Fulbright grew up in Marionville working sparingly on a one-hundred forty-six acre farm that Neely Fulbright owned on Buck Prairie, in Lawrence County.[4] The Fulbright family name locally went all the way back to the founding of Springfield, Missouri. The first Fulbright settled near a local water source that became Fulbright Spring, hence the name Springfield.[5] Another branch of the same Fulbright family made Arkansas home. The Arkansas line included United States Senator J. William Fulbright of Fayetteville, Arkansas, known among other things for the creation of the Fulbright Scholarship Program and the student exchange legislation that opened the world to culture as a commodity of trade among nations.

Harry Fulbright contemplated becoming a lawyer like his famous cousin would become one day; although, in Harry's case, to become whatever it took to leave farming behind, a perplexing choice because he personally owned seventy acres of good land that his father had deeded him when he graduated from high school.[6] Never mind that Mr. Fulbright failed to record the transaction; he could tear up the deed at any time.[7]

Harry and Mildred temporarily set aside marriage plans to attend college. Their engagement was tentative and no announcements made for a wedding date. Mildred began work on her teaching degree. Meanwhile, Harry enrolled in Drury

College in the college's School of Bible and Christian Training, a course of study for students of mature judgment and experience fitting themselves for Christian service looking to the ministry.[8] He graduated with the class of 1915, a college graduate that affirmed him as a suitable catch for a young woman of Mildred's status just entering college.[9] Harry did not go into the ministry but instead set his eye on law school. Later claims by his estranged descendants that he went to Harvard Law School carried about the same amount of validity as the story that he was a javelin thrower on the Olympic team.[10]

Harry went to St. Louis, settled into an apartment on Westminster Place, and enrolled in classes at nearby Washington University.[11] No letters survive of the long distance courtship between Harry and Mildred. They saw each other sparingly during their three years of college, although the Frisco ran regularly from St. Louis to Springfield and on down the line to Billings and Marionville.

Harry never completed his initial course of study at Washington University. He later admitted that he had not finished his first course, and, according to one source, "that he had no intention of practicing law, only took the course for business reasons and to gain a practical knowledge of the law."[12]

The United States entered World War I in April of 1917. Harry made application for officer training school. Neely Fulbright, sitting at home in Marionville, heard of his son's plans and devised a scheme to try to keep his only son out of the war. He called Harry home from St. Louis and insisted he obtain a deferral from the draft to take care of the Fulbright homestead. Harry came home, and on June 5, 1917, three days shy of his twenty-fourth birthday, traveled to Mt. Vernon, Missouri, to register for the draft, as all males eighteen and older were required to do.[13] Harry claimed to be a farmer and thus exempt from the draft for agricultural reasons. A potential draftee could claim II-C draft status as necessary for farm labor. Ordained ministers were also exempt, recalling Harry's course of study at Drury College. More to the moment, however, was a clause in the selective service regulations that allowed a Class III deferment that exempted any registrant "who had aged infirm or invalid parents." Better still, a Class IV exemption said, "Any married registrant whose wife or children were mainly dependent on registrant's labor for support." Class IV draftees rarely were called into military service.

Harry and Mildred married November 18, 1917, at Ash Grove, in Greene County, Missouri.[14] The inexplicable circumstances of traveling from Billings, in Christian County, to Greene County for a wedding that was then recorded in Dallas County gives the impression of an elopement whereby the two families may not have been in full agreement about the union, notwithstanding Harry's link to one of Springfield's more prestigious families.

The newlyweds moved into the old Fulbright family log cabin, circa 1853, that Harry's father had helped to restore to a suitably comfortable abode. Mildred went about the chores of being a homemaker, and Harry embraced his newly acquired occupation of farmer. The year 1917 rolled over to 1918, farm crops were good, and there was a new member of the family on the way. Harry went back to St. Louis to work on his law degree for a semester, long enough to count in the Middle Law Class of 1918 before coming back to Marionville.[15] Then the military deferment plan started to go awry.

For quite a while, and for several miles out around Marionville, there was a general discussion about the unfairness of Harry Fulbright being placed in deferred class when other men's sons had been sent to war, including two of Mildred's brothers and two or three of her cousins. The complaints grew to a point that something needed done. Several reliable men of the community, most of whom had sons in the Army, signed a petition, and sent it to the Bureau of Investigation office in Springfield, Missouri, alleging false representation by Harry W. Fulbright for deferred classification. (Before it was the FBI, the Bureau of Investigation investigated real and perceived threats to the nation and its citizens.) The Bureau thought Harry's case of sufficient interest to send someone to look into it.

Agent Fred S. Dunn arrived in Aurora, Missouri, on August 18, 1918, to begin a series of interviews. It became apparent right away that the people placed the blame on Harry's father who they called a "Charity Howler" complaining about the price of wheat and growling about prices being too high, war or no war. Mr. Fulbright seemed particularly exercised about President Woodrow Wilson and criticized the President for vetoing the $2.40 wheat bill.[16] The people in Aurora posed a simple solution to the Bureau's investigation: send Harry to war, have the old man buy Liberty Bonds, and make him shut his mouth. Others thought old man Neely very peculiar and that he complained more than he should but most considered him a loyal citizen.[17]

Agent Dunn went out to see Neely Fulbright who in the course of Dunn's visit acknowledged that his son was not a farmer and had gone to school most of his life until the spring of 1917 when he came home from St. Louis to take care of the farm. Neely tried to make the case that on account of his age—Neely was age sixty at the time—and sickness he had to give up farming. He produced the deed made to Harry five years previous that made Harry a landowner but did not mention to Agent Dunn that no record was ever made of the deed. Mr. Fulbright proceeded to confirm by his comments that he— Neely—was indeed the problem. Dunn wrote in his report, "He

[Neely Fulbright] stated he would rather have his son run the farm than go to war; that subject [Harry] was married Nov. 18, 1917 to Mildred Kasendeck [sic] of Billings, Missouri; that I would prefer his wife staying with her father, in a way I am not willing to take care of her." It came out in the course of the interview that no one had lived on the farm for many years but had instead always lived in town until Mildred and Harry recently moved into the old Fulbright cabin. Mr. Fulbright argued that Harry was doing his patriotic duty by staying home and raising crops.[18] Agent Dunn noted in his report, "The father's story sounded mighty sorrowful." It came to light later, that Neely had withheld his wheat crop to leverage the price while in the meantime refusing to sell any wheat to neighbors for seed, all of which undermined his claim of wartime patriotic duty. He pointed out though that he had bought $100 in Liberty Bonds and given ten or fifteen dollars to the Red Cross.

Agent Dunn next drove out to the farm to interview Harry. He found a strapping, one-hundred-eighty-pound man, in good health, fine physic, and "fairly well-educated." Harry said he knew some people had criticized him and his father because of his deferred status but he thought the majority of people had a different view of it. Nevertheless, he and Mildred had concluded, he said, that he should after all enlist in the Officers' Training School as soon as the wheat crop was in and Mildred had the baby.[19]

Harry followed through on his promise to enlist. On October 22, 1918, he entered Officers' Training School at Camp Zachary Taylor near Louisville, Kentucky, a month past the birth of his first child.[20] On September 19, 1918, Mildred gave birth to Harry Wilks Fulbright, Jr., great grandson of the immigrant John Herman and Bridget Kastendieck and a new addition to the Kastendieck legacy, a legacy little Harry, Jr., would uphold as no descendant before him had done. Meanwhile, the baby's father, training in Kentucky and dreaming of the time when he would again see his new son, suddenly contracted a serious case of influenza, a disease in 1918 that took about as many lives during World War I as combat did. As events dictated it, Harry Fulbright's war career was short-lived. The War ended soon after Harry, Jr., was born. The army discharged Harry, Sr., in December 1918, and sent him home.

Mildred Kastendieck. This portrait taken at Billings, Missouri, was about the time of her high school graduation and about the time of her engagement to marry Harry Wilks Fulbright of Marionville. She married in 1917. Collection of Dee Willauer.

40

The Divorce

The War being over and a career on the farm no longer in demand, Mildred and Harry moved into a house near Harry's family in Marionville, Missouri. Harry managed the farm off and on and took a job at his alma mater, as a physical education teacher at Drury College in Springfield.[1] Mildred was finishing college on her way to becoming a schoolteacher.[2] In time, a second child came along, this time a daughter Mary Jane, namesake of each of her two grandmothers. Things seemed to be looking up. The War was over, the deferment controversy behind them, Harry had a teaching job, and Mildred soon would as well. They had two healthy children, a caring extended family (at least on the Kastendieck side), and a promising future was on the horizon. Nevertheless, Harry had an itch, or was it Mildred who wanted more?

Harry became acquainted with a student in one of his physical education courses, and the two struck up a friendship. Gladys Jewell Garrison, twelve years Harry's junior, had come north from Russellville, Arkansas, to study music at Drury College.[3] Diminutive in stature, pretty, with alert brown eyes, she immediately caught Harry's eye. He found himself hanging around different places on campus to catch a glimpse of her, or going by the Music Hall now and then to listen to her play. Everyone agreed Gladys was a remarkable musician. Whether a romance grew out of these contacts will never be known because tongues were wagging abut Mildred, too.

One farm over from the Fulbright place lived Joy Lyial Brown, reputed to be a one-time beau of Mildred's before she married Harry. The story goes that Mildred and Joy had an affair. Harry's family maintained that Harry caught the two of them in an embracing position. One family member wrote a book in which he imagined a bawdy encounter complete with squeaky springs, a door kicked in, bare-breasted Mildred, and a scene where Harry screamed "Damn you!, and stormed out of the house and never went back, ignoring Mildred's pleas to forgive her."[4]

Harry and Mildred divorced, the first and only divorce up until then in the Kastendieck family going back at least to the days of Morsum, Germany, and the immigrant Missouri Kastendiecks. Mildred filed the legal papers for a divorce. Harry's biographer maintained that she did so at Harry's urging "for the sake of the children" who he allegedly felt belonged with their mother. The contention that Harry demanded that Mildred file for a divorce would explain why Mildred was the legal plaintiff, but it seems equally probable that all of the imagined prosaic gyrations in defense of Harry and condemnation of Mildred were attempts to veil the other possibility: Mildred caught Harry in a tryst with one of his students.[5]

Gladys Garrison left Drury to move to St. Louis. At the same time, coincidentally, that Harry moved to St. Louis, also, ostensibly to finish his law degree at Washington University.[6] Back home in Arkansas rumors circulated about Gladys and her older divorcee man friend.[7] Harry finished his business in St. Louis and returned to southwest Missouri to tend to his ailing parents. With the help of a few Fulbright family connections—his Uncle James Fulbright was a State Judge—he found a job with a law firm in Springfield.[8]

Neely and Jane Fulbright died within weeks of each other in 1925. Harry, at a loss without his parents, wrote to Gladys and proposed marriage, putting an end to the long speculation about their relationship. Gladys accepted by mail, took a bus to Marionville, and by the end of the year, she was the second Mrs. Harry Fulbright.[9]

Harry opened a law practice in Aurora, Missouri, expecting to remain in southwest Missouri. However, Lawrence County was not a fertile place for a law practice unless one could be content as a passable country lawyer. Being a fancy attorney from Aurora had its drawbacks. For example, in a case that went before Judge S.L. Henson in Barry County, Harry tried to defend George Shoemaker for killing Walter Heatherly in a dispute that involved Mr. Heatherly attacking Shoemaker with a hoe and Shoemaker fatally stabbing his attacker. The judge found Shoemaker guilty of murder and sentenced him to fifteen years in the penitentiary.[10] Thus, Harry lost a high-profile case.

It was 1927. With the Fulbright family all gone from Marionville, Harry sold the farm, divided the inheritance among his siblings, abandoned the historic Fulbright log cabin, and moved his new family to St. Louis, later to take up residence in Pine Lawn, Normandy Township, in north St. Louis County, in a two-story brick house set in a pleasant suburban neighborhood. His second family now included two children.[11] He went to work in the law offices of Stanley Sidman located in the community of Wellston, St. Louis.[12]

Meanwhile, through all of Harry's comings and goings, Mildred remained detached from it all. She did not remarry, not to Joy Brown her alleged lover nor anyone else in the aftermath of her divorce. [13] Ironically, she found a good position teaching in the St. Louis Public Schools, gathered up the children, and moved away from southwest Missouri, good memories and bad left behind. By 1929, she and the kids lived comfortably in an apartment at 6128 Waterman Avenue, a stone's throw from Forest Park, in St. Louis. [14] The following year they moved a few blocks north into a house at 5804 Maple Avenue on the edge of Wellston, just south of where her ex-husband lived at 3840 Oakridge. Mildred's name and Harry's name appeared next to each other in the 1930 city directory. [15] They lived separate lives in St. Louis never more than a few miles apart.

Mildred stayed in close contact with the Kastendieck family. She remained especially close to Minnie, her older sister living in Joplin. Mildred enjoyed playing bridge, and on regular visits to Joplin, Minnie would host a gathering to treat Mildred to several rounds of Bridge. The social page of the local newspaper always took note of the visits of Mildred coming to Joplin to see her sister all the way from St. Louis. [16]

We do not know if any contact actually existed between Mildred and Harry after their divorce, or if Harry maintained a relationship with his children. It appears the two households remained estranged although at times they lived within a few blocks of each other. Years later, Harry's granddaughter by his second marriage tried to contact her father's half-brother, Harry, Jr., by telephone. She never had a response. Sadly, it seems that none of the half-siblings on either side ever met the other. [17]

Meanwhile, Mary Jane Fulbright, Mildred and Harry's daughter, was by all indications a brilliant student who put her education above many other things in her life. Soon after the family arrived in St. Louis, Mary Jane enrolled in St. Elizabeth's Academy on Arsenal Street. St. Elizabeth's was a prestigious school for girls run by the Catholic Church but open to children of any faith.[18]

Living in St. Louis could be dangerous, especially at a time when the country was struggling as it was in the 1930s to recover from the Great Depression. People were desperate to regain a foothold in life. Mildred was the object of one such incident in February 1934 when a petty criminal by the name of Herbert Renaldi accidentally shot Mary Jane and then tried to extort money from Mildred to cover up the shooting. According to the Associated Press who reported on the story, Renaldi intended to rob a house in University City (St. Louis) where Mildred and the children were living at the time. He fired a shot to see whether anyone was home. The stray bullet slightly wounded Mary Jane returning home from a neighborhood drug store. To cover up the shooting, Renaldi wrote two extortion notes to Mildred demanding $2,000 to avoid any future violence. He scrawled one particularly menacing missive with the lead of a .38-caliber bullet. Renaldi later told the police, "I figured give them something really to worry about so they would forget the shooting." Police caught him a month later when he shot at another citizen while stealing a car. He later confessed to several burglaries.[19]

Harry Wilks Fulbright, Sr., died unexpectedly in the winter of 1936. He suffered from Hodgkin's disease, which contributed to heart failure.[20] He died at home on November 14. His burial was in the National Cemetery at Jefferson Barracks with military honors rightly earned in World War I despite the efforts of his family to avoid the draft and his own brief service of less than a month in uniform.[21] We do not know if Mildred and the children attended his funeral. His second family mourned the fact that he had not made suitable arrangements for the care of his family he left behind. At age forty-three, he surely did not anticipate the end of his life so soon. The other regret expressed years later by his second family lamented that the scandalous secrets of Marionville and the circumstances of his divorce would probably never be known because his other family—Mildred and her children—were likely never to confirm nor deny the true cause of the failed marriage. The monument engraver of Harry's tombstone added an unintended insult to the prestigious Fulbright name when he misspelled Fullbright.[22]

By the year 1940 Mildred had all but completed her determination to afford the best possible education for her children, holding to the same values long maintained by the Kastendieck family; a good education is the key to a life worth living. Harry Wilks, Jr., twenty-one, had graduated from University City High School and finished his third year of college; Mary Jane, nineteen, was a sophomore. Mildred, now age forty-three and still a single mom, managed on a teacher's salary and a few dollars from Harry's part time job as a lab assistant at State University. Mildred expected to teach a few more years. She had recently moved to an apartment on Clemens Avenue where rent was a little high but affordable at $60 a month. She had a good job teaching in the St. Louis Public Schools making $2,075 a year. The memory of her ex-husband faded; she knew of his passing because on the 1940 census in the column for marital status she entered "widowed" although as a matter of correct form she was divorced and not widowed. Harry's second wife Gladys was his widow, a mere technicality in the larger scheme of things.[23]

Mildred stayed in touch with Kastendieck family members. Her mother still lived on Oak Street in Billings (John Herman,

Jr., had died in 1936); her siblings were geographically located in three different states. She wrote to her cousin Verda in Wisconsin in 1942 to express her sorrow upon the death of Aunt Mollie Kastendieck, Verda's mother. Mildred had hoped that Mollie would be able to come to Missouri to visit and to reminisce about all the wonderful times Mildred had when she visited Mollie and Andrew as a child at their Billings farm. Mildred brought Verda up to date on current Kastendieck news. She [Mildred] was in summer school—not her favorite thing to be doing, but Washington University was across the street from where she now lived at 6645 University Drive and courses kept her teaching credentials fresh. Mary Jane had graduated and was working at a bank downtown. Harry, Jr., had completed his master's degree the past spring at Washington University and would get his Ph.D. in two more years "if he can go on through," Mildred added.[24]

Mildred did not mention in her letter to Verda that she had decided to remarry to Dr. Timothy Edwin Collins, a St. Louis dentist who went by the name T.E. Collins and who had been in practice in the city for more than twenty years. Born in 1899, he hailed originally from Dell Rapids, South Dakota. He had family ties in Springfield, Missouri.[25] He opened a dental office in Springfield in 1926 and practiced at various locations in Springfield until the year 1930 when he moved to St. Louis.[26]

We know very little about the professional life of T.E. Collins, except his detractors once accused him and his business associate of violations of statutes covering the advertising of professional services. The Missouri Dental Board ordered them to show legal cause why it should not revoke the license of him and his associate for the alleged illegal marketing practices. In those days, it was illegal for professionals like dentists and doctors to advertise their services in any way that conflicted with the ethics of the profession. Dr. Collins denied the charges claiming that he and his partner were victims of a conspiracy. They convinced a court to issue a restraining order against the dental board and nothing more came of it.[27]

The public record on Mildred goes silent after her marriage to Dr. Collins. She made a couple of visits to see Minnie in Joplin, on one occasion with her mother to attend the wedding of Minnie's son in the summer of 1946. The *Joplin Globe* reported that among the wedding guests were Dr. and Mrs. T.E. Collins of Clayton, Missouri.[28] Mildred came to Billings the next year when her mother died. She had been with her father when he died and arranged his funeral. Now, many years later, she came home to spend the last days with her mother.[29] The *Christian County Republican* mentioned her among the survivors that included all the Kastendieck siblings: Roy, Minnie, Ray, and Mildred, the last time they would be together.

Mildred's name appeared intermittently from time to time, mentioned, for instance, in Roy Kastendieck's obituary in 1954, still living as Mrs. Collins in St. Louis.[30]

Dr. T.E. Collins died in late January of 1964, in St. Louis, and for the second time Mildred was a widow.[31] Dr. Collins' interment was in Springfield, Missouri, in Saint Marys Cemetery.[32] Following T.E.'s death, Mildred M.—in later life she went by her middle name Margaret—moved to Florida in 1964 at the age of sixty-seven to a small two-bedroom retirement home in Lauderhill, Florida, west of Ft. Lauderdale in the greater metropolitan area of Miami, a place greatly different from where she grew up in Billings, Missouri.[33]

Lauderhill sat at the tip of the Florida Peninsula, in the narrow band of real estate that lines the eastern edge of the peninsula between the vast Everglades National Park on the west and the Atlantic Ocean on the east. She likely divided her time for a while between living in St. Louis during the seasonal warm months and wintering in Florida.

Many years passed.

The end came for Mildred in 1982. She became ill in Florida and hospitalized at Broward General Medical Center in Ft. Lauderdale. She died there on the evening of June 27, 1982, exactly seven months to the day past her eighty-fifth birthday. Her son Harry was with her, having flown in from his home in Rochester, New York. He took care of final arrangements with Fairchild Crematory, in Ft. Lauderdale.

Remembered as a schoolteacher in the public schools, in the end she did not forget her Kastendieck roots. Her name in life was Mildred M. for Margaret, but in death, she chose as her memorial Mildred K. for Kastendieck, and that is what her son indelibly entered on her death certificate.[34]

The characters in this book end with the third generation of Kastendiecks with one exception, Harry Wilks Fulbright, Jr., son of Mildred (Kastendieck) and Harry Fulbright. The great grandson of the immigrant John Herman Kastendieck, he became by all accounts the most accomplished Kastendieck descendant of three generations if measured by his professional achievements.

Harry got his Ph.D. degree in physics at Washington University. In the period from 1942 until 1944, during World War II, he was in charge of the university's cyclotron under contract to the Manhattan District Project that developed the atomic bomb. When he graduated in 1944, he transferred as a group leader to the Los Alamos Scientific Laboratory in New Mexico, site of the bomb project. His part in engineering the bomb remains a secret. So secret was his work at the time that there was no published copy of his doctoral thesis. He spoke of this later when Washington University could not find a copy in the university's library collection. As Harry described it in a 1998 letter to the Washington University archivist, "wartime secrecy had prevented its normal appearance...the thesis topic was a study of Neptunium 239 decaying to Plutonium 239...to establish an energy level scheme for Plutonium."[35] Plutonium 239 was the primary fissile element used for the production of nuclear weapons.

The United States dropped two atomic bombs on Japan in 1945, which ended the war. Dr. Fulbright left Los Alamos in the summer of 1946 to accept a position as assistant professor at Princeton University.[36] In 1950, he joined the faculty at the University of Rochester. His accomplishments in physics gained attention around the world. Holder of a Fulbright Fellowship (named for his famous Senator cousin) and a Guggenheim Fellowship, he was Fellow at Copenhagen, Denmark; Visiting Professor at Strasbourg, France, and Chandigarh, India; and a Visiting Professor at Leningrad.[37] An expert in nuclear physics, he later turned his attention to Astronomy. The United States National Register of Scientific and Technical Personnel Files noted that he held three advanced degrees: Ph.D., Sc.D., and Ed.D.[38] The Doctor of Science degree (Sc.D.) was in recognition of a substantial and sustained contribution to scientific knowledge beyond that required for a Ph.D. His education degree (Ed.D.) meant he met the advanced qualifications as an educator. He retired as Professor Emeritus in 1989 but continued to work with advanced students at Rochester. His name frequently appeared in the pedigree of noted contemporary physicists who studied at Princeton and Rochester.[39] One writer said of him, "Harry Fulbright was a brilliant and versatile experimentalist, and passed on these skills to the present generation...Harry was not only an exceptional scientist, but he brought his 'hands-on' skills to his teaching."[40]

The circumstances of his early life left him mostly estranged from the extended Kastendieck family, particularly in later years when relatives went their separate ways and the old ties at Billings were no more.

Harry Fulbright lived a quiet life in the suburbs of Rochester, New York. The modest Fulbright home sat nestled in a landscape of trees and open land, on an uncrowded section of Castle Road, in Rochester. There he entertained students and spent many years in the twilight of his retirement. He died after a brief illness at Rochester on May 16, 2009, at the age of ninety.[41] Surviving him was his wife of sixty-four years, Marion Jones Fulbright. They had no children; thus, another line of Kastendieck descendants ended.

Harry Wilks Fulbright, Jr., Two portraits show Dr. Fulbright at very different times in his life. The great grandson of John Herman and Bridget Kastendieck, he was born in Springfield, Missouri, and spent the first years of his life in a log cabin at Marionville. He became a nationally known physicist whose work contributed to the development of the atomic bomb. A graduate of Washington University, he taught at the faculties of Princeton University and the University of Rochester, New York. Photos courtesy of Science & Business Media; private collection.

41

The Hansons

When the Hanson children—George, Cecelia, and Henry—were orphaned by the death of their mother, the oldest was eleven years old. Their seafaring father had died five years before, leaving them stranded in Brooklyn, New York.[1] There were others of the Hanson name living in Brooklyn. However, no extended family lived nearby that they could turn to. Both deceased parents were recent immigrants to America.

When their mother died, the children faced an uncertain future with only the state of New York standing between them and life in an orphanage. John Herman kept them in the Kastendieck family and raised them as his own. When he moved to Billings, Missouri, they moved with him. Their formative years were in Christian County parallel to their stepbrothers and stepsisters all under the Kastendieck roof.

George Hanson was the oldest of the three Hanson children. He came to Billings at the age of seventeen. In a brief space of less than two years, he met, courted, and wed the amenable Sarah Ann Keithley before a justice of the peace in the fall of 1879.[2] They had much in common, George of Brooklyn roots and Sarah Ann a native of Albany, New York, she coming to Missouri by way of Brooklyn, too. The 1880 census found them living in Polk Township seven months into marriage and having a go at the noble trade of farming.[3] The couple went on to rear five children.

Farming did not turn out to be of George Hanson's liking. He quit farming and took up the occupation of house plasterer, a skill trade that required a good measure of technical ability aided as it were by his Norwegian artisanship ancestry. Plastering was a skill in heavy demand around the growing town of Billings, and George was seldom out of work. The couple took out a mortgage and bought a house in Billings.[4]

George Hanson fell out of favor with the Kastendieck clan around 1891 when he, his wife, and other Keithleys testified against Caroline Kastendieck in her lawsuit with a Springfield wholesaler when the rest of the family came to her defense. It never came to light why George felt estranged enough from Caroline, who had helped to raise him, to try to do her harm.

Time passed and by 1910, Billings had lost some of its luster for George and Sarah. All but two of their kids were out of the house and on their own. George quit the building trade, sold his home in Billings, and moved to Kansas City where he went into the grocery business, recalling the years of his childhood when he grew up in the Kastendieck grocery business in Brooklyn. He and Sarah bought a house on East Eighteenth Street in Kansas City and lived there for more than a decade.[5] In the interim, George picked up his plastering tools again to make plastering once more his means of livelihood, working mostly as a wage earner in the construction business.

Kansas City was home. As late as January 1920 George and Sarah still lived in the same house on Eighteenth Street.[6] Then suddenly for unspecified reasons, whether retirement, health concerns, or just to follow grandchildren, George and Sarah left Kansas City and moved to Los Angeles, California. Within six months of their move, George died on June 4, 1920, a month short of his fifty-ninth birthday, with interment in the Los Angeles Odd Fellows Cemetery.[7] Sarah Ann carried on alone until the early spring of 1925 and passed at the age of sixty-five.[8] She went to rest next to her husband in Los Angeles far from Kansas City and far from the memories of their first home in Billings, Missouri, many years before.

The middle Hanson child was Cecelia Bertha Hanson or Celia, as people sometimes knew her. When she arrived at Billings with the Kastendieck family, she wasted no time in going out on her own. She found a job in Marionville a few miles down the Frisco track doing housework for Jesse and Ann Rauch, an older North Carolina couple living alone on Buck Prairie who needed a cook. Celia was sixteen years old.[9]

A few years passed doing domestic work. In 1884, she married a Pennsylvania-born farm boy name George W. Beck, recently moved to Billings with his parents from Sumner County, Kansas.[10] They skipped a Sabbath wedding and married on a Tuesday.[11] George was a wanderer. The couple spent five years at Billings, had a couple of kids, and then moved away to Dixon, Illinois. Three more children were born in Illinois before the family packed up and moved back to Missouri. They bought a house and some land in Polk Township, Christian County. George opened a butcher shop and went into the meat packing business. Before long, two more offspring came along.[12] Before they finished, George and Celia had ten children in a period of less than fifteen years, eight of them while Celia was still in her thirties.[13]

Sometime around 1907, George Beck quit the meat business and moved his family to Mecosta County, Michigan, where he bought a farm. George and Celia's last child was born in Michigan. When George's father died, his aging mother came to live with the Beck family in Michigan, bringing the number of people under one roof to thirteen. By now, the oldest kids were starting to leave the nest to begin their own lives. George again occupied himself in the honorable art of farming, assisted by his grown boys still at home.[14]

Michigan would be the last move the Beck family would make together. Celia died in the fall of 1910, at Chippewa Lake, Michigan, in Mecosta County. She was fifty-five. She had dutifully followed her husband back and forth through three states in the thirty-four years of their marriage. The strain eventually became too much and she succumbed after a lengthy battle with heart disease.[15] George informed officials of her death; Dr. Grant made the necessary entries on her death certificate; and the undertaker came out from Grand Rapids to make final arrangements. They buried her in the Chippewa Lake Cemetery.[16]

After Celia's death, and for unknown reasons, George Beck moved back to Lee County, Illinois, where he worked briefly as a laborer in Dixon.[17] He lived on for several more years—some say until 1939—but his wandering ways caused history to lose track of his final resting place.[18]

The one Hanson who stayed closest to home was Henry Hanson. Orphaned at the age of six and adopted into the Kastendieck home, he never knew any father besides John Herman. He was a stepson but a stepson raised as a Kastendieck. He was a teenager when the Kastendiecks moved to Billings, a young man who fitted comfortably into the middle of the Kastendieck clan with stepbrothers older and stepsisters younger than he was.[19] He married in 1888 at the age of twenty-two to the indefatigable Alma Evadna Marsh; a Billings girl newly arrived in Christian County from Tioga County, New York.[20] They had three children with the colorful names of Bertha Etta, Jetta Estelle, and Ora Edward, names that rolled off the tongue like poetry.

The happiness that comes with the discoveries of raising children came to an abrupt end when Alma died at the age of thirty-three on December 8, 1899, a Friday, only days until the calendar rolled over to the 20th Century. She went to rest in Rose Hill Cemetery.[21] Alma's death was a crushing blow to Henry. He never remarried. Nevertheless, in a curious relationship, Etta Marsh, Alma's sister, moved into the Hanson home to care for the children of her deceased sister. The youngest child was two years old. This au pair arrangement lasted for almost thirty years.[22]

Henry Hanson took up the trade of plasterer with the same Norwegian skill that had helped his older brother enter the same career. He rented a house in Billings and went about the task of raising his family as a widowed single parent under the watchful eye of his sister-in-law.[23]

The next decade in Henry's life went by quickly. He moved to Greene County, Missouri, where the demand for a plasterer was as strong as it was in Billings and where the schools afforded a better opportunity for the education of his children. By 1910, the kids were growing, Bertha the eldest had finished high school, Jetta about to finish, and Ora was just entering, all under the exacting tutorials of Aunt Etta.[24]

Bertha Hanson married George Howcroft in 1914, a Woodmen of the World fraternity-man, and all seemed to be proceeding according to plan.[25] Then, the unthinkable happened. Ora Hanson, Henry's youngest son, was crossing the railroad tracks in Republic, Missouri, in Greene County, when a passenger train struck and killed him instantly. The coroner ruled his death accidental. There was seemingly no explanation for how it could have happened in broad daylight at midday. He was eighteen years old, a student in school, and about ready to take on whatever life intended to serve up.[26] Ironically, when he died on December 3, 1915, it was five days short of the sixteenth anniversary of his mother's death and eerily on a Friday the same day of the week as her passing. They buried him in Rose Hill Cemetery near his mother's grave.[27]

Henry moved back to Billings and bought a house on Pine Street. Greene County was no longer a place he wanted to be. Aunt Etta, still unmarried and in her late fifties, continued as the lifelong companion of the Hansons.[28] Bertha and her two small children moved in, too, following the premature death of her husband in 1919 and lived once again with her father and Aunt Etta.

The decade of the twenties rolled over to the thirties. Henry worked on as a plasterer. His widowed daughter Bertha and her kids stayed on with him in the house on Pine Street. (Bertha later moved to California and died in Los Angeles.)[29] Aunt Etta eventually left, too, her work done in the Hanson household. She bought a house in Springfield, at 733 South Main Avenue. To the surprise of many, she paid cash to the tune of $4,000, a tidy sum for a house in those days, leading to speculation that her lifelong service in the Hanson home may have been a pecuniary one.[30]

Henry Edward Hanson died on October 7, 1932, from apoplexy as the result of a stroke. His son-in-law Sherwood Schmill, husband of his daughter Jetta, handled the arrangements.

Henry was the last of the Hanson stepchildren to pass. There was no one left to remember his life. The part of his death certificate that usually contained a deceased's family history said simply "unknown".[31] After more than thirty years as a widower, he went to rest in Rose Hill beside Alma, his beloved wife of eleven years.[32]

Aunt Etta lived on in Springfield for another dozen years. She died on January 17, 1947, four days past her eighty-fifth birthday of heart failure.[33] She passed away on North Campbell Street, in Springfield, at the home of Jetta her niece, the daughter of her sister Alma—the sister who Etta replaced as surrogate mother. The surrender of her personal life to an unselfish purpose in her youth thus returned to Etta in her old age living out her last years in the care of one she loved.

Notes

Preface

1. *Brooklyn Eagle,* May 23, 1880, p. 4.

Chapter 1. Introduction

1. Kastendieck, Biography of John D. Kastendieck, p. 1. Marriage and death certificates confirm the ancestral seat of the Kastendieck family at Morsum, Germany.

2. David Gay Genealogy, 2014. Johann Kastendieck 16 Jul 1789-12 Oct 1816.

3. Kastendieck, Biography of John D. Kastendieck.

4. Missouri Death Certificate No. 35748, dated 1923, Missouri Secretary of State. The John Dietrich Kastendieck, Sr. death certificate names Johann as his father. This document gives Johann's birthplace and that of his wife Trina as Meinheim, Germany. It is generally accepted, however, that both were born in Morsum. The name Gömann is spelled Gorman on the death certificate.

5. David Gay Genealogy, 2014; Tombstone Inscription, Green-Wood Cemetery, Brooklyn, NY.

6. Kastendieck, Biography of John D. Kastendieck; 1855 New York Census, New York, Kings, Ward 8 Brooklyn City. John Kastendieck; Kenneth J. Gruschow Correspondence, 1 Apr 2011. Gruschow lists a seventh child of John and Trina Kastendieck; viz., Diedrich [sic] "Richard" Kastendieck b Feb 1829, in Hanover, Germany, d bet 1911-1919, Platteville Ulster, New York. He married Eugenie F. Swenson 30 Nov 1876, in Brooklyn, Kings, New York. His birthdate fits into birthdates of other offspring but lacks independent verification. The general record does not support a seventh child.

Chapter 2. John Herman and Steerage Class

1. Obituary of John Herman Kastendieck, newspaper clipping, unidentified source, n. d., collection of the author.

2. *Chamber's Edinburgh Journal*. Vol. 5, June 13, 1846.

3. Fuer, *The Germans in America 1607-1970*, p. 33.

4. Baptism Certificate of Andrew Kastendieck, dated 13 Dec 1863, Brooklyn, New York, gives the native homes of John Herman Kastendieck and Bridget Ford Kastendieck. Dee Willauer collection.

Chapter 3. Aunt Dora

1. Rose Hill Cemetery Tombstone Inscription. Aunt Dora's identification as the daughter of Johann Dietrich and Trina Kastendieck comes from known relationships to her siblings.

2. National Archives and Records Administration, microfilm M237, Reel 67, List 356, Ship *Emma*, Bremen, Germany to New York, New York, 9 June 1847, #66 Joh Castendyck [*sic*] age 26 m farmer #67 Dorothea Castendyck age 29 f [no occupation listed]

3. Kenneth J. Gruschow, Find A Grave Memorial 147791724, Jun 12, 2015; BK Genie, Find A Grave Memorial 126936459, Mar 26, 2014; Green-Wood Cemetery Register Lot 9625 Section 116. The burials of Alice and Hermina Kastendieck occurred January 11, 1857,

4. Green-Wood Cemetery Register, Bovers [*sic*], Alice 1857-01-11 Lot 9625 Section 116, Bovers, Hermina 1857-01-11 Lot 9625 Section 116. The Boevers name appears in records as both Boevers and Bovers, the latter being an Americanized version of the German Bövers.

5. Green-Wood Cemetery Register Lot 9625, Section 116; Kenneth J. Gruschow, Find A Grave Memorial 67424420.

6. 1870 US Census, New York, Kings, Brooklyn Ward 12, Series M593 Roll 953, 480B, National Archives.

7. 1875 New York State Census, New York, Kings, Brooklyn, New York State Library. John Kastendiek [*sic*].

8. 1880 US Census, Missouri, Christian, Polk, Series T9 Roll 681, 7C, National Archives.

9. Tombstone Inscription, Rose Hill Cemetery, Christian County, Missouri. Anna D. Kastendieck wife of Henry Boevers Feb 2 1818 Feb 28 1894.

10. Augusta Kastendieck Family Album, photo inscription "Aunt Dora."

Chapter 4. John Friedrich Wilhelm Kastendieck

1. National Archives and Records Administration, microfilm M237, Reel 67, List 356. Ship *Emma*, Bremen, Germany to New York, New York, 9 June 1847, #66 Joh Castendyck [*sic*] 26 farmer #67 Dorothea Castendyck 29 [no occupation listed].

2. "Collision and Loss at Sea," *The New Monthly Magazine and Universal Register*, 23 April 1847, "The barque 'Emma,' Captain D. Edzard, of and from Bremen, bound to New York with emigrants, April 9, 1847."

3. 1855 New York State Census, New York, Kings, Ward 8 Brooklyn City, New York State Library. John Kastendieck Head 33, Diedrick Kastendieck Brother 21, Mary Kastendieck Sister 24, Mary Kastendieck Mother 70. Brothers Herrman and Henry Kastendieck appeared elsewhere in the census; their sister Dora did not.

4. 1870 US Census, New York, Kings, 8-WD Brooklyn, Series M593 Roll 950, 100, National Archives.

5. *Smith's Brooklyn Directory, 1856-1858*, subsequently *Lain's Brooklyn Directory*, published by Lain and Company, Brooklyn Public Library.

6. Andrew Kastendieck baptismal certificate 13 Dec 1863, Dee Willauer Collection.

7. 1870 US Census, New York, Kings, 8-WD Brooklyn, Series M593 Roll 950, 100, National Archives. Cassendick [*sic*] John, Wife Mary 30, Maggie 8, Annie 4, Dora 2.

8. *Smith's Brooklyn Directory, 1856-1858*, subsequently *Lain's Brooklyn Directory*, published by Lain and Company, Brooklyn Public Library.

9. 1880 US Census, New York, Kings, Brooklyn, Series T9 Roll 844, 349A, National Archives. John Kastendieck.

10. 1875 New York State Census, New York, Kings, Brooklyn, 35, New York State Library. John Kastendick [*sic*].

11. New York, Kings County Estate Files, 1866-1923, Surrogate Court, Brooklyn.

12. Kenneth J. Gruschow, Find A Grave Memorial 38066035, Jun 08, 2009. Children of John F. and Marie Kastendieck: 1. Margaretha Kastendieck (1862-1884), 2. Annie Kastendieck Leonhauser (1865–1929), 3. Dorothy "Dora" Kastendieck Holzer (1868-1934), 4. John Diedrich Kastendieck (1872-1892, 5. Amelia M. Kastendieck Gerken (1875-1913), 6. Henrietta A. Kastendieck (1879-1881). Details of family data for the Kastendieck family

are available from Find A Grave based on the genealogical research of Ken Gruschow.

13. 1880 US Census, New York, Kings, Brooklyn, Series T9 Roll: 844, 349A, National Archives.

14. New York, Kings County Estate Files, 1866-1923, Surrogate Court, Brooklyn, Margarette [*sic*] Kastendieck, 3 Apr 1890; New York City Municipal Deaths, 1795-1949, Margaretha Kastenduck [*sic*], 25 Dec 1884, Brooklyn.

15. *The Brooklyn Daily Eagle*, 18 Dec 1889, p. 1.

16. New York, Kings County Estate Files, 1866-1923, Surrogate Court, Brooklyn, 3 Apr 1890.

17. The name of John Friedrich Kastendieck's son John appeared in the 1855 New York Census as John F. Jr.; as John D. in the probate record of Margaretha Kastendieck on file in the New York Municipal Archives; and again as John D. on his tombstone in Greenwood-Cemetery. It follows that three of the Kastendieck men named their first-born sons John D., presumably after their grandfather Johann Dietrich Kastendieck.

18. 1892 New York State Census, Brooklyn, Ward 08, Enumeration District 07, p. 7., New York State Library. John F Kaslenctieck [*sic*].

19. New York City Municipal Deaths, 1795-1949, New York Municipal Archives. John F.W. Kastendieck, 5 Mar 1893.

20. New York, Kings County Estate Files, 1866-1923, John Friedrich Wilhelm Kastendieck, 1893, Surrogate Court, Brooklyn, pp. 404-414.

21. New York, Kings County Estate Files, 1866-1923, John Friedrich Wilhelm Kastendieck, 1893, Surrogate Court, Brooklyn, p. 405.

22. *Brooklyn Daily Eagle*, 22 Jul 1901, p. 5.

23. Haberstroh, *The German Churches of Metropolitan New York*. Today St. John's German Evangelical Lutheran Church is a consolidation of three separate congregations known as St. John–St. Matthew–Emanuel Lutheran Church.

24. 1920 US Census, New York, Kings, Brooklyn Borough, Series T625 Roll 1162, p. 1751, National Archives.

25. 1930 US Census, New York, Rockland, Orangetown, Series T626, Roll 1640, p. 138, National Archives. Charles Holzer in household of Charles Krimmel.

26. Find A Grave Memorials 102626999 and 67736514. All of John F.W. Kastendieck's family was buried in the Kastendieck plot except Emilie. She

was buried in Green-Wood beside her husband, Charles Gerken, at a different location from the Kastendieck plot; viz., Sec. 138, Lot 29524.

27. Find A Grave Memorial 67736692.

28. New York City Municipal Deaths, 1795-1949, New York Municipal Archives. John Kastendiech [*sic*] in entry for Amelia Gerken, 15 Sep 1913, citing Death, Brooklyn, Kings, New York.

29. *Brooklyn Daily Eagle*, 24 Apr 1889, p. 1.

30. 1920 US Census, New York, Kings, Brooklyn Assembly District 12, T625, roll 1163, p. 11B, National Archives. George D. Gerken.

Chapter 5. John Henry Kastendieck

1. Kastendieck, Biography of John D. Kastendieck, p. 1; 1855 New York State Census, Enumeration District 5, Ward 11, New York State Library. Henry Counrich [*sic*]. The name Kastendieck was transcribed as Counrich in the census index. Henry Kastendieck had been in the city for three years prior to the census.

2. *Smith's Brooklyn Directory, 1856-1858*, subsequently *Lain's Brooklyn Directory*, published by Lain and Company, Brooklyn Public Library.

3. 1850 US Census, New York, Ward 11, Series M432 Roll 547, p. 495B, National Archives. Charles Windler [*sic*].

4. New York City Marriage Records, 1829-1940, New York City Municipal Archives. John H. Kastendeich [*sic*] and Cath. Benthia [*sic*], 31 Dec 1854.

5. Kenneth J. Gruschow, Find A Grave Memorial 13215318, 2006. Gruschow traces his ancestry through the Henry and Catharine (Benthen) Kastendieck line.

6. 1855 New York State Census, Enumeration District 5, Ward 11, New York State Library. Henry Counrich [*sic*].

7. 1865 New York State Census, New York, Kings, Brooklyn, Ward 12, New York State Library. Henry Kastendike [*sic*].

8. Kenneth J. Gruschow, Find A Grave Memorial 13215318.

9. 1875 New York State Census, New York, Kings, Brooklyn, New York State Library. Emile Zollinger.

10. 1875 New York State Census, New York, Kings, New Lots, New York State Library. Henry Kastendick [*sic*].

11. 1880 US Census, New York, Kings, New Lots, Series T9 Roll: 857, p. 434C, National Archives. Henry Kastendeick [*sic*].

12. Kenneth J. Gruschow, Find A Grave Memorial 13215393.

13. Green-Wood Cemetery Register, Kastendieck, John H. 1885-10-23 Lot 9625 Section 116; Kenneth J. Gruschow, Find A Grave Memorial 38066089; New York City Municipal Deaths, 1795-1949, Brooklyn, Kings, New York Municipal Archives. John Henry Kastindeeck [sic], 20 Oct 1885.

14. New York City Municipal Deaths, 1795-1949, Brooklyn, Kings, New York Municipal Archives, John D. Kastendick [sic], 11 Apr 1899.

15. New York, Kings County Estate Files, 1866-1923, 1900, Surrogate Court, Brooklyn. Catherina Kastendieck's will was dated 18 Apr 1899 and signed by P.A. Nolan of No. 114 9th Street, Brooklyn and D. [Dietrich] Ficken 449 3rd Ave, Brooklyn, p. 3 [Green-Wood Cemetery lot co-owner].

16. New York City Municipal Deaths, 1795-1949, New York Municipal Archives. Henry Kastendick [sic] in entry for Mary Gruschow, 22 Oct 1900.

17. Kenneth J. Gruschow, Find A Grave Memorial 13215218, 2006.

18. Kenneth J. Gruschow, Find A Grave Memorial 5205785, 2001.

19. Kenneth J. Gruschow, Find A Grave Memorial 5039493, 2000. Kenneth Gruschow descends from Charles Gruschow and Mary (Kastendieck) Gruschow.

20. New York City Municipal Deaths, 1795-1949, Brooklyn, Kings, New York Municipal Archives. Mary Katstendick [sic] in entry for Charles Gruschow, 05 Jun 1917; Green-Wood Cemetery Register, Brooklyn, Kings County, New York, Lot 21877, Sec. 176, 5 Jun 1917.

21. Kenneth J. Gruschow Find A Grave Memorial 13215500, 2006. Henry Kastendieck, Jr., 5 Feb 1920, Park Slope, Kings County (Brooklyn).

22. *Smith's Brooklyn Directory, 1856-1858*, subsequently *Lain's Brooklyn Directory*, published by Lain and Company, Brooklyn Public Library.

23. New York, Kings County Estate Files, 1866-1923, probate of Henry Kastendieck Jr, Kings County Surrogate's Court 23 Apr 1920. At the time of his death Henry Kastendieck Jr., was a resident of 149 Seventh Ave, Borough of Brooklyn.

24. Probate of Henry Kastendieck Jr, Kings County Surrogate's Court 23 Apr 1920.

Chapter 6. John Dietrich Kastendieck

1. Kastendieck, Biography of John D. Kastendieck. Augusta Kastendieck gives Dietrich Kastendieck's birth year as 1833.

2. Kastendieck, Biography of John D. Kastendieck.

3. 1855 New York State Census, New York, Kings, Brooklyn City, Ward 8, New York State Library. John Kastendieck.

4. Kastendieck, Biography of John D. Kastendieck.

5. Kastendieck, Biography of John D. Kastendieck.

6. David Gay Genealogy, 2013.

7. 1860 US Census, New York, Kings, Brooklyn Ward 12 District 1, Series M653 Roll pp. 771, 766, National Archives.

8. John Dietrich Castendick [sic] and Rebecka Röpke Marriage Certificate, Zion Church, Brooklyn, New York, 30 May 1862, David Gay Collection.

9. Kastendieck, Biography of John D. Kastendieck.

10. New York City Municipal Deaths, 1795-1949, Brooklyn, Kings, New York. Helena Dorothea Kastenbrick [sic], 11 Dec 1865.

11. 1875 New York State Census, New York, Kings, Brooklyn, New York State Library. Alice Kastendiek [sic] in household of John Kastendiek.

12. 1880 US Census, Missouri, Christian, Polk, Series T9 Roll 681, p. 7C, National Archives. John D. Kastendirk [sic].

13. Inscription, Rose Hill Cemetery, Billings, Missouri; Find A Grave Memorial 14778728.

Chapter 7. Trina

1. Kastendieck, Biography of John D. Kastendieck., p. 1.

2. 1855 New York State Census, New York, Kings, Ward 8 Brooklyn City, National Archives. John Kastendieck.

3. Green-Wood Cemetery Register. Kastendieck, Mary C. 1856-02-24 Lot 9625 Section 116.

4. Tombstone Inscription, Green-Wood Cemetery, Brooklyn, New York. T.M. Kastendieck 7 Sep 1731-17 Jul 1857. John Friedrich Wilhelm Kastendieck and John Herman Kastendieck purchased the cemetery lot.

5. New York Deaths and Burials 1795-1952, New York Municipal Archives. Maria Kastendieorr [sic] 17 Jul 1857, Brooklyn, Kings, New York, 1857, p. 77. Trina gave her age on the 1855 New York State Census as 70. Based on her birthdate on her tombstone of 1791 she would have been 64. A New York death record lists her as age 65 at the time of her death.

6. Green-Wood Cemetery Register, Maria Kastendieck Lot 9625 Section 116; Find A Grave, Memorial 59488843; Ken Burchett Correspondence with Green-Wood Executive Office, Green-Wood Cemetery, 500 25th Street, Brooklyn, New York, 25 Mar 2011. Trina probably died at the home of her eldest son, John Friedrich Kastendieck who lived at 19th Street and Third Avenue and not Fifth Avenue as the transcribed record showed.

7. Find A Grave Memorial 59286150; Green-Wood Cemetery Register. Kasdendick [*sic*], John 1892-04-20 Lot 9625 Section 116.

8. Green-Wood Cemetery Register. Kastendiek [*sic*], Bridget 1869-08-06 Lot 9625 Section 116.

9. Marriage Certificate of John Herman Kastendieck and Elida Nilson; Ken Burchett Correspondence with Bob Collins, Find A Grave, 23 Mar 2011; Find A Grave, Memorial 67424420; Ken Burchett Correspondence with Ken Gruschow, 1 Apr 2011. Gruschow prefers Marie to Maria. The burial record gives her name as Maria. Gruschow is the third great grandson of Trina by her son Henry Kastendieck. In 2011, Trina's gravesite, heretofore unknown by her descendants, was rediscovered in Green-Wood Cemetery in the Kastendieck plot, Section 116, Lot 9625. When the gravestone marked T.M. Kastendieck was first noticed, the 1791 birth date carved on the stone coincided with the matriarch's known birthdate, suggesting that it could be the German-born mother of the Brooklyn Kastendiecks, many of whom were interred in Green-Wood Lot 9625. However, the Green-Wood Cemetery directory showed only the burial of Maria Kastendieck 1857-07-20, Section 116, Lot 9625; and not, the name on the tombstone of T. M. Kastendieck. Her name originally was interpreted in family records as "Irina" Kastendieck based on an entry on the marriage certificate of one of her sons, but not heretofore as T. M. or Trina Maria Kastendieck.

Chapter 8. Brooklyn, New York

1. Burrows and Wallace, *Gotham.*

Chapter 9. Red Hook and the Atlantic Basin Riot

1. Red Hook today is an eclectic mix of industry, private residences, and artists. Home to about 11,000 people, the area is working to restore its past reputation as a desirable place to live. Deteriorated neighborhoods in the 1990s harbored drug-related activities that gained Red Hook a reputation as the crack capital of America.

2 The *Brooklyn Daily Eagle* newspaper began publication in October of 1841 and chronicled the growth of Brooklyn for more than a hundred years. The *Eagle* published until 1955, with a brief revival in 1962–1963 and again after 1996 by different owners. It is the primary source of information on the growth and development of Brooklyn, New York.

3. Information on the early formation of Brooklyn comes from an article that appeared in the *Brooklyn Daily Eagle,* 2 Dec 1872, page 4. The delivery of German immigrants in the fall of 1845 raises the possibility that contrary to family tradition, John Herman may have immigrated in 1845 and not 1846, or he came in a second wave of German workers.

4. *Brooklyn Daily Eagle,* Apr 15, 1846, p. 2.

5. *Brooklyn Daily Eagle,* Apr 24, 1846, p. 2.

6. *Brooklyn Daily Eagle,* Apr 24, 1846, p. 2.

7. *Brooklyn Daily Eagle,* Apr 20, 1846, p. 2.

Chapter 10. Corner of Van Brunt and Wolcott

1. Stiles, *History of the City of Brooklyn,* 1870.

2. *Brooklyn Daily Eagle,* 20 Mar 1846, p. 2.

3. *Brooklyn Daily Eagle,* 19 Jul 1896, p. 20.

4. *Brooklyn Daily Eagle,* 2 Aug 1846, p. 2.

5. *Brooklyn Daily Eagle,* 22 Nov 1849, p. 3.

6. *Smith's Brooklyn Directory,* 1856-1858.

7. *Brooklyn Daily Eagle,* 14 Mar 1851, p. 3.

8. *Brooklyn Daily Eagle,* 13 May 1851, p. 3.

9. *Brooklyn Daily Eagle,* 26 Jan 1852, p. 3.

10. *New York times,* 23 May 1853.

11. *Brooklyn Daily Eagle,* 23 Apr 1853, p. 3.

12. *Brooklyn Daily Eagle,* 18 Jul 1854, p. 3.

13. *Brooklyn Daily Eagle,* 23 Apr 1853.

Chapter 11. The Liquor License

1. *Smith's Brooklyn Directory,* 1856-1858.

2. *New York City Directory 1852,* p. 286.

3. *Brooklyn Daily Eagle,* 15 Sep 1854; p. 1.

4. *Brooklyn Daily Eagle,* 15 Sep 1854, p. 1.

5. *Brooklyn Daily Eagle,* 9 Nov 1858, p. 2.

6. *Brooklyn Daily Eagle,* 24 May 1860, p. 3.

7. *Brooklyn Daily Eagle,* 15 Jun 1867, p. 3.

Chapter 12. Bridget Ford of Ireland

1. Kastendieck Family Bible, Jayme Burchett Collection; Ken Burchett Correspondence from Bob Collins, 2 Apr 2011, "Bridget Ford Wife of J.H.

Kastendieck, born Sept. 11, 1836, died Aug. 3, 1869;" Bridget Ford death certificate, "33 years, 7 months, 18 days." The marriage record of Bridget and John Herman's marriage has not been located. The New York City archives for Brooklyn go back only to 1866. They were married in 1855.

2. Baptismal Certificate of Andrew Kastendieck, Dee Willauer Collection; Copy of grant of badge to Lt. Col. George Robert Gayre of Galval, Cornwall, Sept. 30, 1948, Dublin, National Library of Ireland, Genealogical Office, Ms. 111g, fol. 59. The name Galval appears one other time on an unrelated certificate issued in 1948 on file in Dublin.

3. At the time of Brooklyn's consolidation with New York City in 1898, there were 32 wards.

4. Naturalization Index, dated 7 Dec 1854, City Court, Brooklyn, New York; Vol. 17, Record Number 261. John Herman Kastendieck, Kingdom of Hanover, witness Herman Mahnken. Most 19th Century petitions for naturalization showed the applicant's name, country of birth or allegiance, signature, and date of naturalization. Seldom did the date or port of arrival appear on these records. Family information (including spouse and children info) was not included on these early records.

5. 1855 New York Census, New York, Brooklyn City, Ward 12, New York State Library. Therman [*sic*] Kastendieck, 29, Bridget Kastendieck, wife, 20; 1855 New York Census, New York, Kings, Brooklyn City, Ward 8, New York State Library. John Kastendieck, 33, Diedrick Kastendieck, brother, 21, Mary C. Kastendieck, sister, 24, Mary [Trina Marie] Kastendieck, mother, 70; 1855 New York Census, New York, New York City, Ward 11, New York State Library. Henry Counrich [Kastendieck], 30, Catharine Counrich, wife, 33, Adeline Winale [Windeler], daughter, 9. The names cited are those transcribed for the 1855 New York Census. Henry Kastendieck's name is barely recognizable but it was clearly the census entry for him based on his age, origin, and the name of his wife Catharine and stepdaughter Adeline. The indexed transcriptions are to enable future references to the census records.

Chapter 13. Death and Life in Brooklyn

1. Kastendieck Family Bible, John Herman Kastendieck 6 Dec 1855.

2. Kastendieck Family Bible, William Henry Kastendieck, 27 Nov 1857-8 Jan 1858.

3. Kastendieck Family Bible, Heinrich Kastendieck, 13 Nov 1858-19 Nov 1858; New York City Municipal Deaths, 1795-1949, New York Municipal Archives, "Henry Kastendych [sic] 19 Nov 1858 Van Brunt and Dykeman.

4. Kastendieck Family Bible, Belinda Kastendieck, 25 Nov 1859-15 Nov 1859; New York City Municipal Deaths, 1795-1949, New York Municipal Archives, "Kastendyck [sic] 30 Nov 1859 Brooklyn.

5. Green-Wood Cemetery Records, Sec 116, Lot 9625; confirmed by Bob Collins email Apr 2, 2011; posted on Find A Grave by Ken Gruschow under John F. W. Kastendieck.

6. *1859 Brooklyn City Directory.*

7. *Brooklyn Daily Eagle,* 19 Aug 1877, p. 4.

8 Stiles, *History of Kings County,* 806-807; New York City Landmarks Preservation Commission, Designation List 332, LP-2108, 18 Dec 2001.

9. 1860 U.S. Census, New York, Kings, 1st District, 12th Ward, Brooklyn. Series M653 Roll 771, p. 766. Dwelling #156 Family #313, "John H. Kasteindeick [sic], 34, grocer, $4,000 real $1,000 personal, b. Hanover; Bellinda [sic], 25, b. Ireland; John H., 4, b. NY; Harmon Schule, 16, clerk, b. Hanover; Rebecka Röpke, 19, servant, b. Hanover.

10. *The Eagle and Brooklyn*, Vol. 1, Fall 1861.

11. Brooklyn Collection, Brooklyn Public Library.

12. Kastendieck Family Bible, George Kastendieck, 18 May 1861.

13. *Brooklyn Daily Eagle*, 31 Mar 1862, p. 10.

14. *New York Times*, 19 May 1894.

15. *Brooklyn Daily Eagle,* 15 Jan 1862, p. 4.

Chapter 14. The Civil War

1. Brooklyn Collection, Brooklyn Public Library.

2. *Brooklyn Daily Eagle,* 13 Jul 1863, p. 3.

3. *Brooklyn Daily Eagle*, 10 Jul 1863, p, 2.

4. Kastendieck Family Bible, Andrew Kastendieck 18 Sep 1863.

5. Baptism Certificate of Andrew Kastendieck 13 Dec 1863, Brooklyn, New York, Dee Willauer Collection.

6. Brooklyn Collection, Brooklyn Public Library.

Chapter 15. Post-War Episodes

1. Kastendieck Family Bible "Amelyia [sic] Maria Dorothea Kastendieck b. 6 Aug 1866 d. 1 Jul 1918." The spelling of Amelyia is incorrect. Her name always appeared as Amelia.

2. *New York Times*, Jul 28, 1866.

3. *Brooklyn Daily Eagle*, 5 Jun 1867, p. 2.

4. *Brooklyn Daily Eagle*, 15 Apr 1861.

5. *Brooklyn Daily Eagle*, 31 Jul 1867, p. 3.

6. *Brooklyn Daily Eagle*, 22 Sep 1869, p. 2.

7. *Brooklyn Daily Eagle*, 9 Feb 1870, p. 2.

8. *Brooklyn Daily Eagle*, 21 Jun 1867, p. 3.

Chapter 16. The Death of Bridget Kastendieck

1. Eberle, *A Treatise on the Theory and Practice of Medicine*, pp. 213-223.

2. Eberle, *A Treatise on the Theory and Practice of Medicine*, p. 215.

3. 1870 US Census. New York, Kings County, 3-WD Brooklyn, Series M593 Roll 946, p. 202.

4. Stiles, *A History of the City of Brooklyn*.

5. *New York Times*, 12 Feb 1901. Dr. Bond became a rich man and continued to practice medicine in Brooklyn alongside his other business interests that included real estate and banking. He died at home on 10 Feb 1901.

6. *Brooklyn Daily Eagle*, 24 Jun 1869, 2.p.

7. Smith. *A Treatise on the Diseases of Infancy and Childhood*.

8. Bridget Kastendieck Death Certificate 5816, New York City Municipal Archives. The death certificate contains three questionable entries. Somone initially wrote Bridget's length of time as a resident of Brooklyn as 10 years, and then overwrote it with 13. Her age at the time of death they recorded as 33 years 7 months 18 days. However, according to her date of birth recorded in the Kastendieck Family Bible, she was 33 years 10 months and 18 days. Her place of burial, listed as Holy Cross Cemetery, was in fact Green-Wood Cemetery.

9. New York City Municipal Deaths, 1795-1949, New York Municipal Archives. Bridget Kastenbeck [sic] 3 Aug 1869 Van Brunt & Wolcott, 12 Ward, age 33, housekeeping, burial 6 Aug 1869 Holy Cross Cemetery [sic], parents born in Ireland [names not provided].

10. *Brooklyn Daily Eagle*, 3 Aug 1869, p. 3.

11. Death Certificate of Bridget Kastendieck; *Lain's Directory of Brooklyn Undertakers* for 1979-1880 lists William Cody at 506 Court Street. The *Brooklyn Daily Eagle* of 1872 places him at 463 Court Street.

12. *Brooklyn Daily Eagle,* 18 Aug 1870, p. 4.

13. *Brooklyn Daily Eagle,* 31 Dec 1872, p. 4 and 4 Jun 1873, p. 4.

14. *Brooklyn Daily Eagle*, 4 Aug 1869, p. 3 and 5 Aug 1869, p. 3.

15. *Brooklyn Daily Eagle*, 29 Jul 1848, p. 3.

16. Green-Wood Cemetery Index of Burials.

Chapter 17. Green-Wood Cemetery

1. Burrows and Wallace, *Gotham,* a *History of New York City to 1898.*

2. *Brooklyn Daily Eagle*, 4 Sep 1854, p. 2.

3. *Brooklyn Daily Eagle,* 17 Sep 1869, p. 2.

4. *Brooklyn Daily Eagle,* 13 Jun 1859, p. 3.

5. *Brooklyn Daily Eagle,* 7 Sep 1842, p. 2.

6. Burrows and Wallace, *Gotham: a History of New York City to 1898*, p. 719.

7. *Brooklyn Daily Eagle,* 31 Jul 1877, p. 2.

Chapter 18. The Seventies

1. *Brooklyn Daily Eagle,* 9 Aug 1869, p. 2.

2. 1870 U.S. Census. New York, Kings, 12th Ward Brooklyn, Series M593, Roll 953, p. 480. Dwelling #805 Family #1754. Kastendieck, John, 44, Ret[ail] Grocer, $30,000 Real $2,000 Personal, b. Hanover, parents of foreign birth; John, 14, [occupation illegible?], b. NY attended school within the year; George, 9, b. NY attended school; Andrew, 7, b. NY attended school; Amelia, 4, b. NY; [living in the same household on the following census page] Kastendieck, Dorris, 54, Keeping House, b. Hanover, parents foreign born; Richard, 19, clerk in store, b. Hanover, parents foreign born; Behru, Herman, 23, clerk in store, b. Hanover, parents foreign born.

3. *Brooklyn Daily Eagle*, 27 Jul 1870, p. 4.

4. *Brooklyn Daily Eagle,* 9 Apr 1872, p. 5.

5. *Brooklyn Daily Eagle,* 20 Sep 1871, p. 4.

6. "Red Hook Point," *Brooklyn Daily Eagle,* 2 Dec 1872, p. 4.

7. *Boyd's Brooklyn Directory,* 1873. The directory erroneously listed J.D. Kastendieck as I.D. Kastendieck.

Chapter 19. Out of Brooklyn

1. Marriage Certificate 2133, City of New York Municipal Archives; copy obtained 7 May 2011.

2. 1870 US Census, New York, Brooklyn. The name Hannah is taken from the 1870 census, 12-Ward of Brooklyn, which lists Hannah Hansen [sic], 29, dressmaker, born in Norway, with a son Henry, age 4; Cecelia, age 7; and George, age 9. The 1880 US Census for Christian County, Missouri, lists Henry Hansen, 14, stepson of John Kastendieck. Subsequent research connected Henry Hanson and his twin siblings to John Herman's marriage to Hannah Hanson.

3. Certificate of Marriage 218, 2 Feb 1873, New York City Municipal Archives; Find A Grave Memorial 62799026; John Herman and Bridget Kastendieck Family Bible; 1900 US Census, Texas, Lamar, Series T623 Roll 1652, p. 8A, National Archives, Andy J. Riggins. These sources give the birth of Hermina Kastendieck on different dates of 24 Sep 1872, 16 Sep 1873, and Sep 1874.

4. John Herman and Bridget Kastendieck Family Bible.

5. Doris Kastendick [sic] came to our attention as the child of John H. Kastendieck through the research of Jim Murray, a New York historian who specializes in family history. He discovered a record of her death in the New York Archives, Death Certificate 5435, Kings County. She died June 19, 1876, age 7 months. The death certificate gives the cause of death as Cholera Infantum, date of birth of [Dec] 1875 and burial in Green-Wood Cemetery on June 20. The certificate does not name her parents but gives the birthplace of her father as Germany and of her mother as Schweden (German for Sweden). The certificate gives the place of Doris' death as 370 Van Brunt Street, Brooklyn, the same address as John Kastendieck's grocery store and the address from which Bridget Kastendieck's funeral started in 1869. In later years, Minnie Kastendieck gave the birthplace of her mother variously as Sweden, Norway, and Switzerland.

6. Tilden, *The Etiology of Cholera Infantum.*

7. *Real Estate Record and Builders' Guide*, Vol. 16, No. 381 (July 3 1875) & No. 393, p. 631; No. 406 (Dec. 25 1875). Kings County, New York, Sept 17, westerly cor. Van Brunt and Wolcott sts, 50 x 90; Van Brunt St., w. s., 50 s. Wolcott st., 25 x 90, hs. & ls; John H. Kastendieck to John Dietrich Kastendieck, $20,000.

8. *Real Estate Record and Builders' Guide,* v. 16 no. 381 (July 3 1875), no. 406 (Dec. 25 1875). [Brooklyn, N.Y.]: C.W. Sweet & Co., 1868-1884; v. 16, no. 393, p. 631.

9. John Herman Kastendieck may have owned more than one store on Van Brunt because the 1878 *Brooklyn City Directory* listed John H. Kastendick [*sic*], grocer, at 370 Van Brunt Street, and two years earlier had listed him at 396 Van Brunt.

10. *Brooklyn Daily Eagle,* 4 Feb 1876, p. 2.

11. *Brooklyn Daily Eagle,* 14 Feb 1876, p. 4.

12. *Brooklyn Daily Eagle,* 24 May 1876, p. 4.

13. *Brooklyn Daily Eagle,* 21 Jun 1876, p. 4.

14. *Brooklyn Daily Eagle,* 5 July 1876, 2, p. 4

15. *Brooklyn Daily Eagle,* 7 Mar 1877, p. 4.

Chapter 20. Sorting of Kastendiecks

1. *1878 Brooklyn City Directory.*

2. 1870 US Census, New York, Kings, 8th Ward Brooklyn. Series M593 Roll 950, p. 100. Dwelling #1298 Family #1596. Cassendick [*sic*], John 50, milkman, $600 personal property b. Hanover, parents of foreign birth; Mary, 30, housekeeping, b. Hanover, parents of foreign birth; Maggie, 8, b. NY; Annie, 4, b. NY; Dora, 2, b. NY.

3. 1870 US Census New York, Kings, Ward 12 Brooklyn, pp. 207-208.

4. *Brooklyn Daily Eagle,* 22 Aug 879, p. 3; 29 Sep 1879, p. 4.

5. *1879/80 Lain's Brooklyn Directory.*

6. *1888-1890 Brooklyn Directories; 1897 Lain's Brooklyn Directory.*

7. Augusta Kastendieck Family Album, David Gay Collection.

8. *Brooklyn Methodist Episcopal Churches History.*

9. *Brooklyn Daily Eagle,* 30 Mar 1872, p. 2.

10. *Brooklyn Daily Eagle,* 13 Sep 1877, p. 3.

Chapter 21. Wives of John Herman

1. Hazel Kastendieck Shafer Notes (no date). Two pages of handwritten notes by Hazel Shafer found in the John Herman Kastendieck Family Bible, Jayme Schaumann Burchett Collection.

2. Analysis of dates in the Family Bible shows that at the time of their marriage John Herman was 28 years 11 months old; Bridget was 19 years 4 months 29 days. Their marriage lasted 14 years 5 months and 20 days.

3. Bridget Kastendieck Death Certificate 5816, New York City Municipal Archives.

4. Civil registration of Brooklyn marriages began in April of 1866. Marriages prior to that time depended on church, newspaper, Bible, or census records. The city of Brooklyn began civil marriage registration upon passage by the New York State Legislature of an act that created a Metropolitan Sanitary District and formed a Board of Health to oversee it.

5. *Brooklyn Daily Eagle*, 22 Nov 1856, p. 3.

6. *Brooklyn Daily Eagle*, 22 Nov 1856, p. 3.

7. Zion German Evangelical Lutheran Marriage Records Index; John D. Kastendieck and Rebecca Röpke Marriage Certificate, David Gay Collection.

8. Kenneth Gruschow, Find A Grave Memorial 5205785. Mary Kastendieck, Charles Gruschow.

9. Andrew Kastendieck Baptismal Certificate, Dee Willauer Collection.

10. Spelled as Wyckoff and Wycoff in newspaper listings, the name of the Wyckoff Methodist Episcopal Church appeared in the *New York Times* as late as 1897.

11. *Brooklyn Methodist Episcopal Churches History.*

12. John Herman and Bridget Kastendieck Family Bible. John Herman Kastendieck, Jr., b. 6 Dec 1855.

13. 1870 US Census, New York, Kings, Brooklyn Ward 12, Series M593 Roll 953, pp. 207-208, enumerated 12 Jul 1870. John Kastendeick [*sic*]. Bridget died 3 Aug 1869. From the time from her death until the census enumeration, it was 11 months 9 days. Dorris gave her age as 54 on the census but according to her tombstone inscription, she would have been 52. Her name appeared alternately in the records spelled as Dora and Dorothea; full name Anna Dorothea Kastendieck Boevers.

14. Find A Grave Memorial 147791724, Kenneth J. Gruschow, 2015. Anna Dorothea's two children died in 1857. We know nothing of her husband, Henry Boevers. In the 1870 census, she had reverted to using her maiden name, Kastendieck. Her tombstone lists her as Anna D. Kastendieck, wife of Henry Boevers. Her infant children were buried in Green-Wood Cemetery under the surname Boevers.

15. 1870 US Census, New York, Kings, Brooklyn Ward 12, Series M593 Roll 953, p. 203. Hannah Hansen [*sic*].

16. Marriage Certificate 2133 of Johann H. Kastendieck and Hannah Hanson, dated 27 Nov 1870, New York City Department of Records and Information Services, New York Municipal Archives. Officials added

important family information to New York marriage certificates in the year 1866. Several details regarding the lives of John Herman and Hannah are from this document despite its deteriorated and sometimes illegible condition. For example, in addition to the rare signatures of John Herman and Hannah, Dorothea [Aunt Dora] Boevers, sister of John Herman, signed as witness to their marriage.

17. New York City Death Index, Kings County, certificate 549, New York Municipal Archives. Hansen [*sic*], Bernard F. 35 y Jan 25 1867; Michigan Deaths and Burials 1800-1995 film number 1004850. Cecelia Hanson in later life married a Beck and moved to Michigan. Her death certificate names her parents as Bernard Hanson and Hannah Gyridahl. The spelling of the name Gyridahl appears in other records as Gerdahl.

18. 1870 US Census, New York, Kings, 12-Ward, Brooklyn, Series M593 Roll 953, 203. Hannah Hansen.

19. New York City Marriage Records, 1829-1940, New York City Municipal Archives. Peder Geselahl [*sic*] and Jiagina Swensen [*sic*].

20. Helland, "Work among the Scandinavian Seamen," p. 314.

21. New York City Municipal Deaths, 1795-1949, Kings, Brooklyn, cn8213, New York Municipal Archives. Johanna H. Kastendeick [*sic*], 23 Jul 1872, 307 Van Brunt.

22. Green-Wood Cemetery Index. The record of her burial at Green-Wood was indexed as Kastendieck, Johanna H. 1872-07-25, Lot 9625 Section 116, the Kastendieck plot.

23. *Brooklyn Daily Eagle*, 20 Mar 1875, p. 1.

24. 1875 New York State Census, New York, Kings, Brooklyn, 32, New York State Library. John Kastendieck.

25. Certificate of Marriage State of New York 218, dated 12 Feb 1873, New York City Department of Records and Information Services, New York City Municipal Archives; New York City Municipal Deaths, 1795-1949, Elida Sophia Kastendieck.

26. Stiles, *A History of the City of Brooklyn*, 1870.

27. 1870 US Census, New York, Kings, 11-WD Brooklyn [South half of the 11th ward of Brooklyn] Series M593 Roll 952, p. 228. Hunt, Albert S.

28. Brown, *The Cyclopaedia of American Biography*, pp. 241-242.

29. *Brooklyn Daily Eagle*, 7 Mar 1871, p. 8.

30. Hunt, "Introduction," 1885.

31. Hunt, "Sermon 18," 1865, pp. 317-327.

32. 1880 US Census, New York Kings 7-WD, Brooklyn, Series T9 Roll 843, p. 94. Hunt, A. S.

33. John Herman and Bridget Kastendieck Family Bible, Jayme Burchett Collection.

34. New York City Municipal Deaths, 1795-1949, cn2057, New York Municipal Archives. Elida Sophia Kastendieck, 29 Feb 1876

35. Find A Grave Memorial 59492258 and 59624592. Doris and Edward Kastendick [sic].

36. Green-Wood Cemetery Index of Burials. Kastendieck, Elida S. 1876-08-12 Lot 21709 Section 63. Her infant children were buried in this same lot.

37. New York City Municipal Deaths, 1795-1949, cn2057. Elida Sophia Kastendieck, 2 Mar 1876, Green-Wood.

38. Ken Burchett Correspondence from Jane Cuccurullo, Green-Wood Cemetery, 2010.

39. Find A Grave Memorials 120859178 and 120859653. Casper and Anna Röpke Ficken; Green-Wood Cemetery Burial Index. Ficken, Casper 1893-11-03, Lot 21709 Section 63.

40. John Herman and Caroline Wingood Kastendieck Marriage Certificate 2196, dated 3 Dec 1876, New York City Department of Records and Information Services, New York City Municipal Archives. Costendieck [sic] John, Wingood, Caroline.

Chapter 22. Into Missouri

1. Stern, Mellins, and Fishman, *New York 1880*.

2. Kastendieck, Biography of John D. Kastendieck.

3. Kastendieck, Biography of John D. Kastendieck.

4. Faust, *The German Element in the United States*, 1:538.

5. Goodrich, "Gottfried Duden," 145.

6. Faust, *The German Element in the United States*, 1:441.

7. Goodrich, "Gottfried Duden," pp. 131-146.

8. US Census German States; United States. Secretary of the Interior. "Table LL—Nativity of foreigners residing in each state and territory." *Statistics of the United States in 1860.* Washington, D.C.: Government Printing Office, 1866; Richardson, *The Secret Service, the Field, the Dungeon, the Escape,* p. 161.

9. *Brooklyn Daily Eagle*, 3 Aug 1877, p. 2.

10. *Brooklyn Daily Eagle*, 3 Aug 1869, p. 2.

11. *Brooklyn Daily Eagle*, 4 Oct 1869, p. 1.

12. *Brooklyn Daily Eagle*, 20 May 1877, p. 2.

13. *Brooklyn Daily Eagle*, 1 Oct 1880, p. 4.

14. *100 Years of Service: Frisco Centennial Year 1860-1960*. St. Louis: Frisco Veterans' Reunion, 1960.

Chapter 23. Christian County

1. *Christian County*, p. 80.

2. Poken, Steve. "Why does Christian Co. have a Panhandle?" *Springfield News-Leader*, (10 Aug 2018): 6A.

3. *Christian County*, pp. 2-3, 80.

4. *Christian County*, pp. 2-3.

5. Rennick, *Kentucky Place Names*, pp. 97–98.

6. *Christian County*, p. 81.

7. Rauch, *125 Years of Ministry*.

8. Rauch, *125 Years of Ministry*.

9. 1880 US Census, Missouri, Christian County, Polk Twp, Series T9 Roll 681, p. 6D. John H. Kastendirk [*sic*]; p. 7A John D. Kastendirk; p. 9A George Hansen; 1880 US Census, Missouri, Lawrence County, Marionville, Series T9 Roll 698, p. 547A Celia Hanson in household of Jesse Rouk [*sic*], National Archives.

10. *Christian County*, pp. 16, 82; *The Billings Times* discontinued publication in 1954.

11. *Brooklyn Daily Eagle*, 20 Apr 1879, p. 2.

12. 1880 US Census.

Chapter 24. Taxes, Churches, and Bald Knobbers

1. Kastendieck, Biography of John D. Kastendieck, p. 2.

2. Missouri State Archives, Trans. by Mabel Phillips, Christian County Library, Ozark, Missouri. Assessment day was June 1 of the previous year. Taxes due in 1880 were assessed on June 1, 1879.

3. 1875 New York State Census, Kings, Brooklyn, Ward 12, E.D. 02, New York State Library; 1870 US Census, New York: (2nd) City of Brooklyn, ward 12, Series M593, Roll 953, National Archives. The value of John Herman's personal estate was $2,000, real estate $30,000; projected to 1880 the same property would have grown in value to more than $40,000.

4. Hutter, "History of Billings."

5. *Christian County*, pp. 11, 85.

6. *Christian County*, p. 83.

7. Hutter, "History of Billings;" Funeral announcements dating to as late as 1912 confirm the Billings Methodist Episcopal Church as the Kastendieck worship preference. The name of the Methodist Episcopal Church was later changed to the Wesley Methodist Episcopal Church some time prior to 1921 before becoming known as the Billings Methodist Church and then as the Billings United Methodist Church. Sanborn Map, 1921. Missouri Secretary of State.

8. Rauch, *125 Years of Ministry; Christian County*, p. 87.

9. *Christian County*, pp. 11, 84.

10. Upton, *Bald Knobbers*.

11. *Abilene Reflector* [Abilene, Kansas], 8 Sep 1887.

12. *Christian County*, pp. 184-198.

13. Kastendieck, Biography of John D. Kastendieck, p. 2.

14. Rauch, *125 Years of Ministry*.

Chapter 25. Caroline's Court Case

1. Keet and Rountree Mercantile Company vs. Caroline Kastendieck, Circuit Courts of Christian, Greene, and Webster counties, Christian County Library and Missouri State Archives; Christian County Circuit Court Box 12 Folder 31, p. 2, Christian County Library. Keet and Rountree Mercantile sued Caroline Kastendieck—attachment in a civil action for $270.44 debt, which in today's dollars would be approximately $7,000.

2. Christian County Circuit Court Box 12 Folder 31, Christian County Library, p. 3.

3. Christian County Circuit Court Box 12 Folder 31, Christian County Library, p. 4.

4. Christian County Circuit Court Box 12 Folder 31, Christian County Library, p. 6.

5. Christian County Circuit Court Box 12 Folder 31, Christian County Library, p. 7.

6. Christian County, Missouri, Index to Circuit Court Records 1859-1899, Christian County Library.

7. *Springfield Leader* (Weekly), Greene County, Missouri 18 Jun 1891. Josiah T. Keet was the son of Charles T. Keet, a wealthy citizen of Greene County, Missouri. The elder Keet died in 1890, the year before the lawsuit against Caroline Kastendieck.

8. *Greene County, Missouri*, St. Louis, Mo.: Western Historical, 1883.

9. Christian County, Missouri, Personal Property Tax Index 1879-1900, Christian County Library.

10. Christian County Circuit Court Box 12 Folder 31, Christian County Library.

11. Christian County Circuit Court Box 12 Folder 31, Christian County Library, p. 8.

12. Christian County Circuit Court Box 12 Folder 31, Christian County Library.

13. Christian County Circuit Court Box 12 Folder 31, Christian County Library.

14. Christian County Circuit Court Box 12 Folder 31, Christian County Library.

15. Greene County Record Circuit Court Box 28 Folder 47, Missouri State Archives.

16. Christian County Circuit Court Box 12 Folder 31, Christian County Library.

17. Greene County Record Circuit Court Box 28 Folder 47, Missouri State Archives.

18. Greene County Record Circuit Court Box 28 Folder 47, Missouri State Archives, p. 10.

19. Greene County Record Circuit Court Box 28 Folder 47, Missouri State Archives, p. 13.

20. Greene County Record Circuit Court Box 28 Folder 47, Missouri State Archives.

21. Greene County Record Circuit Court Box 28 Folder 47, Missouri State Archives.

22. Greene County Record Circuit Court Box 28 Folder 47, Missouri State Archives, p. 14-15. The transcript of the Christian County proceedings was filed in Greene County but not Christian County where the record is incomplete because some of the original documents were required by law to accompany the transcript.

23. Greene County Record Circuit Court Box 28 Folder 47, Missouri State Archives, p. 18.

24. Greene County Record Circuit Court Box 28 Folder 47, Missouri State Archives, p. 19.

25. Greene County Record Circuit Court Box 28 Folder 47, Missouri State Archives, p. 20.

26. *Revised Statutes of the State of Missouri, 1879* (Vol. 1), Jefferson City, Mo.: Carter and Regan, 1879, p. 204.

27. Webster County Circuit Court Box 26 Folder 45, Missouri State Archives.

28. Greene County Record Circuit Court Box 28 Folder 47, Missouri State Archives.

29. Christian County, Missouri, Personal Property Tax Index 1879-1900, Christian County Library.

30. Find A Grave Memorial 84218208.

Chapter 26. Rose Hill

1. *Brooklyn Daily Eagle*, 31 May 1883, p. 24 Sep 1883, p. 4.

2. *Brooklyn Daily Eagle*, 5 Feb, 1889, p. 6.

3. *Brooklyn Daily Eagle,* 8 Mar 1887, p. 4

4. Brooklyn Daily Eagle, 20 Apr 1890, p. 20.

5. Rauch, 125 *Years of Ministry,*

6. John Herman and Bridget Kastendieck Family Bible. Receipt from Rose Hill Cemetery Association; Perpetual Maintenance Trust Fund for Lot 36, Block 2, 23 May 1968, $100 paid by Frank A. Kastendieck, Geo. H. Kastendieck, Katherine Andrews, Hazel Shafer, Pauline Jeidy, and Oscar Brandemuehl.

7. Rose Hill Cemetery. From the intersection of Highways 60 & 14 in Billings, Missouri, go east on Highway 60 1.7 miles. Turn left on Rose Hill Road. Go 1.5 miles, the cemetery is on the right. Rose Hill closed in 1983, when replaced by a second Rose Hill, Rose Hill West.

8. "*Christian County,*" pp. 88-89.

9. Funeral Announcement and Obituary of John H. Kastendieck. Found pressed between pages 472 and 473—Psalms—in the John Herman and Bridget Kastendieck Family Bible. The funeral announcement measures 6.25 x 3.0 inches. The origin of the obituary clipping is unknown. It may have been placed in the Bible by John Herman Kastendieck, Jr., who inherited the Bible or by Caroline Kastendieck, wife of John Herman, Sr.

10. Billings Special Road District 1897-1900, p. 119, Christian County Library.

11. *Brooklyn Daily Eagle*, 6 Feb 1896, p. 7.

12. *Brooklyn Daily Eagle*, 1 Nov 1894, p. 6.

13. *Official Record Minutes of the St. Louis German Conference of the Methodist Episcopal Church*, 41 (September 8-13, 1920): 8; Find A Grave Memorial 99185668. Jacob Frederick Froeschle 1854-1912.

14. 1900 US Census, Missouri, Franklin, Washington Twp, Washington, Series T623 Roll 854, p. 28B, National Archives. Caroline Kascudick [*sic*].

15. *Rand-McNally Official Railway Guide and Hand Book.* Chicago: American Railway Guide, 1902, lxxxv.

16. Welty, Ruth. "Place Names of St. Louis and Jefferson County." M.A. thesis. University of Missouri-Columbia, 1939. The surviving institutions of the original Bethesda complex are known today as the Bethesda Health Group.

17. *Medical Forthnightly*, 16 (September 15, 1899): 538.

18. "Richard M. Scrugg's Gift on Behalf of Incurables Represents an Outlay of $73,000: Presents New Building to the Bethesda Home." *St. Louis Republic*, 7 April 1901, p. 9.

19. *New York Times*, 24 May 1897.

20. 1910 US Census, Missouri, St. Louis, Ward 16, Series T624 Roll 817, p. 15A, National Archives. Carrie V. Kastendick [*sic*].

21. Virginia Caroline Kastendieck Death Certificate 6706, filed 1 Feb 1912. Missouri State Board of Health, Secretary of State Archives. Caroline died 31 Jan 1912; *St. Louis Post-Dispatch* 1912 Burial Permit 2/3 p. 11, St. Louis Public Library. Virginia [*sic*] Kastendick [*sic*] 67 Billings, Mo. cancer.

Chapter 27. The Last Immigrant

1. Diedrich Kastendieck Application for Passport, New York City, 29 Apr 1869, Passport Applications 1795-1905, Series M1372 Roll 160, National Archives. Diedrich Kastendieck, age 35.

2. Kastendieck, Biography of John D. Kastendieck, pp. 1-2.

3. Kastendieck, Biography of John D. Kastendieck, p. 2.

4. Kastendieck, Biography of John D. Kastendieck, p. 1.

5. Kastendieck, Biography of John D. Kastendieck, p. 1.

6. Kastendieck, Biography of John D. Kastendieck, pp. 1-2.

7. Diedrich Kastendieck Application for Passport, New York City, 29 Apr 1869, Passport Applications 1795-1905, Series M1372 Roll 160, National Archives. Diedrich Kastendieck, age 35. The age of daughter Alice Kastendieck given on Diedrich Kastendieck's passport application was ten months, which raises the possibility that she was born in 1868 and not 1867 as given on her tombstone in Rose Hill Cemetery.

8. Kastendieck, Biography of John D. Kastendieck, p. 2.

9. Kastendieck, Biography of John D. Kastendieck, p. 2.

10. Christian County Centennial, *Christian County, Its first 100 years,* Jefferson City, MO: Von Hoffman, 1959, p. 81; Kastendieck, Biography of John D. Kastendieck, p. 2.

11. *Jefferson City Daily Tribune* 4 Sep 1892 p. 1, col. 3; *Official Manual, Missouri Office of the Secretary of State*, 1893, p. 317. The Kastendieck-Blades Milling Company incorporated as a flourmill, filed in Jefferson City, Missouri, 3 Sep 1892, issuing 150 shares of stock.

12. *Modern Miller*, St. Louis, 23 (August 14, 1897), p. 24 (11 June 1898). The Kastendieck-Blades Mill name appeared regularly in the *Modern Miller* and other trade magazines often endorsing mill equipment like Beall Wheat Temperer, a machine used to add moisture to wheat to improve the flour product, a machine the company used in its milling operations.

13. *Billings Weekly Times*, 1 Dec 1898.

14. Christian County Circuit Court Case Files 1860-1899, Box 255 Doc 20, microfilm 721.28, Missouri State Archives, Christian County Library.

15. Kastendieck, Biography of John D. Kastendieck, pp. 3-4. Noted taxidermist A. Russell Smith, of Pennsylvania, took note of the Kastendieck Bird Collection. Ornithologist Otto Widmann of St. Louis included frequent references to his collection in a 1907 publication, *A Preliminary Catalogue of the Birds of Missouri*; and Rudolf Bennett, well-known bird enthusiast from the University of Missouri, relied significantly on the Kastendieck collection in his *Catalog of Birds of Missouri*, also published in 1907.

16. Kastendieck, Biography of John D. Kastendieck, p. 4.

17. Kastendieck, Biography of John D. Kastendieck, pp. 2-3.

18. Kastendieck, Biography of John D. Kastendieck, p. 3.

19. Kastendieck, Biography of John D. Kastendieck, p. 4.

20. Kastendieck, Biography of John D. Kastendieck, p. 4.

21. Death Certificate of John D. Kastendieck, Christian County, File No. 35748, dated 8 Dec 1923, Missouri Board of Health, Missouri Secretary of State.

Chapter 28. Children of Diedrich and Rebecka

1. Kastendiok [*sic*], Charlotte, Froeschle, D., 10/12/1892, License No. ML000R0340, Christian County Recorder of Deeds; Christian County, Missouri, Marriages 1859-1940, Book 5, p. 114. Froeschle D. Charlottie [*sic*] Kastendieck 12 Oct 1892 Official: Schurtz William m g; *Minutes of the*

Seventy-Fifth Session of the Southern Illinois Conference Methodist Episcopal Church (September 21-26, 1926): 68. Ministerial assignments of Rev. David Froeschle up to the year 1905: 1891, St. Louis Ger., Billings, Mo.; 1893, New Melle, Mo.; 1895, Owensville, Mo.; 1899, Berger, Mo.; 1905, Jamestown, Mo.; "Our Honored Dead," *Official Minutes of the St. Louis German Conference,* 41-45 (August 1919): 303.

2. Genealogists sometimes attribute a daughter named Ruby to David and Charlotte Froeschle but no record of her birth confirms this.

3. 1900 US Census, Missouri, Franklin County, Boeuf Twp., Berger, Series T623 Roll 854, p. 11B; Find A Grave Memorial 26866386. Clarence Walter Froeschle b 10 Aug 1893 d 11 Jan 1973; Find A Grave Memorials 58639704 and 58639705. Edgar Froeschle b 6 Mar 1897 d 17 Mar 1977 and Ethyl Rebecca Froeschle b 14 Jan 1900 d 7 Sep 1992.

4. Find A Grave Memorial 13081572, b 20 Jun 1870 d 10 Apr 1905.

5. *Pulse Yearbook, 1907,* Central Wesleyan College, p. 126, Minnie Schumacher; 1919, p. 41, Edgar D. Froeschle. Central Wesleyan College was founded in 1854 to train ministers for the German Methodist Episcopal Church. The college closed in 1941.

6. 1930 US Census, Illinois, Madison County, Granite City, Series T626 Roll 542, p. 5B; *Pulse Yearbook, 1907,* p. 121; Find A Grave Memorial 142099425. Rev. David Daniel Froeschle b 1864 d 25 Jan 1949.

7. Christian County, Missouri, Marriages 1858-1940. Froeschle Clarence W Elizabeth Peiter 5 Sep 1919 Official: Orlowsky Geo pastor, Book 10, 166; 1930 US Census, Missouri, Stone, Grant, Series T626 Roll 1248, p. 1B; Find A Grave Memorial 25534692. Elizabeth Peiter Froeschle b 8 Dec 1891 d 14 Jul 1950.

8. *Pulse Yearbook, 1923,* p. 174; *South Orange County Directory,* 1932, p. 351. Froeschle, Edgar D. (Ruby R) teacher Willard Jr., High School, Santa Ana; Froeschle, Ethel teacher Franklin School, Santa Ana.

9. License No. ML000Z0072, Christian County Recorder; Louisa Kastendieck Death Certificate 38001, filed 4 Dec 1943, Missouri Board of Health, Secretary of State Archives; Christian County, Missouri, Marriages-1859-1940, Christian County Library. Kastendick [sic] J.D., Jr., Louisa Franck 30 Mar 1893 Book 5 p. 147 Sandmeyer J.J. rev.

10. Find A Grave Memorial 14778673, Clara M. Kastendieck b 5 Oct 1855, d 23 Apr 1943; Karl Dietrick [sic] Kastendieck b 5 Oct 1897 d 1 Nov 1953; Paul J. Kastendieck b 11 Feb 1899 d 24 Aug 1986; Willie Andrew Kastendieck b 25 Feb 1903 d 28 Feb 1904.

11. Christian County, Missouri-Businesses Listed on Personal Property Tax Lists 1879-1900: An Index, Christian County Library. Kastendieck, J.D., Jr., 1899 Polk #1833 value $668 tax $7.84 date 30 Dec 1899 J.D. Kastendieck; Merchant.

12. 1900 US Census, Missouri, Christian, Polk, Series T623 Roll 848, p. 3A, National Archives. John D. Kastendieck, Jr.,

13. Statement of Billings Creamery from 1 May 1907 to 1 May 1908, Dee Wilhaur Collection.

14. 1940 US Census, Missouri, Christian, Polk, Series T627 Roll 2096, p. 6A, National Archives. Jno. D. Kastendieck.

15. Clara M. Kastendieck Death Certificate 14023, filed 13 May 1943, Missouri Board of Health, Secretary of State Archives.

16. John D. Kastendieck Death Certificate 24694, filed 19 Jul 1943, Missouri Board of Health, Secretary of State Archives.

17. Obituary of Louisa (Franck) Kastendieck, *Christian County Republican*, 4 Nov 1943.

18. License No. ML000Z0125, Christian County Recorder; Christian County, Missouri Marriages-1859-1940, Christian County Library. Karl Kastendieck, Minnie Peiter 10 Dec 1919 Book 10 p. 189 Brown, Roy S. preacher.

19. Karl Detrick [sic] Kastendieck Death Certificate 35613, filed 9 Nov 1953, Missouri Board of Health, Secretary of State Archives.

20. Obituary of Karl Dietrick Kastendieck, *Christian County Republican*, 12 Nov 1953; Obituary of Minnie (Peiter) Kastendieck, *Ozark Headliner*, 12 May 1988

21. License No. ML000Z0200, Christian County Recorder; Christian County, Missouri Marriages-1859-1940, Christian County Library. Paul J. Kastendieck, Maud E. Wolf 13 May 1922 10/398, Young, John T. rev.

22. 1930 US Census, Missouri, Stone, Grant, Series T626 Roll 1248, p. 3A, and Christian, Polk Twp., Series T 626 Roll 1122, p. 5A, National Archives. Paul J. Kastendicok [sic] and Karl D. Kastiondist [sic].

23. Kastendieck, Biography of John D. Kastendieck. The Kastendieck biography referred to the writing of Dr. Rudolf Bennett "published last year'. He published his *Check-List of the Birds of Missouri* in 1932.

24. 1920 US Census, Missouri, Christian, Polk, Series T625 Roll 911, p. 4A, National Archives. Augusta Kastendieck was recorded in the household of John D Kastendieck, Sr.

25. Honorable Mention, Notable Paintings from the 84th Annual Exhibition of the National Academy of Design, New York 1909. *The Burr McIntosh Monthly*, Vol. 19, 1909.

26. American Civil Liberties Union, *Annual Report*, 1921, p. 23.

27. *Springfield Leader* (Springfield, Missouri), 6 Jan 1927, p. 10.

28. *Joplin Globe* (Joplin, Missouri), 28 Dec 1929, p. 2.

29. 1930 US Census, Missouri, Jasper, Carthage, Series T626 Roll 1206, p. 25A, National Archives. Augusta Kastendiesk [*sic*] 1804 Grand Avenue, in Carthage.

30. 1940 US Census, Missouri, Jasper, Marion Twp., Carthage, Series T627 Roll 2118, p. 1A, National Archives. Augusta Kastendiech [*sic*]; 1937 *Carthage, Missouri, City Directory*, p. 108.

31. *Wilson Bulletin*, Vols. 34-36 p. 205; *Transactions of the Academy of Science of Saint Louis*, 1907 p. 96; *National Historical Magazine* Vol. 77 1943, p. 590.

32. Kastendieck, Augusta M. *The Jew: The Hub of the Nations*. Chicago: New Covenant Testimony, 1945, p. 21.

33. *Joplin Globe* (Joplin, Missouri), 16 May 1948, p. 18; Kastendieck, Augusta M. *The Power of Life*. Boston: Christopher Pub. House, 1961; *Catalog of Copyright Entries: Musical compositions* [American drama], Part 1, Vol. 42, U.S. Government Printing Office, 1945.

34. 1947 *Carthage, Missouri, City Directory*, p. 112, Kastendieck, Augusta M. 1143 South Main.

35. 1953 *Springfield, Missouri, City Directory*, p. 272, Kastendieck, Augusta 509 South Market Avenue; 1955 *Springfield, Missouri, City Directory*, p. 266, Kasendick [*sic*], Augusta 827 E. Walnut.

36. Hensley, John. "The Kastendieck Bird Collection," *The Ozarks Mountaineer*, July-August 1985, pp. 38-39. Ralph Foster Museum, School of the Ozarks.

37. Obituary of Augusta A. Kastendieck, *Ozark Headliner*, 11 Apr 1974, at Sunshine Acres Nursing Home, Springfield, Missouri.

Chapter 29. Kastendieck Family Bible

1. Brown, John, and Cooke, H. *The Self-Interpreting Bible, Containing the Old and New Testaments According to the Authorized Version; with an Introduction, Marginal References and Illustrations; a Summary of The Several Books; an Analysis of Each Chapter; a Paraphrase and Evangelical*

Reflections upon the Most Important Passages; and Numerous Explanatory Notes. New York: Johnson, Fry & Co., [1875].

2. Collection of Jayme Schaumann Burchett. The family pages of the Bible were scanned in 2010. The full-size digital reproduction produced a nearly perfect color rendition. Five hard copies of the digital scan were made in actual size and color in 2010. Digital copies were furnished to Ken Gruschow, David Gay and family members. No other copies to exist outside the original.

3. Tabulation of adult male and female grandchildren of John Herman Kastendieck, grandsons/granddaughters: John Herman Kastendieck, Jr., 2/2; George Dietrich Kastendieck 2/2; Andrew Kastendieck 0/2; Amelia (Kastendieck) Kinloch 0/3; and Hermina (Kastendieck) Riggins 3/0.

<h3 style="text-align:center">Chapter 30. Andrew</h3>

1. John Herman and Bridget Kastendieck Family Bible.

2. Baptism Certificate of Andrew Kastendieck, 13 December 1863, Brooklyn, New York. Dee Willauer Collection, Dodgeville, Wisconsin, great granddaughter of Andrew Kastendieck.

3. 1880 US Census, Missouri, Christian, Polk, Series T9 Roll 681, p. 7; Kastendirk [sic], Andrew.

4. Christian County, Missouri, Personal Property Tax Index, 1879-1900, Missouri State Archives.

5. License ML000Z0034, Christian County Recorder; Christian County, Missouri, Marriages, 1859-1940, Andrew Kastendieck, Mollie Dewey, 28 Nov 1894, Christian County Library; Obituary of Mary A. Kastendieck. *Fennimore Times*, 20 May 1942. Molly Kastendieck's obituary says she and Andrew Kastendieck married 27 Nov and not 28 Nov. The spelling of Molly Dewey's name appears in the records as both Molly and Mollie, more frequently as the latter.

6. 1900 US Census, Missouri, Christian, Polk Twp., Series T623 Roll 848, p. 133. Kastendick [sic] Andrew.

7. Christian County Plat Map, 1912. Sections 16, 20, and 21 of Township 27N, Range 24W.

8. Inscription on the back of a postcard addressed to Mrs. Andrew Kastendieck; Billings, Mo. R.F.D. No. 1. Dee Willauer Collection.

9. John Hutter. History of Billings, Mo. *Billings Times* (Vol. 33, No. 39), Thursday, October 15, 1914, Billings, Missouri.

10. Letter from Pauline (Kastendieck) Jeidy to Deanne (Dee) Lombard Willauer describing Andrew Kastendieck's love of music; dated 27 Sep 1975.

2 pp. on 1, handwritten on blue paper front and back. 8 x 6.75 in. Collection of Dee Willauer, Dec 2010.

11. Andrew Kastendieck Select Knights of America sword. Dee Willauer Collection.

12. David Rauch, *125 Years of Ministry*, manuscript, n. d.

13. 1910 US Census, Missouri, Christian, Polk Twp., Series T624 Roll 776, p. 139. Kandendick [*sic*] Andrew.

14. Andrew Kastendieck Death Certificate 16520, filed 3 May 1912, Bureau of Vital Statistics, Missouri State Board of Health.

15. Funeral Announcement of Andrew Kastendieck, found in the John Herman and Bridget Kastendieck Family Bible. Jayme Burchett Collection.

Chapter 31. Three Women

1. Death Certificate of Andrew Kastendieck 16520. Missouri Secretary of State Archives.

2. Rose Hill Cemetery visit, 2010.

3. John Hutter. "History of Billings, Mo." *The Billings [Missouri] Times*, 15 Oct 1914.

4. Statement of Billings Creamery; 1 May 1907 to 1 May 1908. David Gay Collection.

5. John Hutter. "History of Billings, Mo." *The Billings [Missouri] Times*, 15 Oct 1914.

6. John Hutter. "History of Billings, Mo." *The Billings [Missouri] Times*, 15 Oct 1914.

7. Verda and Pauline Kastendieck photograph taken about 1915 in Missouri, Robert E. Hinchey studio Aurora, Missouri. Dee Willauer Collection.

8. Billings High School Graduating Class of 1914, photograph 6" x 8", Dee Willauer Collection.

9. 1920 US Census, Missouri, Christian County.

10. Obituary of Celestine Leitensdorfer 27 Dec 1896-22 Jul 1964. *Christian County Republican*, 30 Jul 1964.

11. Springfield Normal School became Southwest Missouri State Teacher's College in 1919. After several name changes, it is today Missouri State University.

12. Background on the teaching career of Pauline Kastendieck comes from a Ventura County School memorandum prepared February 4, 1963, in response to a request January 15, 1963, for information from the Association

of California Educators that was considering her for honorary membership in the organization. The memorandum came from the Ventura superintendent's office, probably written by Pauline who was serving then as assistant superintendent in the final year before her retirement.

13. Obituary of Mary A. Kastendieck. *Fennimore Times*, 20 May 1942.

14. Dee Willauer notes.

15. Mary A. Kastendieck Obituary. *Fennimore Times*, 20 May 1942.

16. Public Sale flyer, 20 Apr 1918. Dee Willauer Collection.

17. Funeral Announcement of Mrs. M. Kastendieck. *The Fennimore (Wisconsin) Times*, 20 May 1942.

18. Obituary of Mrs. Mary Kastendieck. *Fennimore (Wisconsin) Times*, 27 May 1942.

19. Two pages of handwritten notes by Hazel Kastendieck Shafer, found in the John Herman and Bridget Kastendieck Family Bible. Jayme Burchett Collection.

20. Mossberg, Midge, "High Honor Given Venturan: Mrs. Pauline Jeidy to Aid McArthur," *Ventura (California) County Star-Free Press*, 6 Dec 1947. Dee Willauer Collection.

Chapter 32. Amelia

1. John Herman and Bridget Kastendieck Family Bible; New York City Births, 1846-1909, ref. cn1212 New York Municipal Archives. John Hammond [sic] Kastendieck in entry for Kastendieck, 06 Aug 1866. This entry in the New York City birth records coincides with the date of Amelia Kastendieck's birth. It listed her mother's name as Malinda Ford of Ireland instead of Bridget. Malinda and Bridget was unquestionably the same person. The death certificate of her son Andrew in 1912 referred to her Belinda.

2. 1875 New York State Census, Kings, Brooklyn, Ward 12, family 310, p. 32. New York State Library, Albany. The census taker mistakenly entered her name as Amelia Hansen [sic], stepdaughter. The Hanson siblings were John Herman Kastendieck's stepchildren. Amelia was a Kastendieck and not Hanson.

3. 1880 US Census, Missouri, Christian, Polk, Series T9 Roll 681, p. 6D. National Archives. Emilie Kastendirk [sic].

4. Wesleyan Methodist Church in Canada Baptismal Registers, 1825-1910, FLM 592 Vols. 1 & 2, Victoria University Archives.

5. 1870 US Census, Illinois, Fayette, Laclede Twp., Series M593 Roll 220, p. 28, National Archives. Kinlock, George; 1870 US Census Missouri, Phelps,

Arlington Twp., Series M593 Roll 797, p. 643, National Archives. Kinlock, Geo. Enumerators counted the George Kinlock family twice in the 1870 census; first in Illinois in June 1870 and again in Missouri in August 1870.

6. 1880 US Census, Missouri, Christian, Polk Twp., Series T9 Roll 681, p. 3, National Archives. Kinlock, Sherman.

7. Wesleyan Methodist Church in Canada Baptismal Registers, 1825-1910, FLM 592 Vols. 1 & 2, Victoria University Archives.

8. 1870 US Census, Missouri, Phelps, Arlington Twp., Series M593 Roll 797, p. 643. Kinlock, Geo. Demographics of the Kinlock family come from birthplaces and other data recorded on census records.

9. State Historical Society of Missouri; Columbia, Mo.; Chronicling America, Library of Congress.

10. License No. ML000Z0061, Christian County Recorder, Christian County, Missouri, Marriages, Bk 04/093, 24 Jul 1887. Amelia Kastendrick [sic], Sherman Kinlock, Welker, John Justice of the Peace.

11. 1900 US Census, Indian Territory, Choctaw Nation, South McAlester, Series T623 Roll 1851, p. 7A. Kinlock, Sherman.

12. 1910 US Census, Oklahoma, Pottawatomie, Shawnee, 2-WD, Series T624 Roll 1271, p. 81. Kinlock, Sherman T.

13. The history of Shawnee, Oklahoma, is excerpted from Ernestine Gravley's "Fifty Years Ago in Shawnee and Pottawatomie County," in *Chronicles of Oklahoma*, 31 (No. 4, 1953): 381.

14. Pottawatomie County Oklahoma Marriages, Pottawatomie Marriage Indexes, Pottawatomie Genealogy Club. Kinlock, Lela Pearl to Fleming, Francis J., 14 Apr 1909, Bk 12, p. 159.

15. 1920 US Census, Oklahoma, Okmulgee, Series T625 Roll 1476, p. 3A, National Archives. Fleming, Francis; 1930 US Census, Oklahoma, Oklahoma City, Series T626 Roll 1918, p. 4B, National Archives, Francis J. Fleming.

16. Pottawatomie County Oklahoma Marriages, Pottawatomie Marriage Indexes, Pottawatomie Genealogy Club. Kinlock, Nellie J. to Williams, Horvorne L. [sic] 22 Nov 1911, Bk 14, p. 422; 1920 US Census, Oklahoma, Oklahoma City Ward 1, Series T625 Roll 1473, p. 6A, National Archives. Norborne L Williams.

17. 1930 US Census, Oklahoma, Pittsburg, Bucklucksy, Series 626 Roll 1926, p. 12B, National Archives. Williams, Nellie V.

18. Shawnee High School Fifteenth Annual Commencement, 23 May 1913; 1920 US Census, Oklahoma, Pottawatomie, Shawnee, Series T625 Roll 1485, p. 3A, National Archives. Thomas S. Kenlock [sic].

19. Fairview Cemetery, Shawnee, Oklahoma. Kinlock, Amelia 20 Jul 1918 Blk 5 Lot 148 E½.

20. Hazel Kastendieck Shafer Notes.

21. Fairview Cemetery, Shawnee, Oklahoma. Kinlock, Amelia 20 Jul 1918 Blk 5 Lot 148 E½.

22. 1920 US Census, Oklahoma, Pottawatomie, Shawnee 2-WD, Series T625 Roll 1485, p. 71, National Archives. Kenlock [*sic*], Thomas S.

23. 1910 US Census, Oklahoma, Pottawatomie, Shawnee Ward 2, Series T624 Roll 1271, p. 7B, National Archives. Mennie Wilkenson [*sic*] in household of Edward H. Wilkenson.

24. Old Records System City of Shawnee Fairview Cemetery Records, Pottawatomie County, Oklahoma.

25. Marriage records, 1890-1951, Oklahoma District Court (Oklahoma County), vol. 46, 1923, p 10. Thomas Sherman Kinlock and Minnie Wilkinson, 1 Oct 1923.

26. 1930 US Census, Oklahoma, Pottawatomie, Shawnee, Series T626 Roll 1928, p. 9A, National Archives. Thomas S. Kinlock.

27. Find A Grave Memorial 100695970. Minnie Wilkinson Kinlock 22 Sep 1932 Block 5 23, E.H. Wilkinson bur. 31 Mar 1911, Block: 5, Lot: 23.

28. Old Records System City of Shawnee Fairview Cemetery Records, Pottawatomie County, Oklahoma. Thomas S. Kinlock bur. 28 Dec 1944 Block 5 148 E ½, Amelia Kinlock bur. 20 Jul 1918 Block 5 148 E ½.

29. Fairview Cemetery, Shawnee, Pottawatomie County, Oklahoma, Plot B5A-R3-17.

Chapter 33. George Dietrich

1. Kastendieck Family Bible. The spelling of George's middle name appears as Dietrich in the Family Bible and Detrick on his death certificate. Typical German spelling is Dietrich. His name usually appeared in documents as George D. Kastendieck or simply George Kastendieck. Various transcriptions of the Kastendieck surname appear as Kastendirk, Kastnedieck, Kastendick, Kasteindeick, and Kastendeick.

2. Obituary of George D. Kastendieck, *Billings Times,* 10 Nov 1927.

3. Obituary of George D. Kastendieck, *Billings Times,* 10 Nov 1927; Article, *Billings Times,* 10 Nov 1927.

4. 1880 US Census, Missouri, Christian, Polk, Series T9 Roll 681, p. 7. Kastendirk [*sic*], George.

5. Obituary of George D. Kastendieck, *Billings Times,* 10 Nov 1927.

6. License No. ML000Z0079, Christian County Recorder; Christian County, Missouri Marriages 1859–1940, Book 5 Page 16. Missouri State Archives. George D. Kastenedieck [sic], Billings, Elizabeth A. Keast, Billings; 13 May 1891, Rev. P. C. Mooney.

7. Keast Family Record, Unknown Source and Date.

8. Keast Family Record, Unknown Source and Date.

9. Genealogy of the Keast family is from "The Kastendieck/Keast/Hayes Families of Missouri" by Roy Steel Reynolds, manuscript, March 29, 2005; Keast Family Record, Unknown Source and Date; Corinne Stanley Correspondence to Bob Kastendieck 30 Sep 1996. Corinne Stanley claimed that George Lord Keast immigrated first to Eaton, Pennsylvania, in 1872, and then to Pen Argyl, in Plainfield Township, Northampton County, Pennsylvania, in the Lehigh Valley region of the state known as Pennsylvania's Slate Belt. Conflicting information places the Keast immigrant family at two different locations in Pennsylvania, seventy-five miles apart. A family tradition claims that Elizabeth Keast kept a diary of the Keast family's ocean voyage. It seems unlikely, however, that a five-year-old would keep a diary. Nevertheless, this diary was last in the possession of Joe Kastendieck, grandson of Elizabeth Keast. If such a diary existed, it casts doubt on the immigration date of George Lord and his family.

10. Obituary of Elizabeth Ann Kastendieck, *Billings Times,* 6 Apr 1939.

11. Keast Family Record. Unknown Source and Date.

12. Billings History 1882-1989, Billings-Mt. Olive United Methodist Churches Archives.

13. Hazel Kastendieck School Report Cards 1908, 1909, Jayme Burchett Collection.

14. 1900 US Census, Missouri, Christian, Polk Twp., Series T623 Roll 848, p. 152. Keast, George L. The 1910 census asked for the number of children born and how many were surviving. Catherine Keast listed six children with two living.

15. Keast Family Record. Unknown Source and Date.

16. Christian County, Missouri Personal Property Tax Index 1879-1900, Missouri State Archives.

17. Hutter, John. "History of Billings, Mo," *Billings Times,* 15 Oct 1914.

18. Christian County Circuit Court 1860-1899, Series 721 Roll 28, Box 12 Folder 62, Missouri State Archives. Kastendieck Milling Company vs. Marion Stone, 1894.

19. 1900 US Census, Missouri, Christian, Polk Twp., Series T623 Roll 848, p. 143. Kasendieck [sic], George D.

20. Obituary of George D. Kastendieck, *Billings Times,* 10 Nov 1927.

21. 1910 US Census, Missouri, Christian, Polk Twp., Billings, Ward 2, Series T624 Roll 776, p. 3A, Kastendick [sic], George D.; Missouri, Greene, Campbell Twp., Series T624 Roll 782, p. 10B, Henry Hanson; Missouri, Lawrence, Marionville, Series T624 Roll 795, p. 3A, George Keast.

22. The description of George Dietrich Kastendieck's shop comes from contemporary photographs.

23. Sanborn Fire Insurance Maps for Missouri, Billings, Aug 1921, Ellis Library Special Collections, University of Missouri-Columbia.

24. 1910 US Census, Missouri, Christian, Polk Twp., Billings, Ward 2, Series T624 Roll 776, p. 3A. Kastendick [sic], George D.

25. Bill and Penny Kastendieck Correspondence to Ken Burchett, 10 Nov 2010.

26. Obituary of George D. Kastendieck, *Billings Times,* 10 Nov 1927.

27. 1900 US Census, Missouri, Christian, Billings Ward 2, Series T623 Roll 848, p. 3A, National Archives. Kastendieck, George D.

Chapter 34. Good Times and Bad Times

1. *Springfield Missouri Republican,* 23 Jan 1915, p. 5. Hazel Kastendieck is identified as the "diminutive" Billing's basketball star by process of elimination of other possibilities. Her cousin Mildred was 18 in 1915, Katherine 18, Verda 18, and Pauline 16 going on 17. Clara, daughter of John D. Kastendieck, Jr., was 19, Mildred, Katherine and Pauline all graduated in 1914, Verda graduated the year before that. This leaves Hazel who would have been approximately in her sophomore year in 1915. This assumes that only high school-eligible girls played on the team.

2. Family Bible of James Keatts, *Holy Bible,* Philadelphia: John E. Potter & Co., 1880, Possession of Jayme Schaumann Burchett.

3. Selective Service Registration Cards, World War II: Fourth Registration (Old Man's Draft), 1942, National Archives. Frank Andrew Kastendieck.

4. World War I Selective Service System Draft Registration Cards, 1917-1918, National Archives.

5. 1920 US Census, Missouri, Christian, Polk, Series T625 Roll 911, p. 7A, National Archives. Frank A Kastendieck.

6. Soldiers' Records: War of 1812-World War I, Missouri Secretary of State.

7. *Springfield Missouri Republican*, 22 Oct 1918, p. 3.

8. US Army WWI Transport Service, Passenger Lists, National Archives. George Herman Kastendieck

9. *The Springfield Leader*, 23 Jul 1920, p. 1.

10. 1920 US Census, Missouri, Greene, Springfield Ward 5, Series T625 Roll 915, p. 11A, National Archives. George Kastendieck in household of P.L. Hayes.

11. 1920 US Census, Missouri, Christian, Polk, Billings, Ward 2, Series T625 Roll 911, p. 234. Kastendieck, George D.

12. *The Springfield Leader*, 23 Apr 1922, p. 20; 1940 US Census, Oklahoma, Tulsa, Tulsa City, Series T627 Roll 3351, p. 2A. Walter L Shafer.

13. Obituary of Frank Andrew Kastendieck, *Christian County Republican*, 13 Mar 1969, p. 4.

14. Obituary of George D. Kastendieck, *Billings Times*, 10 Nov 1927.

15. 1910 US Census, Missouri, Christian, Polk Twp. Series T624 Roll 776, p. 144. Brown, Eli B.

16. Hirschfelder, Arthur D., *Diseases of the Heart and Aorta*. Lippincott, 1910.

17. Smith, William M., and Wilbur, "The Practice of Medicine in Greene County," in *Past and Present of Greene County, Missouri,* compiled by Fairbanks and Tuck ca. 1915.

18. A.S. Wallace Funeral Home Records 1926-1945, Library Center, Springfield, Mo. "[blank] George 66 yr 5 mo 6 da, b 18 May 1861, married, carpenter; religion [blank], d 24 Oct 1927 in Billings, father: John Herman Kastendieck b Germany, mother: Bridget Ford b Ireland.

19. Obituary of George D. Kastendieck, *Billings Times, 10* Nov 1927.

20. *Billings Times,* Article, 10 Nov 1927, Jayme Burchett Collection.

21. Elizabeth Ann Kastendieck Death Certificate 10477, dated 30 Mar 1939, Missouri State Board of Health.

22. Obituary of Elizabeth Ann Kastendieck, *Billings Times*, 6 Apr 1939.

23. Hazel Kastendieck School Report Cards 1908, 1909.

24. *Billings Times*, 6 Apr 1939.

25. Record of Public Auction, 25 May 1939. Typewritten list of 105 items sold at public auction with prices paid. Jayme Burchett Collection.

26. 1940 US Census, Oklahoma, Tulsa, Tulsa City, Area G, Series T627 Roll 3351, p. 2A, National Archives. Walter L Shafer.

27. 1940 US Census, Iowa, Van Buren, Jackson Twp., Milton, Series T627 Roll 1208, p. 1A. William Andrew [*sic*].

28. Find A Grave Memorial 97849603; Van Buren County Genealogical Society Obituary Scrapbook A, p. 356, Keosauqua Public Library, Keosauqua, Iowa.

29. *Engineering World: A Journal of Engineering and Construction*, 20-21 (June 1922): 385.

30. *Sedalia Democrat*, 26 Feb 1939.

31. 1940 US Census, Missouri, Cole, Jefferson Twp., Jefferson City, Ward 2, Series T627 Roll 2099, p. 6A, National Archives. Geo. Kastendieck, lodger.

32. *Springfield Missouri Republican*, 28 Aug 1918, p. 6;1940 US Census, Missouri, Greene, Pond Creek Twp., Series T627 Roll 2109, p. 6B, National Archives. Frank Kastendicek [*sic*].

33. 1930 US Census, Missouri, Greene, Pond Creek, Series T626 Roll 1189, p. 5B, National Archives. Frank Kastendick [*sic*].9

34. Selective Service Registration Cards, World War II: Fourth Registration (Old Man's Draft), 1942, National Archives. Frank Andrew Kastendieck.

35. Obituary of Frank Andrew Kastendieck, *Christian County Republican*, 13 Mar 1969, p. 4 and 20 Mar 1969, p. 8. Frank Andrew Kastendieck died at 7 p.m. Tuesday, March 11, 1969, at his home at Route 2, Billings. Services were at 2 p.m. March 13, burial under the direction of Cantrell of Billings.

36. John Herman and Bridget Kastendieck Family Bible, receipt from the Rose Hill Cemetery Association Perpetual Maintenance Trust Fund for Lot 36, Block 2, 23 May 1968, $100 paid by Frank A. Kastendieck, Geo. H. Kastendieck, Katherine Andrews, Hazel Shafer, Pauline Jeidy and Oscar Brandemuehl. Pauline Jeidy was the daughter of Andrew Kastendieck; Oscar was Andrew Kastendieck's son-in-law, husband of Verda.

Chapter 35. Hermina Elida

1. John Herman and Bridget Kastendieck Family Bible.

2. Find A Grave Memorial 62799026; John Herman and Bridget Kastendieck Family Bible; 1875 New York State Census, Kings, Brooklyn, p. 32; 1880 US Census, Missouri, Christian, Series T9 Roll 681, p. 13, National Archives; 1900 US Census, Texas, Lamar, Series T623 Roll 1652, p. 8A, National Archives. Andy J. Riggins.

3. New York City Municipal Archives, Certificate of Marriage State of New York #218, 12 Feb 1873.

4. Death Certificate 5435, Kings County, New York Archives. Dora Kastendieck died June 19, 1876, age 7 months. Find A Grave Memorials

59624592 and 59624592. Green-Wood Cemetery, Edward (Infant) Kastendick [sic] and Doris (Infant) Kastendick [sic].

5. 1880 US Census, Missouri, Christian, Series T9 Roll 681, p. 13, National Archives.

6. *Frisco Employees' Magazine*, March 1934, p. 13; 1910 US Census, Oklahoma, Le Flore, Talihina, Series T624 Roll 1258, p. 5B. Andrew J. Riggins.

7. *Frisco Employees' Magazine*, March 1934, p. 13.

8. License No. ML00CC0031, Christian County Recorder; Christian County, Missouri, Marriages, 1859-1940, Christian County, Missouri, Library. Kastendieck, H.R. [sic], Billings, (m) [?] Riggins [A.J.], Lamar County, Texas (m); 26 Nov 1893, 05/211, Hall, A.M., m g.

9. *Minutes of the St. Louis Annual Conference, Methodist Episcopal Church* (Vols. 25-33), [March] 1893, p. 23.

10. Roberts, Campbell, "History of Lynchings in the South Documents Nearly 4,000 Names," *New York Times*, 10 Feb 2015.

11. 1900 US Census, Texas, Lamar, Justice Precinct 1 (north of R.R. & west of Frisco Rys excl. Paris city), Series T623 Roll 1652, p. 8A, National Archives. Andy J. Riggins. This census record listed "Minnie" with a birthdate of Sept. 1874 and not 1872 recorded on her gravestone. Omer Riggins (born 1 Nov 1898) was listed as "Oma, daughter" causing biographers to later think that Hermina and Andrew had a daughter.

12. Find A Grave Memorials 69740139, 69740139, and 69740191. Omer b. 1 Nov 1898, Harry b. 24 Sep 1900, Paul b. 5 Dec 1902.

13. Peck, Henry L., *The Proud Heritage of Le Flore County: A History of an Oklahoma County*, Van Buren, Ar.: Press Argus, 1963.

14. 1920 US Census, Oklahoma, Le Flore, Talihina, Series T625 Roll 1468, p. 7B, National Archives. Andrew J. Riggins. Hermina revealed in this census that she grew up in a German-speaking household and her mother spoke Swedish.

15. *Talihina Tribune* (Talihina, Okla.), 24 Mar 1916 p. 8.

16. *The Owl*, 1923 Paris High School Alumni Roll Class of 1916.

17. *Talihina Tribune* (Talihina, Okla.), 24 Mar 1916 p. 8.

18. *Talihina Tribune* (Talihina, Okla.), 20 Jul 1917 p. 4.

19. *Talihina Tribune* (Talihina, Okla.), 4 May 1917 p. 6.

20. 1920 US Census, Oklahoma, Le Flore, Talihina, Series T625 Roll 1468, p. 7B, National Archives. Andrew J. Riggins. In the 1920 census, Hermina's

date of birth is back to 1874. Census enumerators entered her birthday differently on three successive censuses from 1900 to 1920.

21. Oklahoma School Records, 1895-1936. A.J. Riggins in entry for Paul Riggins, 1922.

22. *Talihina Tribune* (Talihina, Okla.), 22 Feb 1918 p. 1; 1910 US Census, Oklahoma, Le Flore, Talihina, Series T624 Roll 1258, p. 5B, National Archives. Andrew J. Riggins.

23. Pushmataha County, Oklahoma Marriages, Book 4, 1919-1921, 24 Nov 1921.

24. Graham, Bernice. *Graham; Descendants of William and Dinah Ann (Wilson) Graham.* Marietta, Oh.: Richardson, 1967.

25. Choctaw Nation, Choctaw Roll, Shade County, Tuskahoma, Indian Territory, Field 2011, Dawes' Roll No. 5752; Department of the Interior Commission to the Five Civilized Tribes, Choctaw Nation, 15 Jul 1901, approved 16 Jan 1903. Effie McGee, 1/8 Blood; Effie was enrolled as Choctaw with a blood quantum, thus her descendants were eligible to apply for a CDIB (Certificate of Degree of Indian Blood) and tribal membership.

26. Culberson, James, "The Fort Towson Road: A Historic Trail," *Chronicles of Oklahoma,* 5 (December 1927): 418.

27. *Official Report of Agreements Made Between the Officials of the Roads Named Herein and the B. of L.E. Committees Representing the Engineers Employed Thereon.* 1 Nov 1907.

28. *Frisco Employees' Magazine,* Nov 1926.

29. *Frisco Employees' Magazine,* Apr 1927.

30. 1930 US Census, Oklahoma, Le Flore, Talihina Town, Series T625 Roll 1468, p. 7B, National Archives. Andrew J. Riggins, Harry B. Riggins.

31. 1930 US Census, Oklahoma, Bryan, Bokchito, Series T626 Roll 1894, p. 1A, National Archives. Omer Riggins.

32. 1930 US Census, Oklahoma, Bryan, Durant, Series T626 Roll 1894, p. 7A, National Archives. P.A. Riggins.

33. *Frisco Employees' Magazine,* Jun 1933, May 1934.

34. *Talihina American,* Le Flore County, Oklahoma, 4 May 1933; *Frisco Employees' Magazine,* May 1933, Oct 1933.

35. *Frisco Employees' Magazine,* Mar 1934, p. 13.

36. Arkansas Death Index, 1914-1950, Arkansas Department of Health. Andrew Jac [*sic*] Riggins, 20 Oct 1939.

37. 1940 US Census, Oklahoma, Choctaw, Hugo, Series T627 Roll 3283, p. 15A. Omer E. Riggens [*sic*]

38. 1940 US Census, Oklahoma, Pushmataha, Kosoma, Series T627 Roll 3329, p. 1B. Harry B. Riggins; Oklahoma School Records, H.B. Riggins in entry for Lillie Jean Riggins, 1942.

39. 1940 US Census, Oklahoma, Cleveland, Norman, Series T627 Roll 3284, p. 22A. Nell Riggins.

40. Graham, Bernice. *Graham; Descendants of William and Dinah Ann (Wilson) Graham.* Marietta, Oh.: Richardson, 1967, p. 145.

41. 1940 US Census, Oklahoma, Seminole, Wewoka, Series T627 Roll 3332, p. 61A. Paul Riggins.

42. Arkansas, [Polk] County Marriages, 1837-1957, Book T p. 412. Paul Andrew Riggins and Cora Bell Freeman, 14 Jul 1941.

43. United States Social Security Death Index, US Social Security Administration, Paul Riggins, Mar 1970; Find A Grave Memorial 69740191. 25 Mar 1970.

44. United States Social Security Death Index, US Social Security Administration. Nell Riggins May 1980.

45. Find A Grave Memorial 103473663, 17 May 1980.

46. Find A Grave Memorial 69740139, 18 May 1951.

47. Find A Grave Memorial 160697733, 27 Apr 1968.

48. Funeral Announcement, *Houston Chronicle*, 26 Mar 2008; Find A Grave Memorial 25552074. 26,Mar 2008; Obituary of Lillie Jean Riggins-Doyle, *Bishinik, the Official Publication of the Choctaw Nation*, Durant, Okla. Jun 2009, p. 16.

Chapter 36. John Herman, Jr.

1. John Herman and Bridget Kastendieck Family Bible, John Herman Kastendieck, Jr., b. 6 Dec 1855.

2. 1870 US Census, New York, Kings, WD-12-Series M593 Roll 953, p.480. John Kastendeick [*sic*].

3. Kastendieck, Biography of John D. Kastendieck.

4. *Brooklyn Daily Eagle,* Sep 13, 1877, p. 3. John Kasondick [*sic*]

5. 1880 US Census, Missouri, Christian, Polk, Series T9, Roll 681, p. 7A. John H. Kastendirk [*sic*]. The 1880 census began on 1 June 1880 and ended within thirty days. It was the first census to identify relationship to the head of household.

6. *1879/80 Lain's Brooklyn Directory.*

7. 1870 US Census, Illinois, Jackson, Series M593, Roll 232, p. 10, National Archives. Thomas Stone.

8. *Christian County*, p. 81.

9. *Portrait and Biographical Record of Clinton, Washington, Marion and Jefferson Counties, Illinois*; Chicago, Il.: Chapman, 1894.

10. 1870 US Census, Illinois, Jackson, Series M593, Roll 232, p. 10, National Archives. Thomas Stone.

11. Christian County, Missouri, Personal Property Tax Index, 1879-1900. Kastendick [*sic*], J.H. Jr., 1884, #1090, value $75; tax $0.91 28 Oct 1884.

12. Kastenderck [*sic*], John, Stone, Mary M., 06/17/1885, License No. ML000Z0112, Christian County Recorder; Find A Grave Memorial 14778764; Obituary of Mary Stone Kastendieck, *Christian County Republican*, 5 Jun 1947, p. 1; Christian County, Missouri, Marriages. Kastendieck John H. Mary M. Stene [*sic*] 17 Jun 1885 Book 03 p. 216 Miller Jacob m g.

13. Find A Grave Memorial 14778764.

14.. Land Patents 1831-1961, Township School Land Patents, Vol. Z, p. 157, reel s00200, Certificate #157, date 18 Aug 1885. Missouri State Archives, Office of Secretary of State. The record is unclear on whether this land patent belonged to John Herman, Sr. or John Herman, Jr.

15. Kastendieck, Biography of John D. Kastendieck.

16. Christian County, Missouri, Personal Property Tax Index, 1879-1900. Kassendeick [*sic*], John H., 1886, #1248, value $91, tax $0.82, 27 Oct 27 1886.

17. 1900 US Census, Missouri, Christian, Polk Twp., Billings, Series T623 Roll 848, p. 6A, National Archives. Kasendiech [sic] John H.

18. Rauch, *125 Years of Ministry*.

19. Find A Grave Memorial 14778654. Ceceil Kastendieck.

20. Rose Hill Cemetery Visit; Hazel Kastendieck Biography; Find A Grave Memorial 14778654. Ralph Kastendieck. The tombstones of Ralph and Ceceil Kastendieck are located in the John Herman Kastendieck, Jr., plot. Birth association and age proximity to the marriage of John Herman, along with the biography of Hazel Kastendieck, confirm them as the infant children of John Herman, Jr., and Mary Kastendieck.

21. Rauch, *125 Years of Ministry*.

22. Rauch, *125 Years of Ministry*

23. Rauch, *125 Years of Ministry*. Church records do not stipulate if this was John Herman, Jr., or John Herman Sr. However, John Herman, Sr. would have been age 66 when construction began and died four years after it was completed. John Herman, Jr., was a successful carpenter and house builder. Other claims that a Kastendieck built the old St. Peter's Church are incorrect.

According to church records cited by Rauch, Edward Schmidt and Benedict Hutter constructed the old St. Peter's, two immigrant farmers living in Polk Township, Christian County. See the 1880 census; Edward Schmidt and Benedict Hutter were neighbors ages 37 and 49 respectively.

24. Rauch, *125 Years of Ministry. Bolivar Herald-Free Press,* May 20, 2005. According to Rauch, the corner stone bore the founding date of the church in 1880 and date of the laying of the stone in 1892. It contained a copper box containing information for future generations. In 2005, the box was removed and opened on the 125th anniversary of the founding of St. Peter's Church. One of the participating church members was Sam Schaumann, great grandnephew of John Herman Kastendieck, Jr.,

25. Rauch, 125 *Years of Ministry.* Rauch did not give the name of the local newspaper but attributed the source to Fredrick De Brunner, one of the founding members of St. Peter's Church and Secretary of the Building Committee.

26. Rauch, 125 *Years of Ministry*

27. *"Christian County,"* p. 85.

28. *Portrait and Biographical Record of Clinton, Washington, Marion and Jefferson Counties, Illinois;* Chicago, Il.: Chapman, 1894.

29. Christian County Circuit Court, 1860-1899, Box 50 Folder 19, Series 721 Roll 78, Missouri State Archives.

30. *Springfield Missouri Republican* (Springfield, Missouri), 16 Dec 1915, p. 4.

Chapter 37. Life on Oak Street

1. Kastendieck tax receipts appeared filed variously under the names Kastendeick, Kassendeick Kassendeik, Kastendick, Keastendick, and Kastenick.

2. Christian County, Missouri Personal Property Tax Index-1879-1900, Missouri State Archives.

3. 1900 US Census, Missouri, Christian, Polk, Series T623 Roll 848; p. 6A, National Archives. John H. Kasendiech [*sic*].

4. Harper, Kimberly, *White Man's Heaven: The Lynching and Expulsion of Blacks in the Southern Ozarks, 1894–1909,* Fayetteville, Ar.: University of Arkansas Press, 2010.

5. 1910 US Census, Missouri, Christian, Polk, Series T624 Roll 776, p. 5B, National Archives. John H. Kastendick [*sic*].

6. 1930 Christian County, Missouri, Census Index, Christian County Library; 1930 US Census, Missouri, Christian, Billings, Series T626 Roll 1182, p. 1B, National Archives. John Kastendich [*sic*].

7. 1920 US Census, Missouri, Christian, Polk, Series T625 Roll 911, p. 6A, National Archives. John H. Kastendieck.

8. John Herman Kastendieck [Jr.] Death Certificate No. 25894, filed 15 Aug 1935, Missouri State Board of Health.

9. A.S. Wallace Funeral Home Records 1926-1945.

10. Mary Kastendieck Death Certificate No. 17133, filed 9 Jun 1947, State Board of Health of Missouri.

11. 1940 US Census, Missouri, Christian, Polk, Series T627 Roll 2096, p. 3A, National Archives. Mary Kastendieck.

12. Obituary of Mary Kastendieck, *Christian County Republican*, 5 Jun 1947, p. 1; Find A Grave Memorials 14778737 and 14778764.

13. Hazel Kastendieck Shafer Notes, undated prior to 1980.

14. 1940 US Census, Oklahoma, Creek, Bristow, Series Roll, p. 11A, National Archives. John L. Kastendieck.

15. Find A Grave Memorial 22791963. John L. Kastendieck b. 4 May 1890 d. 12 Feb 1954.

16. *Morning Tulsa Daily World*, 30 Nov 1915 p. 3.

17. World War I Selective Service System draft registration cards, 1917-1918, National Archives. John Leroy Kastendieck.

18. Soldiers' Records: War of 1812-World War I, Missouri State Archives; United States World War I Draft Registration Cards, 1917-1918, National Archives. John L. Kastendieck, Army SN 3,230,704.

19. 1920 US Census, Missouri, Christian, Polk, Series T625 Roll 911, p. 6A, National Archives. Roy John Kastendieck.

20. World War I Selective Service System draft registration cards, 1917-1918, National Archives. John Leroy Kastendieck.

21. Creek County Marriage Records (Sapulpa, Oklahoma), 1907-1921, Bk 11 pg. 377.

22. Birth Certificate 78294, Texas Board of Health, 20 Dec 1926; Obituary of Ruth K. Dawson, *Sapulpa Herald*, Sapulpa, Oklahoma, 19 Apr 2004; Find A Grave Memorial 24634023.

23. 1930 Christian County Plat Book, University of Missouri-Columbia, Ellis Library Special Collections.

24. 1930 US Census, Texas, Cameron, Harlingen, Series T626 Roll 2305, p. 12B, National Archives. Leroy Kastendieck.

25. *Valley Morning Star* (Harlingen, Texas), 16 Aug 1931, p. 7.

26. 1940 US Census, Oklahoma, Creek, Bristow, Series Roll, p. 11A, National Archives. John L. Kastendieck.

27. Selective Service Registration Cards, World War II: Fourth Registration, Record Group 147, National Archives.

28. United States, World War II Draft Registration Cards, 1942. John Leroy Kastendieck.

29. Applications for Headstones to Be Provided for Deceased US Military Personnel, 1925-1963, M1916, M2113, Record Group 92, National Archives.

30. *Billings Times*, 18 Feb 1954. The *Times* notice incorrectly listed Roy's surviving wife as "nee Williams" instead of Anderson.

31. Oklahoma State Vital Records Index, Oklahoma State Department of Health.

32. Find A Grave Memorial 22791963; Find A Grave Memorial 22791972. Virgie A. Kastendieck b 25 Dec 1901 d 16 Nov 1991.

33. 1920 US Census, Missouri, Jasper, Webb City Ward 1, Series T625 Roll 922, p. 1B, National Archives. Hermina Kastendieck.

34. 1920 US Census, Missouri, Christian, Polk, Series T625 Roll 911, p. 6A, National Archives. John H. Kastendieck.

35. 1920 US Census, Missouri, Jasper, Webb City Ward 1, Series T625 Roll 922, p. 4B, National Archives. William Weaver Davis in household of Ola Debo.

36. 1940 US Census, Missouri, Jasper, Galena Twp., Joplin, Series T627 Roll 2117, p. 24B, National Archives. W.W. Davis, 230 North Joplin.

37. 1930 US Census, Missouri, Jasper, Galena Twp. Joplin, Series T626 Roll 1205, p. 6A, National Archives. William W. Davis. The Davis home was valued at $2,500 in 1930.

38. *Joplin Globe*, 25 Aug 1946.

39. *Christian County Republican*, 5 Jun 1947.

40. *Billings Times*, 18 Feb 1954.

41. Death Certificate 565-61-041433, filed 5 Dec 1961. William W. Davis, Sr.

42. Death Certificate 0011087, filed 1 Apr 1964. Hermina Davis.

43. Find A Grave Memorials 80941332 and 80612397.

Chapter 38. The Architect

1. 1910 US Census, Missouri, Christian, Polk, Series T624 Roll 776, p. 5B, National Archives. Raymond S. Kastendieck.

2. Gary Rotary Club, *Steuben Republican* (Angola, Indiana), 18 Apr 1951.

3. *Morning Tulsa Daily World*, 30 Nov 1915 p. 3.

4. *Arkansas Democrat* (Little Rock), 27 Jun 1917, p. 5; *Morning Tulsa Daily World*, 14 Aug 1917 p. 3; Obituary of Raymond Kastendieck, *Post-Tribune* (Gary, Indiana), 23 Apr 1983, p. B5, Gary (Indiana) Public Library.

5. United States World War I Draft Registration Cards, 1917-1918, microfilm M1509, National Archives. Raymond Stone Kastendieck, 1917-1918.

6. *Arkansas Democrat* (Little Rock), 27 Jun 1917, p. 5; *Morning Tulsa Daily World*, 14 Aug 1917 p. 3.

7. United States World War I Draft Registration Cards, 1917-1918, microfilm M1509, National Archives. Raymond Stone Kastendieck, 1917-1918.

8. "Fort Logan H. Roots Military Post Historic District," National Register of Historic Places, on file at Arkansas Historic Preservation Program, Little Rock, Arkansas.

9. Lists of Incoming and Outgoing Passengers, 1917-1938, Record Group 92, National Archives. *HMT Lancashire*, 31 Aug 1918.

10. Obituary of Raymond Kastendieck, *Post-Tribune*, Apr 23, 1983, p. B5, Gary Public Library.

11. Lists of Incoming and Outgoing Passengers, 1917-1938, Record Group 92, National Archives. *USAT Martha Washington*, 22 Feb 1919.

12. Form No. 724-1, A.G.O., Soldiers' Records: War of 1812 - World War I, Missouri Secretary of State. Raymond Stone Kastendieck.

13. Obituary of Raymond S. Kastendieck, *Post-Tribune* (Gary, Indiana), Apr 23, 1983, p. B5, Gary Public Library.
1920 US Census, Missouri, Christian, Polk, Series T625 Roll 911, p. 6A. Raymond S. Kastendieck.

14. *Steuben Republican* (Angola, Indiana), 18 Apr 1951; Obituary of Raymond S. Kastendieck, *Post-Tribune* (Gary, Indiana), Apr 23, 1983, p. B5, Gary Public Library.

15. *American Architects Directory* (1st edition), New York: R.R. Bowker, 1955; Obituary of Lillian Kastendieck, *Post-Tribune* (Gary, Indiana), 9 Sep 1931, p. 2.

16. *Sedalia Democrat* (Sedalia, Missouri), 28 Jun 1925, p. 3.

17. *Sedalia Democrat* (Sedalia, Missouri), 26 Apr 1925, p. 8; *Sedalia Weekly Democrat* (Sedalia, Missouri), 30 Apr 1925, p. 4; *Sedalia Democrat* (Sedalia, Missouri), 24 May 1925, p. 2; United States World War I Draft

Registration Card 1917-1918, microfilm M1509, National Archives. Raymond Stone Kastendieck, 1917-1918.

18. 1920 US Census, Missouri, Johnson, Columbus, Series T625 Roll 930, p. 2A. A.F. Pruess.

19. *Sedalia Democrat* (Sedalia, Missouri), 28 Jun 1925, p. 3.

20. *Steuben Republican* (Angola, Indiana). 18 Apr 1951.

21. 1930 US Census, Indiana, Lake, Gary, Series T626 Roll 599, p. 7A. Ray Kastendieck.

22. Death Notice of Lillian Kastendieck, *Post-Tribune* (Gary, Indiana), 9 Sep 1931, p. 2. The history of Mercy Hospital, Gary, Indiana, includes the hospital as the birthplace of Michael Jackson and the Jackson siblings. Later abandoned, it fell into disrepair.

23. Obituary of Lillian Kastendieck, *Post-Tribune* (Gary, Indiana), 9 Sep 1931, p. 2; Funeral Announcement of Lillian Kastendieck, *Post-Tribune* (Gary, Indiana), Sep 10, 1931, p. 18; Find A Grave Memorial 86469812.

24. *Steuben Republican* (Angola, Indiana), 18 Apr 1951; *Steuben Republican* (Angola, Indiana), 22 Oct 1952, p. 2; *Post-Tribune* (Gary, Indiana), 23 Apr 1982, p. B5.

25. *Post-Tribune* (Gary, Indiana), 23 Apr 1983, p. B5, Gary Public Library; 1940 US Census, Indiana, Lake, Calumet Twp., Gary, Series T627 Roll 1119, p. 8B. Marion Williams; Obituary of Marion E. (Williams) Kastendieck, *Post-Tribune* (Gary, Indiana), 6 Nov 2001, p. A9. Wed at Evanston, Illinois, 3 Aug 1941.

26. 1920 US Census, Illinois, McDonough, Bushnell, Series T625 Roll 385, p. 2A, National Archives. Charles Williams; 1910 US Census, Illinois, McDonough, Bushnell, Series T624 Roll 305, p. 1B, National Archives. Charles C. Williams in household of Noah Everly.

27. Obituary of Marion E. Kastendieck, *Post-Tribune* (Gary, Indiana), 6 Nov 2001, p. A9.

28. Selective Service Registration Cards, World War II: Fourth Registration, National Archives. Raymond Stone Kastendieck.

29. *Steuben Republican* (Angola, Indiana), 18 Apr 1951.

30. *Steuben Republican* (Angola, Indiana), 18 Apr 1951.

31. *Steuben Republican* (Angola, Indiana), 22 Oct 1952, p. 1.

32. New York Passenger and Crew Lists, 1909, 1925-1957, Passenger Manifest, Trans World Airlines, Inc., Aircraft 6012 C, National Archives. Raymond S Kastendieck, 1953.

33. Bodenhamer, David J., and Barrows, Robert G, *The Encyclopedia of Indianapolis*, Indiana University Press, 1994, p. 737.

34. *American Architects Directory* (1st edition), New York: R.R. Bowker, 1955.

35. Indiana University Northwest, Calumet Regional Archives, CRA401—M Milan Opacich Papers, Box 2, File 7, Scrapbook, Raymond and Marion Kastendieck, (1938-1998), 3400 Broadway, Library Room 331, Gary, Indiana 46408.

36. Find A Grave Memorial 29284371, Bushnell Cemetery Plot: Blk. 4 Lot 1 Sec C

37. Obituary of Raymond Kastendieck, *Post-Tribune* (Gary, Indiana), 23 Apr 1983, p. B5; *Post Tribune* (Gary, Indiana), 24 Apr 1983, p. A6, col. 1.

38. For a partial list of Raymond Kastendieck's designs, see *American Architects Directory* (3rd edition), New York: R.R. Bowker, 1970.

39. Pauline Jeidy Correspondence to Deanne "Dee" Lombard, about 1975.

40. United States Public Records, 1970-2009, Marion E Kastendieck, Residence, Macomb, Illinois; US Social Security Death Index, US Social Security Administration. Marion W. Kastendieck, 04 Nov 2001.

41. Find A Grave Memorial 29284351, Bushnell Cemetery, McDonough County, Illinois, Plot: Blk. 4 Lot 1 Sec C.

Chapter 39. Mildred and Harry

1. 1900 US Census, Missouri, Christian, Polk Twp., Billings, Series T623 Roll 848, p. 6A, National Archives. Kasendiech [sic] John H.; 1910 US Census, Missouri, Christian, Polk, Series T624 Roll 776, p. 5B, National Archives. John H. Kastendick [*sic*]; Billings High School Graduation Portrait, 1914.

2. Investigative Reports of the Bureau of Investigation [FBI] 1908-1922, Series M1085 Roll 695, p. 3, Case Number 279911, National Archives.

3. 1910 U S Census, Missouri, Lawrence, Marionville Ward 2, Series T624 Roll 795, p. 8A, National Archives. Harry Fulbright in household of Neeley W. Fulbright; Fulbright, *Glimpses of Life,* p. 46. Harry W. Fulbright was born 8 Jun 1893 to William Neely and Jane Wilks Fulbright.

4. Fulbright, *Glimpses of Life,* p. 14; Investigative Reports of the Bureau of Investigation [FBI] 1908-1922, Series M1085 Roll 695, p. 2, Case Number 279911, National Archives.

5. Fulbright, *Glimpses of Life,* p. 43.

Notes

6. Fulbright, *Glimpses of Life*, p. 13.

7. Investigative Reports of the Bureau of Investigation [FBI] 1908-1922, Series M1085 Roll 695, p. 2, Case Number 279911, National Archives.

8. *Bulletin of Drury College Annual Catalogue*, January 1915 [for the academic year 1915-1916], pp. 128-129.

9. *Drury College Bulletin*, July 1915, p. 23.

10 Fulbright, *Glimpses of Life*, pp. 15, 47.

11. *St Louis, Missouri, City Directory*, 1917, US City Directories, 1822-1995. Harry W. Fulbright, 4158 Westminster, St. Louis, student.

12. Investigative Reports of the Bureau of Investigation [FBI] 1908-1922, Series M1085 Roll 695, p. 4, Case Number 279911, National Archives.

13. United States World War I Draft Registration Cards, 1917-1918, Series M1509, National Archives. Harry Wilks Fulbright, 8 Jun 1917.

14. Marriage Records of Dallas County, Missouri Book 9 1913 to 1918, p. 38. 18 Nov 1917, Harry H. [*sic*] Fulbright (age 24) (Billings, Christian, Mo), Mildred Kastendieck (age 20) (Billings, Christian, Mo), Frank P. Hiner, Minister of the Gospel, at Ash Grove, Greene, Mo.

15. Washington University, Middle Law Class of 1918.

16. Investigative Reports of the Bureau of Investigation [FBI] 1908-1922, Series M1085 Roll 695, p. 4, Case Number 279911, National Archives.

17. Investigative Reports of the Bureau of Investigation [FBI] 1908-1922, Series M1085 Roll 695, p. 2, Case Number 279911, National Archives.

18. Investigative Reports of the Bureau of Investigation [FBI] 1908-1922, Series M1085 Roll 695, pp. 2-3, Case Number 279911, National Archives.

19. Investigative Reports of the Bureau of Investigation [FBI] 1908-1922, Series M1085 Roll 695, p. 3-4, Case Number 279911, National Archives.

20. Fulbright, *Glimpses of Life*, p. 13; Social Security Death Index. Harry Fulbright, b. 19 Sep 1918 d. 16 May 2009, SSN 087-26-6512, New York. The author of *Glimpses of Life* gives an incorrect birthdate for Harry Fulbright, Jr., as 10 Nov 1918.

Chapter 40. The Divorce

1. 1920 US Census, Missouri, Lawrence, Buck Prairie, Series T625 Roll 932, p. 18B. Fullbright [*sic*], Harry W.

2. Fulbright, *Glimpses of Life*, pp. 15, 47.

3. Fulbright, *Glimpses of Life*, pp. 16, 55.

4. Fulbright, *Glimpses of Life*, pp. 49-50, 53-54, 107-108.

5. Fulbright, *Glimpses of Life*, pp. 51, 62.

Notes

6. Fulbright, *Glimpses of Life*, pp. 38, 58-59.

7. Fulbright, *Glimpses of Life*, p. 59.

8. Fulbright, *Glimpses of Life*, p. 48.

9. Fulbright, *Glimpses of Life*, p. 60.

10. *Springfield Missouri Republican*, 19 Sep 1926, p. 10.

11. 1930 US Census, Missouri, St. Louis, Series T626 Roll 1225, p. 10A, National Archives. Harry W. Fulbright; Fulbright, *Glimpses of Life*, pp. 38-39, 60.

12. Fulbright, *Glimpses of Life*, p. 63.

13. Keast Family Record. Unknown Source and Date. Joy Brown, Mildred's alleged lover, married Marian Keast in 1923. In the small world that was Billings, Mildred and Marian were cousins by marriage. Marian Keast was the niece of Elizabeth Keast, the wife of Mildred's Uncle George Dietrich Kastendieck. The convoluted relationship enlarged the interest in the reputed scandal but played no known part in it.

14. *St Louis, Missouri, City Directory, 1929*, US City Directories, 1822-1995. Mildred Fulbright, teacher.

15. *St Louis, Missouri, City Directory, 1930*, US City Directories, 1822-1995. Mildred Fulbright, Teacher; Harry W. Fulbright, lawyer.

16. *Joplin Globe* (Joplin, Missouri), 30 Jul 30, 1929, p. 5; 3 Aug 1929, p. 5; 4 Aug 1929, p. 13.

17. Fulbright, *Glimpses of Life*, p. 51

18. 1930 US Census, Missouri, St. Louis (Independent City), St. Louis (Districts 251-500), Series T626 Roll 1236, p. 2A, National Archives. Jane Fulbright. St. Elizabeth's Academy later accepted only students of high school age. After many decades of operation, the school eventually closed due to financial reasons.

19. *Sedalia Democrat* (Sedalia, Missouri), 19 Mar 1934, p. 8.

20. Death Certificate of Harry W. Fulbright 42424, Missouri State Board of Health.

21. Find A Grave Memorial 153019920. Harry W. Fullbright [*sic*].

22. Fulbright, *Glimpses of Life*, pp. 45, 51, 63-64.

23. 1940 US Census, Missouri, St. Louis, Ward 28, Series T627 Roll 2211, p. 6A, National Archives. Mildred Fulbright.

24. Mildred Fulbright Correspondence to Verda (Kastendieck) Brandemuehl, 16 Jul 1942.

25. Death Certificate of Timothy Edwin Collins 0003194, Missouri Division of Health, Department of Public Health and Welfare, Jefferson City.

26. *The Springfield Leader*, Springfield, Missouri, 14 Dec 1926, p. 22. Advertisements for T.E. Collins Dental appeared regularly in the *Springfield Leader* in 1927; 1930 US Census, Missouri, St Louis (Districts 1-250), St Louis (Independent City), ED 55, sheet 11B, line 99, microfilm T626 Roll 1237, Theodore Collins, National Archives and Records Administration.

27. *St. Louis Globe-Democrat* Clippings File, Series Number 1, Box 159/Items 404 and 405, Dr. Collins, T.E., 21 Nov 1937, dentist, Special Collections, St. Louis Mercantile Library.

28. *Joplin Globe*, 23 and 25 Aug 1946.

29. Mary Kastendieck Death Certificate No. 17133, filed 9 Jun 1947, State Board of Health of Missouri.

30. *Billings Times*, 18 Feb 1954.

31. Hazel Kastendieck Shafer Family Notes, c. 1970. Hazel (Kastendieck) Shafer said Mildred went to Florida in later years and that at the time [about 1970] Dr. Collins was deceased.

32. Death Certificate of Timothy Edwin Collins 0003194, Missouri Division of Health, Department of Public Health and Welfare, Jefferson City.

33. Broward County Appraiser, Property ID 4941-35-06-0250. Mildred Collins' property in Florida was located at 1415 Northwest 58th Ave., Lauderhill, FL. It was an 810 square foot house on a 3,256 square foot lot, valued in 2017 at $103,384. Kristen Collins York, thought to have been a relative of Dr. Collins, Mildred's husband, inherited the property. She lived in Los Angeles on Fairview Boulevard and used the Florida property as her second address. Ms. York transferred the property in 2007 to a real estate developer.

34. Mildred Collins Death Certificate No. 82-048807, Bureau of Vital Statistics, State of Florida.

35. Washington University, *Department of Physics Newsletter*, Fall 2010, p. 13.

36. *Albuquerque Journal* (Albuquerque, New Mexico), 25 Aug 1946, p. 13; *Princeton Alumni Weekly*, 46 (May 3, 1945): 7.

37. Bromley, D.A., "Treatise on Heavy-Ion Science: (Vol. 7): Instrumentation and Techniques," *Springer Science & Business Media* (Apr 17, 2013): 178.

38. United States National Register of Scientific and Technical Personnel Files, 1954-1970, Harry W. Fulbright, New York, Nov 1954; citing 1954 National Register of Scientific and Technical Personnel, 622629, National Archives at College Park, Maryland.

39. Mathematics Genealogy Project, North Dakota State University and American Mathematical Society.

40. Pipher, Judy, and Forrest, Bill. "Obituary: Harry W. Fulbright (1918-2009)." *Bulletin of the American Astronomical Society*, 43 (December 2011); University of Rochester, 15 Jun 2009.

41. United States Social Security Death Index, 19 May 2014, Harry W. Fulbright, 16 May 2009; citing U.S. Social Security Administration.

Chapter 41. The Hansons

1. New York City Death Index, Kings County 1862-1948, Death Certificate 549, New York City Municipal Archives; 1865 New York State Census, Kings, Brooklyn, Ward 12, p. 22, New York Archives. Bernard Hansen [*sic*]. The Hanson children in later years used the spelling Hanson instead of Hansen.

2. Christian County, Missouri, Marriages. Hanson George Bernard, Sarah Ann Kieghtly [*sic*] 16 Oct 1879 Book 01 p. 407, officiating: Lumpkin, MT j p.

3. 1880 US Census, Missouri, Christian, Polk, Series T9 Roll 681, p. 9, National Archives. Hansen [sic] George.

4. 1900 US Census, Missouri, Christian, Polk Twp., Series T623 Roll 848, p. 146, National Archives. Harrison [*sic*] [Hanson] George B.

5. 1910 US Census, Missouri, Jackson, Kansas City, 14-Wd, Series T624 Roll 788, p. 286, National Archives. Hanson George B.

6. 1920 US Census, Missouri, Jackson, Kansas City, 15-WD, Series T625 Roll 928, p. 259, National Archives. Hanon [*sic*] [Hanson] George B.

7. Find A Grave Memorial 22809718. George Bernard Hanson.

8. Find A Grave Memorial 22809735. Sarah Ann Keightley Hanson, 28 Mar 1925.

9. 1880 US Census, Missouri, Lawrence, Marionville, Buck Prairie, Series T9 Roll 698, p. 547A, National Archives. Celia Hanson in household of Jesse Rouk [*sic*].

10. 1880 US Census, Kansas, Sumner, Jackson Twp., Series T9 Roll 398, p. 194C, National Archives. George W. Beck in household of Jacob F. Beck.

11. Christian County, Missouri, Marriages. Beck George W. Celia B. Hanson 2 Sep 1884 Book 03 p. 164, Miller Jacob m g.

12. 1900 US Census, Missouri, Christian, Polk Twp., Series T623 Roll 848, p. 56, National Archives. Beck George W.

13. Find A Grave Memorial 158121623.

14. 1910 US Census, Michigan, Mecosta, Grant Twp., Series T624 Roll 663, p. 8A, National Archives. George W Beck.

15. Death Certificate of Death No. 10 dated 5 Nov 1910, Michigan Department of State Division of Vital Statistics. Celia Beck.

16. Michigan Deaths and Burials, 1800-1995; Find A Grave Memorial 158121623. Cecelia Bertha "Celia" Hanson Beck

17. 1920 US Census, Illinois, Lee, Dixon, Series T625 Roll 382, p. 187, National Archives. George Beck.

18. 1939 Deaths as reported in the *Pioneer [Michigan] Newspaper*. 21 Sep 1939 George W. Beck, Colfax Township, Mecosta County, Michigan; FamilySearch LD92-QLG, The Church of Jesus Christ of Latter-Day Saints; *Dixon [Illinois] Telegraph Newspaper* Pre-1948 Index, Lee County, Illinois, Historical and Genealogical Society.

19. 1880 US Census, Missouri, Christian, Polk, Series T9 Roll 681, p. 7, National Archives. Henry Hansom [*sic*].

20. Christian County, Missouri, Marriages. Hanson Henry E. Alma E. Marsh 10 Oct 1888 Book 04 p. 176, Combs C. rev.

21. Find A Grave Memorial 55712084. Alma Evadna Marsh Hanson.

22. The relationship between Etta and Alma presaged the circumstances of another Kastendieck family in 1913 when the nieces of John Herman shared a similar relationship when Anna Kastendieck Leonhauser moved into the household of George Gerken after the death of her sister Emilie left Mr. Gerken with four young sons.

23. 1900 US Census, Missouri, Christian, Polk, Series T623 Roll 848, p. 147, National Archives. Hanson Henry.

24. 1910 US Census, Missouri, Greene, Campbell Twp., Series T624 Roll 782, p. 277, National Archives. Hanson Henry E.

25. Christian County, Missouri, Marriages. Hanson Bertha to George Howcroft 19 Aug 1914 Book 09 p. 254, Heidlebaugh M.V. m g; Find A Grave Memorial 11475401, George Howcroft.

26. Death Certificate No. 36678 filed 3 Dec 1915, Missouri State Board of Health. Ora Hanson, 3 Dec 1915.

27. Find A Grave Memorial 113137194. Ora E. Hanson.

28. 1920 US Census, Missouri, Christian, Polk, Billing's, 2-Wd, Series T625 Roll 911, p. 235, National Archives. Hanson Henry E.

29. California Death Index, 1940-1997, Department of Public Health Services, Sacramento. Bertha Etta Howcroft, 22 Nov 1983.

30. 1930 US Census, Missouri, Greene, Springfield, Series T626 Roll 1188, 3A, National Archives. Etta A Marsh.

31. Death Certificate No. 31730 filed 10 Oct 1932, Missouri State Board of Health. Henry Edward Hanson.

32. Rose Hill Cemetery Tombstone, Christian County, Missouri.

33. Death Certificate No. 818 filed 18 Jan 1947, State Board of Health of Missouri. Etta A. Marsh.

Bibliography

Newspapers

Brooklyn Daily Eagle; Abilene (Kansas) Reflector; Albuquerque Journal; Arkansas Democrat; Billings (Missouri) Times; Billings (Missouri) Weekly Times; Bolivar (Missouri) Herald Free Press; Christian County Republican; Fennimore (Wisconsin) Times; Houston (Texas) Chronicle; Jefferson City (Missouri) Daily Tribune; Joplin (Missouri) Globe; Morning Tulsa Daily World; New York Times; Ozark (Missouri) Headliner; Pioneer (Michigan) Newspaper; Post-Tribune (Gary, Indiana); Sapulpa (Oklahoma) Herald; Sedalia (Missouri) Democrat; Sedalia (Missouri) Weekly Democrat; Springfield (Missouri) Leader; Springfield (Missouri) Republican; St. Louis Globe-Democrat; St. Louis Post-Dispatch; St. Louis Republic; Steuben Republican (Angola, Indiana); Talihina (Oklahoma) American; Talihina Tribune; Valley Morning Star (Harlingen, Texas); and Ventura (California) County Star-Free Press

100 Years of Service: Frisco Centennial Year 1860-1960. St. Louis: Frisco Veterans' Reunion, 1960.

A. S. Wallace Funeral Home Records 1926-1945. Library Center. Springfield, Missouri.

American Architects Directory (1st & 3rd eds.). New York: R.R. Bowker, 1955, 1970.

American Civil Liberties Union. *Annual Report.* New York: Arno & New York Times, [1921] 1970.

Applications for Headstones to Be Provided for Deceased US Military Personnel, 1925-1963. National Archives.

Bibliography

Arkansas Death Index, 1914-1950, Arkansas Department of Health. Little Rock, Arkansas.

Arkansas, County Marriages, 1837-1957. Various County Courthouses in the State of Arkansas.

Bennett, Rudolf. *Check-List of the Birds of Missouri.* Columbia: University of Missouri Press, 1932.

Billings History 1882-1989. Billings-Mt. Olive United Methodist Churches Archives.

Billings Special Road District 1897-1900. Christian County Library.

Bishinik, the Official Publication of the Choctaw Nation (Durant, Oklahoma).

Bodenhamer, David J., and Barrows, Robert G. *The Encyclopedia of Indianapolis.* Indiana University Press, 1994.

Boyd's Brooklyn [New York State] Directory. Syracuse, NY: Andrew Boyd, [1872].

Bromley, D.A. "Treatise on Heavy-Ion Science: (Vol. 7): Instrumentation and Techniques." *Springer Science & Business Media* (Apr 17, 2013): 178.

Brooklyn City Directory, 1859, 1878. Brooklyn [N.Y.]: Lain & Co., 1857.

Brooklyn Daily Eagle. Brooklyn Public Library. Brooklyn, New York, 1841-1955.

Brooklyn Methodist Episcopal Churches History. New York: New York Methodist Conference, 1869.

Brown, John H. *The Cyclopaedia of American Biography.* Boston: Cyclopedia, 1897-1903.

Brown, John H. *The Cyclopaedia of American Biography: Comprising the Men and Women of the United States Who Have Been Identified With the Growth of the Nation* (Vol. 4). Whitefish, Mont.: Kessinger, 2006.

Brown, John, and Cooke, H. *The Self-Interpreting Bible, Containing the Old and New Testaments According to the Authorized Version.* Johnson and Fry: New York, 1875.

Bulletin of Drury College Annual Catalogue, January 1915 [for the academic year 1915-1916].

Bulletin of the American Astronomical Society, 43 (December 2011).

Bureau of Vital Statistics. State of Florida.

Burrows, Edwin G., and Wallace, Mike. *Gotham: A History of New York City to 1898.* New York: Oxford University Press, 1999.

California Death Index, 1940-1997. Department of Public Health Services, Sacramento, California.

Carthage, Missouri, City Directory, 1937, 1947. Kansas City, Mo.: R.L. Polk.

Chamber's Edinburgh Journal. 5 (June 13, 1846).

Choctaw Nation, Choctaw Roll. Shade County, Tuskahoma, Indian Territory.

Christian County Centennial, *Christian County, Its first 100 years,* Jefferson City, Mo.: Von Hoffman, 1959.

Christian County Circuit Court 1860-1899. Missouri State Archives. Christian County Library.

Christian County Marriages. Christian County Recorder.

Christian County Plat Book/Map, 1912, 1930. University of Missouri-Columbia, Ellis Library Special Collections.

Christian County, Missouri, Census Index, 1930. Christian County Library

Christian County, Missouri, Index to Circuit Court Records 1859-1899. Christian County Library.

Christian County, Missouri, Personal Property Tax Index, 1879-1900. Missouri State Archives. Trans. by Mabel Phillips, Christian County Library. Ozark, Missouri.

Christian County, Missouri-Businesses Listed on Personal Property Tax Lists 1879-1900: An Index. Christian County Library.

Chronicling America. Library of Congress.

Circuit Courts of Christian, Greene, and Webster Counties. Missouri State Archives. Christian County Library, Ozark, Missouri.

Cleveland, N., Smillie, James. *Green-Wood Illustrated.* New York: R. Martin, 1847.

Collection of David Gay.

Collection of Dee Willauer.

Collection of Jayme Schaumann Burchett.

Collision and Loss at Sea. *The New Monthly Magazine and Universal Register,* 1847.

Creek County Marriage Records (Sapulpa, Oklahoma), 1907-1921. Creek County, Oklahoma, Clerk.

Culberson, James. "The Fort Towson Road: A Historic Trail," *Chronicles of Oklahoma,* 5 (December 1927): 418.

Dixon [Illinois] Telegraph Newspaper Pre-1948 Index. Lee County, Illinois, Historical and Genealogical Society.

Drury College Bulletin, July 1915. (See also *Bulletin of Drury College*)

Eberle, John. *A Treatise on the Theory and practice of Medicine,* (Vol. 1, 3rd ed.). Philadelphia: Grigg & Elliott, 1835.

Bibliography

Engineering World: A Journal of Engineering and Construction, 20-21 (June 1922): 385.

Family Bible of James Keatts, *Holy Bible*. Philadelphia: John E. Potter, 1880.

FamilySearch. Online Database. Salt Lake City, Utah: The Church of Jesus Christ of Latter-day Saints, 1999-.

Faust, Albert B. *The German Element in the United States* (2 vols.). New York: Houghton Mifflin, 1909.

Find A Grave Memorial. Online Database. Salt Lake City, Utah: Ancestry.com, 1998-.

Frisco Employees' Magazine (May 1933, Oct 1933).

Fuer, Howard B. *The Germans in America 1607-1970,* Dobbs Ferry, N.Y. [n. p.], 1973

Fulbright, James S. *Glimpses of Life*. Bloomington, In.: iUniverse, 2014.

Goodrich, James W. "Gottfried Duden: A Nineteenth Century Missouri Promoter." *Missouri Historical Review* 75 (January 1981): 131-146.

Graham, Bernice. *Graham Descendants of William and Dinah Ann (Wilson) Graham*. Marietta, Oh.: Richardson, 1967.

Gravley, Ernestine. "Fifty Years Ago in Shawnee and Pottawatomie County." In *Chronicles of Oklahoma,* 31 (No. 4, 1953): 381.

Greene County Record Circuit Court. Missouri State Archives.

Greene County, Missouri. St. Louis, Mo.: Western Historical, 1883.

Green-Wood Cemetery Index of Burials and Register. Green-Wood Cemetery. Brooklyn, New York.

Haberstroh, Richard. *The German Churches of Metropolitan New York.* New York: New York Genealogical & Biographical Society, 2000.

Harper, Kimberly. *White Man's Heaven: The Lynching and Expulsion of Blacks in the Southern Ozarks, 1894–1909,* Fayetteville, Ar.: University of Arkansas Press, 2010.

Harper's Weekly. New York: Harper's Magazine, 1859.

Hazel Kastendieck Shafer Family Notes, undated c. 1970, prior to 1980.

Helland, O. "Work among the Scandinavian Seamen: Rev. O. Helland's Report for the Quarter Ending September 1st". *The Sailors' Magazine and Sailors Friend,* 41 (October 1869): 313-314.

Hensley, John. "The Kastendieck Bird Collection," *The Ozarks Mountaineer,* (July-August 1985): 38-39.

Hirschfelder, Arthur D. *Diseases of the Heart and Aorta*. Philadelphia: Lippincott, 1910.

Bibliography

Hunt, Albert S. "Introduction." In *Old Sands Street Methodist Episcopal Church of Brooklyn, NY: An Illustrated Centennial Record, Historical and Biographical*, by Edwin Wariner. New York: Phillips & Hunt, 1885.

Hunt, Albert S. "Sermon 18." In *Our Martyr President, Abraham Lincoln: Voices from the Pulpit of New York and Brooklyn*. New York: Tibbals & Whiting, [1865].

Hutter, John. "History of Billings, Mo." *The Billings [Missouri] Times* 33 (October 15, 1914).

Indiana University Northwest. Calumet Regional Archives. Gary, Indiana.

Investigative Reports of the Bureau of Investigation [FBI] 1908-1922, National Archives.

John Herman and Bridget Kastendieck Bible. (See also Kastendieck Family Bible and Brown & Cooke *Bible*)

Kastendieck Family Bible. Jayme Schaumann Burchett Collection. (See also Brown and Cooke *Bible*.)

Kastendieck, Augusta M. Biography of John D. Kastendieck (four-page typescript). David Gay Collection, n. d.

Kastendieck, Augusta M. *The Jew: The Hub of the Nations*. Chicago: New Covenant Testimony, 1945.

Kastendieck, Augusta M. *The Power of Life*. Boston: Christopher Pub. House, 1961.

Keast Family Record. Jayme Schaumann Burchett Collection, n. d.

Lain's Brooklyn City Directory, 1879/80, 1897. Brooklyn, NY: J. Lain, 1858-1899.

Lain's Directory of Brooklyn Undertakers, 1979-1880. New York Public Library.

Land Patents 1831-1961. Township School Land Patents, Vol. Z. Missouri Secretary of State. Jefferson City, Missouri.

Lists of Incoming and Outgoing Passengers, 1917-1938. Record Group 92. National Archives.

Marriage Records of Dallas County, Missouri.

Marriage records, 1890-1951. Oklahoma District Court (Oklahoma County), Oklahoma.

Mathematics Genealogy Project. North Dakota State University & American Mathematical Society, 2005.

Medical Forthnightly, 16 (September 15, 1899): 538.

Michigan Deaths and Burials, 1800-1995. Michigan Department of State Division of Vital Statistics.

Minutes of the St. Louis Annual Conference, Methodist Episcopal Church (Vols. 25-33), [March] 1893.

Missouri Board of Health. Secretary of State Archives. Jefferson City, Missouri.

Missouri Division of Health, Department of Public Health and Welfare, Jefferson City, Missouri.

Missouri State Archives. Secretary of State. Jefferson City, Missouri.

Modern Miller. St. Louis, 23 (August 14, 1897).

National Historical Magazine Vol. 77 (1943).

National Register of Historic Places. Arkansas Historic Preservation Program. Little Rock, Arkansas.

National Register of Scientific and Technical Personnel. National Archives at College Park, Maryland. Washington, D.C.: Superintendent of Documents, 1954-1970.

New York City Births, 1846-1909. New York City Municipal Archives.

New York City Death Index. New York City Municipal Archives.

New York City Department of Records and Information Services. New York City Municipal Archives.

New York City Directory 1852. New York: Doggett & Rode, [1851]-.

New York City Landmarks Preservation Commission.

New York City Marriage Records, 1829-1940. New York City Municipal Archives.

New York City Municipal Deaths and Burials, 1795-1949. New York Municipal Archives.

New York Passenger and Crew Lists, 1909, 1925-1957. National Archives.

New York State Census, 1855, 1865, 1875, 1892. New York State Library.

New York, Kings County Estate Files, 1866-1923, 1900. Surrogate Court, Brooklyn.

Official Manual, Missouri Office of the Secretary of State. Jefferson City, Missouri, 1893.

Official Record Minutes of the St. Louis German Conference of the Methodist Episcopal Church, 41 (September 8-13, 1920): 8

Official Report of Agreements Made Between the Officials of the Roads Named Herein and the B. of L.E. Committees Representing the Engineers Employed Thereon. Brotherhood of Locomotive Engineers. Cleveland: Gardner, 1907.

Oklahoma School Records, 1895-1936. Multiple County Clerk offices, Oklahoma school district offices, Oklahoma.

Bibliography

Oklahoma State Vital Records Index. Oklahoma State Department of Health. Oklahoma City, Oklahoma.

Old Records System City of Shawnee Fairview Cemetery Records. Pottawatomie County, Oklahoma.

Our Honored Dead. *Official Minutes of the St. Louis German Conference*, 41-45 (August 1919): 303.

Passport Applications 1795-1905. National Archives and Records Administration.

Peck, Henry L. *The Proud Heritage of Le Flore County: A History of an Oklahoma County*, Van Buren, Ar.: Press Argus, 1963.

Poken, Steve. "Why does Christian Co. have a Panhandle?" *Springfield News-Leader*, (10 Aug 2018): 6A.

Portrait and Biographical Record of Clinton, Washington, Marion and Jefferson Counties, Illinois. Chapman Publishing & Mt. Vernon Genealogical Society. Evansville, Ind.: Unigraphic, 1975.

Pottawatomie County, Oklahoma, Marriages. Pottawatomie Marriage Indexes. Pottawatomie Genealogy Club.

Princeton Alumni Weekly 46 (May 3, 1945): 7.

Pulse Yearbook, 1907, 1923. Central Wesleyan College.

Pushmataha County, Oklahoma, Marriages. Pushmataha County Archives.

Rand-McNally Official Railway Guide and Hand Book. Chicago: American Railway Guide, 1902.

Rauch, David. *125 Years of Ministry.* Bolivar, Missouri: Bolivar Herald-Free Press, n. d.

Real Estate Record and Builders' Guide, v. 16 no. 381 (July 3 1875), no. 406 (Dec. 25 1875). [Brooklyn, N.Y.]: C.W. Sweet & Co., 1868-1884.

Rennick, Robert M. *Kentucky Place Names.* Lexington, Ky.: University Press of Kentucky. [1987] 2013.

Revised Statutes of the State of Missouri, 1879 (Vol. 1). Jefferson City, Mo.: Carter and Regan, 1879.

Reynolds, Roy S. "The Kastendieck/Keast/Hayes Families of Missouri." Manuscript, 2005.

Richardson, Albert D. *The Secret Service, the Field, the Dungeon, the Escape.* Hartford: American, 1865.

Roberts, Campbell. "History of Lynchings in the South Documents Nearly 4,000 Names." *New York Times* (10 Feb 2015).

Sanborn Fire Insurance Maps for Missouri, Billings. Special Collections, Ellis Library. University of Missouri-Columbia.

Bibliography

Smith, Job L. *A Treatise on the Diseases of Infancy and Childhood.* Philadelphia: H.C. Lea, 1869.

Smith, William M., and Wilbur. "The Practice of Medicine in Greene County." In *Past and Present of Greene County, Missouri,* compiled by Fairbanks and Tuck, c. 1915.

Smith's Brooklyn Directory, 1856-1858, subsequently *Lain's Brooklyn Directory,* published by Lain and Company. Brooklyn Public Library.

Social Security Death Index. United States Social Security Administration.

Soldiers' Records: War of 1812-World War I. Missouri State Archives. Missouri Secretary of State. Jefferson City, Missouri.

South Orange County (California) Directory. Westminster, Calif.: Contacts Influential, 1932.

Special Collections. St. Louis Mercantile Library.

Springfield, Missouri, City Directory. Kansas City, Mo.: R.L. Polk, 1853, 1955.

St Louis, Missouri, City Directory. St. Louis, Missouri: R.L. Polk, 1917, 1929, 1930

State Historical Society of Missouri. St. Louis and Columbia, Missouri.

Stern, Robert A.M. Mellins, Thomas, and Fishman, David. *New York 1880.* New York: Monacelli, 1999.

Stiles, Henry R. *History of Kings County including Brooklyn, N.Y.* Brooklyn: W. W. Munsell, 1884.

Stiles, Henry R. *A History of the City of Brooklyn: including the Old Town and Village of Brooklyn, the Town of Bushwick, and the Village and City of Williamsburgh.* Brooklyn: [s.n.], [1867] 1870.

Street Index of the City of Brooklyn, 1872. Brooklyn Public Library.

The Eagle and Brooklyn, Vol. 1, (Winter 1852; Fall 1861). Brooklyn Collection. Brooklyn Public Library.

The Owl. 1923 Paris High School Alumni Roll Class of 1916.

Tilden, John H. *The Etiology of Cholera Infantum.* Denver, Co.: Merchants, 1909.

Transactions of the Academy of Science of Saint Louis. [St. Louis, Academy of Science of St. Louis], 1907.

United States Army World War I Transport Service, Passenger Lists. National Archives.

United States Selective Service Registration Cards, World War II: Fourth Registration, Record Group 147. National Archives.

United States World War I Draft Registration Cards, 1917-1918. National Archives.

United States, World War II Draft Registration Cards, 1942.

United States. Census German States. National Archives and Records Administration. Washington, D.C.

United States. Census, 1850, 1860, 1870, 1880, 1900, 1910, 1920, 1930, 1940. National Archives.

United States. Secretary of the Interior. "Table LL—Nativity of foreigners residing in each state and territory." *Statistics of the United States in 1860.* Washington, D.C.: Government Printing Office, 1866

Upton, Lucile M. *Bald Knobbers.* Point Lookout, Mo.: S of O Press, 1970.

Washington University. *Department of Physics Newsletter* (Fall 2010).

Webster County Circuit Court. Missouri State Archives.

Welty, Ruth. "Place Names of St. Louis and Jefferson County." M.A. thesis. University of Missouri-Columbia, 1939.

Wesleyan Methodist Church in Canada Baptismal Registers, 1825-1910. Victoria University Archives.

Widmann, Otto. *A Preliminary Catalogue of the Birds of Missouri.* [S.l.]:[s.n.], 1907.

Wilson Bulletin, Vols. 34-36. White Plains, N.Y.: H.W. Wilson, [1914-1930].

Winks, Robin W. *Frederick Billings: A Life.* Berkeley, Ca.: University of California Press, 1998.

Zion German Evangelical Lutheran Marriage Records Index.

Index

www.ingramcontent.com/pod-product-compliance
Lightning Source LLC
Chambersburg PA
CBHW060233100426
42742CB00011B/1523